Sweetness & Lightning

9

Gido Amagakure

c o n t e n t s

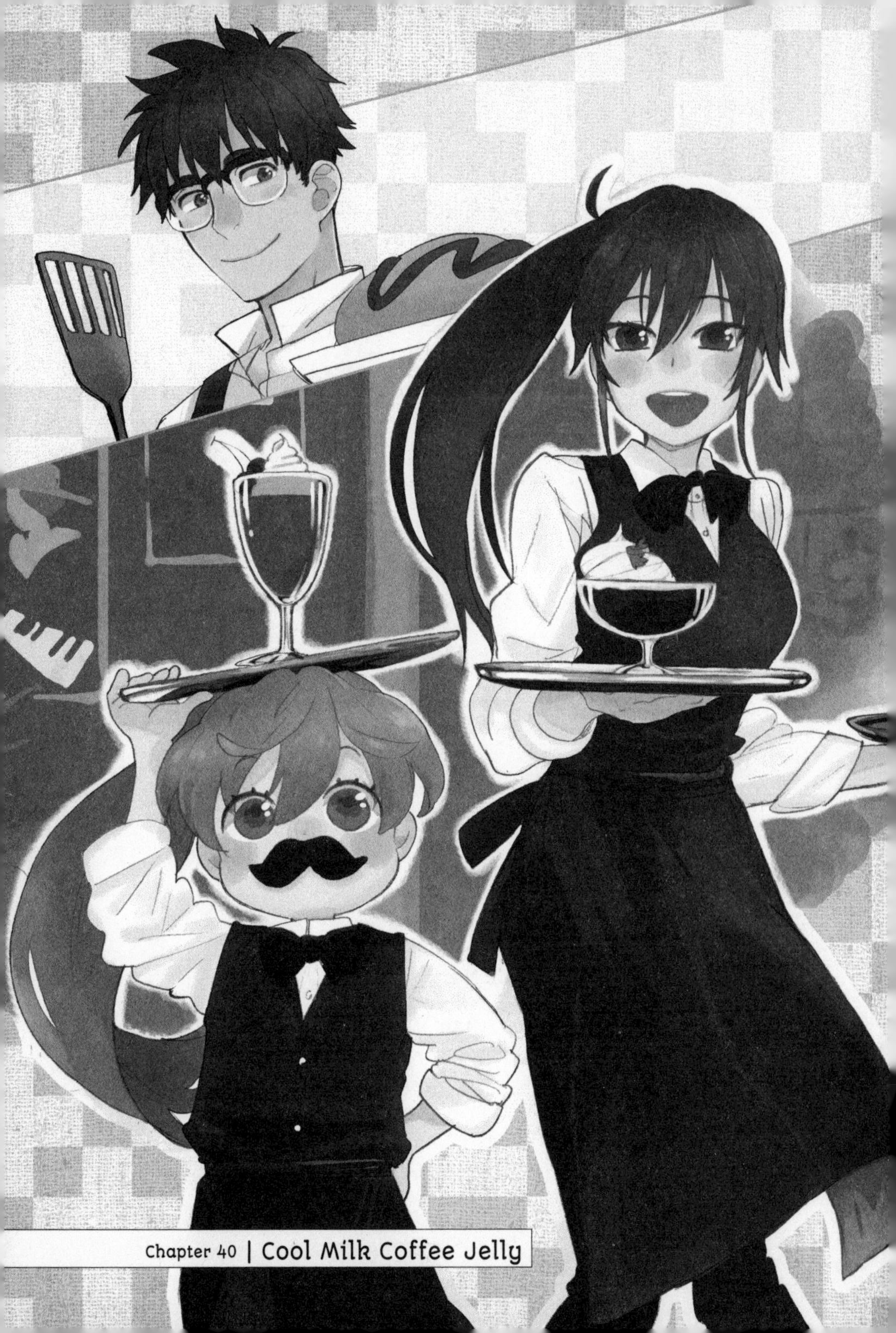

Chapter 40 | Cool Milk Coffee Jelly

sweetness &
lightning

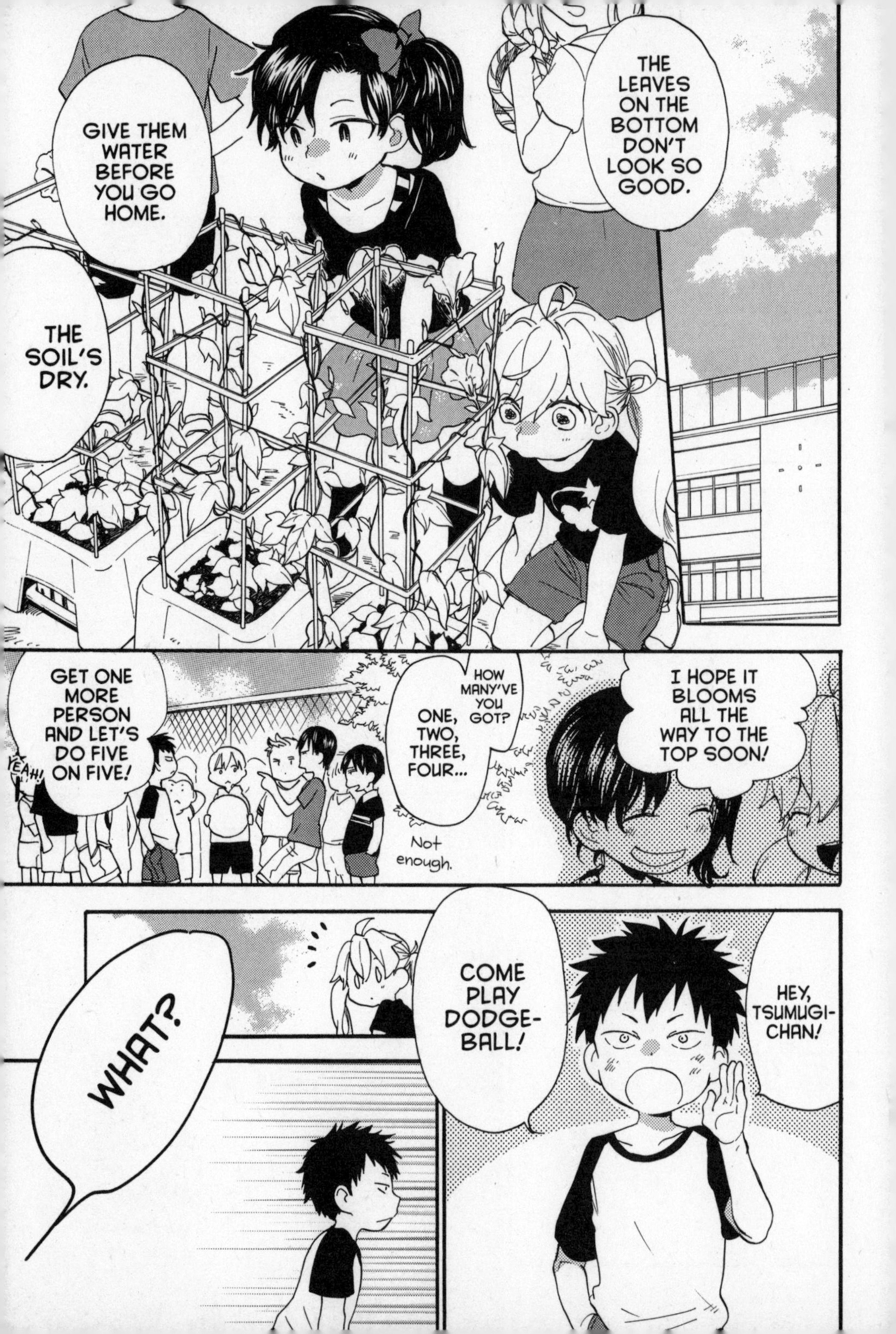
THE LEAVES ON THE BOTTOM DON'T LOOK SO GOOD.
GIVE THEM WATER BEFORE YOU GO HOME.
THE SOIL'S DRY.
I HOPE IT BLOOMS ALL THE WAY TO THE TOP SOON!
HOW MANY'VE YOU GOT?
ONE, TWO, THREE, FOUR...
Not enough.
GET ONE MORE PERSON AND LET'S DO FIVE ON FIVE!
YEAH!
HEY, TSUMUGI-CHAN!
COME PLAY DODGE-BALL!
WHAT?

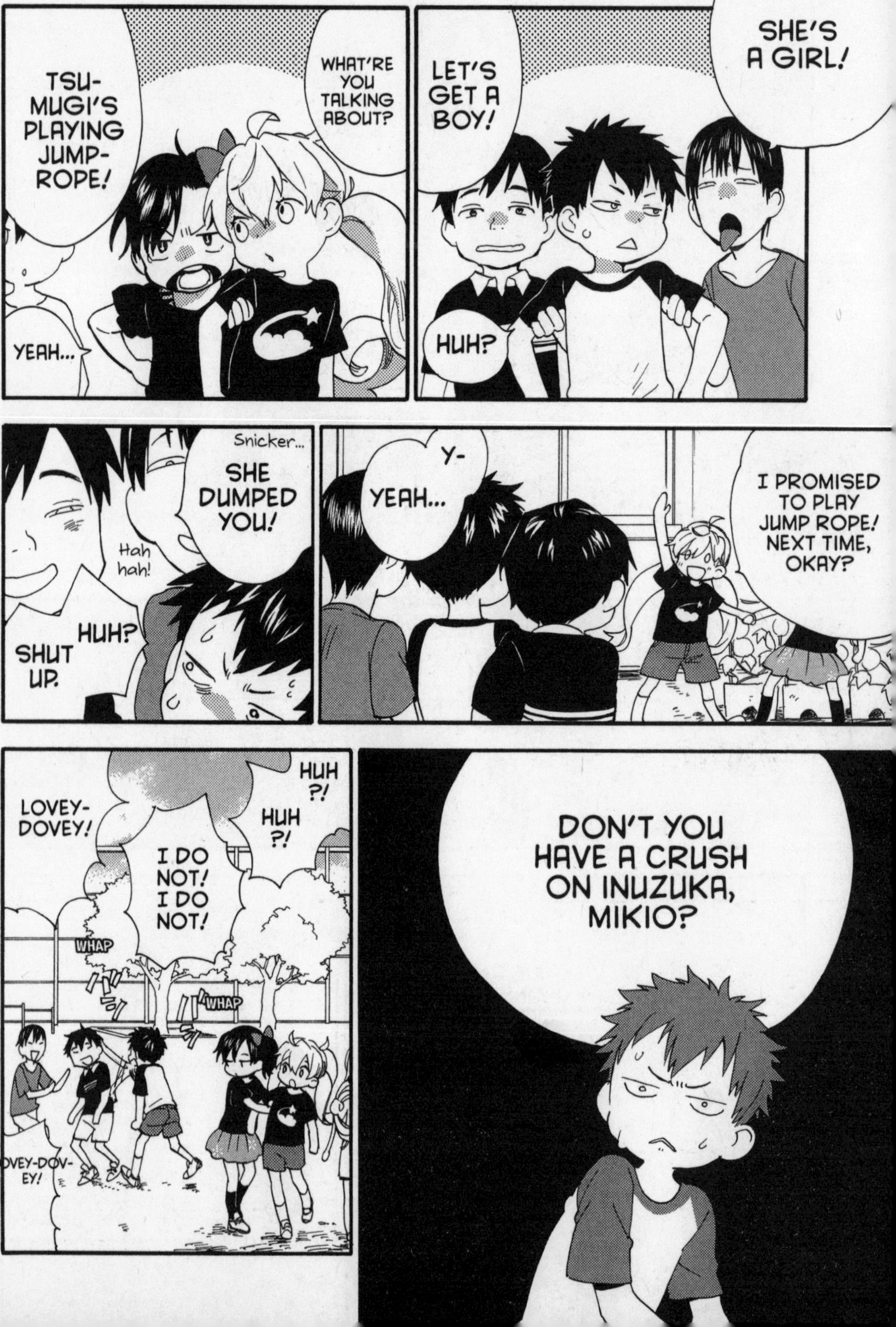
SHE'S A GIRL!
LET'S GET A BOY!
HUH?
WHAT'RE YOU TALKING ABOUT?
TSU-MUGI'S PLAYING JUMP-ROPE!
YEAH...
I PROMISED TO PLAY JUMP ROPE! NEXT TIME, OKAY?
Y- YEAH...
Snicker...
SHE DUMPED YOU!
Hah hah!
HUH?
SHUT UP.
DON'T YOU HAVE A CRUSH ON INUZUKA, MIKIO?
HUH ?!
HUH ?!
LOVEY-DOVEY!
I DO NOT! I DO NOT!
WHAP
WHAP
LOVEY-DOV-EY!

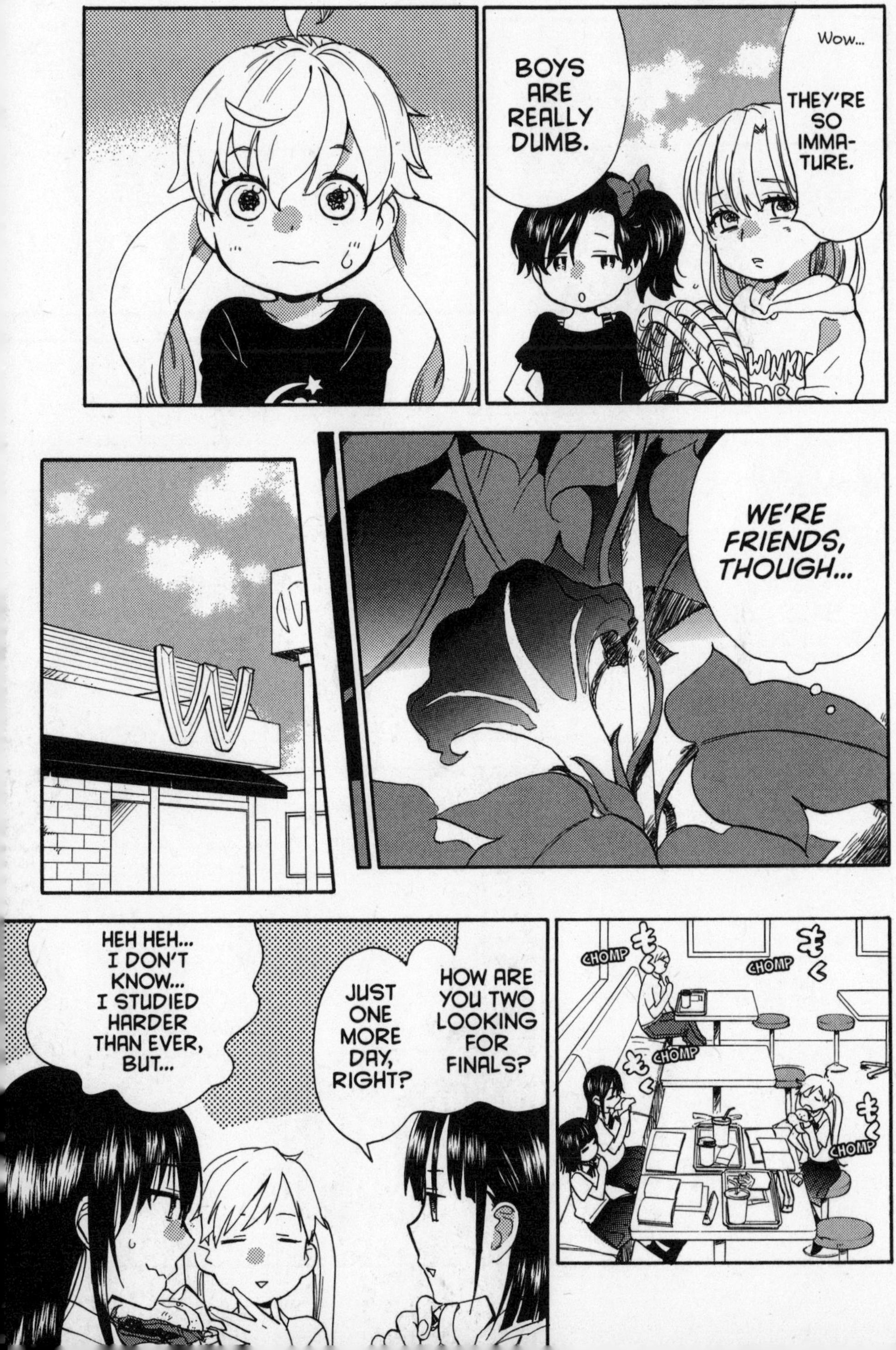

Wow...
THEY'RE SO IMMA-TURE.
BOYS ARE REALLY DUMB.
WE'RE FRIENDS, THOUGH...
CHOMP
CHOMP
CHOMP
CHOMP
HOW ARE YOU TWO LOOKING FOR FINALS?
JUST ONE MORE DAY, RIGHT?
HEH HEH... I DON'T KNOW... I STUDIED HARDER THAN EVER, BUT...

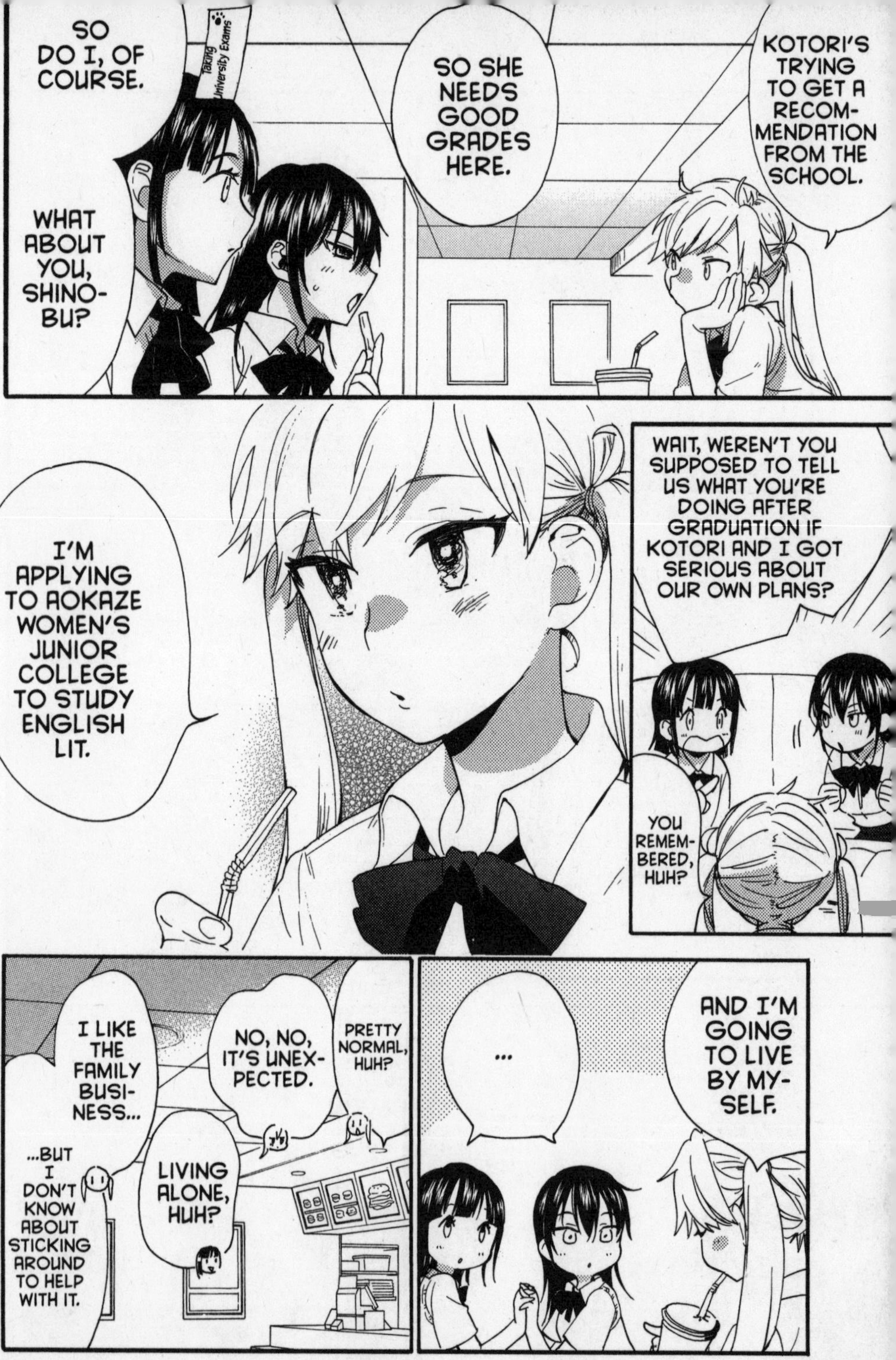
KOTORI'S TRYING TO GET A RECOMMENDATION FROM THE SCHOOL.
SO SHE NEEDS GOOD GRADES HERE.
SO DO I, OF COURSE.
Taking University Exams
WHAT ABOUT YOU, SHINOBU?
WAIT, WEREN'T YOU SUPPOSED TO TELL US WHAT YOU'RE DOING AFTER GRADUATION IF KOTORI AND I GOT SERIOUS ABOUT OUR OWN PLANS?
YOU REMEMBERED, HUH?
I'M APPLYING TO AOKAZE WOMEN'S JUNIOR COLLEGE TO STUDY ENGLISH LIT.
AND I'M GOING TO LIVE BY MYSELF.
...
PRETTY NORMAL, HUH?
NO, NO, IT'S UNEXPECTED.
I LIKE THE FAMILY BUSINESS...
LIVING ALONE, HUH?
...BUT I DON'T KNOW ABOUT STICKING AROUND TO HELP WITH IT.

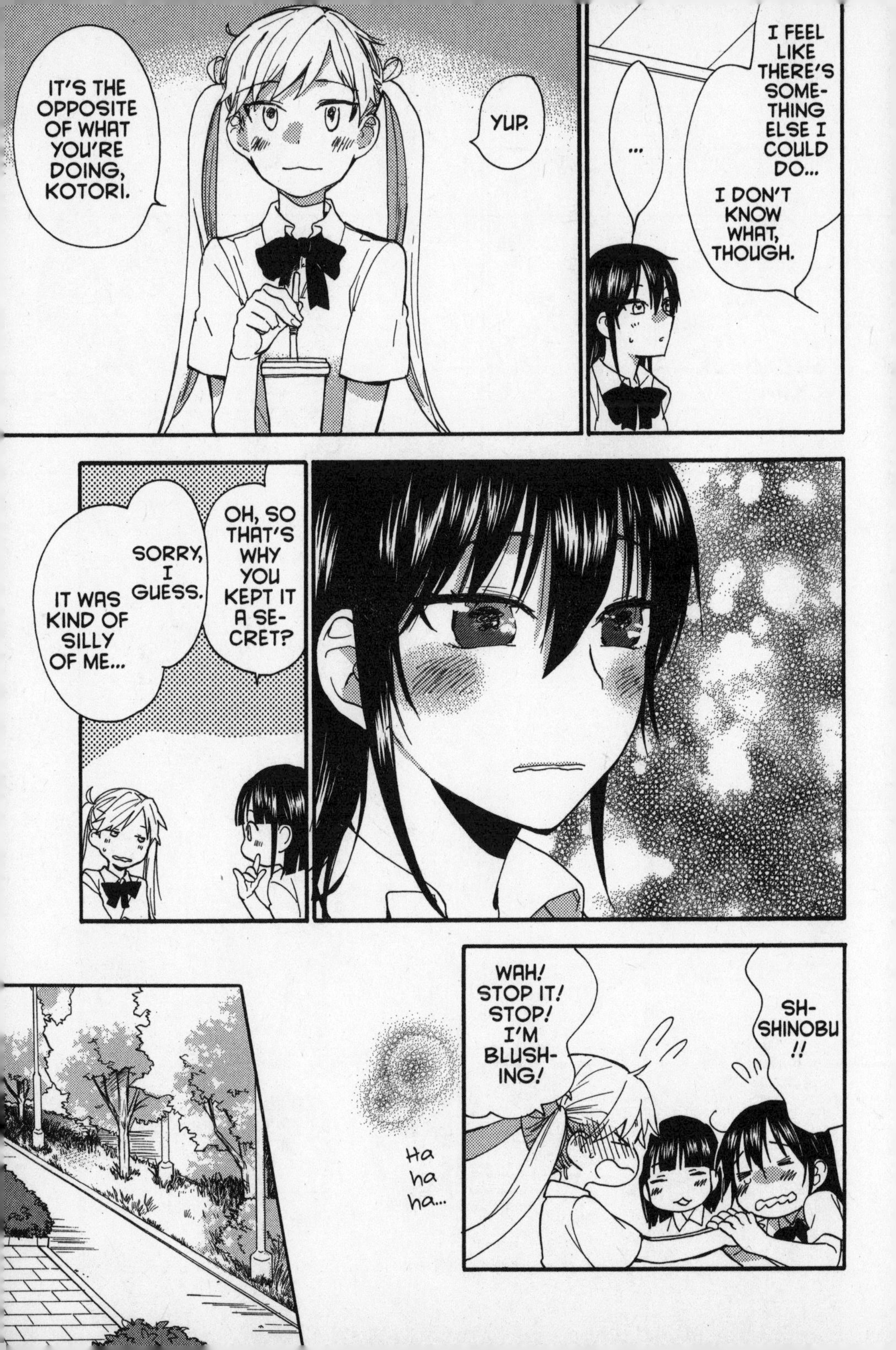
I FEEL LIKE THERE'S SOMETHING ELSE I COULD DO... I DON'T KNOW WHAT, THOUGH.
...
YUP.
IT'S THE OPPOSITE OF WHAT YOU'RE DOING, KOTORI.
OH, SO THAT'S WHY YOU KEPT IT A SECRET?
SORRY, I GUESS. IT WAS KIND OF SILLY OF ME...
SH-SHINOBU!!
WAH! STOP IT! STOP! I'M BLUSHING!
Ha ha ha...

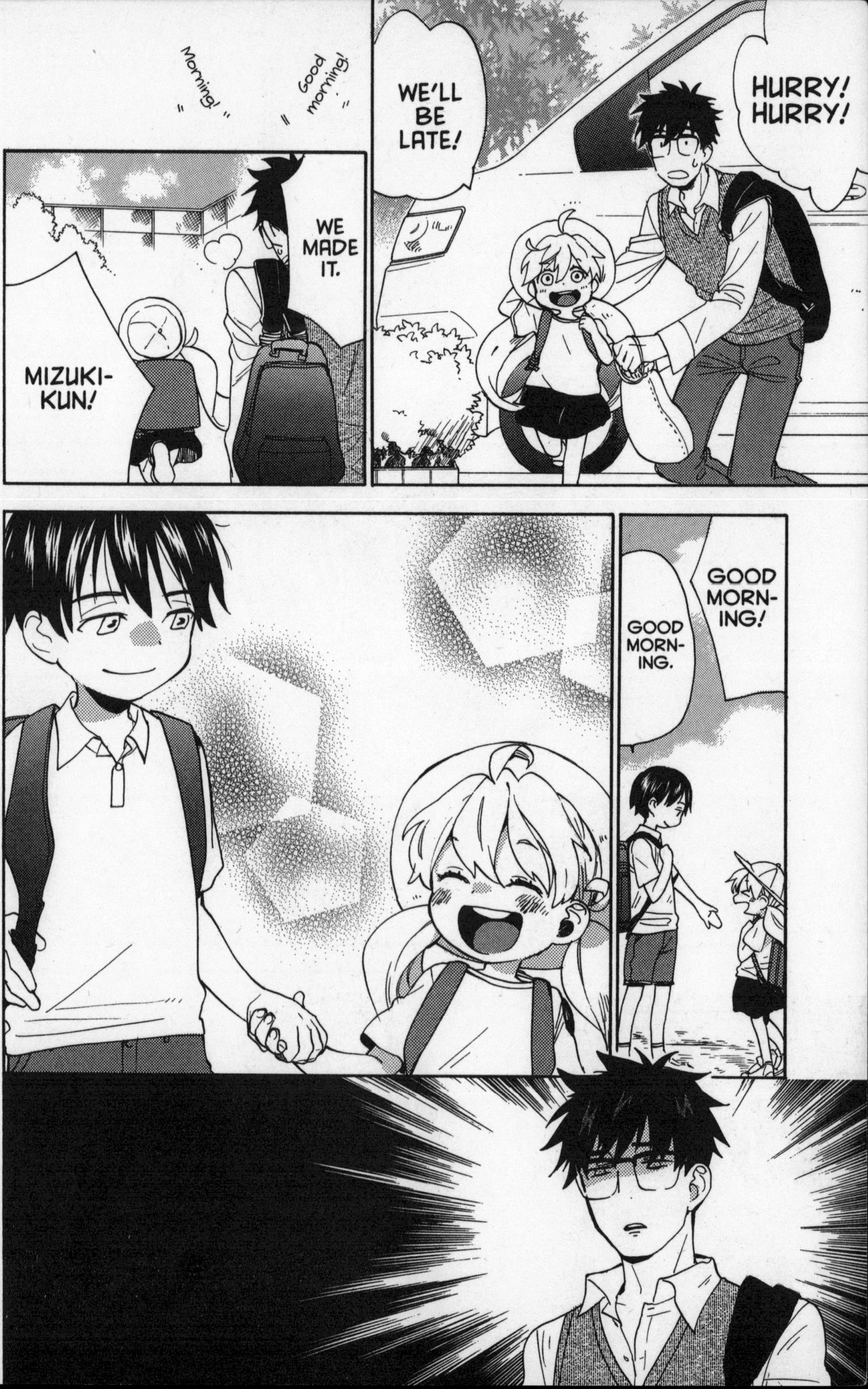
HURRY! HURRY!
WE'LL BE LATE!
Good morning!
Morning!
WE MADE IT.
MIZUKI-KUN!
GOOD MORNING!
GOOD MORNING.

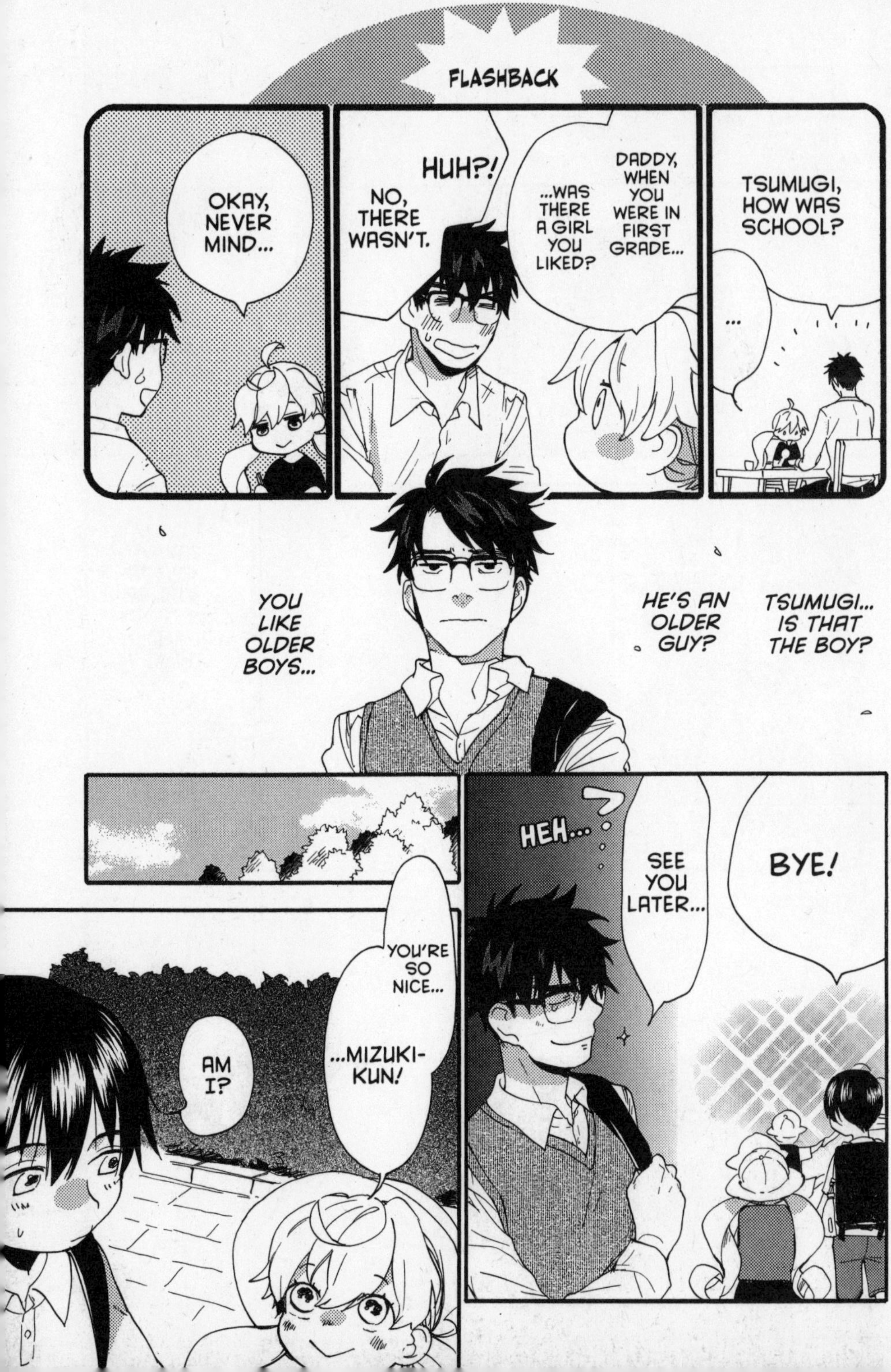
FLASHBACK
TSUMUGI, HOW WAS SCHOOL?
...
DADDY, WHEN YOU WERE IN FIRST GRADE...
...WAS THERE A GIRL YOU LIKED?
HUH?!
NO, THERE WASN'T.
OKAY, NEVER MIND...
TSUMUGI... IS THAT THE BOY?
HE'S AN OLDER GUY?
YOU LIKE OLDER BOYS...
BYE!
SEE YOU LATER...
HEH...
YOU'RE SO NICE...
...MIZUKI-KUN!
AM I?

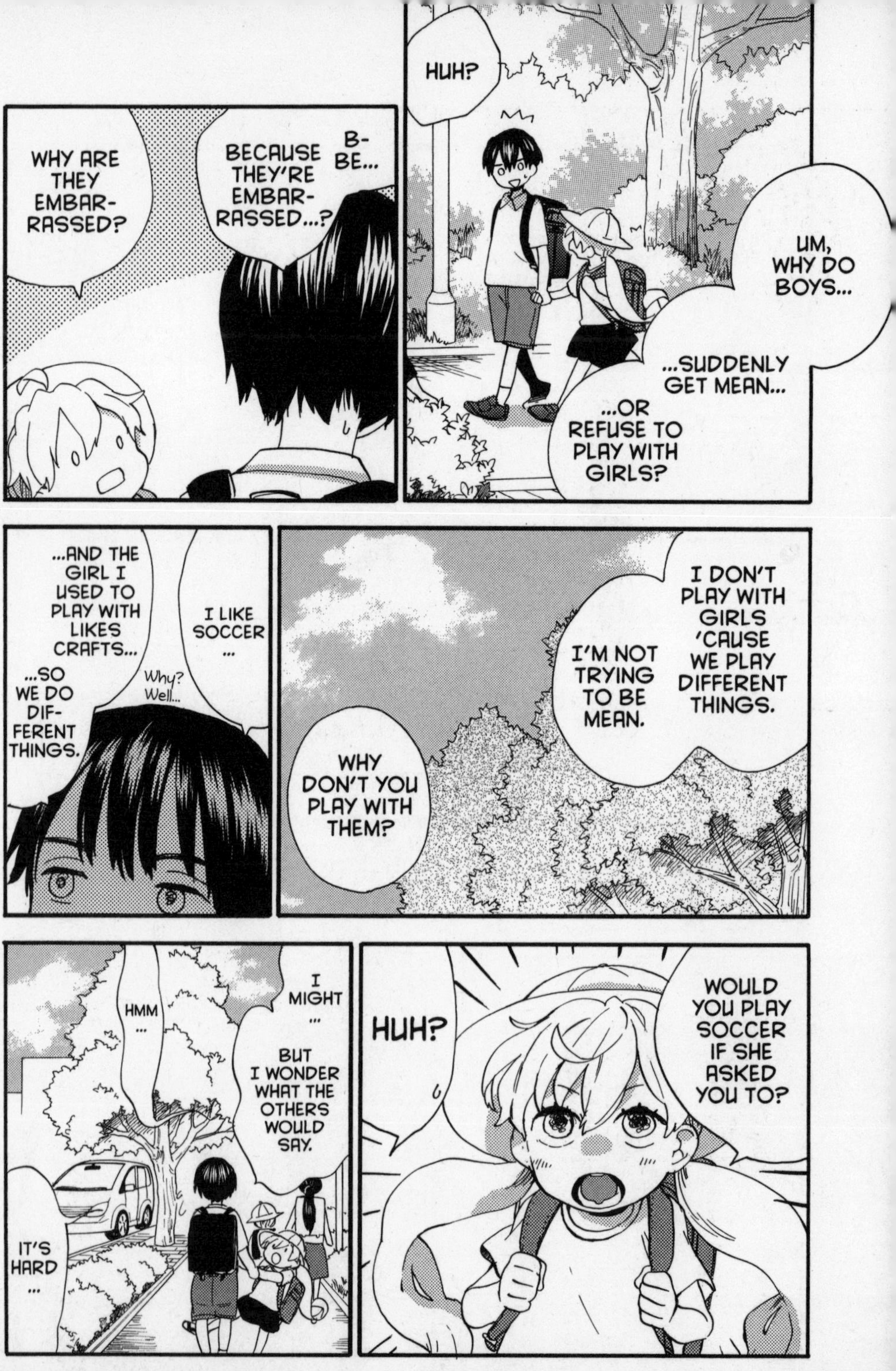
HUH?
UM, WHY DO BOYS...
...SUDDENLY GET MEAN...
...OR REFUSE TO PLAY WITH GIRLS?
B-BE...
BECAUSE THEY'RE EMBARRASSED...?
WHY ARE THEY EMBARRASSED?
I DON'T PLAY WITH GIRLS 'CAUSE WE PLAY DIFFERENT THINGS.
I'M NOT TRYING TO BE MEAN.
WHY DON'T YOU PLAY WITH THEM?
Why? Well...
I LIKE SOCCER...
...AND THE GIRL I USED TO PLAY WITH LIKES CRAFTS...
...SO WE DO DIFFERENT THINGS.
WOULD YOU PLAY SOCCER IF SHE ASKED YOU TO?
HUH?
I MIGHT...
BUT I WONDER WHAT THE OTHERS WOULD SAY.
HMM...
IT'S HARD...

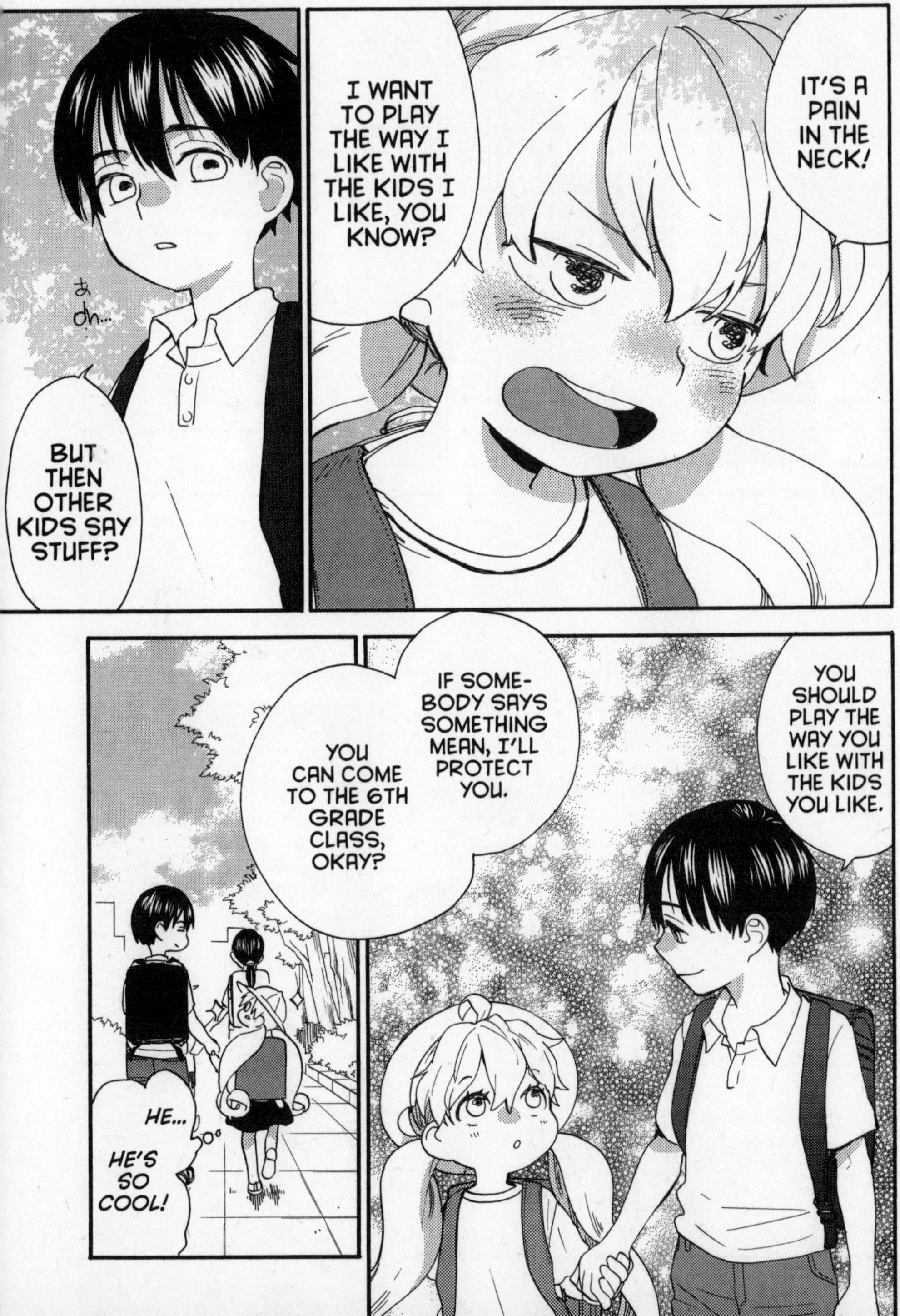
IT'S A PAIN IN THE NECK!
I WANT TO PLAY THE WAY I LIKE WITH THE KIDS I LIKE, YOU KNOW?
あ oh...
BUT THEN OTHER KIDS SAY STUFF?
YOU SHOULD PLAY THE WAY YOU LIKE WITH THE KIDS YOU LIKE.
IF SOME-BODY SAYS SOMETHING MEAN, I'LL PROTECT YOU.
YOU CAN COME TO THE 6TH GRADE CLASS, OKAY?
HE...
HE'S SO COOL!

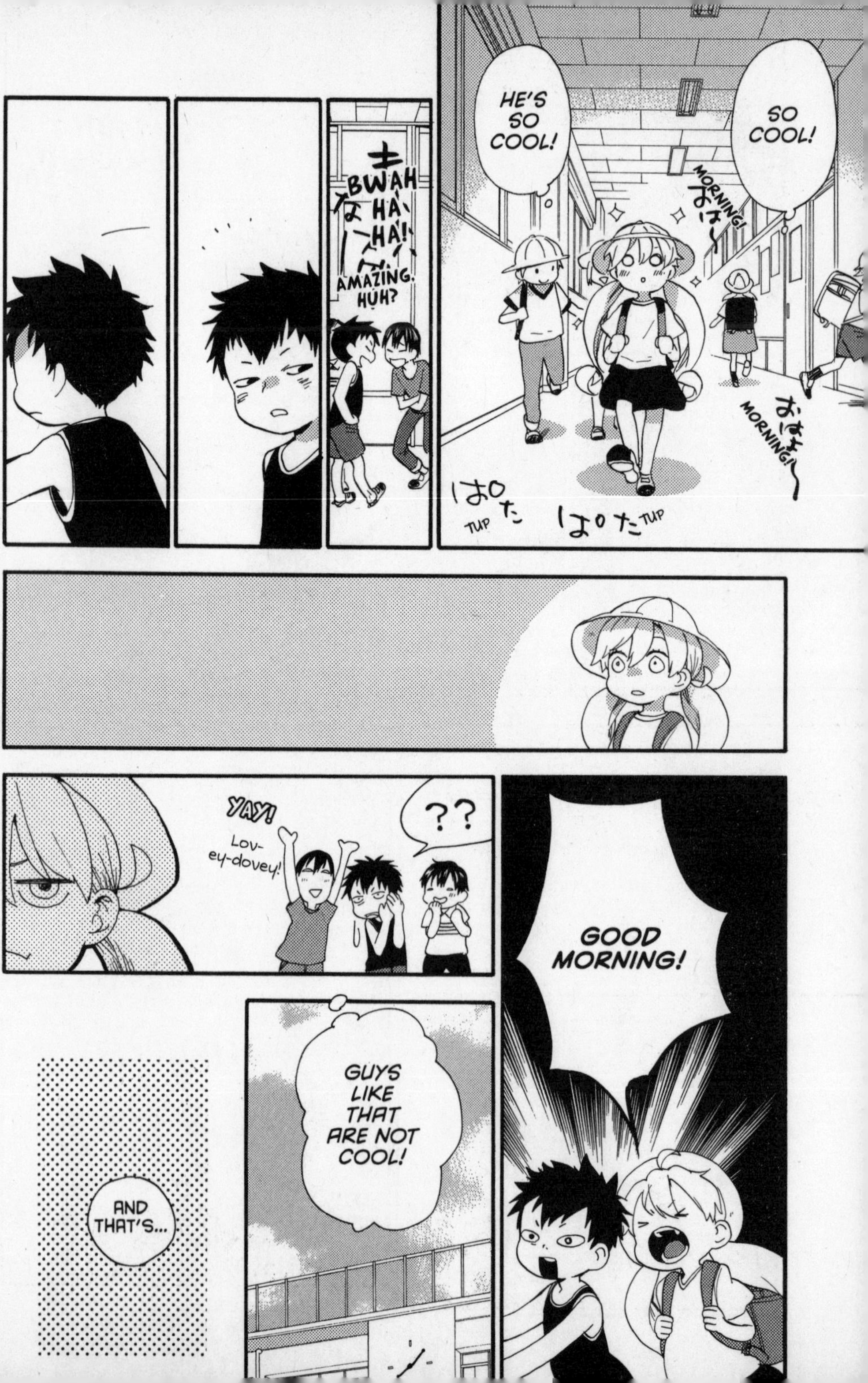
SO COOL!
HE'S SO COOL!
MORNING!
おは~
おはよ~
MORNING!
ぱた ぱた
TUP TUP
BWAH HA HA!
AMAZING, HUH?
GOOD MORNING!
??
YAY!
Lov-ey-dovey!
GUYS LIKE THAT ARE NOT COOL!
AND THAT'S...

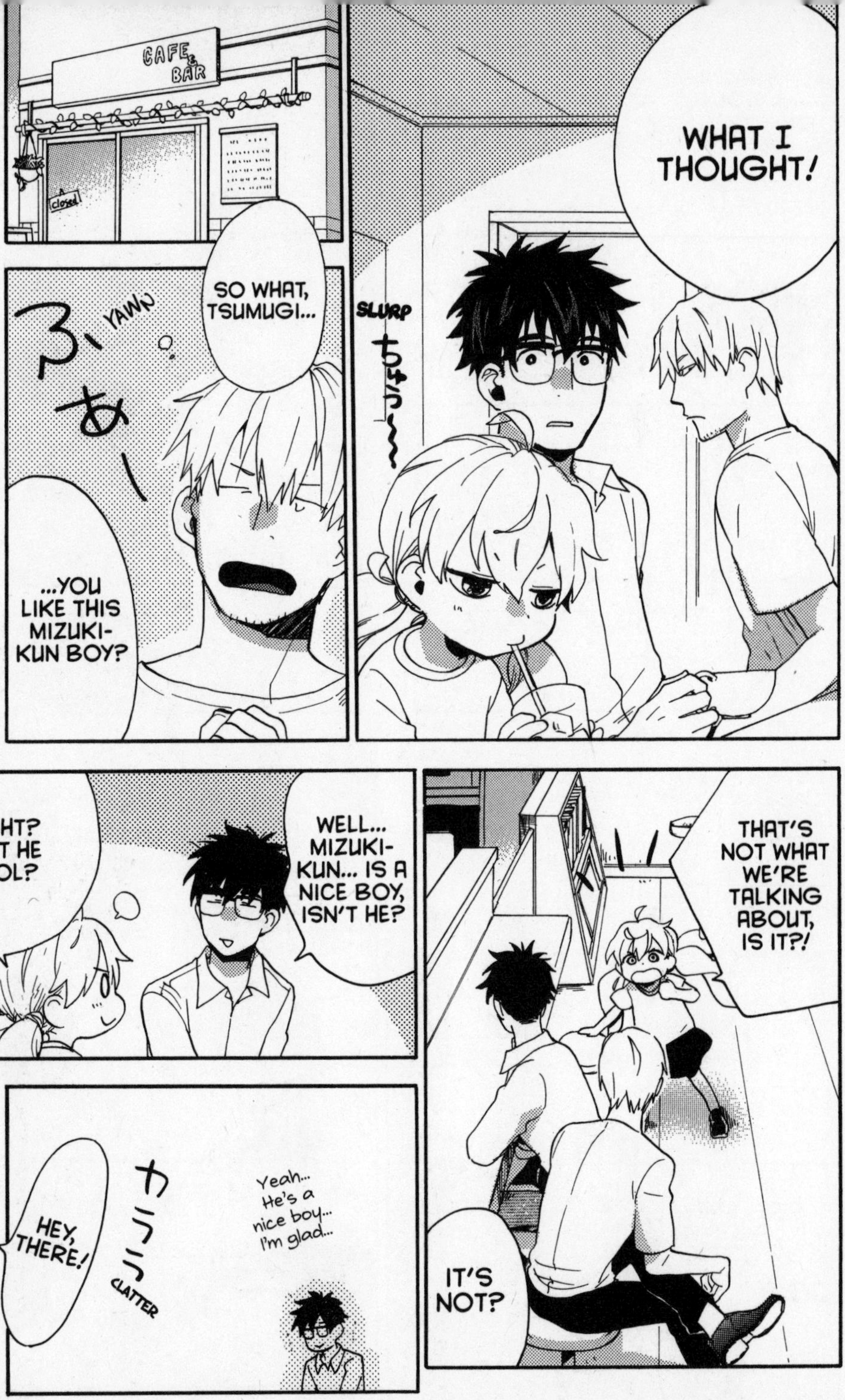

WHAT I THOUGHT!
SLURP
ちゅう〜
CAFE & BAR
closed
SO WHAT, TSUMUGI...
YAWN
ふあ
...YOU LIKE THIS MIZUKI-KUN BOY?
THAT'S NOT WHAT WE'RE TALKING ABOUT, IS IT?!
IT'S NOT?
WELL... MIZUKI-KUN... IS A NICE BOY, ISN'T HE?
RIGHT? ISN'T HE COOL?
Yeah... He's a nice boy... I'm glad...
カララ
CLATTER
HEY, THERE!

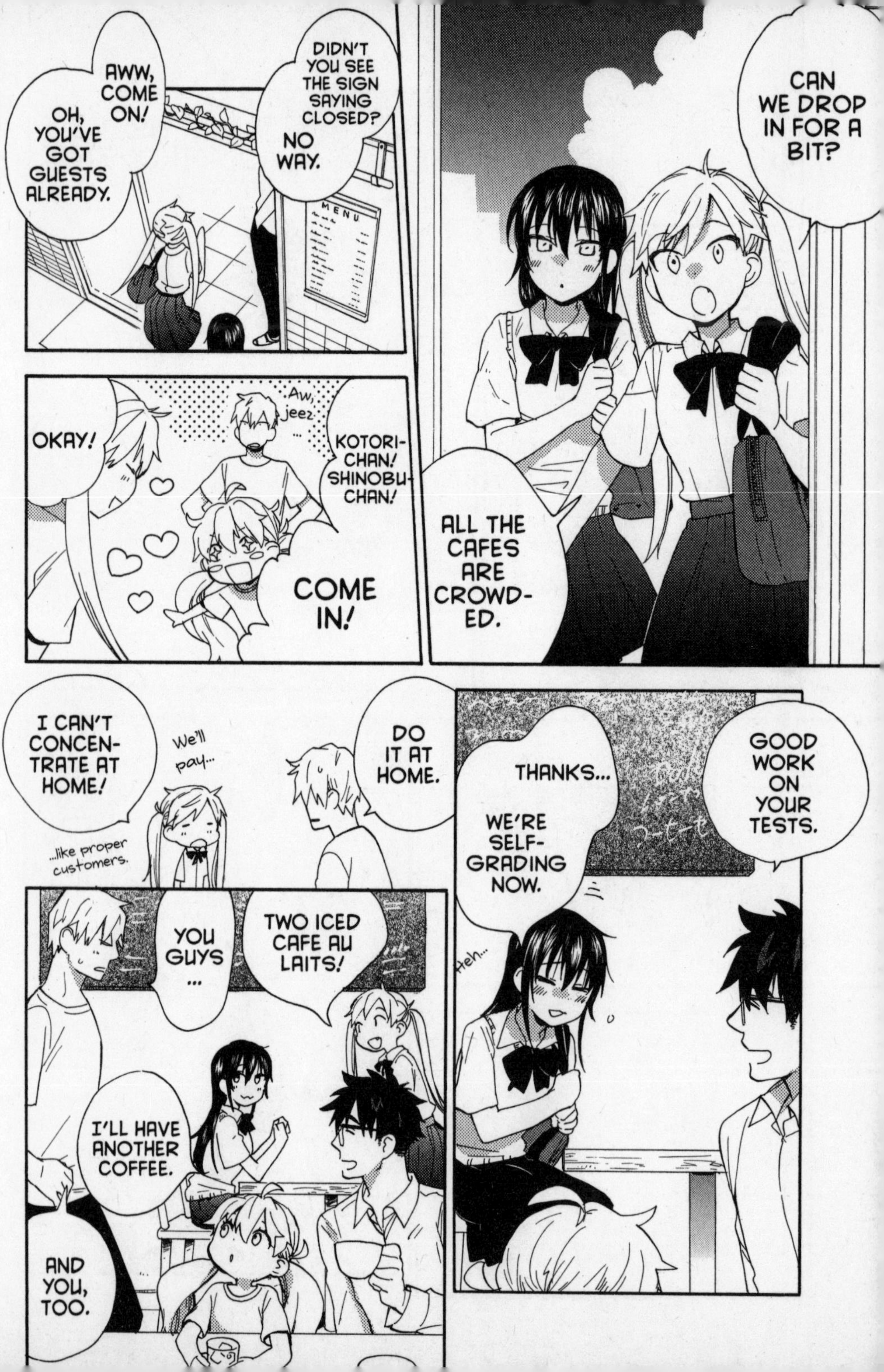
CAN WE DROP IN FOR A BIT?
ALL THE CAFES ARE CROWD-ED.
DIDN'T YOU SEE THE SIGN SAYING CLOSED?
NO WAY.
AWW, COME ON!
OH, YOU'VE GOT GUESTS ALREADY.
MENU
KOTORI-CHAN! SHINOBU-CHAN!
Aw, jeez ...
OKAY!
COME IN!
GOOD WORK ON YOUR TESTS.
THANKS...
WE'RE SELF-GRADING NOW.
Heh...
DO IT AT HOME.
I CAN'T CONCEN-TRATE AT HOME!
We'll pay...
...like proper customers.
TWO ICED CAFE AU LAITS!
YOU GUYS ...
I'LL HAVE ANOTHER COFFEE.
AND YOU, TOO.

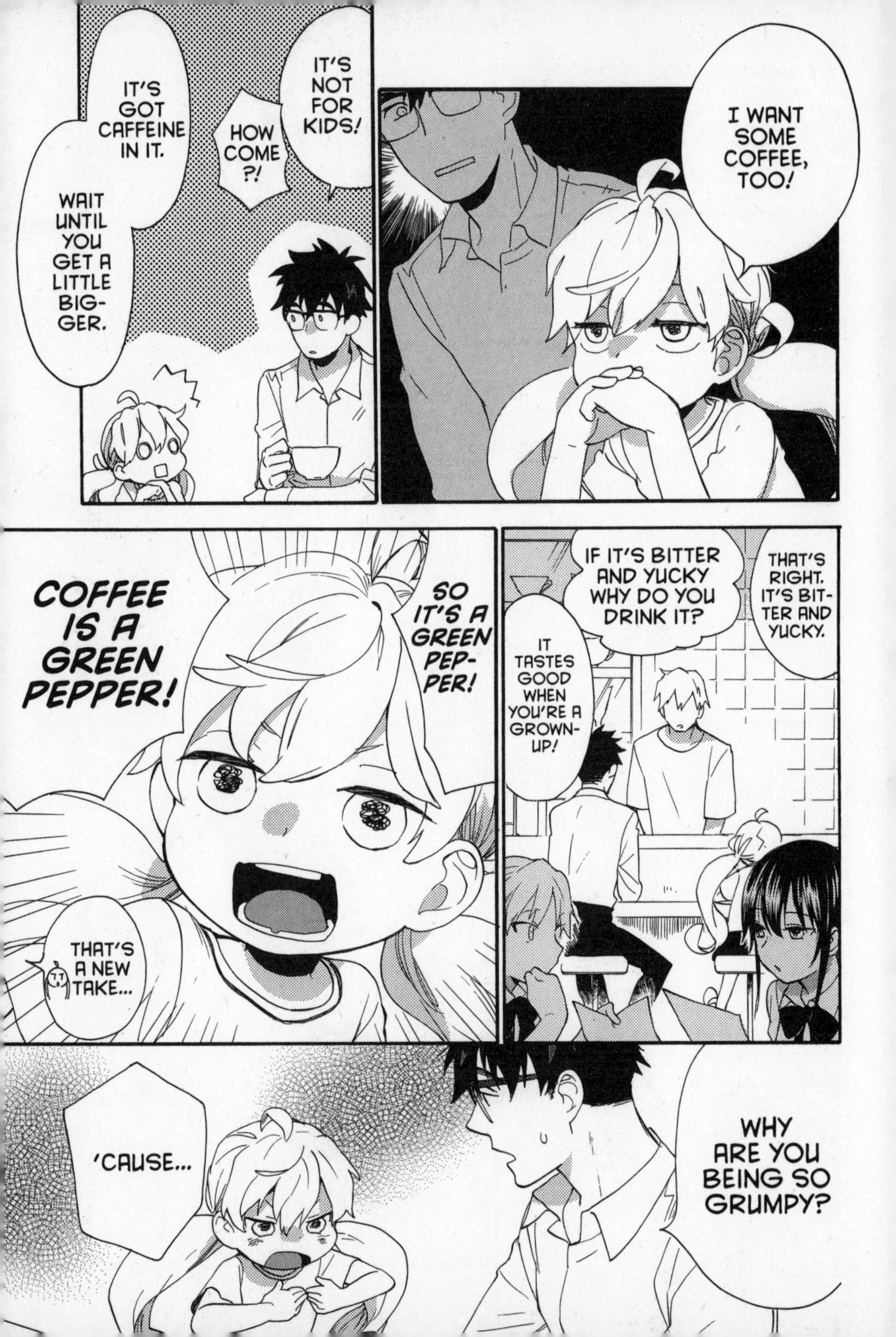
I WANT SOME COFFEE, TOO!
IT'S NOT FOR KIDS!
HOW COME?!
IT'S GOT CAFFEINE IN IT.
WAIT UNTIL YOU GET A LITTLE BIGGER.
THAT'S RIGHT. IT'S BITTER AND YUCKY.
IF IT'S BITTER AND YUCKY WHY DO YOU DRINK IT?
IT TASTES GOOD WHEN YOU'RE A GROWN-UP!
SO IT'S A GREEN PEPPER!
COFFEE IS A GREEN PEPPER!
THAT'S A NEW TAKE...
WHY ARE YOU BEING SO GRUMPY?
'CAUSE...

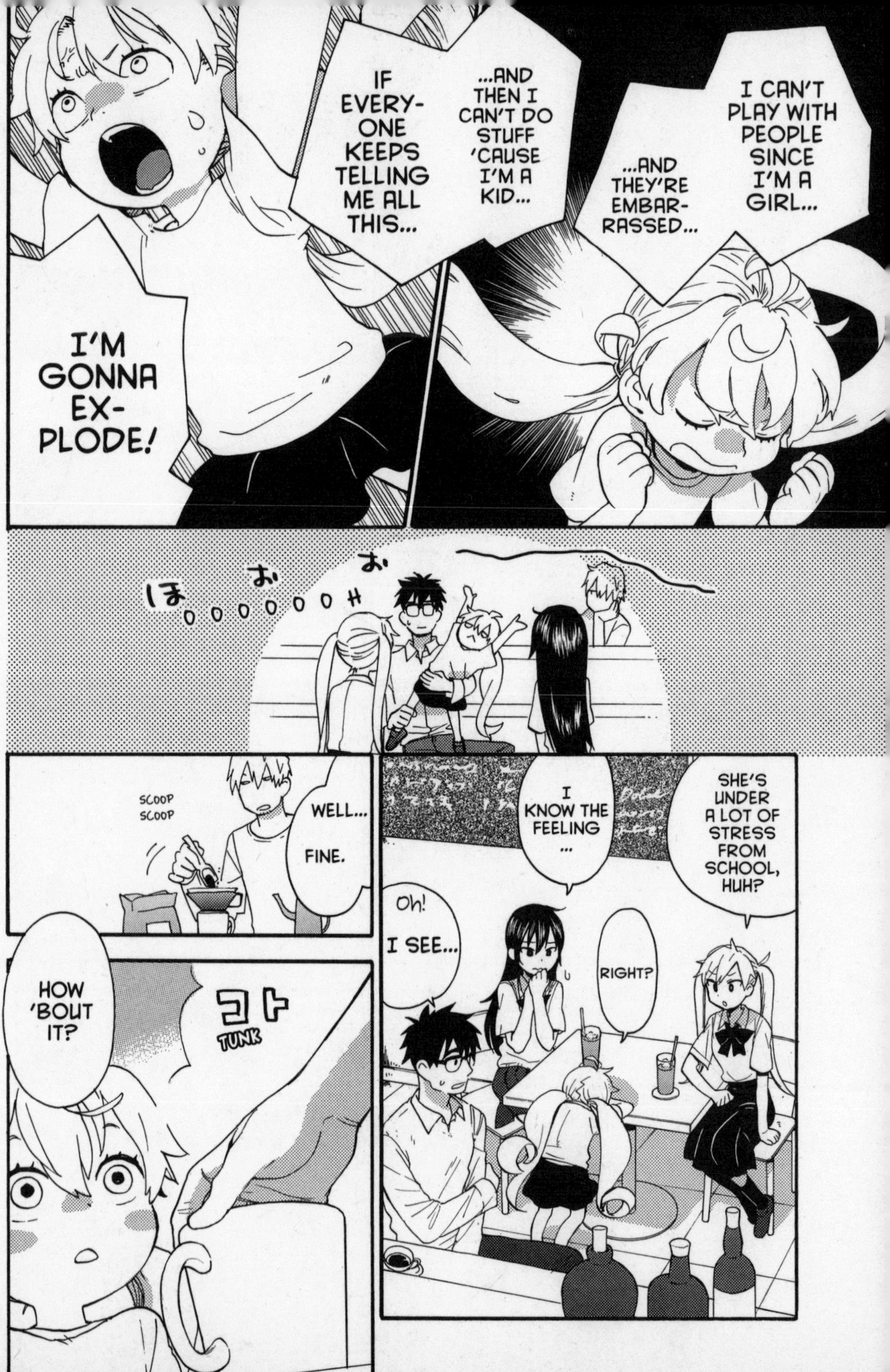
I CAN'T PLAY WITH PEOPLE SINCE I'M A GIRL...
...AND THEY'RE EMBARRASSED...
...AND THEN I CAN'T DO STUFF 'CAUSE I'M A KID...
IF EVERYONE KEEPS TELLING ME ALL THIS...
I'M GONNA EXPLODE!
ほおお
OOOOOOOH
SHE'S UNDER A LOT OF STRESS FROM SCHOOL, HUH?
I KNOW THE FEELING...
RIGHT?
Oh! I SEE...
SCOOP SCOOP
WELL...
FINE.
コト
TUNK
HOW 'BOUT IT?

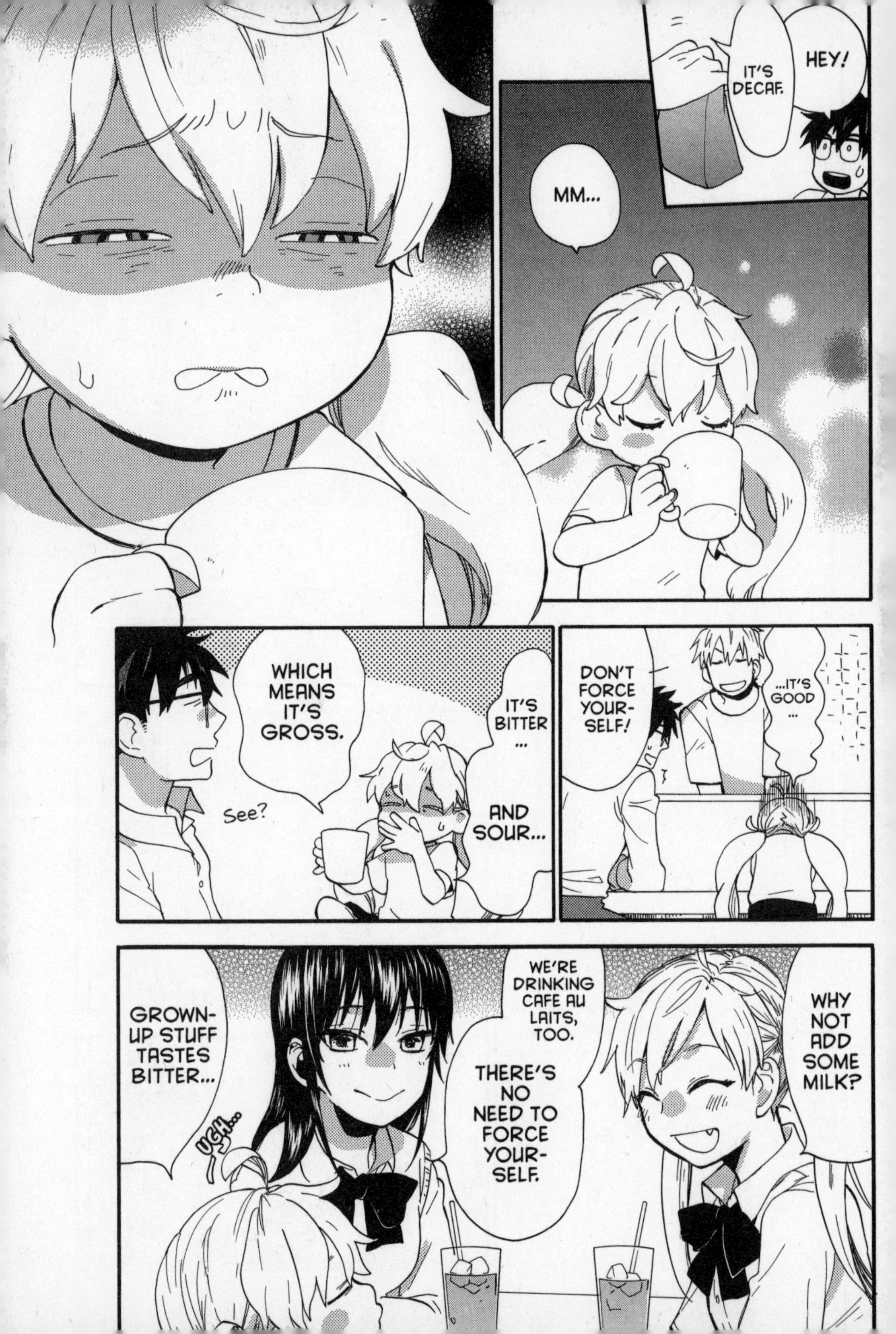
HEY!
IT'S DECAF.
MM...
...IT'S GOOD ...
DON'T FORCE YOUR-SELF!
IT'S BITTER ...
AND SOUR...
WHICH MEANS IT'S GROSS.
See?
WHY NOT ADD SOME MILK?
WE'RE DRINKING CAFE AU LAITS, TOO.
THERE'S NO NEED TO FORCE YOUR-SELF.
GROWN-UP STUFF TASTES BITTER...
UGH...

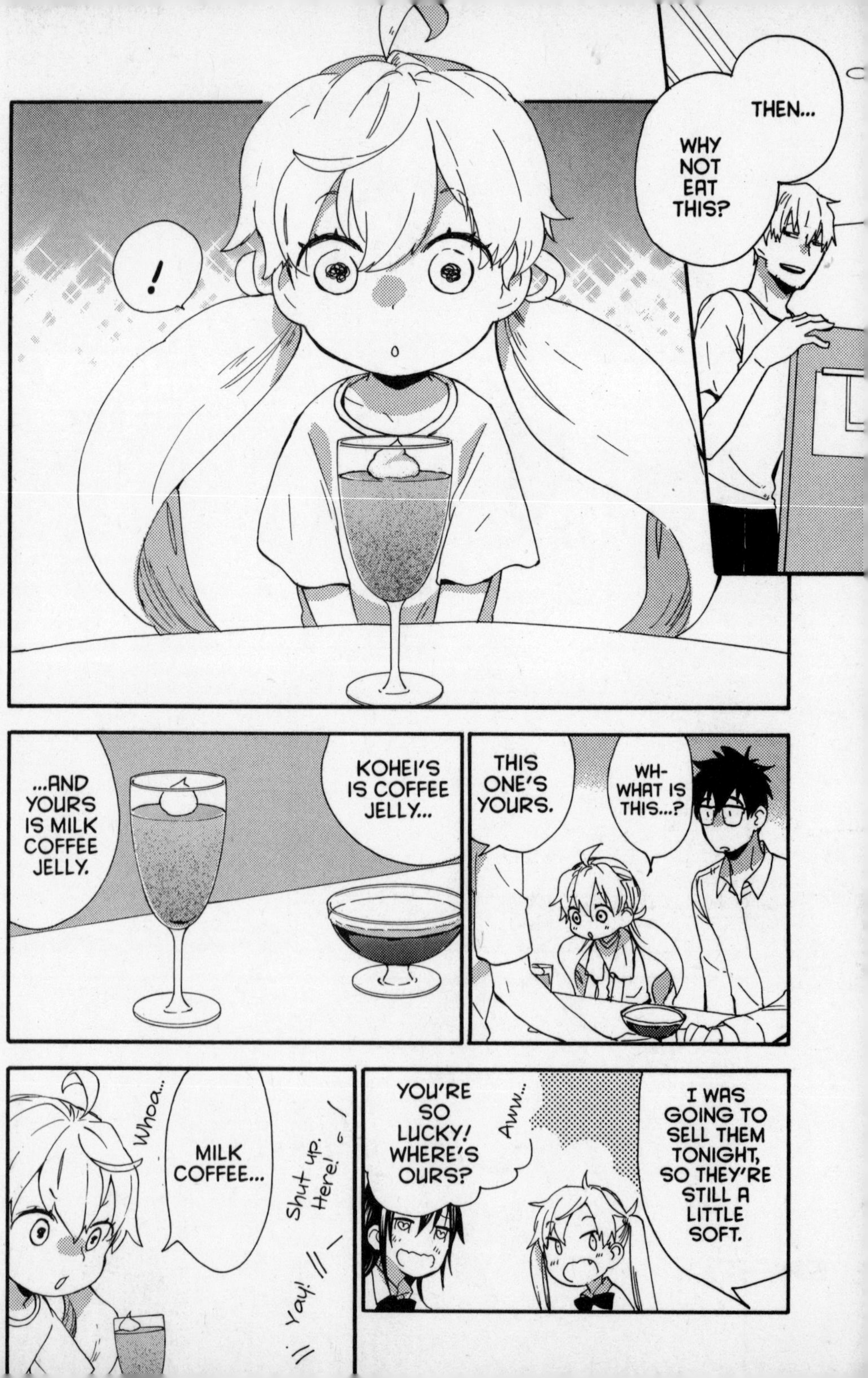
THEN... WHY NOT EAT THIS?
!
WH- WHAT IS THIS...?
THIS ONE'S YOURS.
KOHEI'S IS COFFEE JELLY...
...AND YOURS IS MILK COFFEE JELLY.
I WAS GOING TO SELL THEM TONIGHT, SO THEY'RE STILL A LITTLE SOFT.
Aww...
YOU'RE SO LUCKY! WHERE'S OURS?
Shut up. Here!
Yay!
MILK COFFEE...
Whoa...

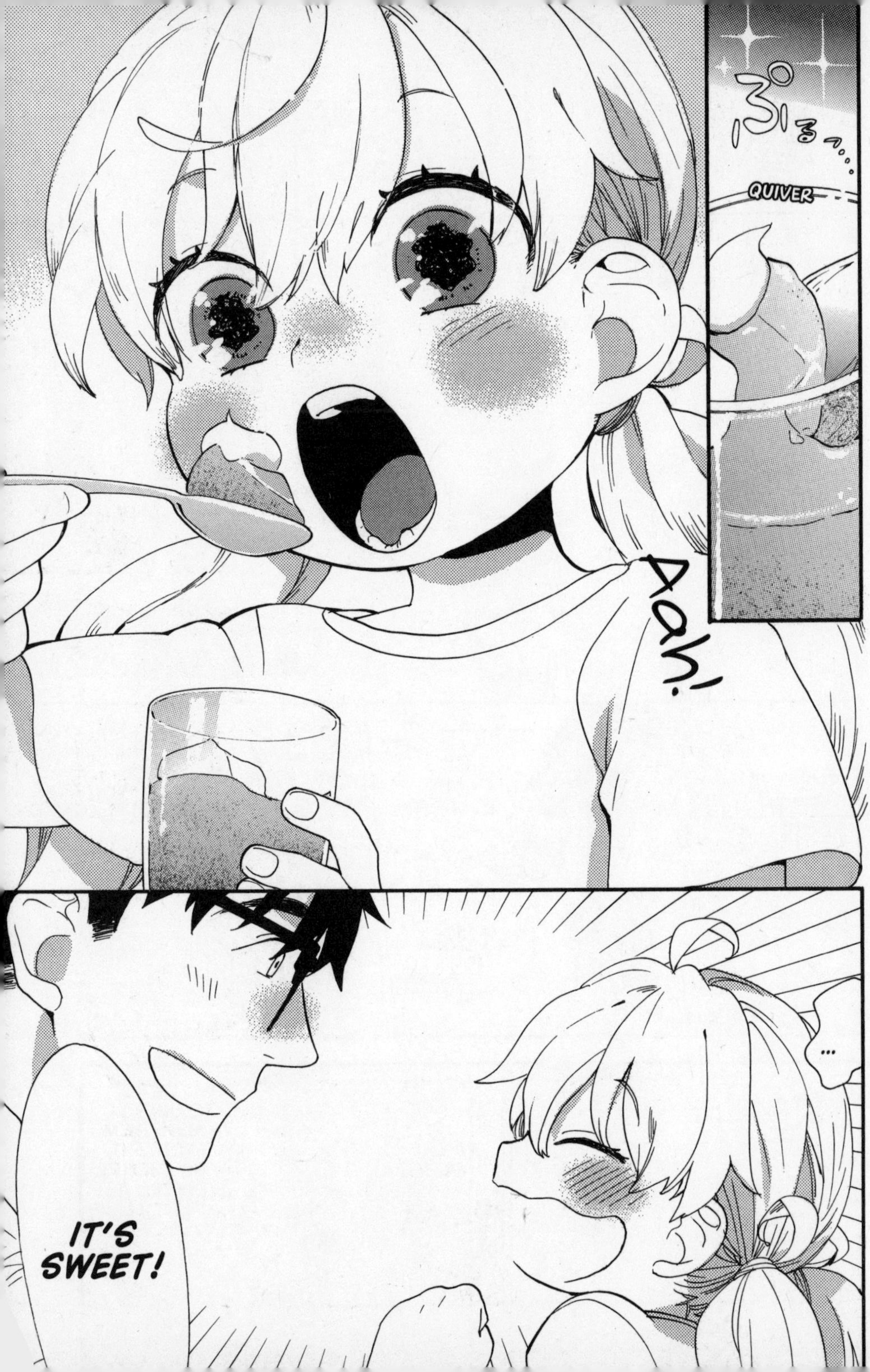
ぷるっ...
QUIVER
Aah!
...
IT'S SWEET!

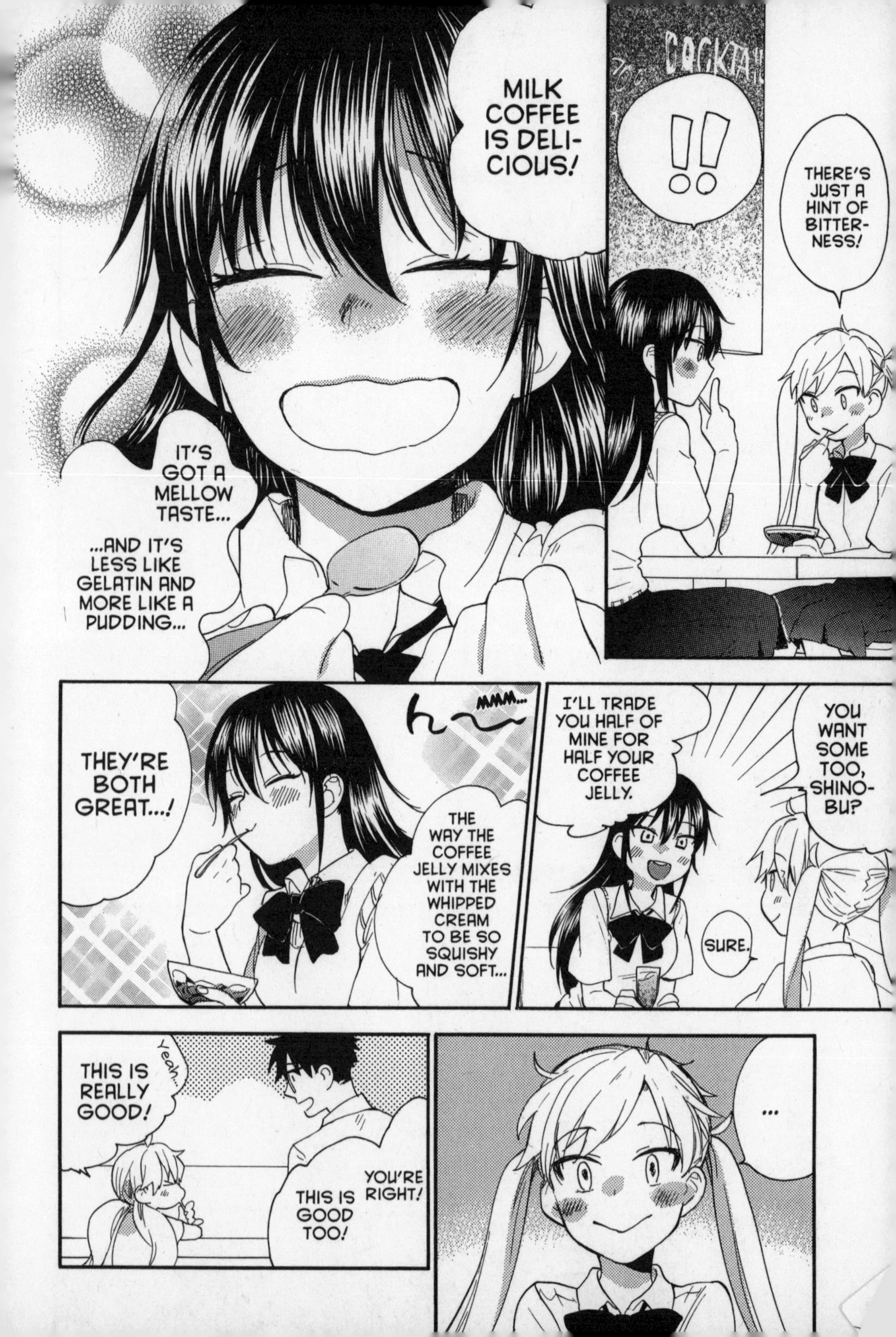

THERE'S JUST A HINT OF BITTERNESS!
!!
MILK COFFEE IS DELICIOUS!
IT'S GOT A MELLOW TASTE...
...AND IT'S LESS LIKE GELATIN AND MORE LIKE A PUDDING...
YOU WANT SOME TOO, SHINOBU?
I'LL TRADE YOU HALF OF MINE FOR HALF YOUR COFFEE JELLY.
SURE.
MMM...
THEY'RE BOTH GREAT...!
THE WAY THE COFFEE JELLY MIXES WITH THE WHIPPED CREAM TO BE SO SQUISHY AND SOFT...
...
THIS IS REALLY GOOD!
Yeah...
YOU'RE RIGHT!
THIS IS GOOD TOO!

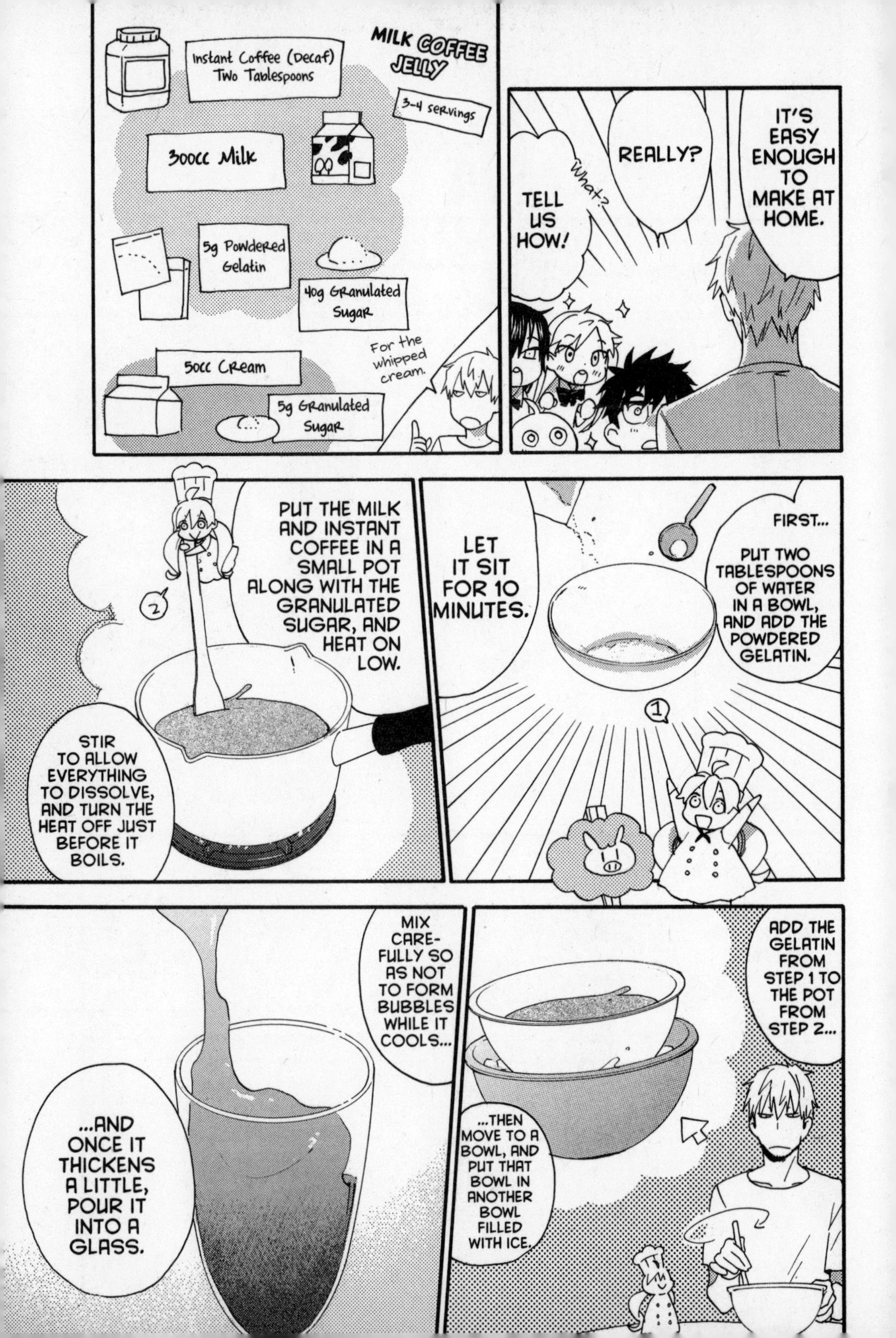

IT'S EASY ENOUGH TO MAKE AT HOME.
REALLY?
What?
TELL US HOW!
MILK COFFEE JELLY
3-4 servings
Instant Coffee (Decaf) Two Tablespoons
300cc Milk
5g Powdered Gelatin
40g Granulated Sugar
For the whipped cream.
50cc Cream
5g Granulated Sugar
FIRST...
PUT TWO TABLESPOONS OF WATER IN A BOWL, AND ADD THE POWDERED GELATIN.
LET IT SIT FOR 10 MINUTES.
1
PUT THE MILK AND INSTANT COFFEE IN A SMALL POT ALONG WITH THE GRANULATED SUGAR, AND HEAT ON LOW.
2
STIR TO ALLOW EVERYTHING TO DISSOLVE, AND TURN THE HEAT OFF JUST BEFORE IT BOILS.
ADD THE GELATIN FROM STEP 1 TO THE POT FROM STEP 2...
...THEN MOVE TO A BOWL, AND PUT THAT BOWL IN ANOTHER BOWL FILLED WITH ICE.
MIX CAREFULLY SO AS NOT TO FORM BUBBLES WHILE IT COOLS...
...AND ONCE IT THICKENS A LITTLE, POUR IT INTO A GLASS.

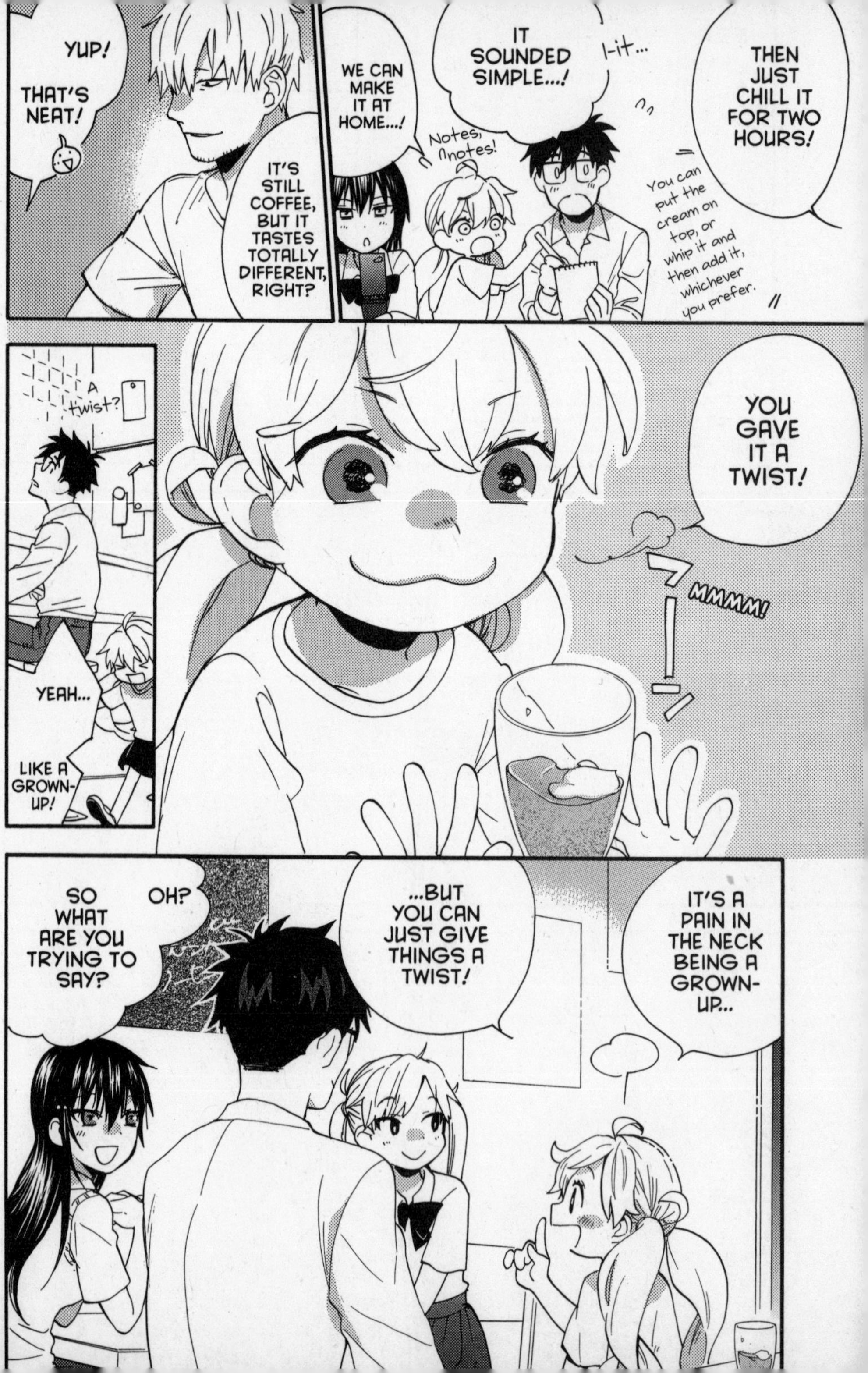
THEN JUST CHILL IT FOR TWO HOURS!
You can put the cream on top, or whip it and then add it, whichever you prefer.
IT SOUNDED SIMPLE...!
I-it...
Notes, notes!
WE CAN MAKE IT AT HOME...!
IT'S STILL COFFEE, BUT IT TASTES TOTALLY DIFFERENT, RIGHT?
YUP!
THAT'S NEAT!
YOU GAVE IT A TWIST!
MMMM!
A twist?
YEAH...
LIKE A GROWN-UP!
IT'S A PAIN IN THE NECK BEING A GROWN-UP...
...BUT YOU CAN JUST GIVE THINGS A TWIST!
OH?
SO WHAT ARE YOU TRYING TO SAY?

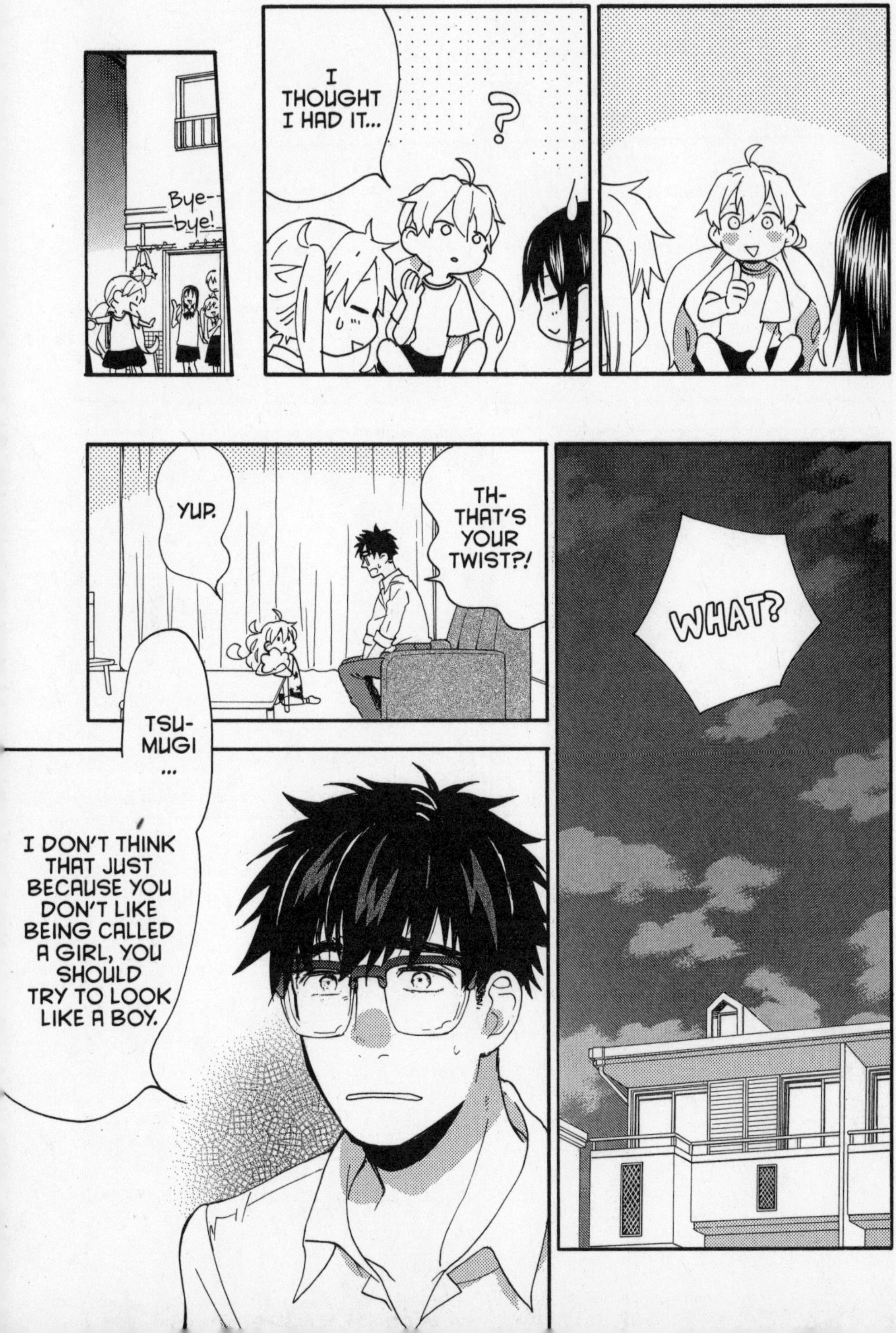
?
I THOUGHT I HAD IT...
Bye-bye!
WHAT?
TH-THAT'S YOUR TWIST?!
YUP.
TSU-MUGI...
I DON'T THINK THAT JUST BECAUSE YOU DON'T LIKE BEING CALLED A GIRL, YOU SHOULD TRY TO LOOK LIKE A BOY.

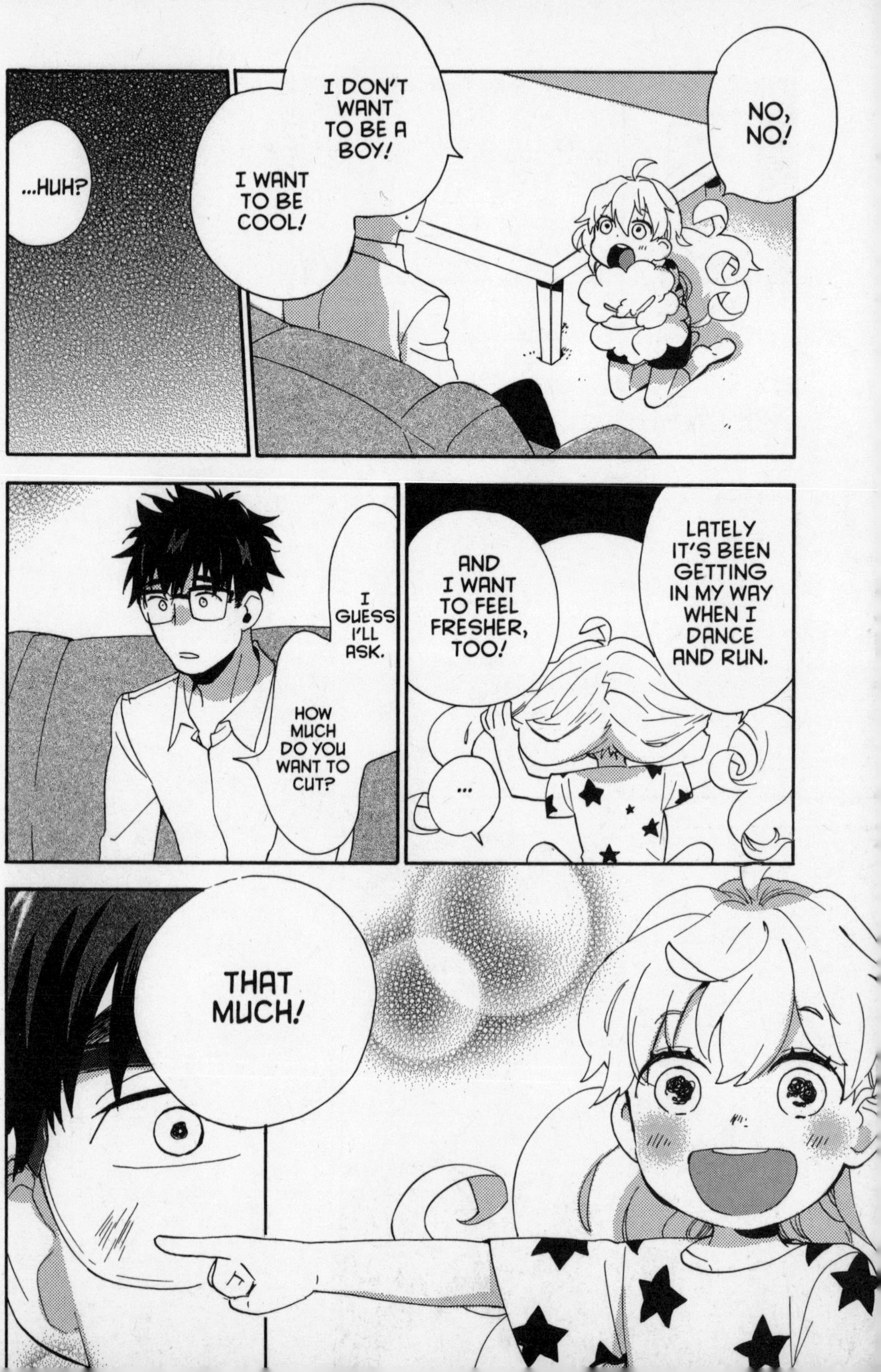
NO, NO!
I DON'T WANT TO BE A BOY!
I WANT TO BE COOL!
...HUH?
LATELY IT'S BEEN GETTING IN MY WAY WHEN I DANCE AND RUN.
AND I WANT TO FEEL FRESHER, TOO!
...
I GUESS I'LL ASK.
HOW MUCH DO YOU WANT TO CUT?
THAT MUCH!

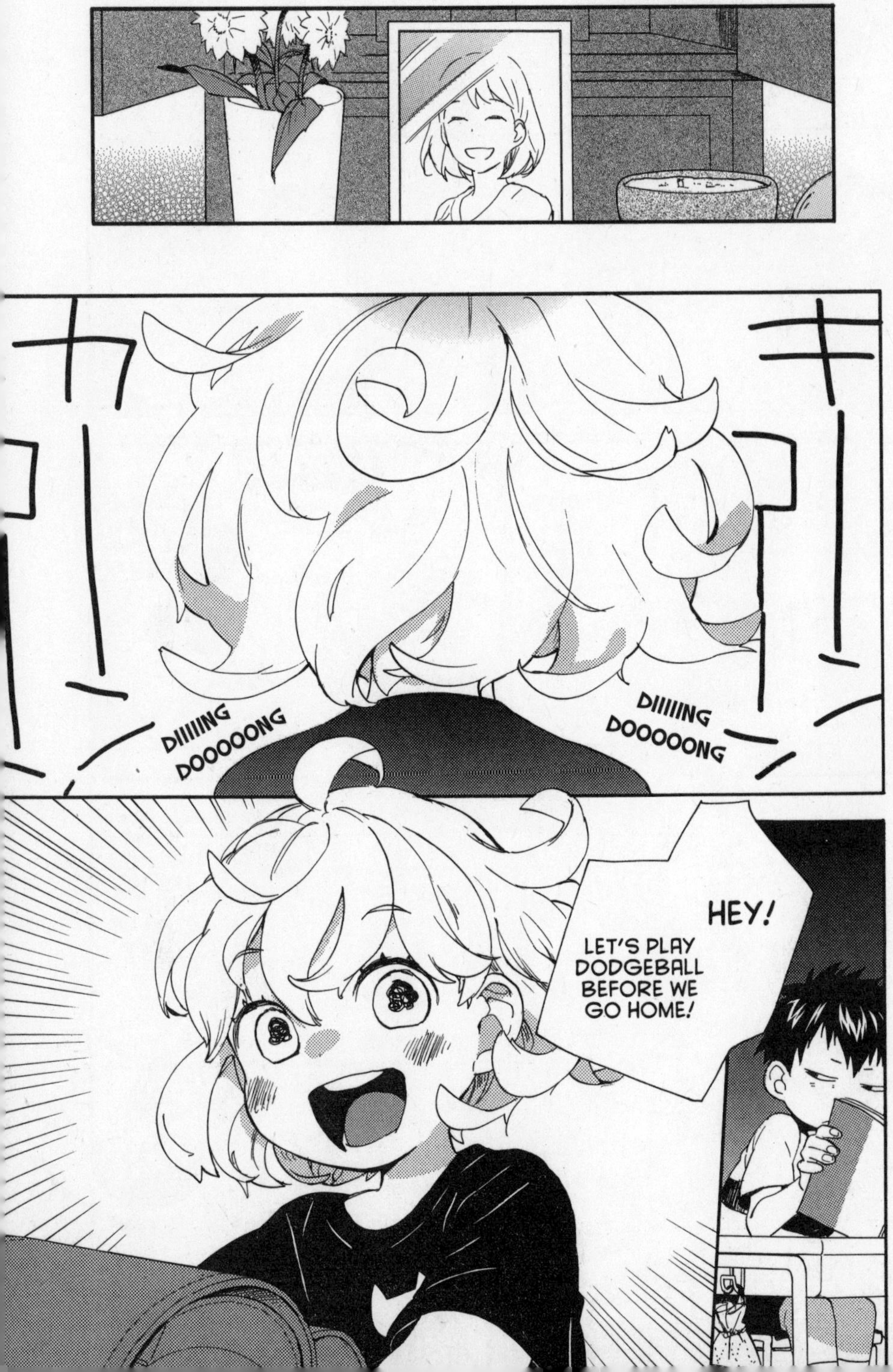
DIIIING DOOOOONG
DIIIING DOOOOONG
HEY!
LET'S PLAY DODGEBALL BEFORE WE GO HOME!

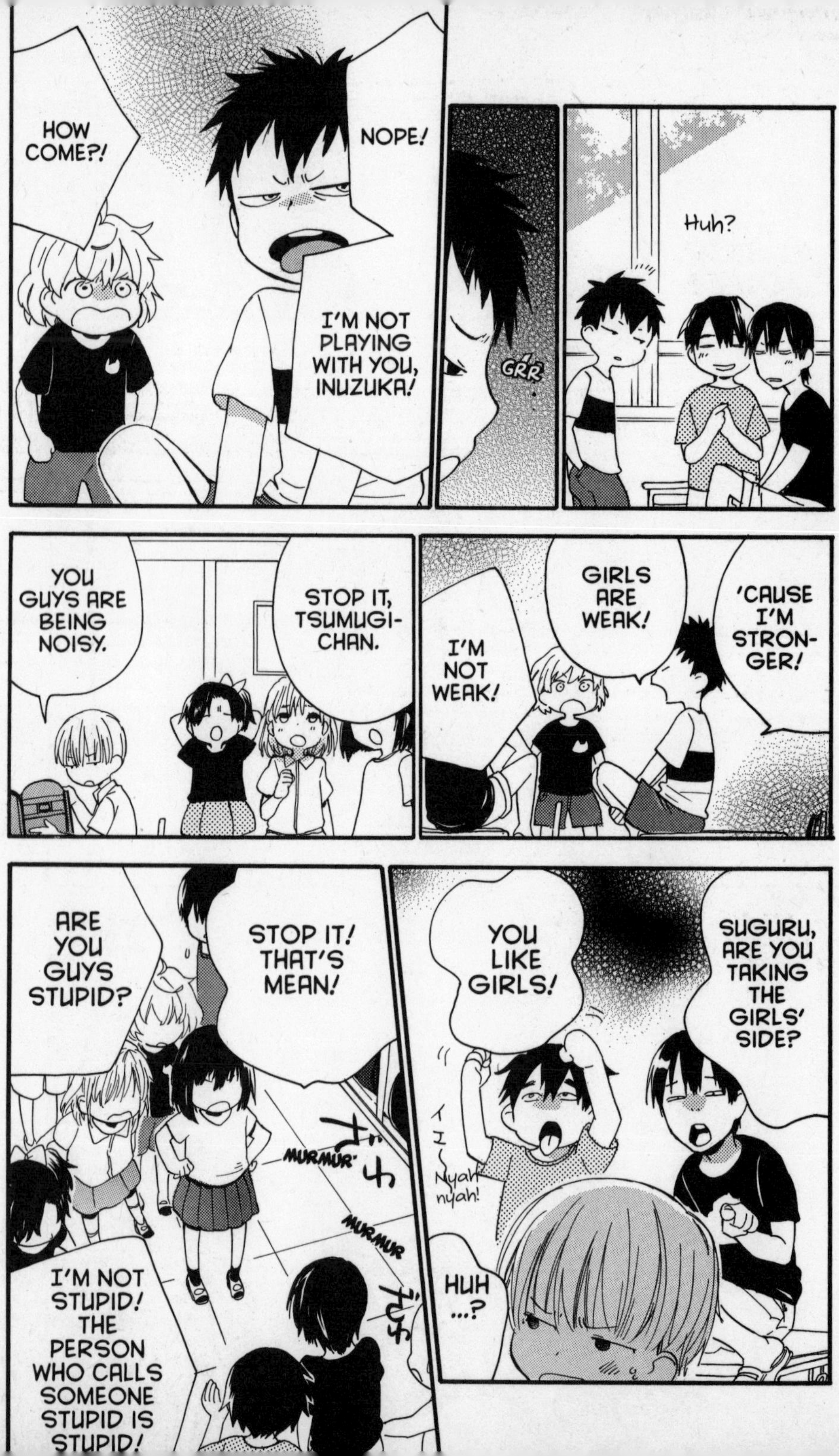
Huh?
GRR
NOPE!
I'M NOT PLAYING WITH YOU, INUZUKA!
HOW COME?!
'CAUSE I'M STRONGER!
GIRLS ARE WEAK!
I'M NOT WEAK!
STOP IT, TSUMUGI-CHAN.
YOU GUYS ARE BEING NOISY.
SUGURU, ARE YOU TAKING THE GIRLS' SIDE?
YOU LIKE GIRLS!
Nyah nyah!
HUH ...?
STOP IT! THAT'S MEAN!
ARE YOU GUYS STUPID?
MURMUR
MURMUR
I'M NOT STUPID! THE PERSON WHO CALLS SOMEONE STUPID IS STUPID!

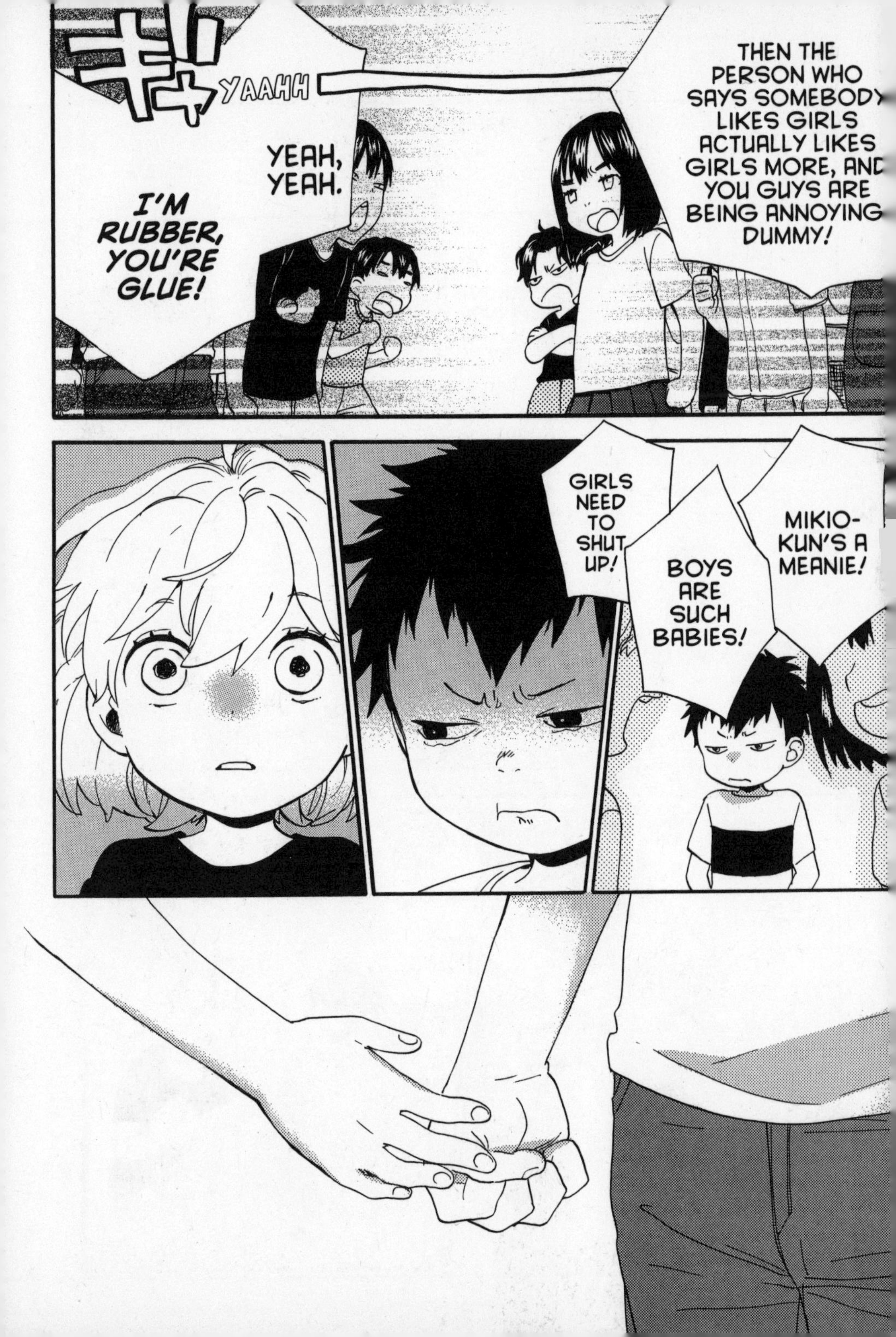
THEN THE PERSON WHO SAYS SOMEBODY LIKES GIRLS ACTUALLY LIKES GIRLS MORE, AND YOU GUYS ARE BEING ANNOYING, DUMMY!
YAAHH
YEAH, YEAH.
I'M RUBBER, YOU'RE GLUE!
MIKIO-KUN'S A MEANIE!
GIRLS NEED TO SHUT UP!
BOYS ARE SUCH BABIES!

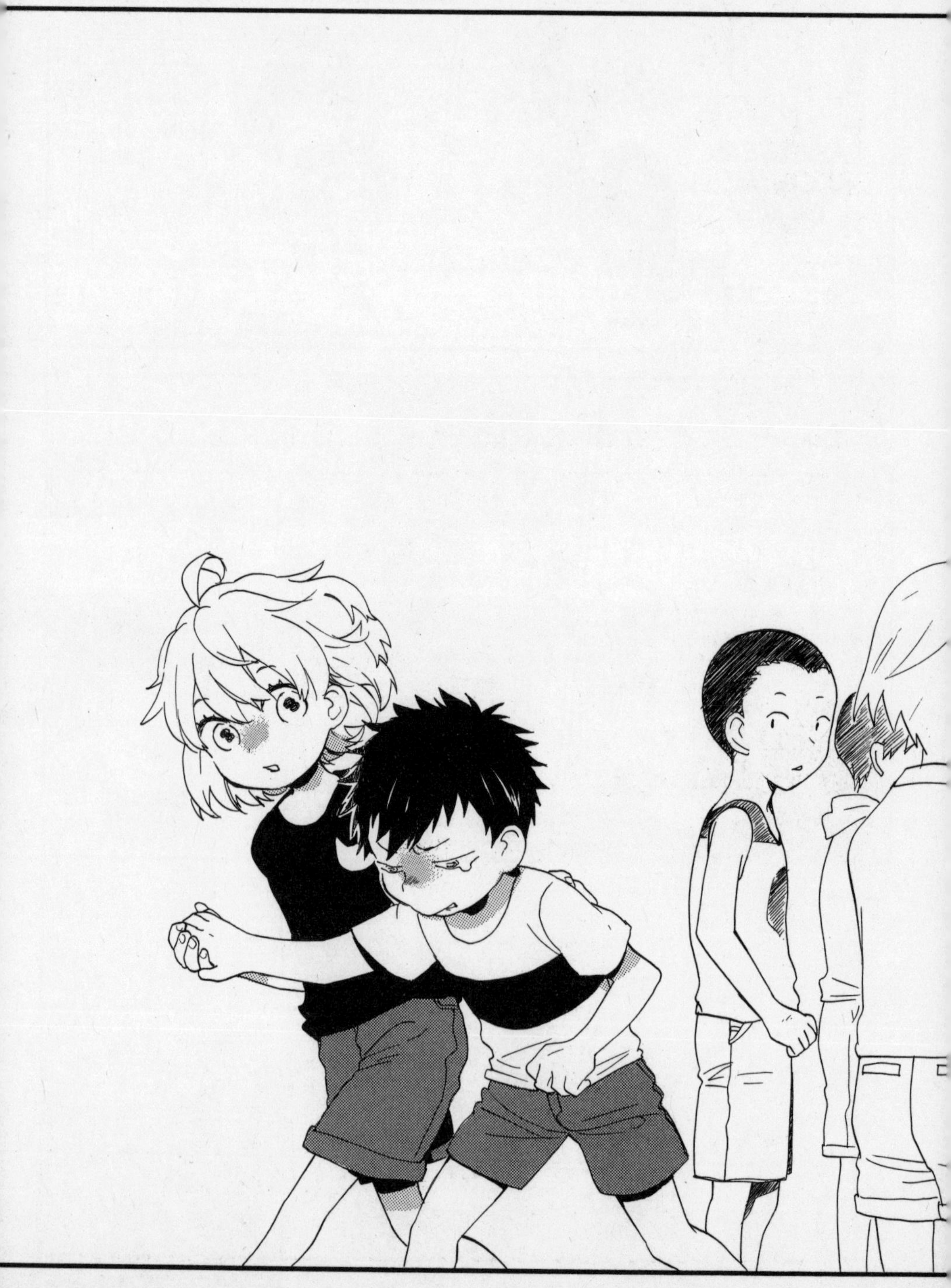

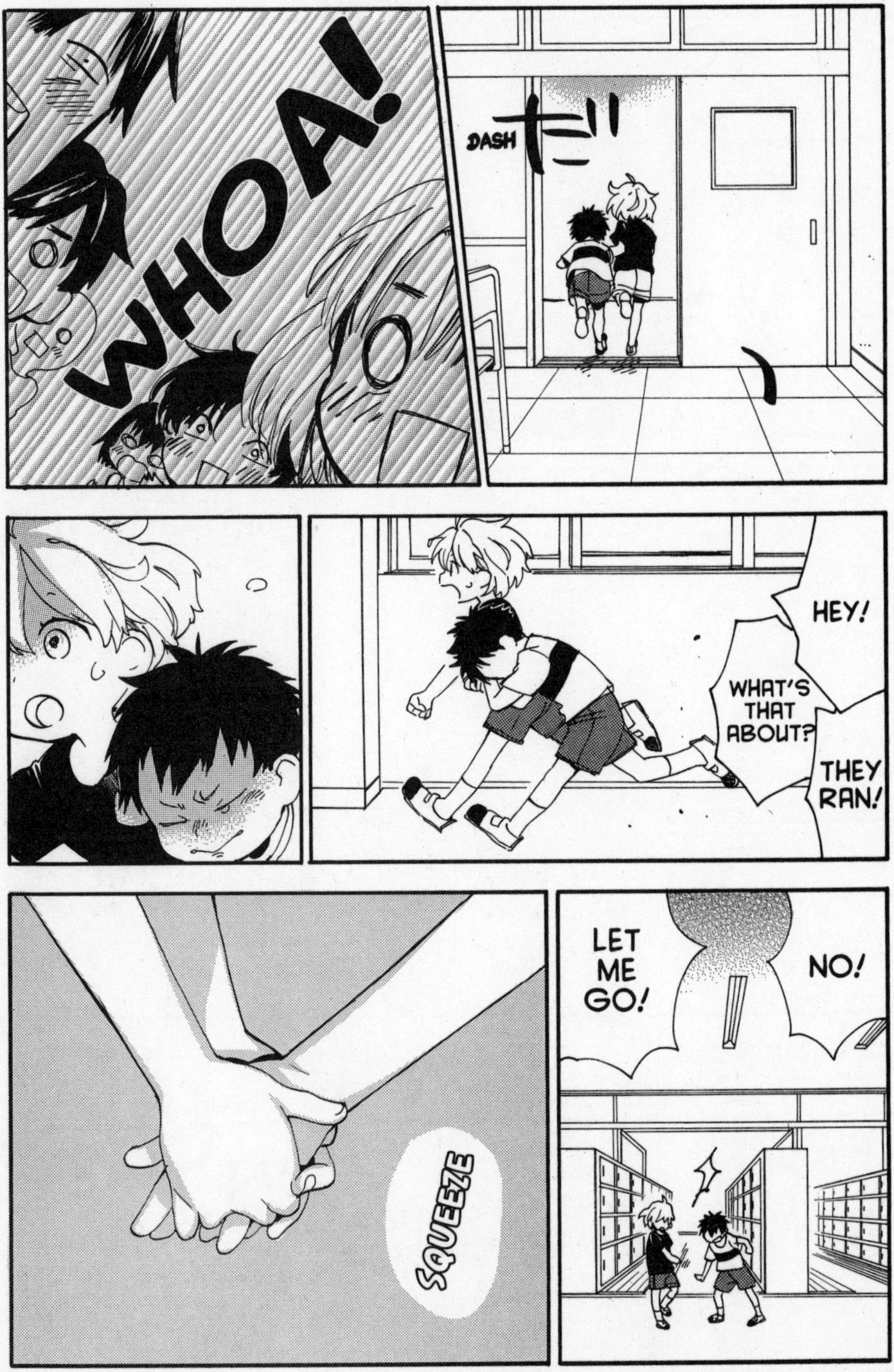
DASH
WHOA!
HEY!
WHAT'S THAT ABOUT?
THEY RAN!
LET ME GO!
NO!
SQUEEZE

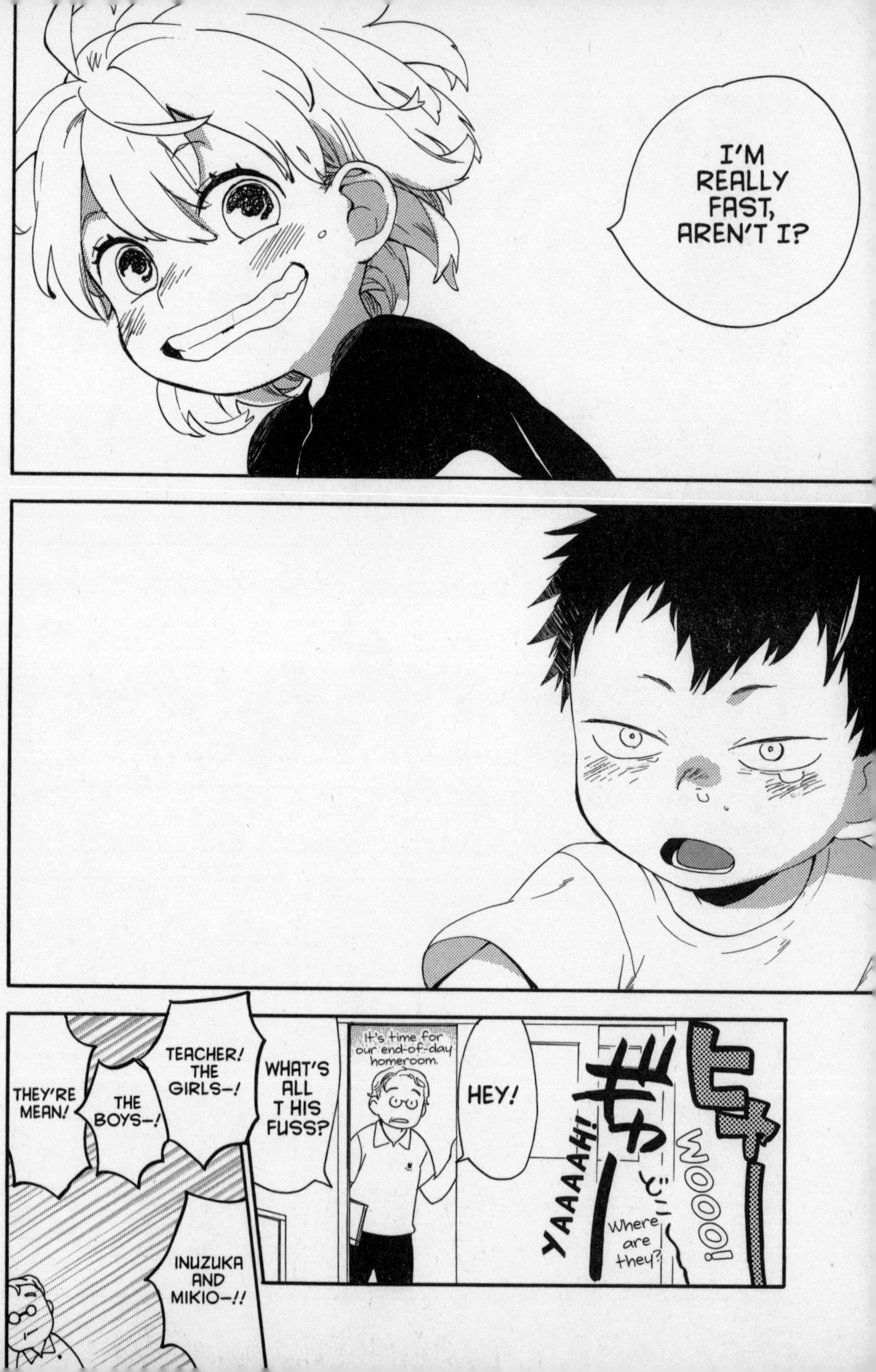
I'M REALLY FAST, AREN'T I?
WOOOO!
YAAAAH!
Where are they?
HEY!
It's time for our end-of-day homeroom.
WHAT'S ALL T HIS FUSS?
TEACHER! THE GIRLS—!
THE BOYS—!
THEY'RE MEAN!
INUZUKA AND MIKIO—!!

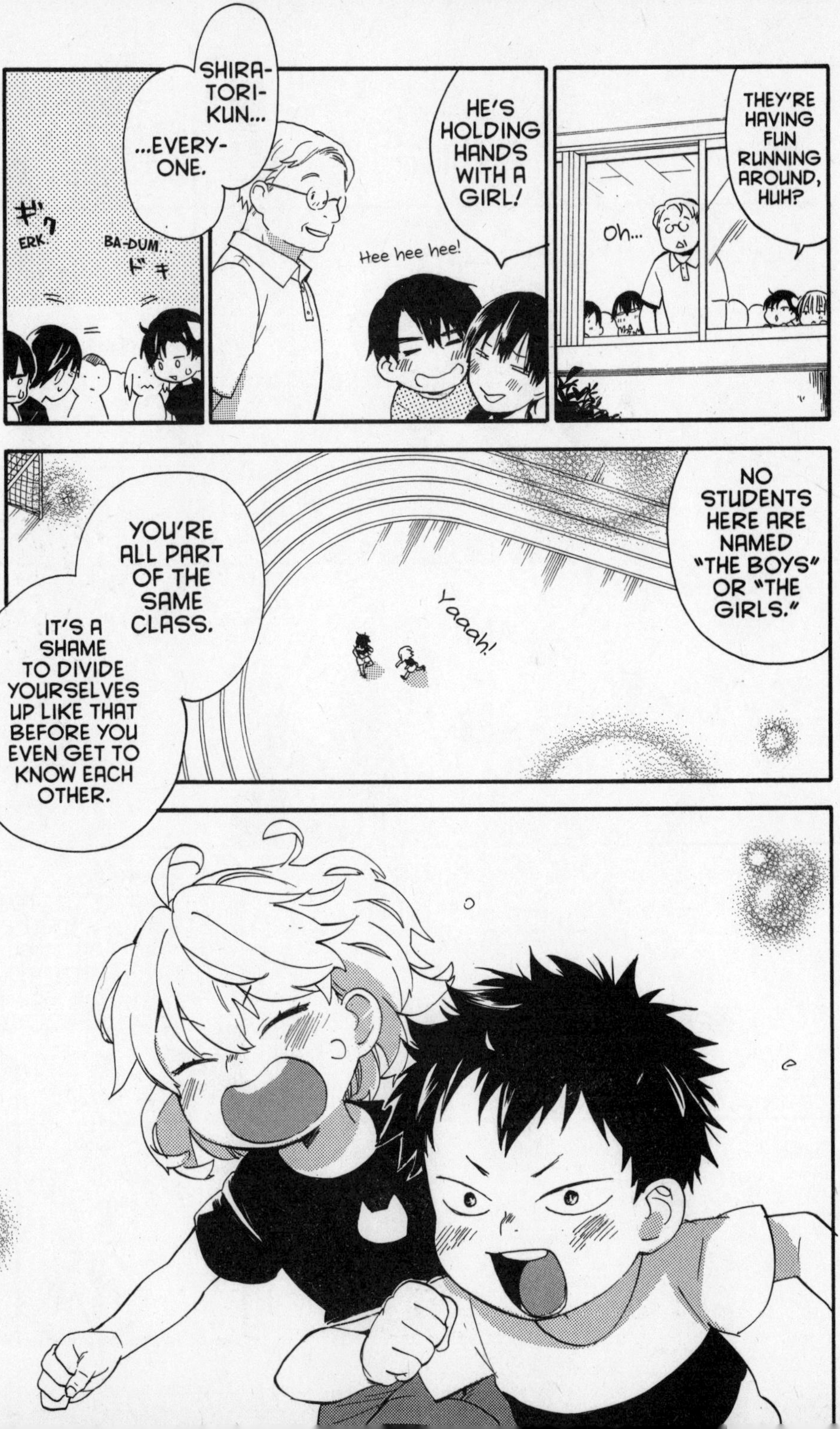
THEY'RE HAVING FUN RUNNING AROUND, HUH?
Oh...
HE'S HOLDING HANDS WITH A GIRL!
Hee hee hee!
SHIRATORI-KUN... ...EVERY-ONE.
ギク ERK.
BA-DUM... ドキ
NO STUDENTS HERE ARE NAMED "THE BOYS" OR "THE GIRLS."
YOU'RE ALL PART OF THE SAME CLASS.
Yaaah!
IT'S A SHAME TO DIVIDE YOURSELVES UP LIKE THAT BEFORE YOU EVEN GET TO KNOW EACH OTHER.

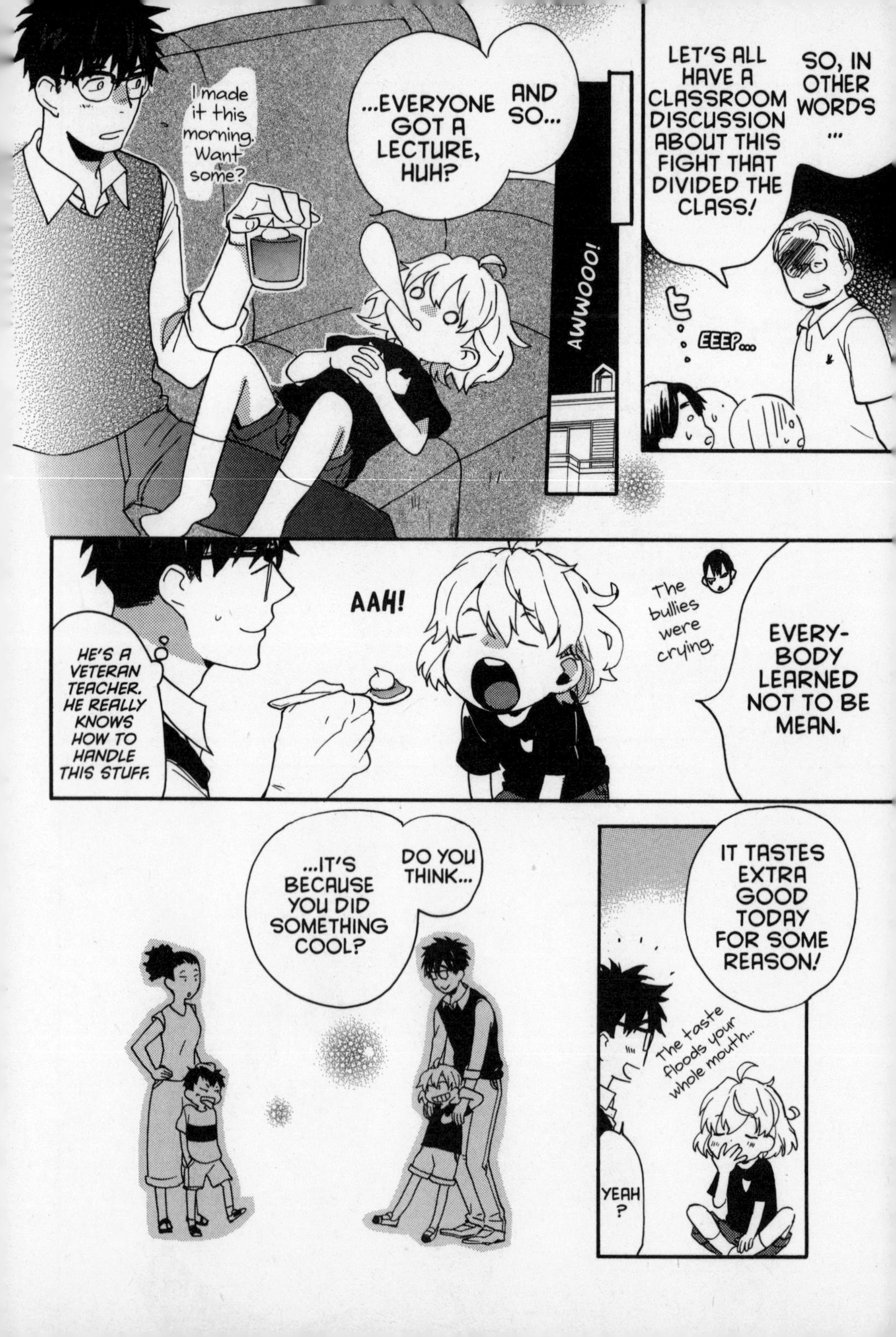
SO, IN OTHER WORDS...
LET'S ALL HAVE A CLASSROOM DISCUSSION ABOUT THIS FIGHT THAT DIVIDED THE CLASS!
EEEP...
AWWOOO!
AND SO...
...EVERYONE GOT A LECTURE, HUH?
I made it this morning. Want some?
EVERY-BODY LEARNED NOT TO BE MEAN.
The bullies were crying.
AAH!
HE'S A VETERAN TEACHER. HE REALLY KNOWS HOW TO HANDLE THIS STUFF.
IT TASTES EXTRA GOOD TODAY FOR SOME REASON!
The taste floods your whole mouth...
YEAH?
DO YOU THINK...
...IT'S BECAUSE YOU DID SOMETHING COOL?

MILK COFFEE JELLY

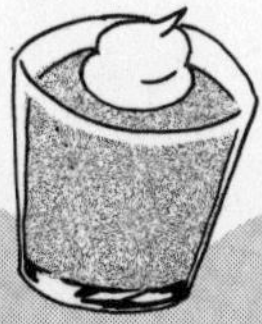

☆ Ingredients (serves 3-4) ☆

- ★ 300cc Milk
- ★ 40g Granulated Sugar
- ★ 50cc Cream
- ★ 2 Tablespoons Instant Coffee (Decaf)
- ★ 5g Powdered Gelatin
- ★ 5g Granulated Sugar

1. Dissolve the granulated gelatin in two tablespoons of water, and let set for ten minutes.
2. In a small saucepan, place milk, instant coffee, and 40g of the sugar and heat over low heat. Stir until they dissolve, and remove from heat before the mixture boils.
3. Mix 1 and 2 together well, and transfer to a bowl. Place base of bowl in ice water.
4. Stir to chill, taking care not to create bubbles.
5. When the mixture thickens, pour into serving cups and chill for at least two hours.
6. Add 5g granulated sugar to the cream, then whip to desired thickness
7. When the gelatin sets, top it with 6 and it's done!

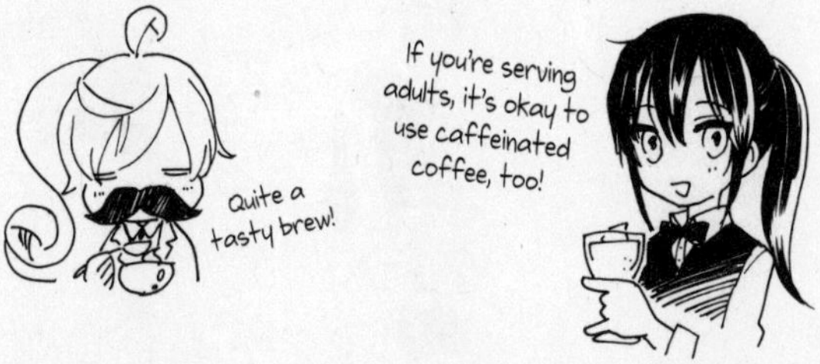
If you're serving adults, it's okay to use caffeinated coffee, too!
Quite a tasty brew!

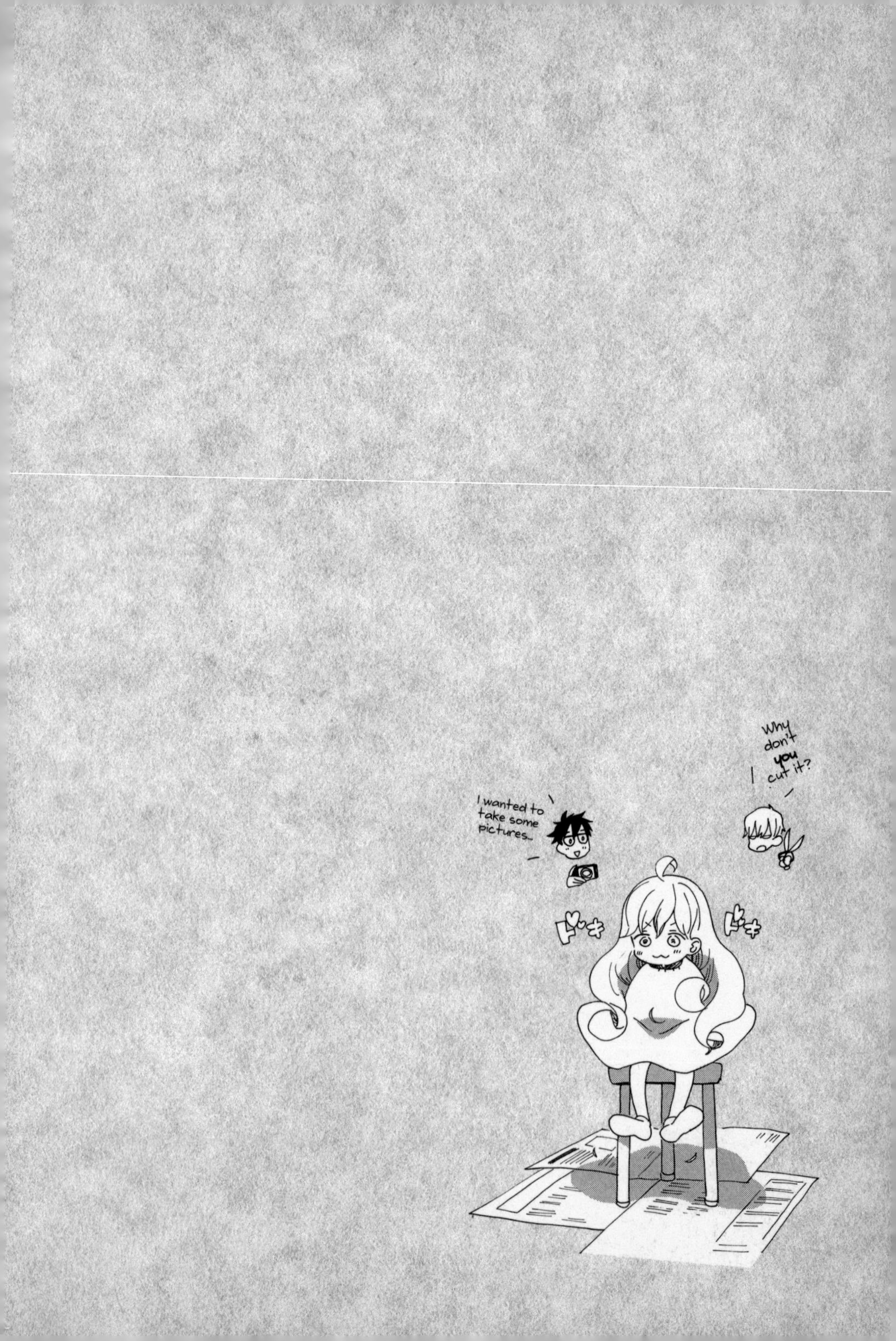
Why don't you cut it?
I wanted to take some pictures...

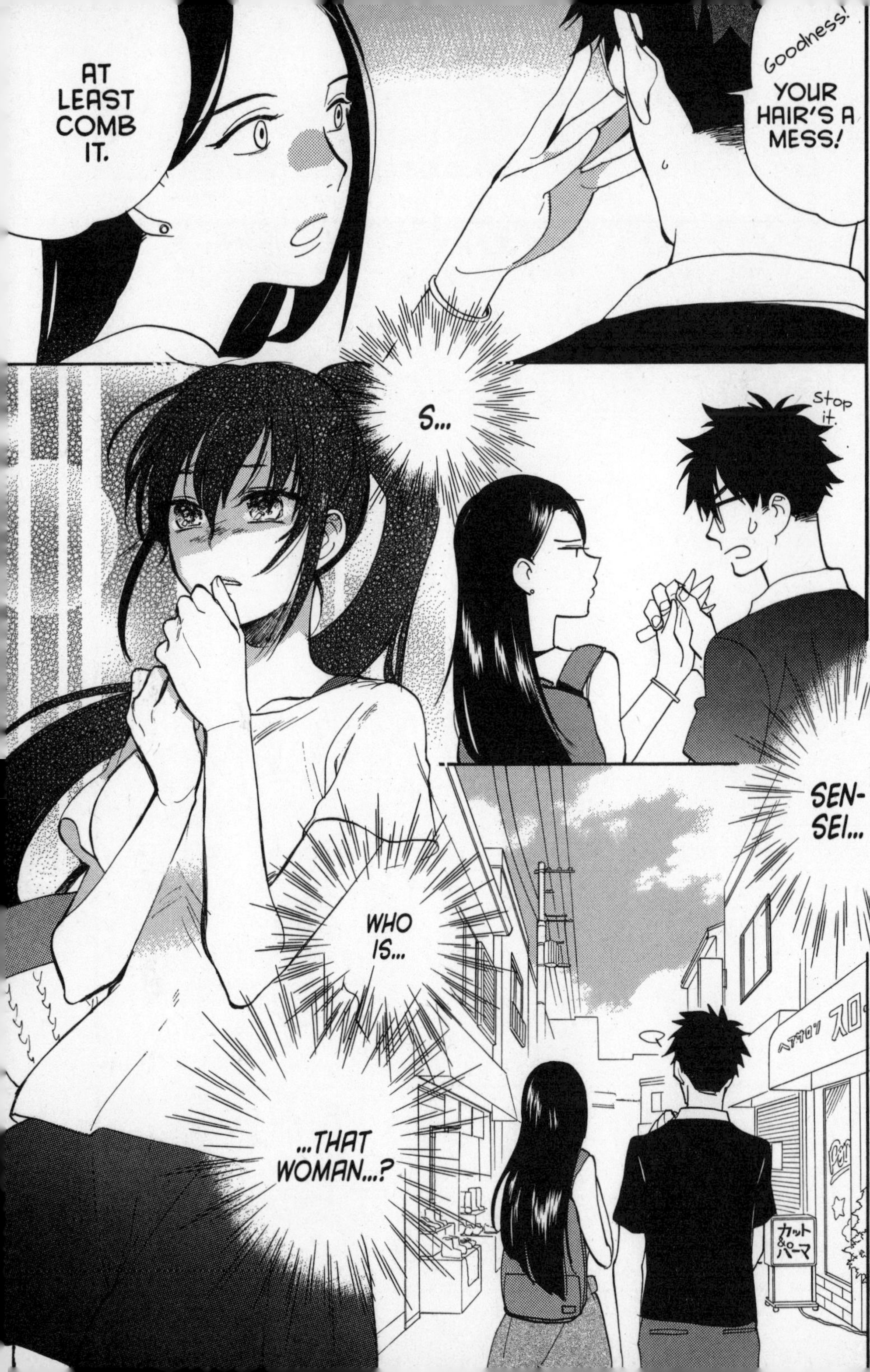

Goodness!
YOUR HAIR'S A MESS!
AT LEAST COMB IT.
Stop it.
SEN-SEI...
カット&パーマ
S...
WHO IS...
...THAT WOMAN...?

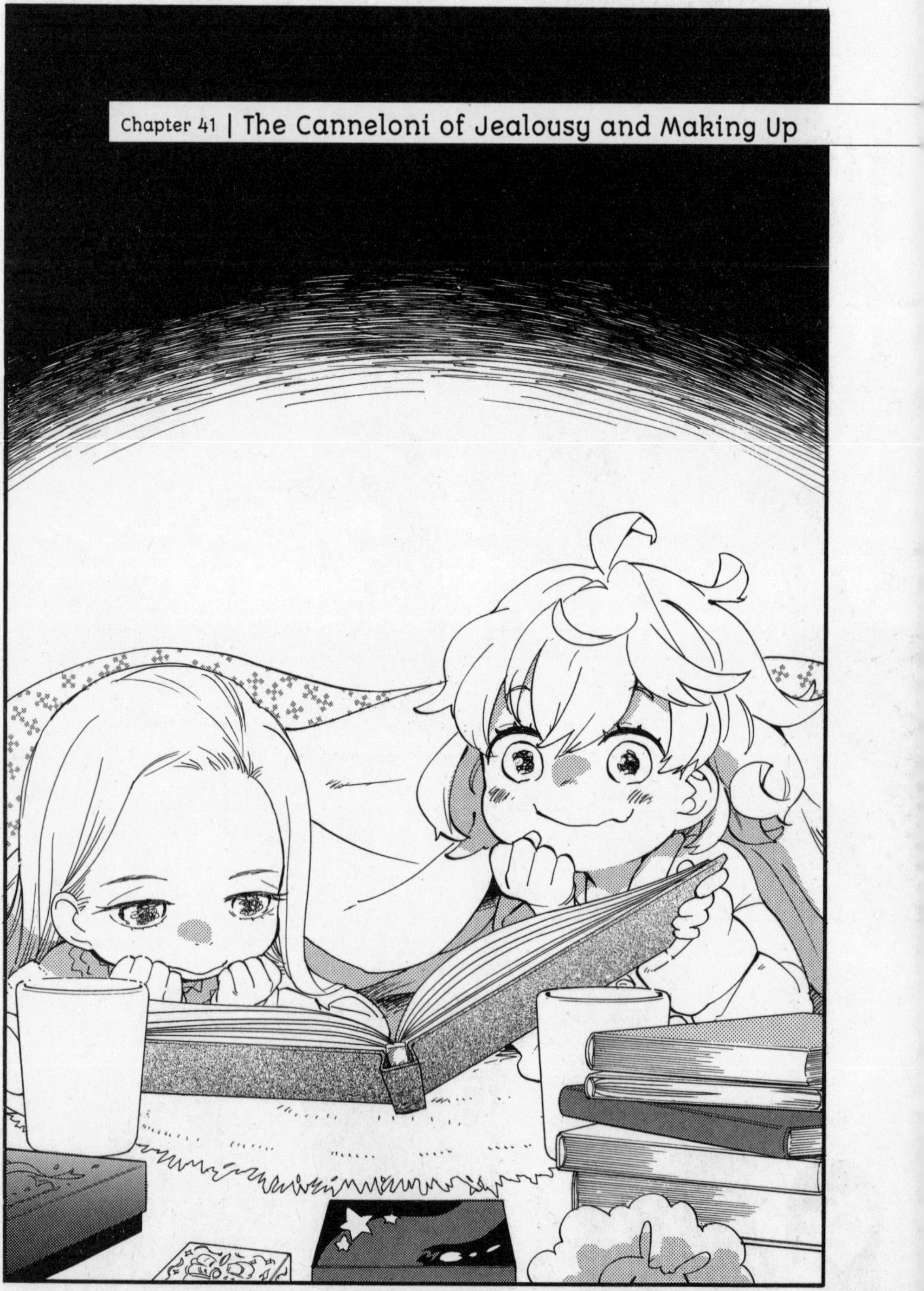
Chapter 41 | The Canneloni of Jealousy and Making Up

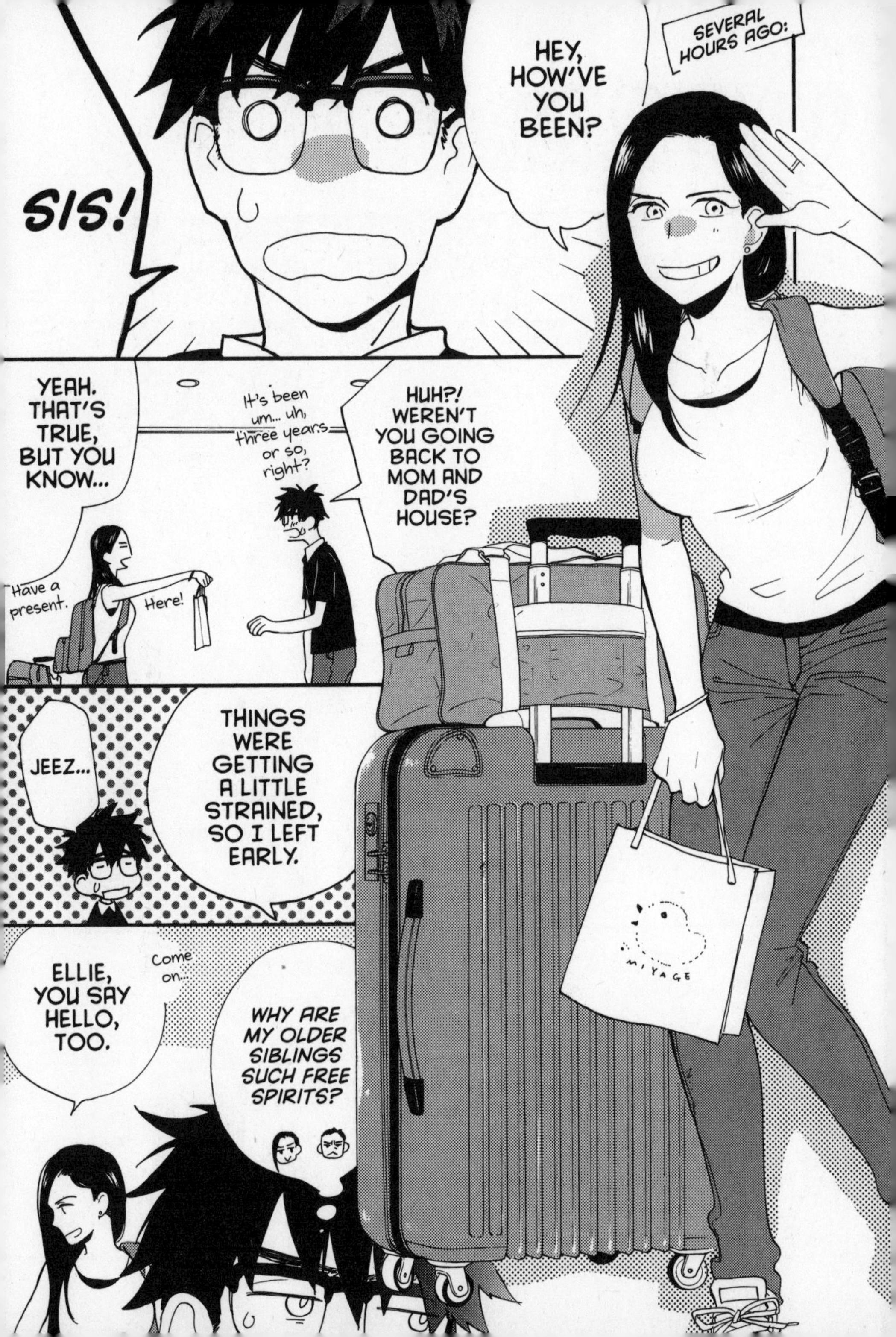
SEVERAL HOURS AGO:
HEY, HOW'VE YOU BEEN?
MIYAGE
SIS!
HUH?! WEREN'T YOU GOING BACK TO MOM AND DAD'S HOUSE?
It's been um... uh, three years or so, right?
YEAH. THAT'S TRUE, BUT YOU KNOW...
Here!
Have a present.
THINGS WERE GETTING A LITTLE STRAINED, SO I LEFT EARLY.
JEEZ...
WHY ARE MY OLDER SIBLINGS SUCH FREE SPIRITS?
Come on...
ELLIE, YOU SAY HELLO, TOO.

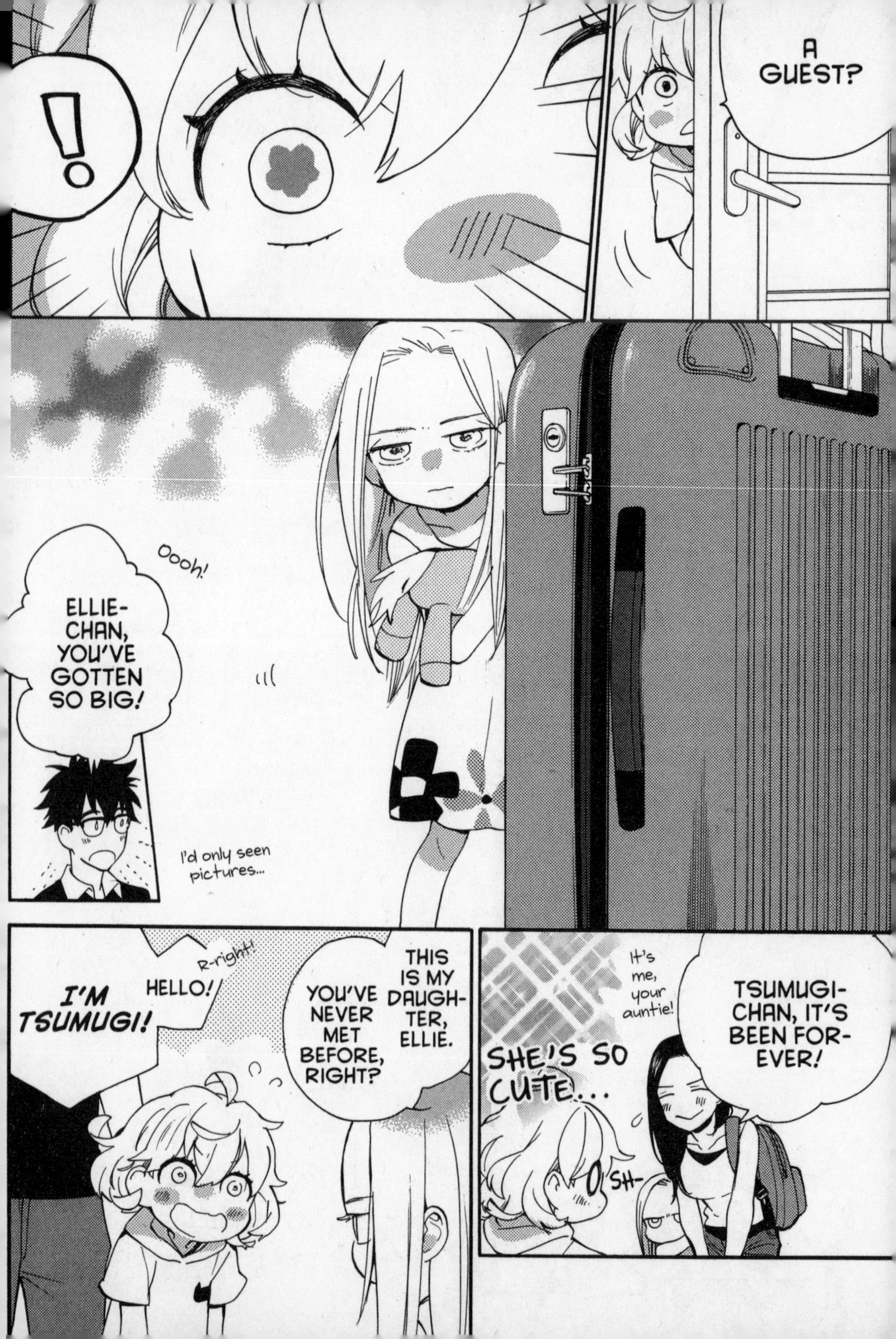

A GUEST?
!
Oooh!
ELLIE-CHAN, YOU'VE GOTTEN SO BIG!
I'd only seen pictures...
TSUMUGI-CHAN, IT'S BEEN FOR-EVER!
It's me, your auntie!
SHE'S SO CUTE...
SH-
THIS IS MY DAUGH-TER, ELLIE.
YOU'VE NEVER MET BEFORE, RIGHT?
HELLO!
R-right!
I'M TSUMUGI!

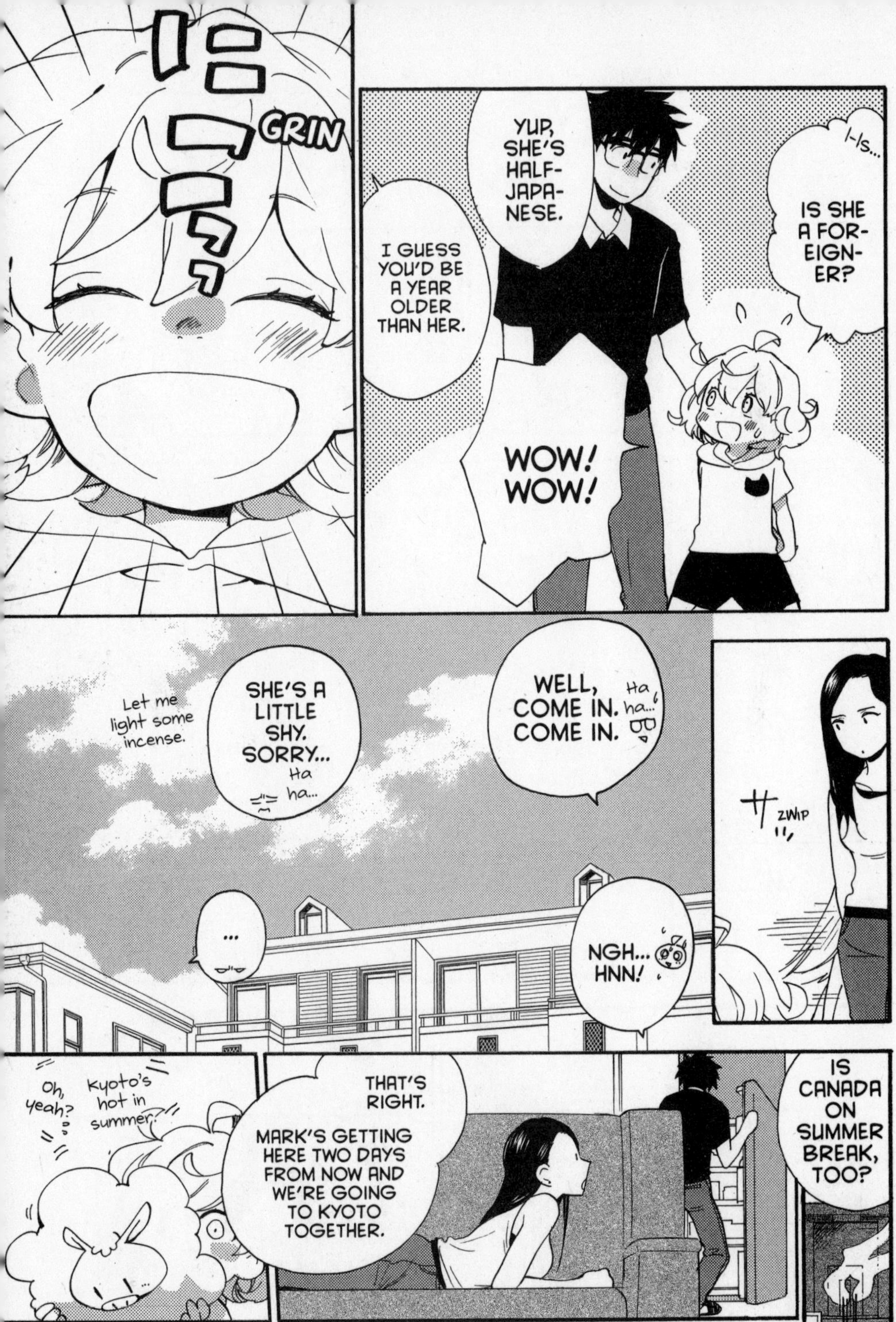
I-Is...
IS SHE A FOR-EIGN-ER?
YUP, SHE'S HALF-JAPA-NESE.
I GUESS YOU'D BE A YEAR OLDER THAN HER.
WOW! WOW!
GRIN
ZWIP
WELL, COME IN. COME IN.
Ha ha...
SHE'S A LITTLE SHY. SORRY...
Ha ha...
Let me light some incense.
NGH... HNN!
...
IS CANADA ON SUMMER BREAK, TOO?
THAT'S RIGHT.
MARK'S GETTING HERE TWO DAYS FROM NOW AND WE'RE GOING TO KYOTO TOGETHER.
Kyoto's hot in summer.
Oh, yeah?

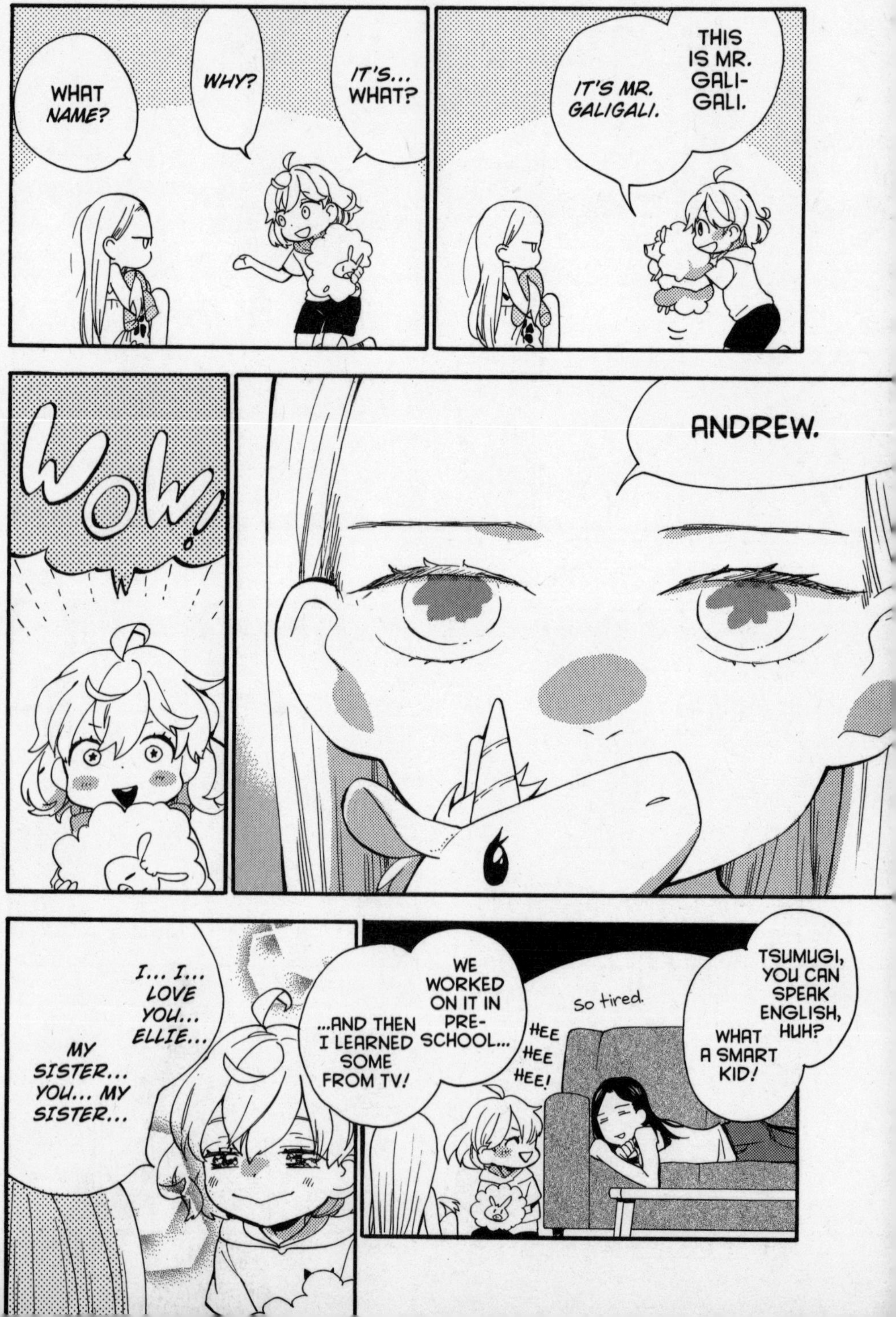
THIS IS MR. GALI-GALI.
IT'S MR. GALIGALI.
IT'S... WHAT?
WHY?
WHAT NAME?
ANDREW.
WOW!
TSUMUGI, YOU CAN SPEAK ENGLISH, HUH?
WHAT A SMART KID!
So tired.
HEE HEE HEE!
WE WORKED ON IT IN PRE-SCHOOL...
...AND THEN I LEARNED SOME FROM TV!
I... I... LOVE YOU... ELLIE...
MY SISTER... YOU... MY SISTER...

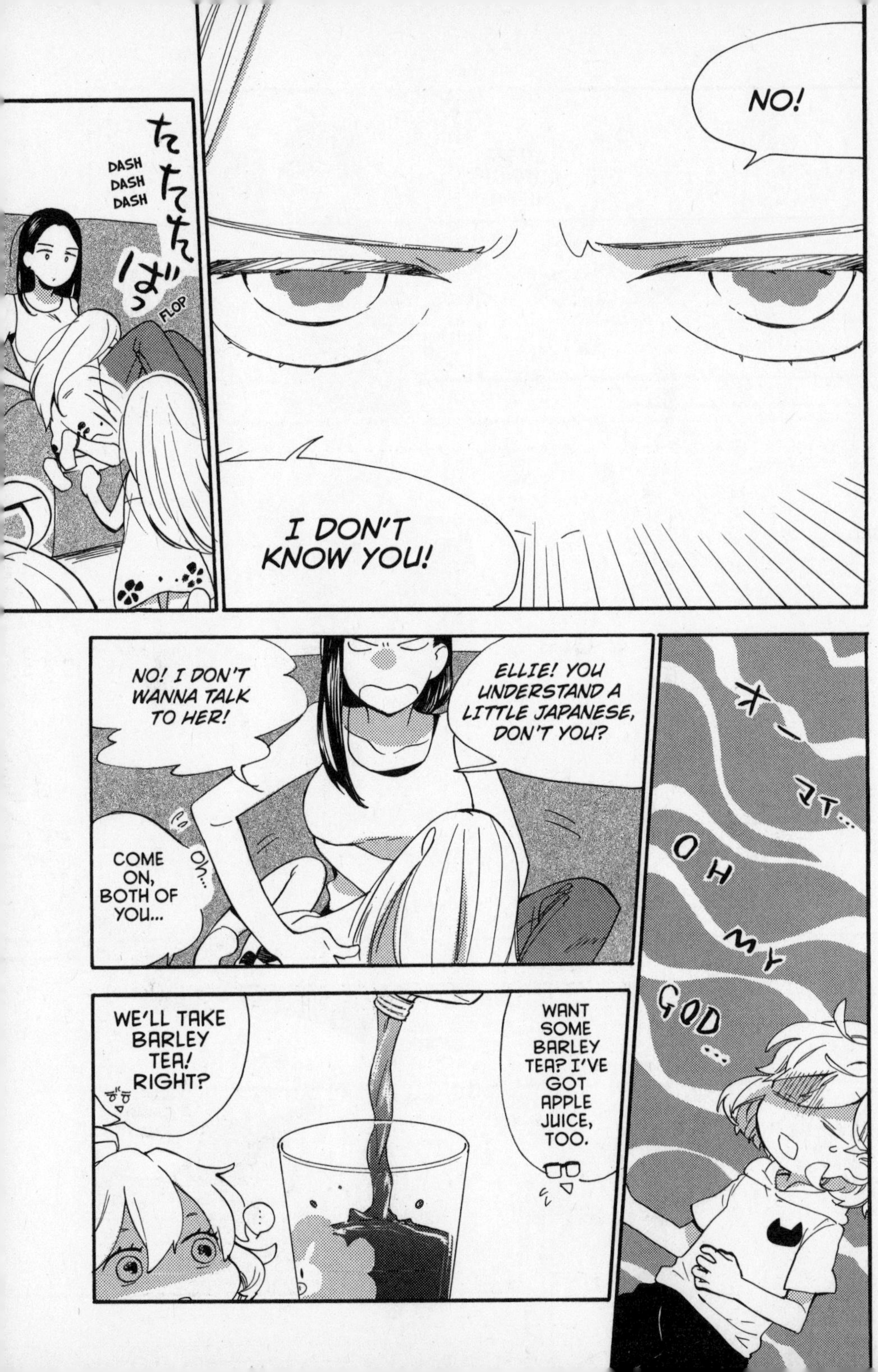
NO!
I DON'T KNOW YOU!
たたた
DASH DASH DASH
ぱっ
FLOP
オーマイ…
OH MY GOD...
ELLIE! YOU UNDERSTAND A LITTLE JAPANESE, DON'T YOU?
NO! I DON'T WANNA TALK TO HER!
Oh...
COME ON, BOTH OF YOU...
WANT SOME BARLEY TEA? I'VE GOT APPLE JUICE, TOO.
WE'LL TAKE BARLEY TEA! RIGHT?
...

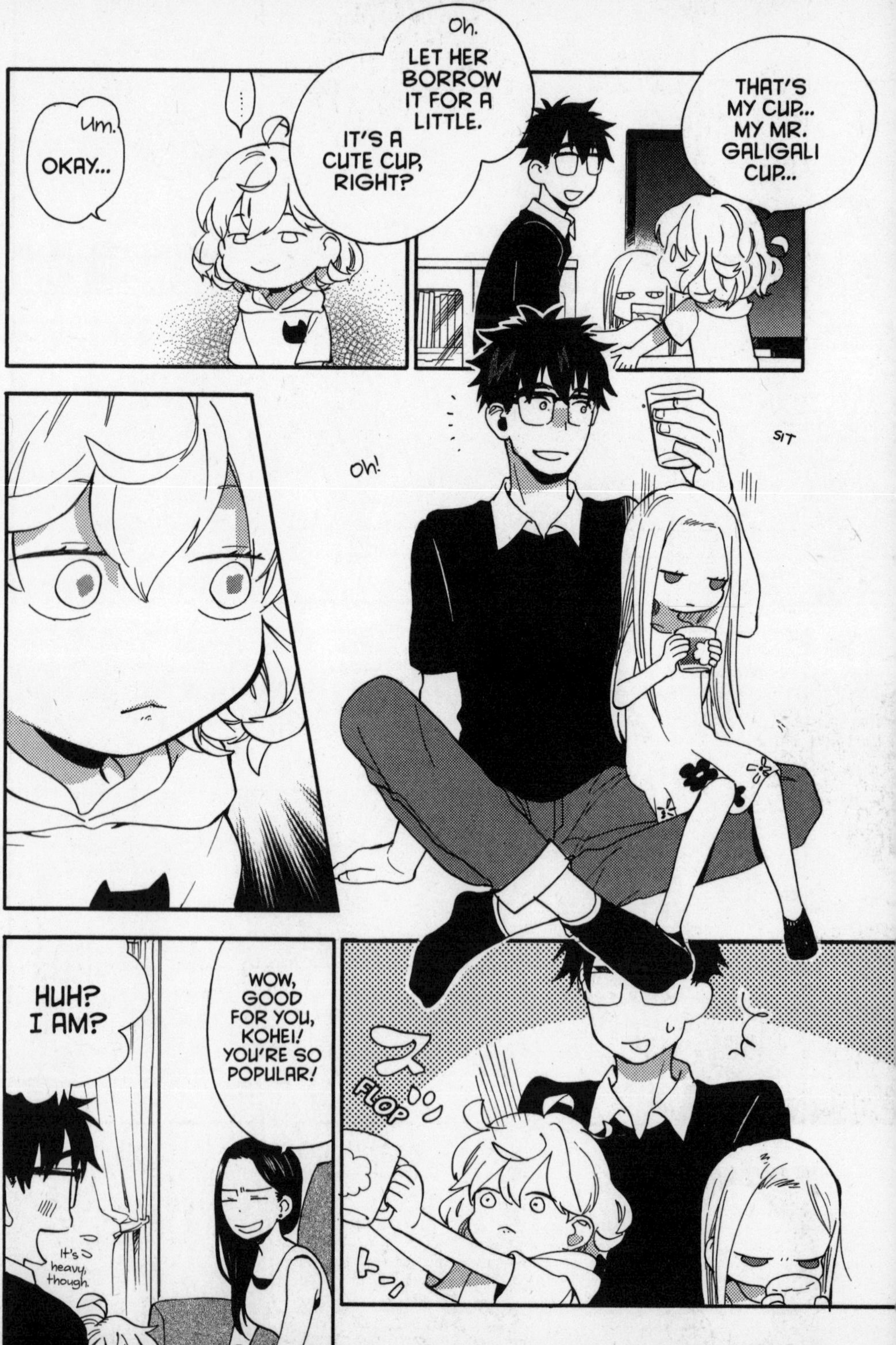
THAT'S MY CUP... MY MR. GALIGALI CUP...
Oh.
LET HER BORROW IT FOR A LITTLE.
IT'S A CUTE CUP, RIGHT?
...
Um.
OKAY...
Oh!
SIT
FLOP
WOW, GOOD FOR YOU, KOHEI! YOU'RE SO POPULAR!
HUH? I AM?
It's heavy, though.

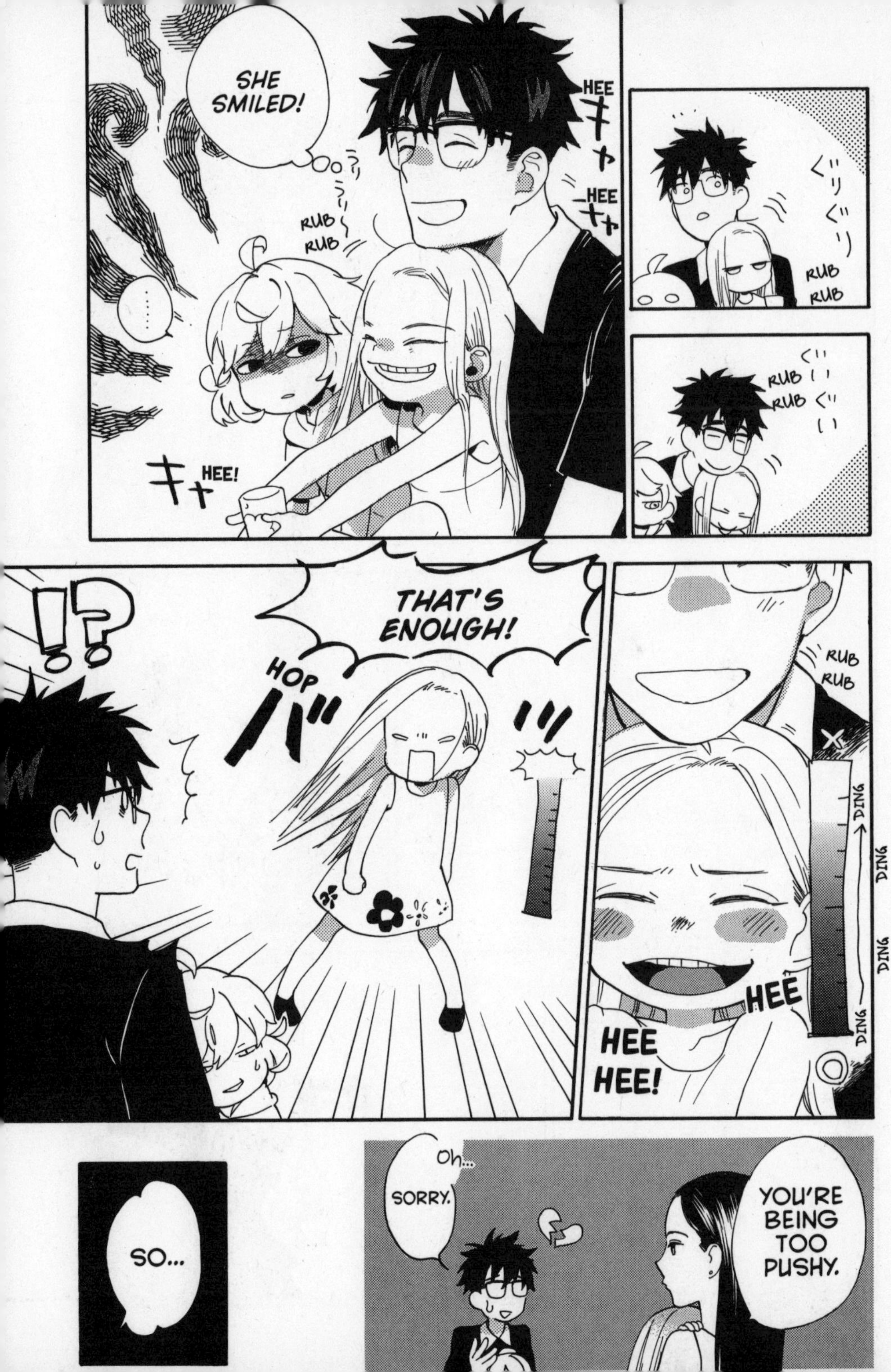
...
ぐりぐり
RUB RUB
RUB RUB
ぐりぐり
SHE SMILED!
HEE キャ
HEE キャ
RUB RUB
......
キャ HEE!
RUB RUB
DING DING DING DING
HEE
HEE HEE!
THAT'S ENOUGH!
HOP バッ
!?
YOU'RE BEING TOO PUSHY.
Oh...
SORRY.
SO...

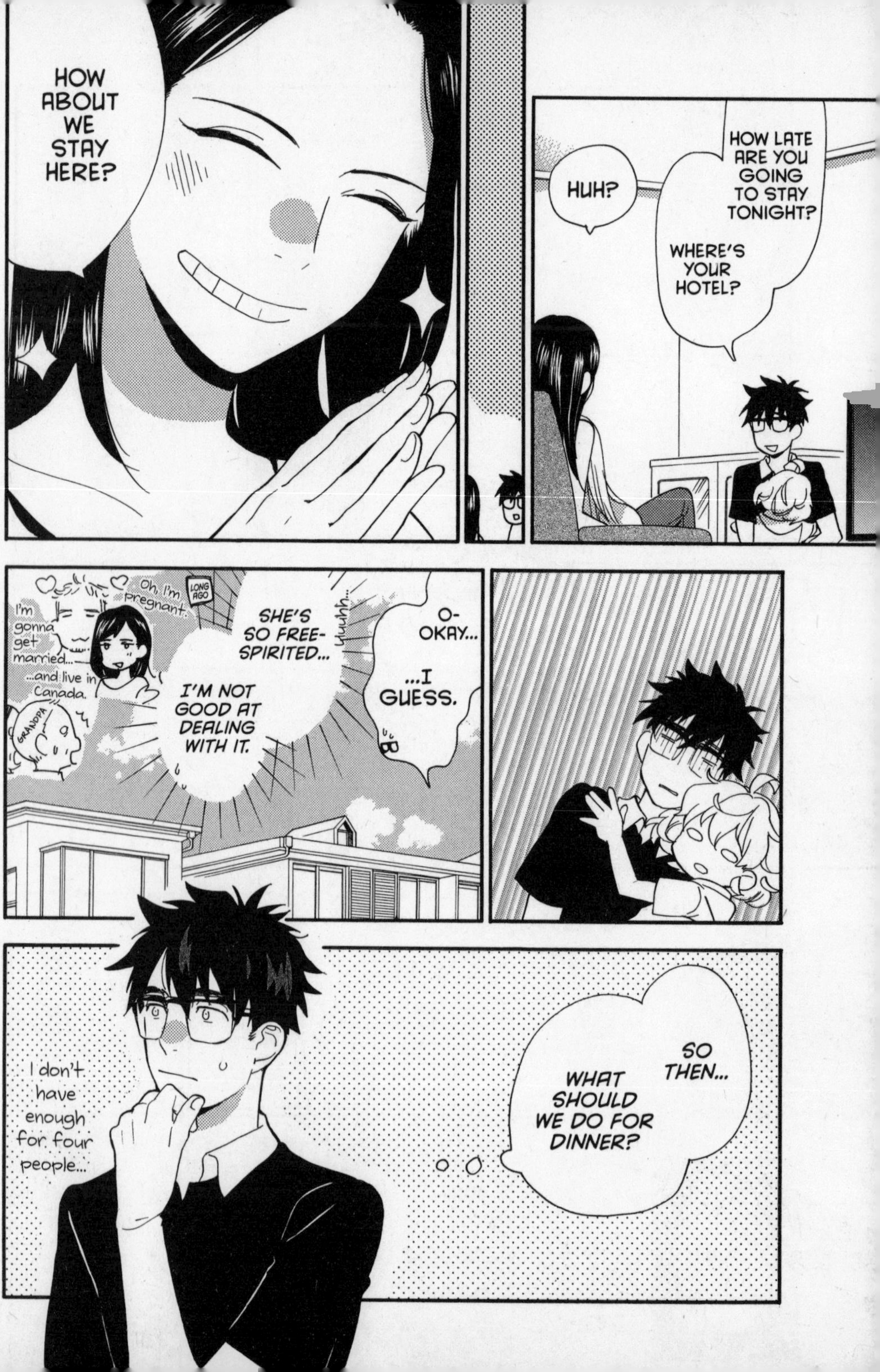
HOW LATE ARE YOU GOING TO STAY TONIGHT?
HUH?
WHERE'S YOUR HOTEL?
HOW ABOUT WE STAY HERE?
O-OKAY...
...I GUESS.
Uuuhh...
SHE'S SO FREE-SPIRITED...
I'M NOT GOOD AT DEALING WITH IT.
LONG AGO
Oh, I'm pregnant.
I'm gonna get married...
...and live in Canada.
GRANDPA
SO THEN...
WHAT SHOULD WE DO FOR DINNER?
I don't have enough for four people...

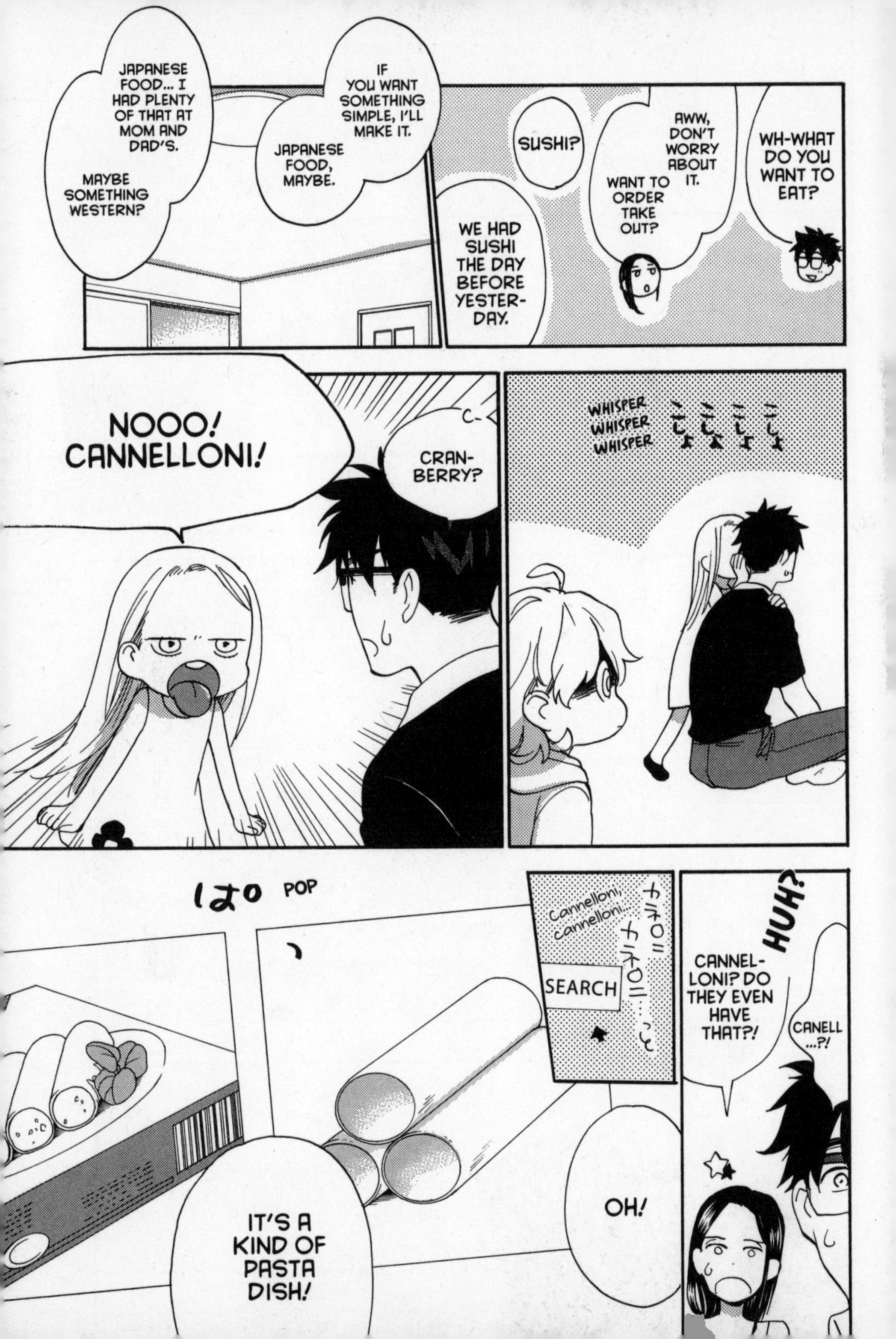
WH-WHAT DO YOU WANT TO EAT?
AWW, DON'T WORRY ABOUT IT.
WANT TO ORDER TAKE OUT?
SUSHI?
WE HAD SUSHI THE DAY BEFORE YESTER-DAY.
IF YOU WANT SOMETHING SIMPLE, I'LL MAKE IT.
JAPANESE FOOD, MAYBE.
JAPANESE FOOD... I HAD PLENTY OF THAT AT MOM AND DAD'S.
MAYBE SOMETHING WESTERN?
WHISPER WHISPER WHISPER
こしょこしょこしょこしょ
C-
CRAN-BERRY?
NOOO! CANNELLONI!
HUH?
CANNEL-LONI? DO THEY EVEN HAVE THAT?!
CANELL ...?!
Cannelloni, cannelloni...
カネロニカネロニ…っと
SEARCH
OH!
はっ POP
IT'S A KIND OF PASTA DISH!

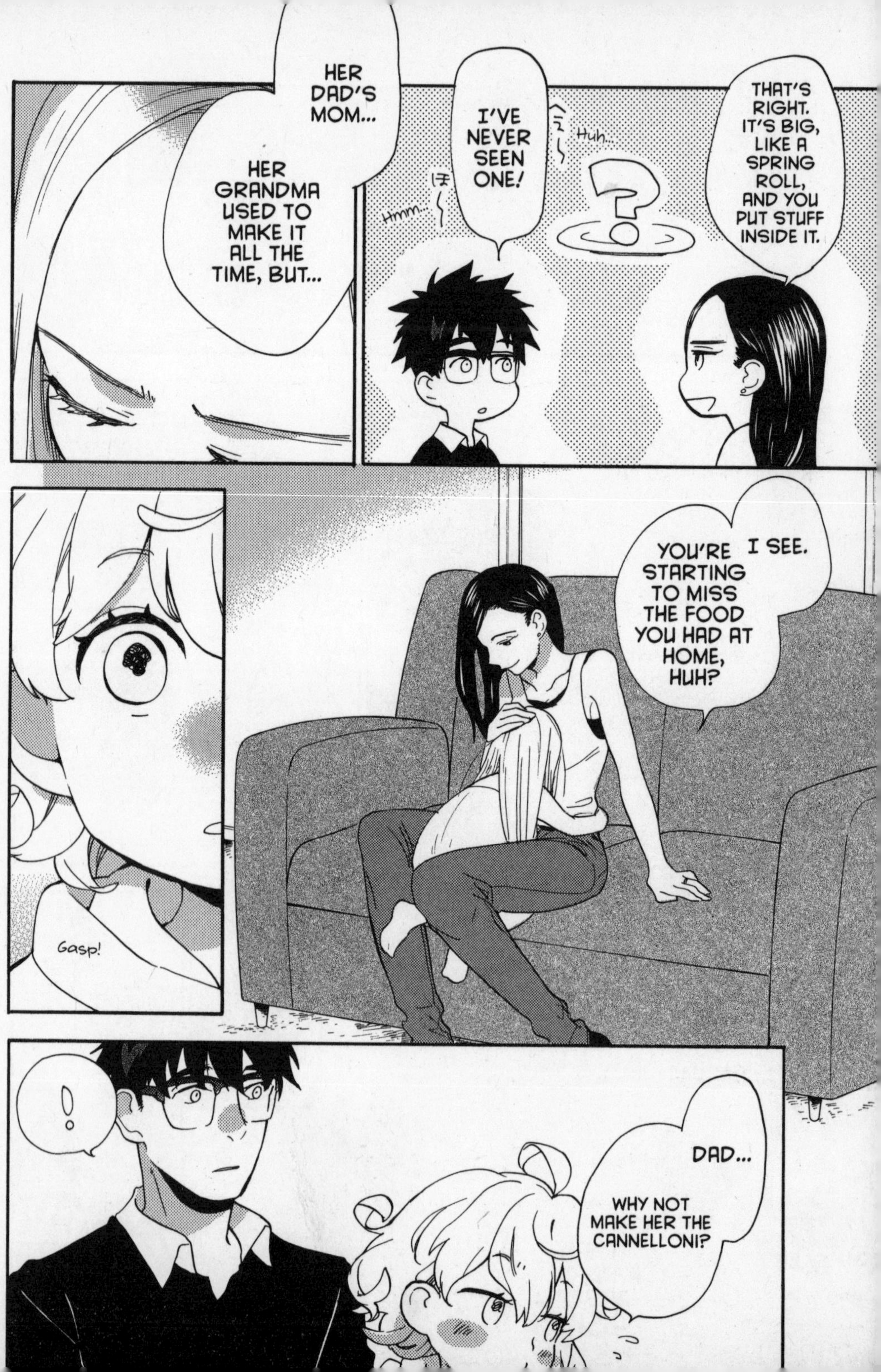
THAT'S RIGHT. IT'S BIG, LIKE A SPRING ROLL, AND YOU PUT STUFF INSIDE IT.
Huh...
I'VE NEVER SEEN ONE!
Hmm...
HER DAD'S MOM...
HER GRANDMA USED TO MAKE IT ALL THE TIME, BUT...
I SEE.
YOU'RE STARTING TO MISS THE FOOD YOU HAD AT HOME, HUH?
Gasp!
DAD...
WHY NOT MAKE HER THE CANNELLONI?
!

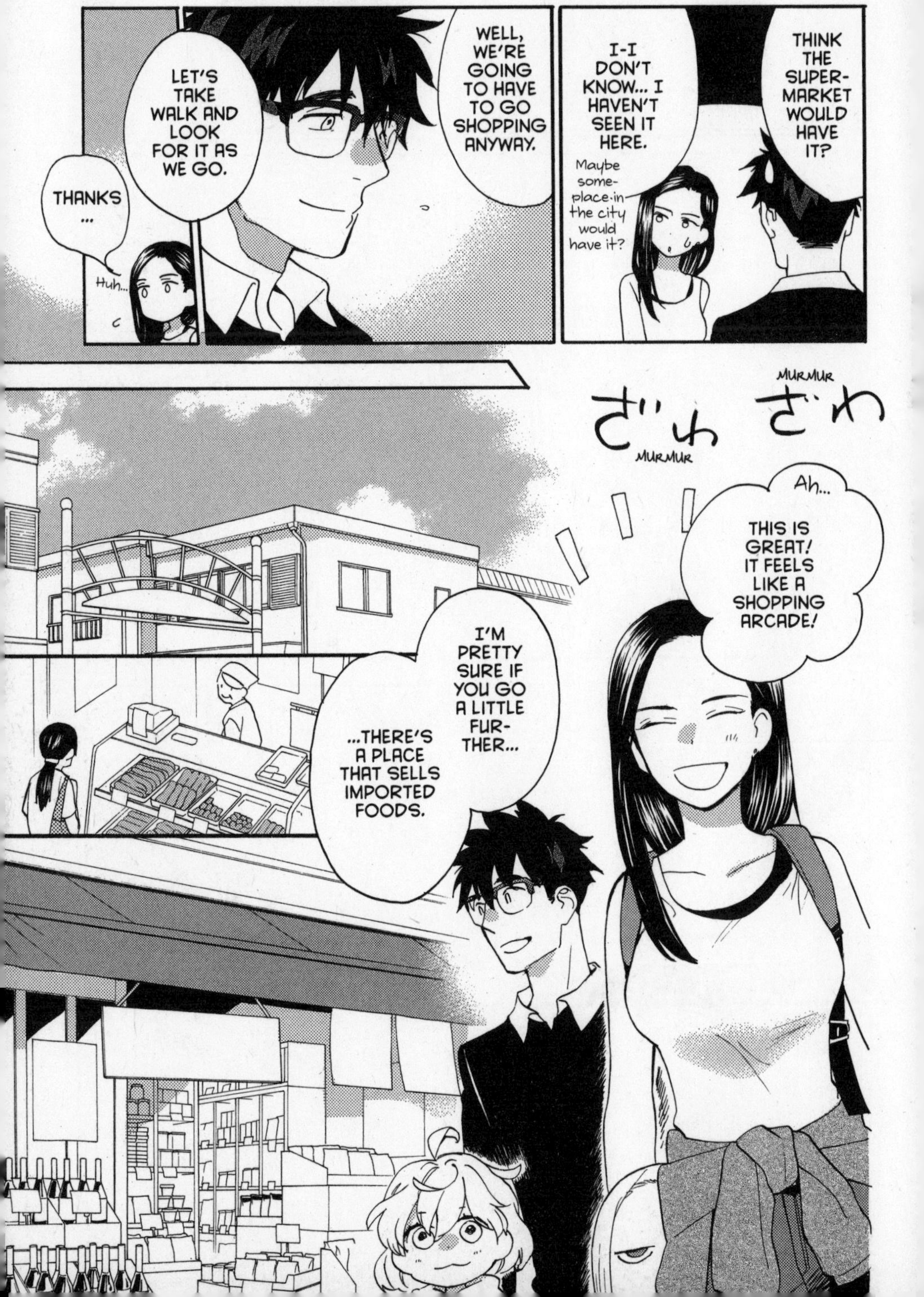
THINK THE SUPERMARKET WOULD HAVE IT?
I-I DON'T KNOW... I HAVEN'T SEEN IT HERE.
Maybe someplace in the city would have it?
WELL, WE'RE GOING TO HAVE TO GO SHOPPING ANYWAY.
LET'S TAKE WALK AND LOOK FOR IT AS WE GO.
THANKS ...
Huh...
ざわ MURMUR
ざわ MURMUR
Ah...
THIS IS GREAT! IT FEELS LIKE A SHOPPING ARCADE!
I'M PRETTY SURE IF YOU GO A LITTLE FURTHER...
...THERE'S A PLACE THAT SELLS IMPORTED FOODS.

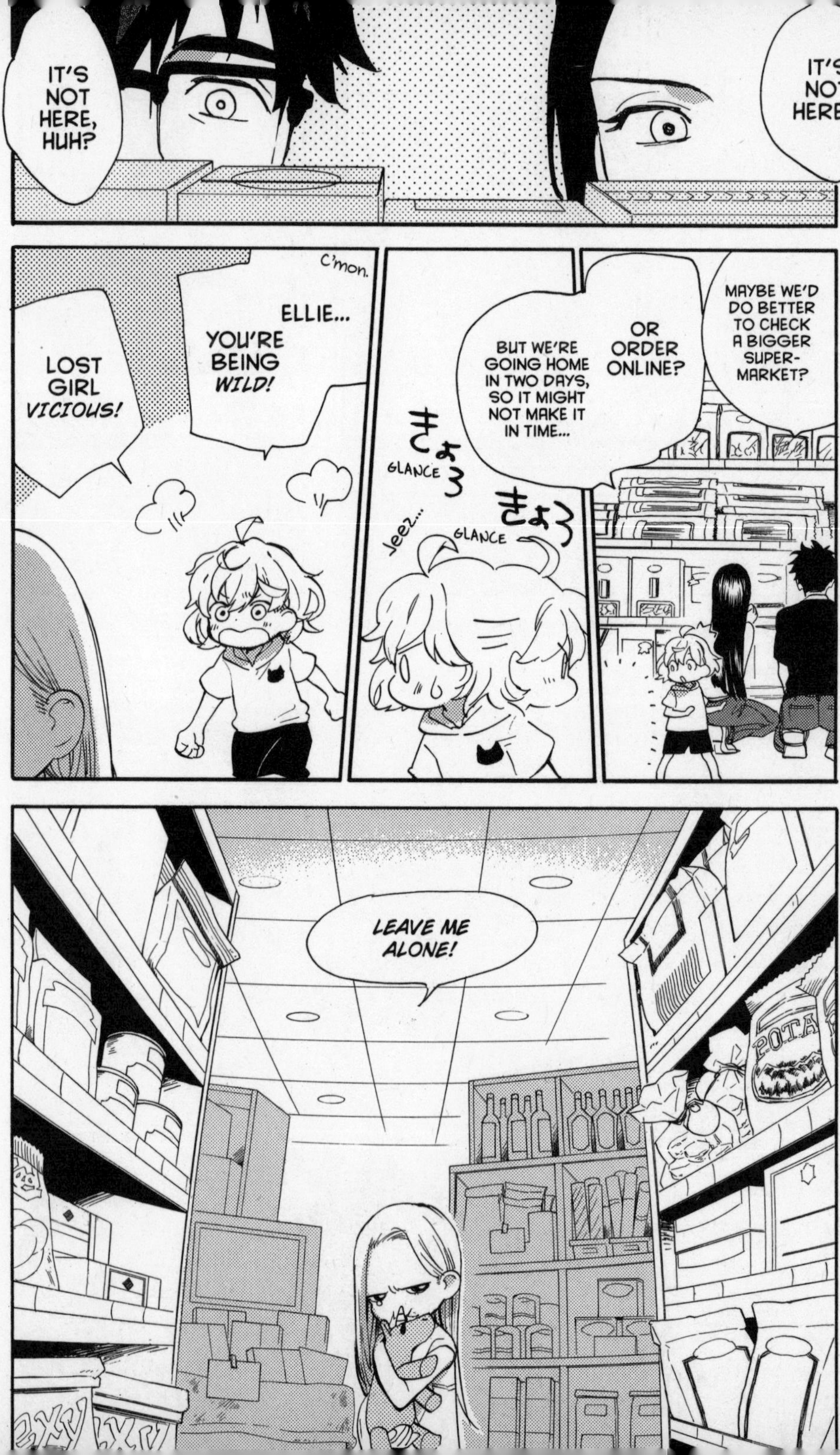
IT'S NOT HERE...
IT'S NOT HERE, HUH?
MAYBE WE'D DO BETTER TO CHECK A BIGGER SUPER-MARKET?
OR ORDER ONLINE?
BUT WE'RE GOING HOME IN TWO DAYS, SO IT MIGHT NOT MAKE IT IN TIME...
きょろ
GLANCE
きょろ
GLANCE
Jeez...
C'mon.
ELLIE...
YOU'RE BEING *WILD!*
LOST GIRL *VICIOUS!*
LEAVE ME ALONE!

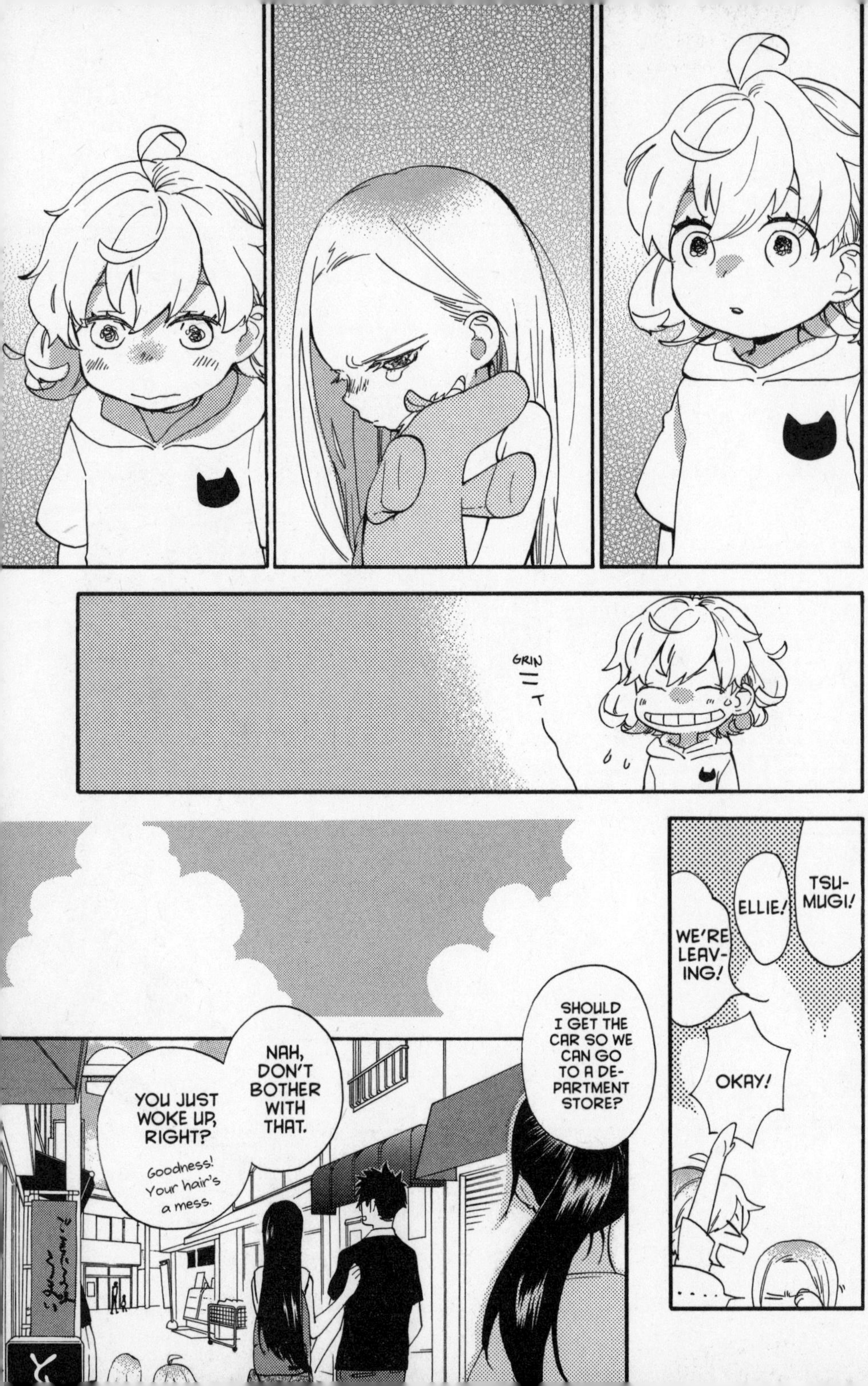
GRIN
TSU-MUGI!
ELLIE!
WE'RE LEAVING!
OKAY!
....
SHOULD I GET THE CAR SO WE CAN GO TO A DEPARTMENT STORE?
NAH, DON'T BOTHER WITH THAT.
YOU JUST WOKE UP, RIGHT?
Goodness! Your hair's a mess.

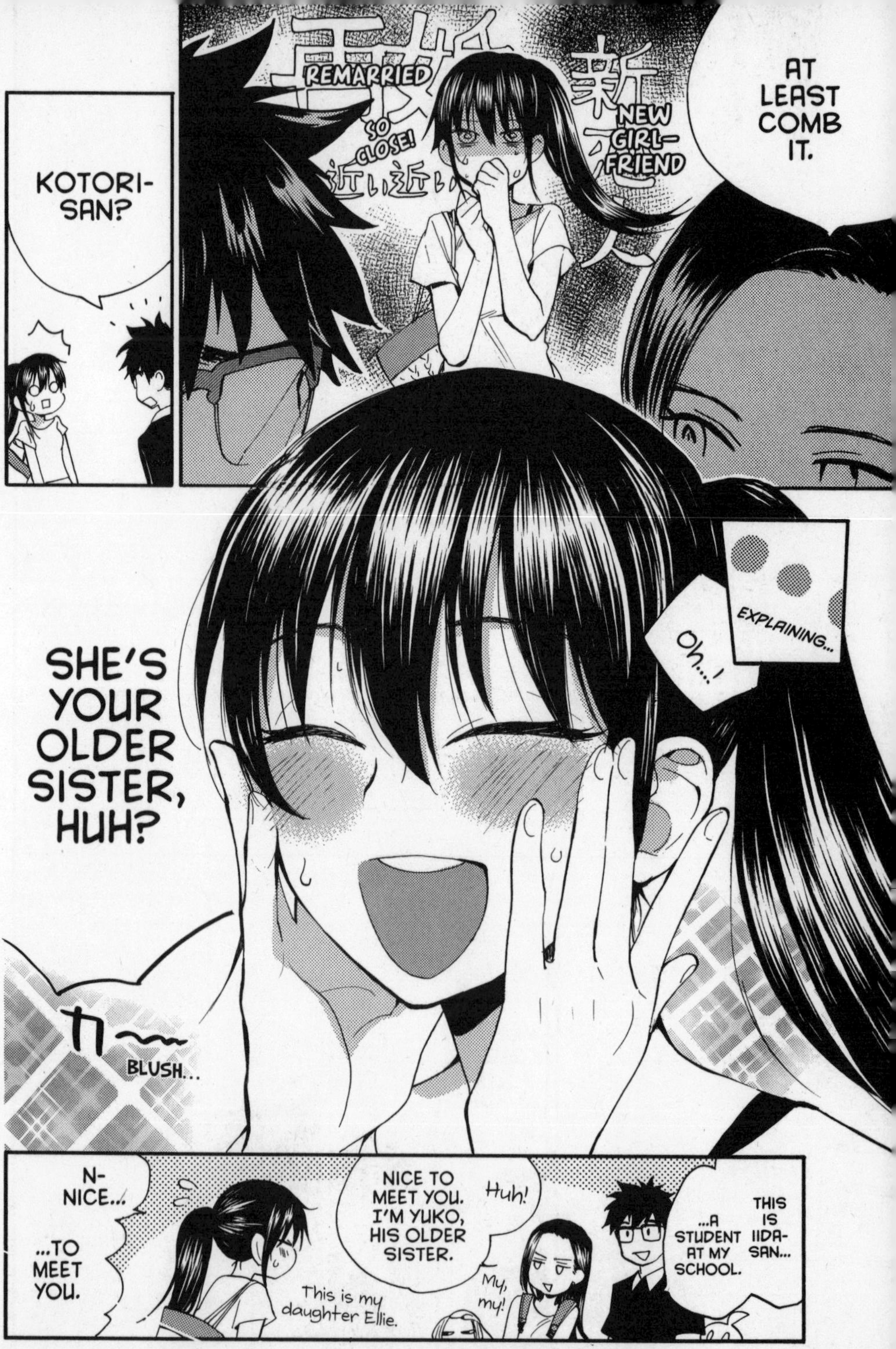
AT LEAST COMB IT.
REMARRIED
NEW GIRLFRIEND
SO CLOSE!
KOTORI-SAN?
Oh...!
EXPLAINING...
SHE'S YOUR OLDER SISTER, HUH?
BLUSH...
THIS IS IIDA-SAN...
...A STUDENT AT MY SCHOOL.
My, my!
Huh!
NICE TO MEET YOU. I'M YUKO, HIS OLDER SISTER.
This is my daughter Ellie.
N-NICE...
...TO MEET YOU.

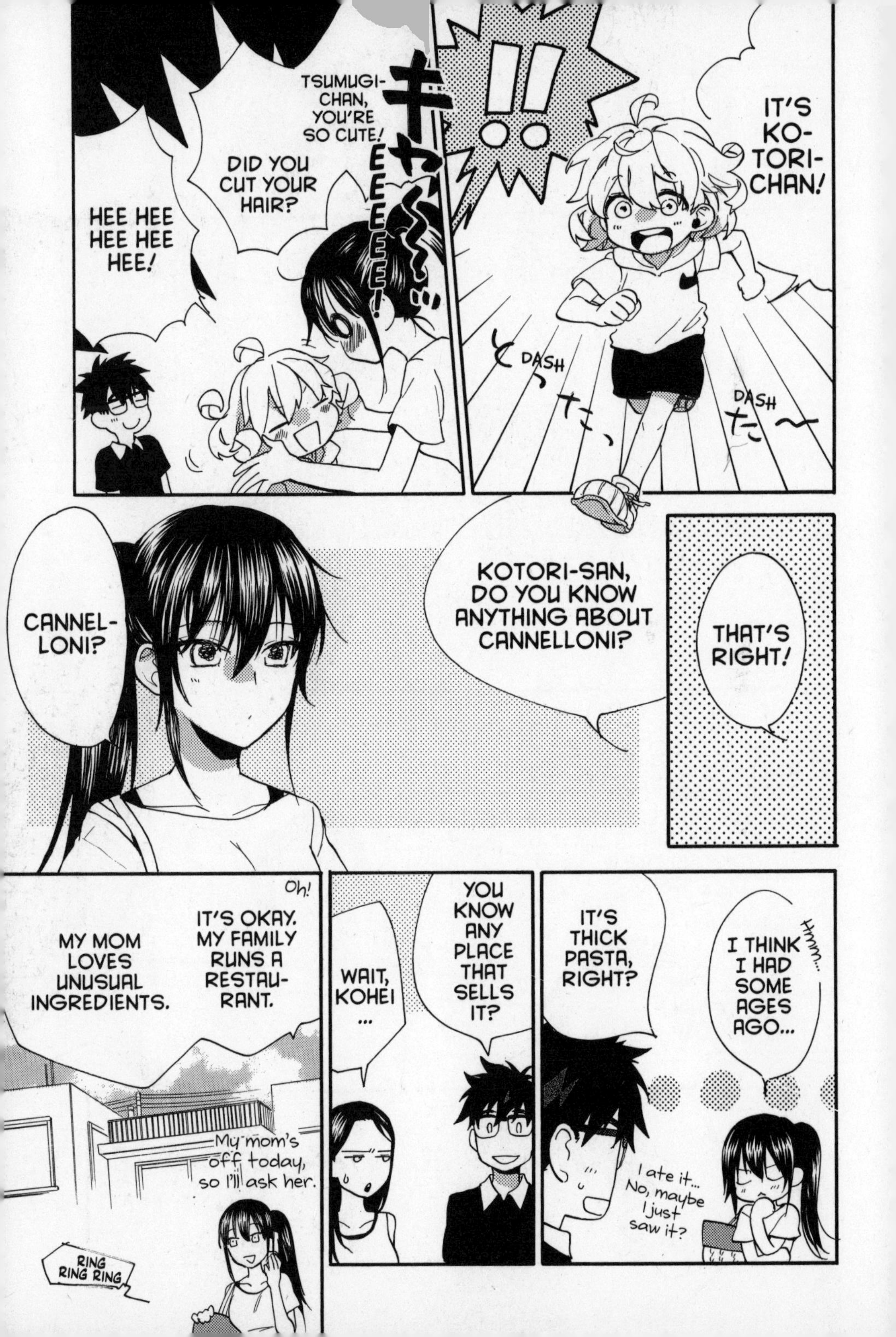
IT'S KO-TORI-CHAN!
DASH
DASH
TSUMUGI-CHAN, YOU'RE SO CUTE!
EEEEEE!
DID YOU CUT YOUR HAIR?
HEE HEE HEE HEE HEE!
THAT'S RIGHT!
KOTORI-SAN, DO YOU KNOW ANYTHING ABOUT CANNELLONI?
CANNEL-LONI?
I THINK I HAD SOME AGES AGO...
Hmm...
IT'S THICK PASTA, RIGHT?
I ate it... No, maybe I just saw it?
YOU KNOW ANY PLACE THAT SELLS IT?
WAIT, KOHEI ...
Oh!
IT'S OKAY. MY FAMILY RUNS A RESTAU-RANT.
MY MOM LOVES UNUSUAL INGREDIENTS.
My mom's off today, so I'll ask her.
RING RING RING

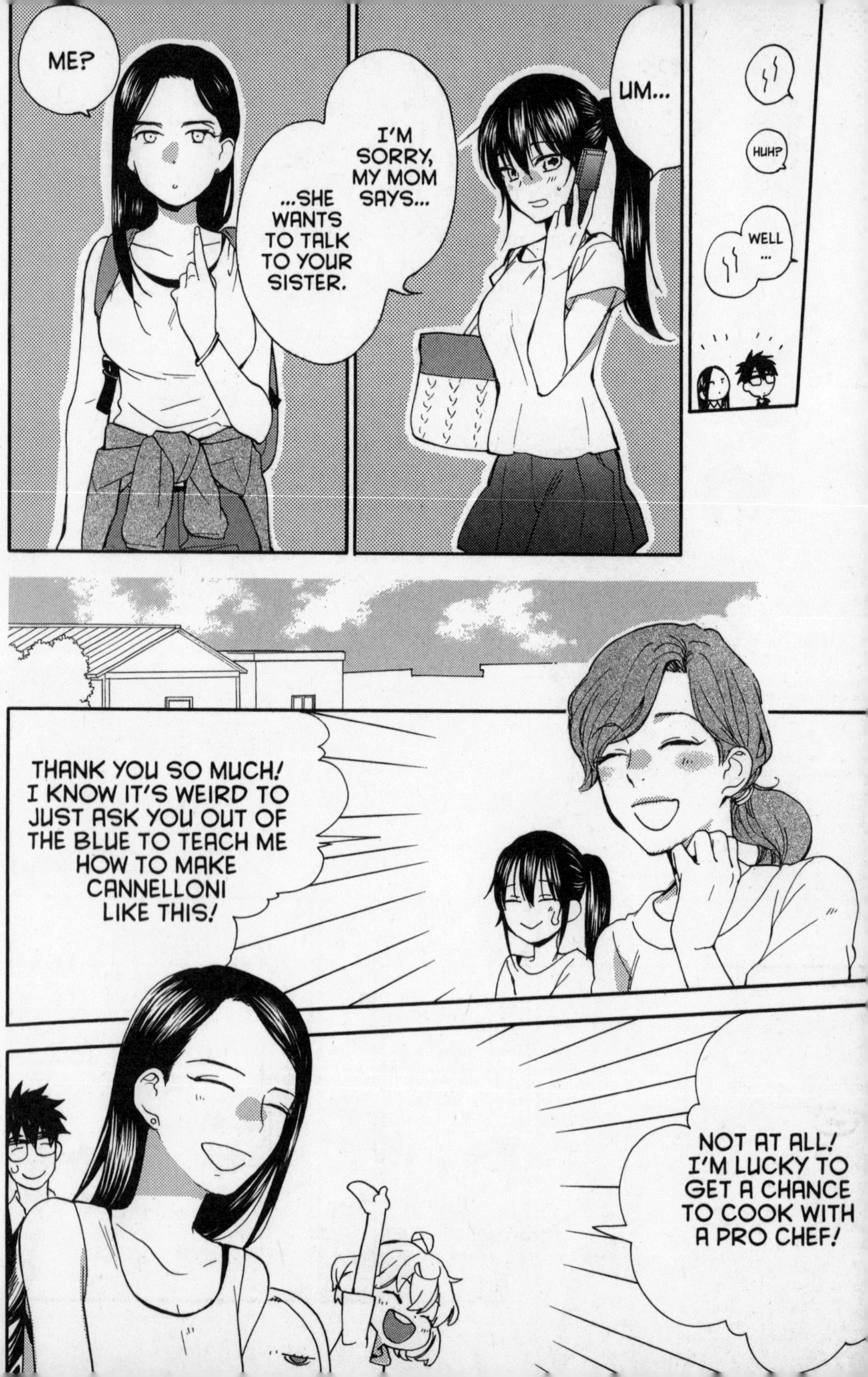
HUH?
WELL ...
UM...
I'M SORRY, MY MOM SAYS... ...SHE WANTS TO TALK TO YOUR SISTER.
ME?
THANK YOU SO MUCH! I KNOW IT'S WEIRD TO JUST ASK YOU OUT OF THE BLUE TO TEACH ME HOW TO MAKE CANNELLONI LIKE THIS!
NOT AT ALL! I'M LUCKY TO GET A CHANCE TO COOK WITH A PRO CHEF!

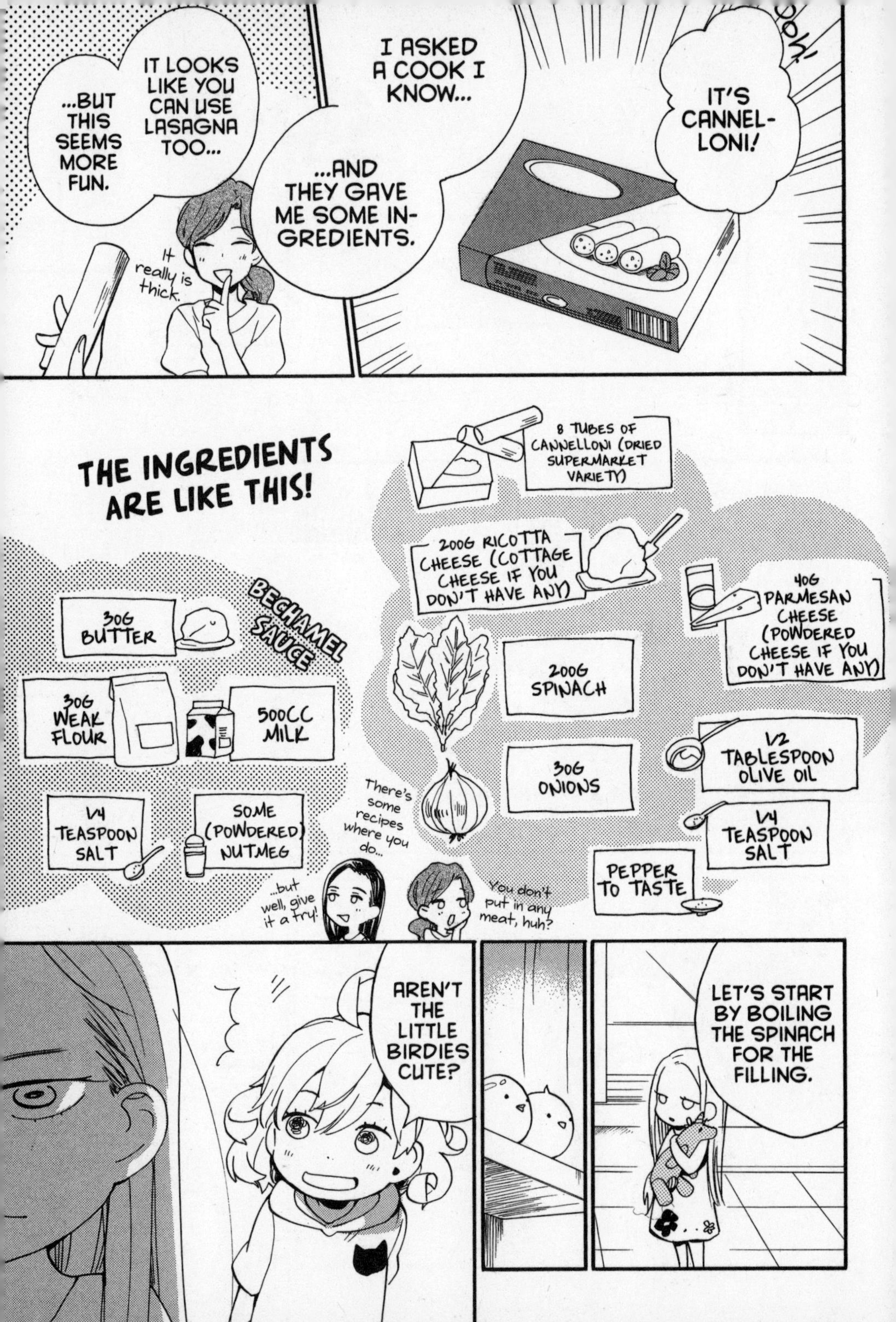
OOH!
IT'S CANNEL-LONI!
I ASKED A COOK I KNOW...
...AND THEY GAVE ME SOME IN-GREDIENTS.
IT LOOKS LIKE YOU CAN USE LASAGNA TOO...
...BUT THIS SEEMS MORE FUN.
It really is thick.
THE INGREDIENTS ARE LIKE THIS!
8 TUBES OF CANNELLONI (DRIED SUPERMARKET VARIETY)
200G RICOTTA CHEESE (COTTAGE CHEESE IF YOU DON'T HAVE ANY)
40G PARMESAN CHEESE (POWDERED CHEESE IF YOU DON'T HAVE ANY)
200G SPINACH
30G ONIONS
1/2 TABLESPOON OLIVE OIL
1/4 TEASPOON SALT
PEPPER TO TASTE
BECHAMEL SAUCE
30G BUTTER
30G WEAK FLOUR
500CC MILK
1/4 TEASPOON SALT
SOME (POWDERED) NUTMEG
You don't put in any meat, huh?
There's some recipes where you do...
...but well, give it a try!
LET'S START BY BOILING THE SPINACH FOR THE FILLING.
AREN'T THE LITTLE BIRDIES CUTE?

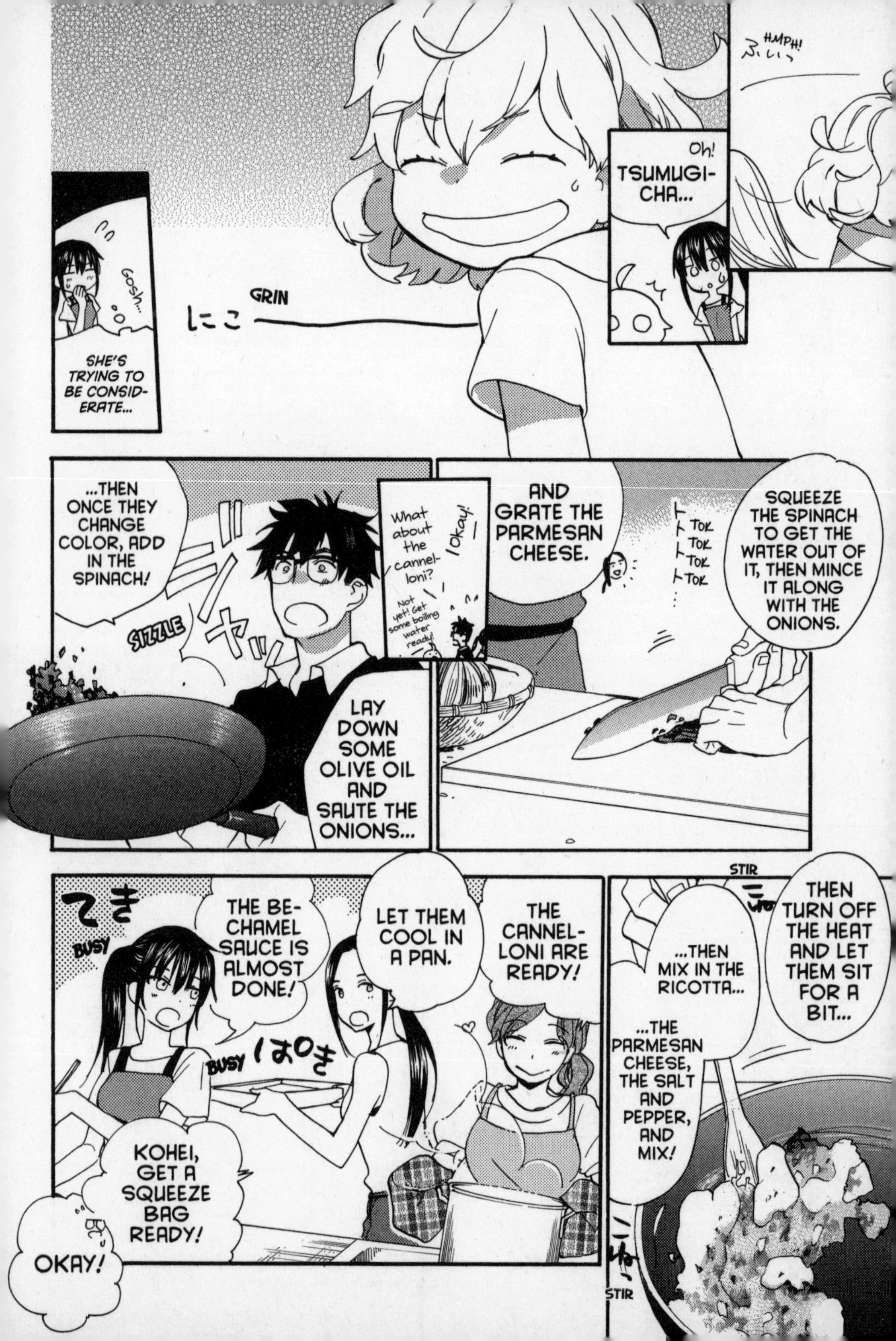
HMPH!
ふいっ
Oh! TSUMUGI-CHA...
GRIN
にこ
Gosh...
SHE'S TRYING TO BE CONSID-ERATE...
SQUEEZE THE SPINACH TO GET THE WATER OUT OF IT, THEN MINCE IT ALONG WITH THE ONIONS.
TOK TOK TOK TOK
AND GRATE THE PARMESAN CHEESE.
What about the canneI-loni?
Okay!
Not yet! Get some boiling water ready!
LAY DOWN SOME OLIVE OIL AND SAUTE THE ONIONS...
SIZZLE
...THEN ONCE THEY CHANGE COLOR, ADD IN THE SPINACH!
THEN TURN OFF THE HEAT AND LET THEM SIT FOR A BIT...
STIR
...THEN MIX IN THE RICOTTA...
...THE PARMESAN CHEESE, THE SALT AND PEPPER, AND MIX!
STIR
THE CANNEL-LONI ARE READY!
LET THEM COOL IN A PAN.
THE BE-CHAMEL SAUCE IS ALMOST DONE!
BUSY
BUSY
KOHEI, GET A SQUEEZE BAG READY!
OKAY!

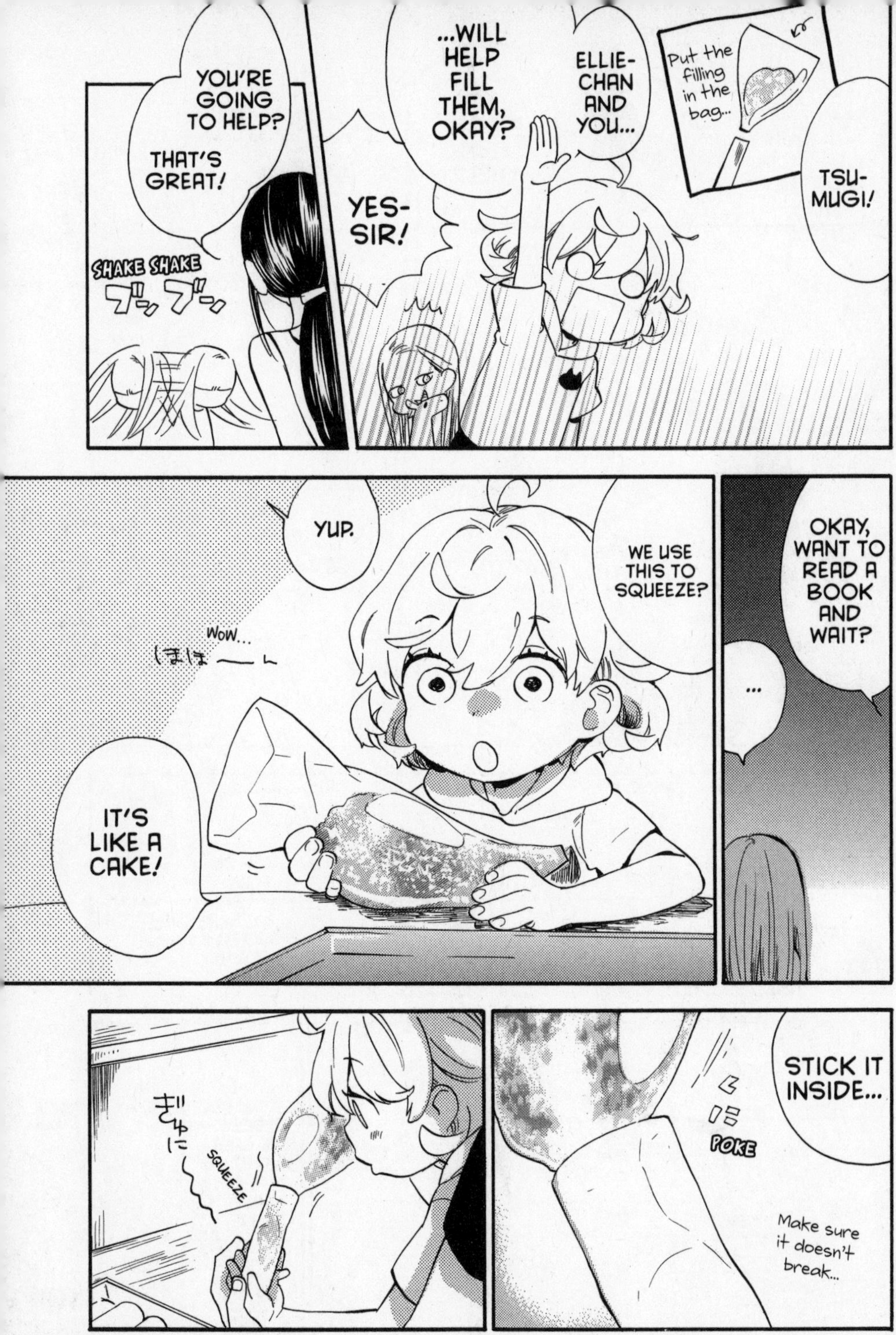
TSU-MUGI!
Put the filling in the bag...
ELLIE-CHAN AND YOU...
...WILL HELP FILL THEM, OKAY?
YES-SIR!
YOU'RE GOING TO HELP?
THAT'S GREAT!
SHAKE SHAKE
OKAY, WANT TO READ A BOOK AND WAIT?
...
WE USE THIS TO SQUEEZE?
YUP.
WOW...
IT'S LIKE A CAKE!
STICK IT INSIDE...
POKE
Make sure it doesn't break...
SQUEEZE

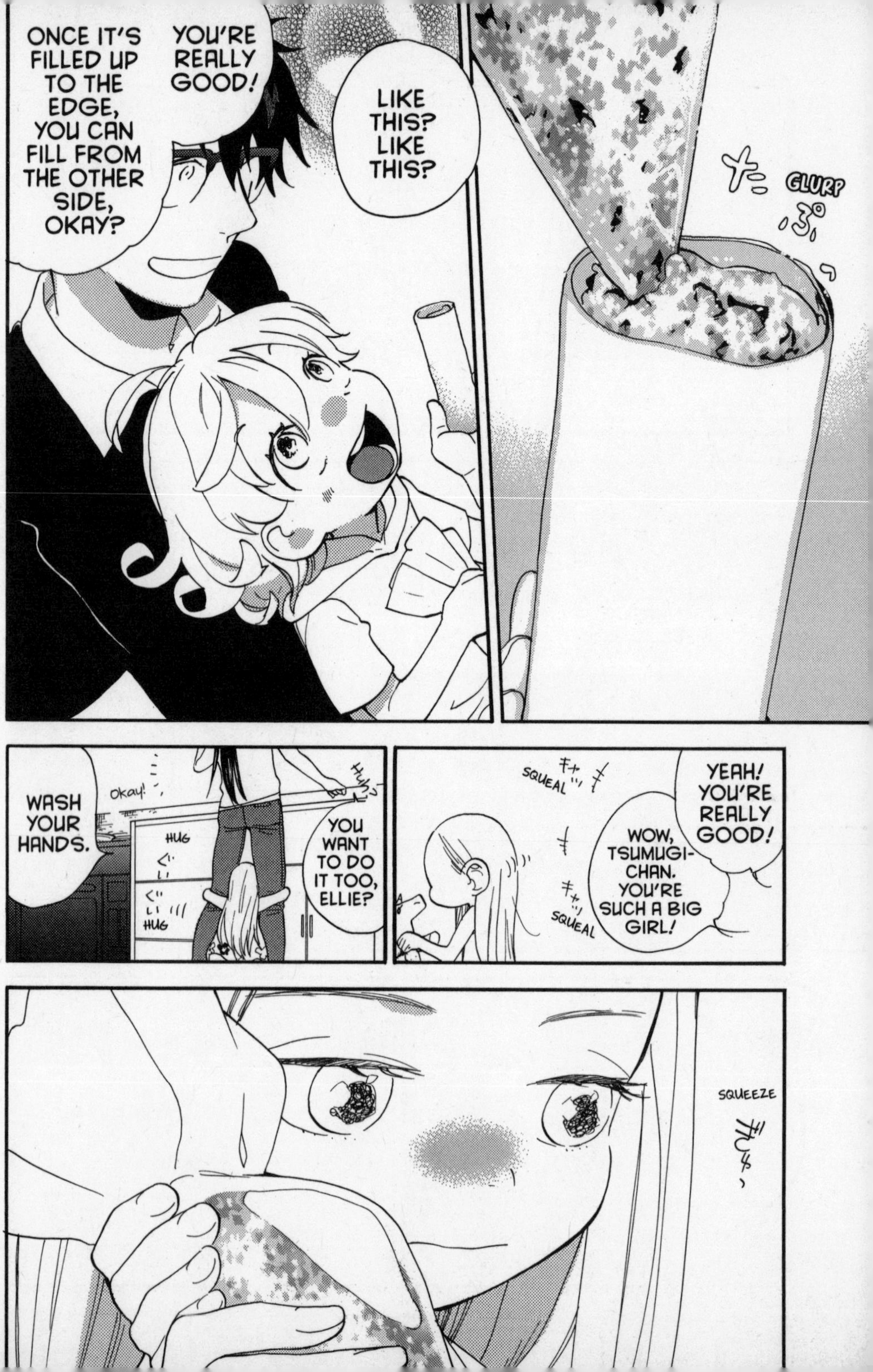
GLURP
LIKE THIS? LIKE THIS?
YOU'RE REALLY GOOD!
ONCE IT'S FILLED UP TO THE EDGE, YOU CAN FILL FROM THE OTHER SIDE, OKAY?
YEAH! YOU'RE REALLY GOOD!
SQUEAL
WOW, TSUMUGI-CHAN. YOU'RE SUCH A BIG GIRL!
SQUEAL
YOU WANT TO DO IT TOO, ELLIE?
Okay!
HUG
HUG
WASH YOUR HANDS.
SQUEEZE

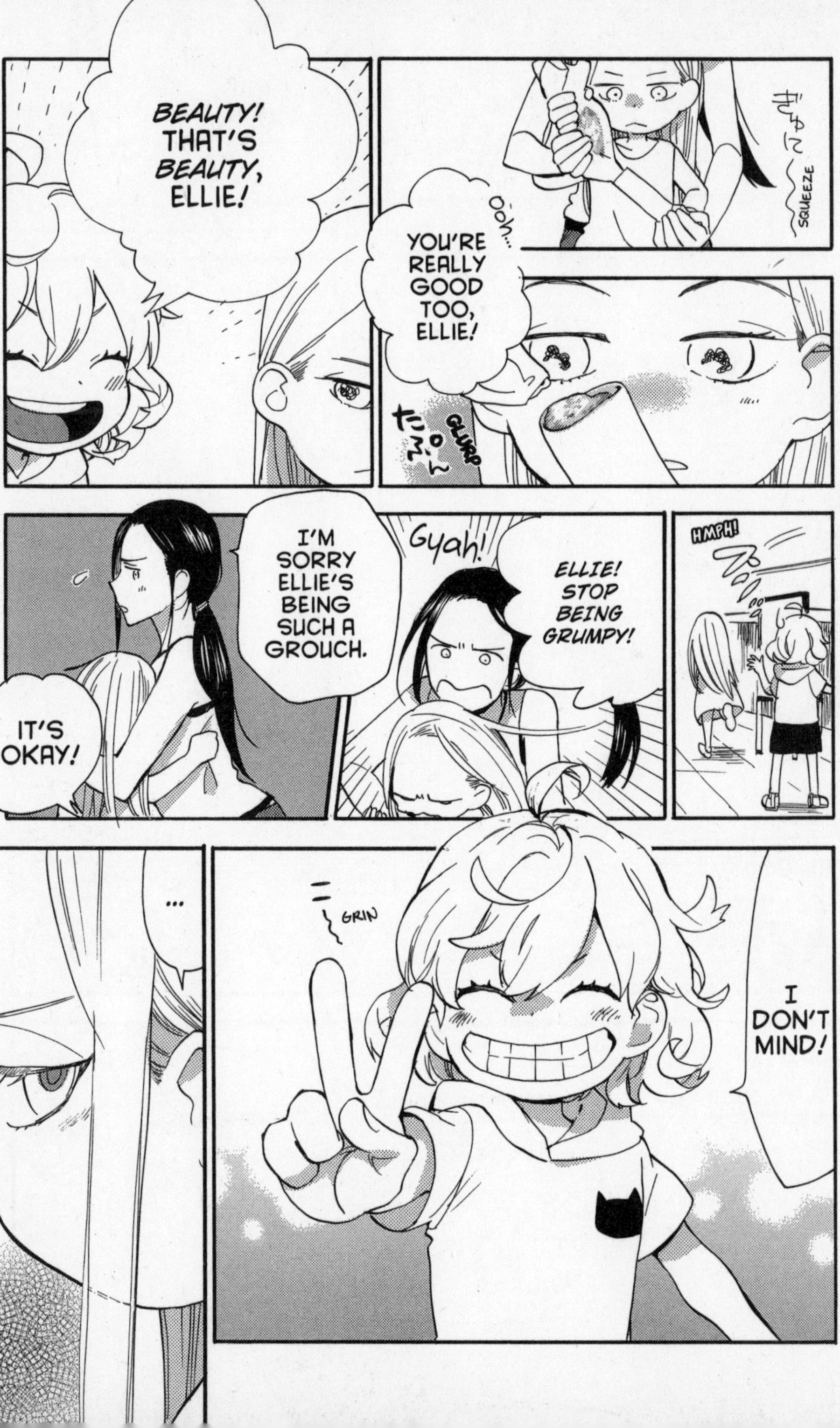
SQUEEZE
Ooh...
YOU'RE REALLY GOOD TOO, ELLIE!
GLURP
BEAUTY! THAT'S BEAUTY, ELLIE!
HMPH!
Gyah!
ELLIE! STOP BEING GRUMPY!
I'M SORRY ELLIE'S BEING SUCH A GROUCH.
IT'S OKAY!
I DON'T MIND!
GRIN
...

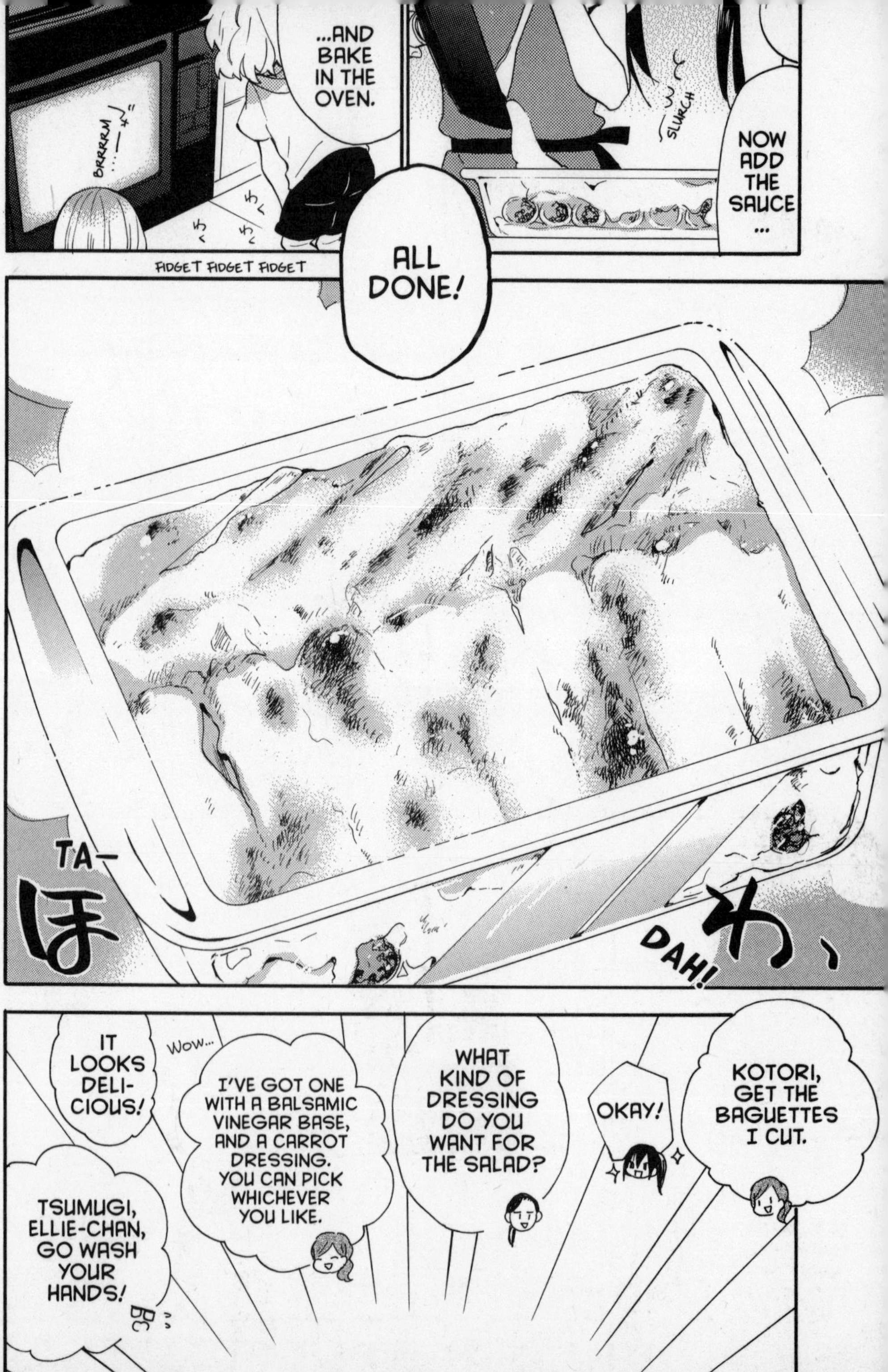
NOW ADD THE SAUCE...
SLURCH
...AND BAKE IN THE OVEN.
BRRRRM...
FIDGET FIDGET FIDGET
ALL DONE!
TA—
ほ
わ、
DAH!
KOTORI, GET THE BAGUETTES I CUT.
OKAY!
WHAT KIND OF DRESSING DO YOU WANT FOR THE SALAD?
I'VE GOT ONE WITH A BALSAMIC VINEGAR BASE, AND A CARROT DRESSING. YOU CAN PICK WHICHEVER YOU LIKE.
WOW...
IT LOOKS DELICIOUS!
TSUMUGI, ELLIE-CHAN, GO WASH YOUR HANDS!

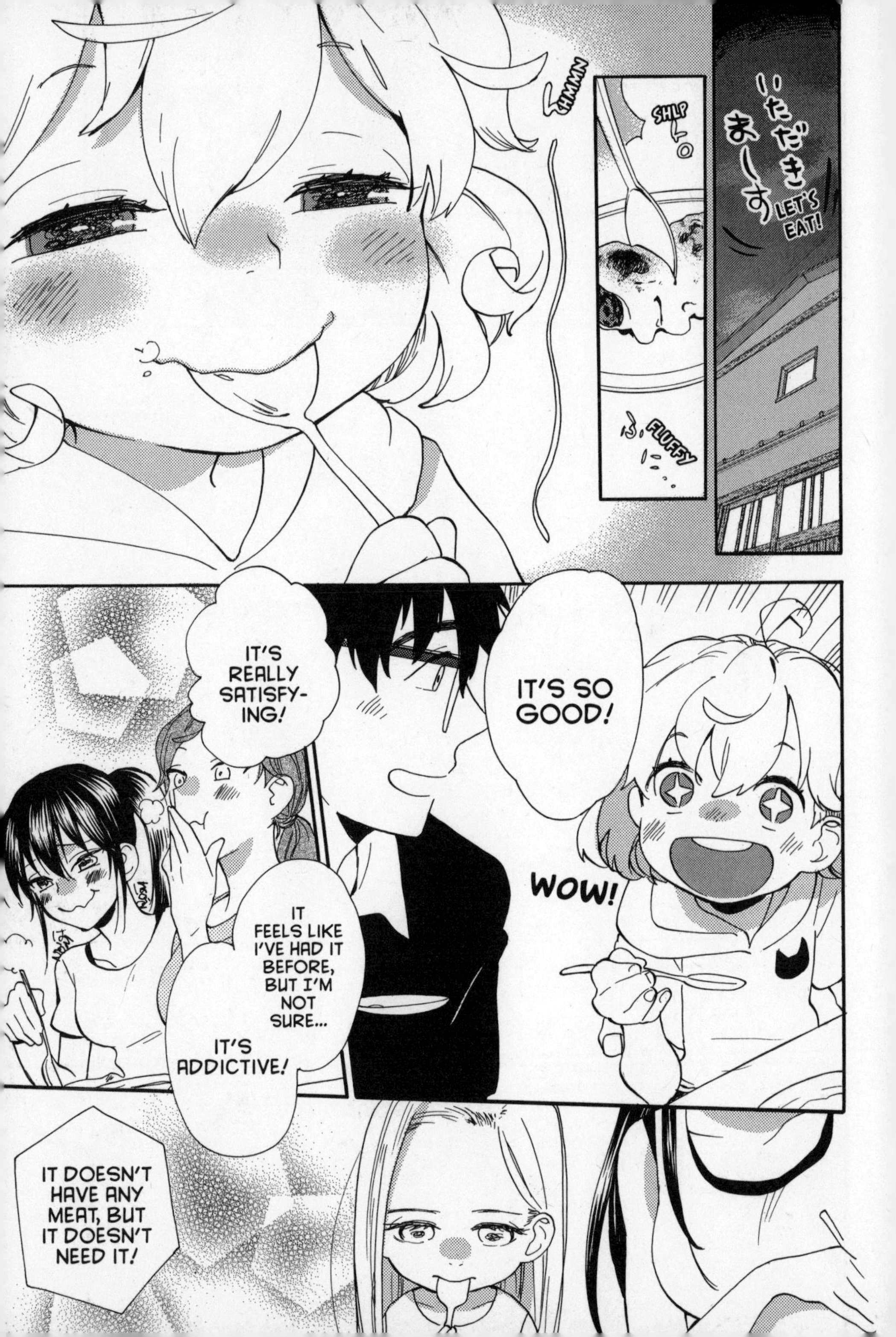

いただきます
LET'S EAT!
SHLP
FLUFFY
HMMN
WOW!
IT'S SO GOOD!
IT'S REALLY SATISFY-ING!
IT FEELS LIKE I'VE HAD IT BEFORE, BUT I'M NOT SURE...
IT'S ADDICTIVE!
IT DOESN'T HAVE ANY MEAT, BUT IT DOESN'T NEED IT!

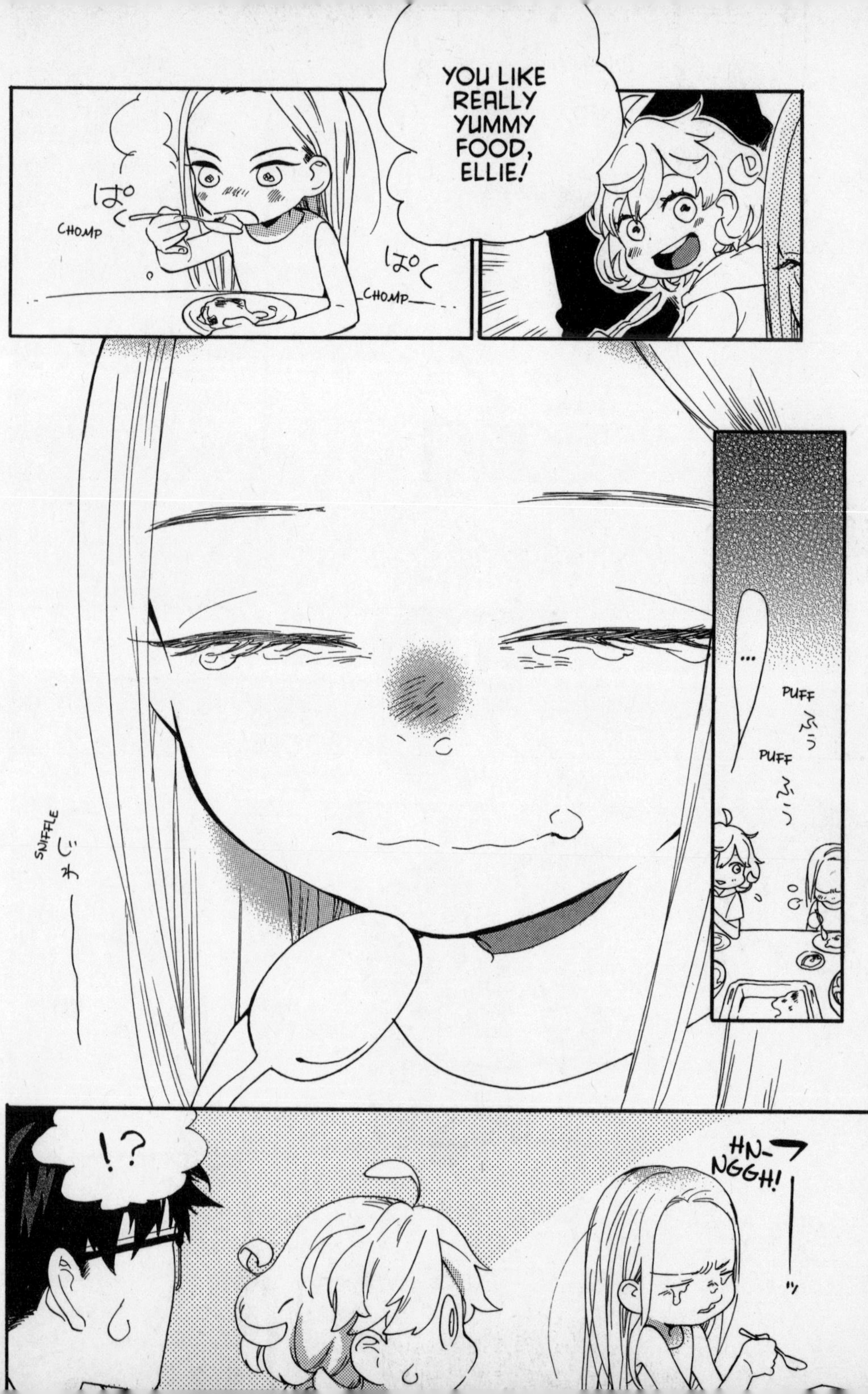

YOU LIKE REALLY YUMMY FOOD, ELLIE!
ぱく
CHOMP
ぱく
CHOMP
...
PUFF
ふぅ
PUFF
ふぅ
SNIFFLE
ずび
HN-NGGH!
!?

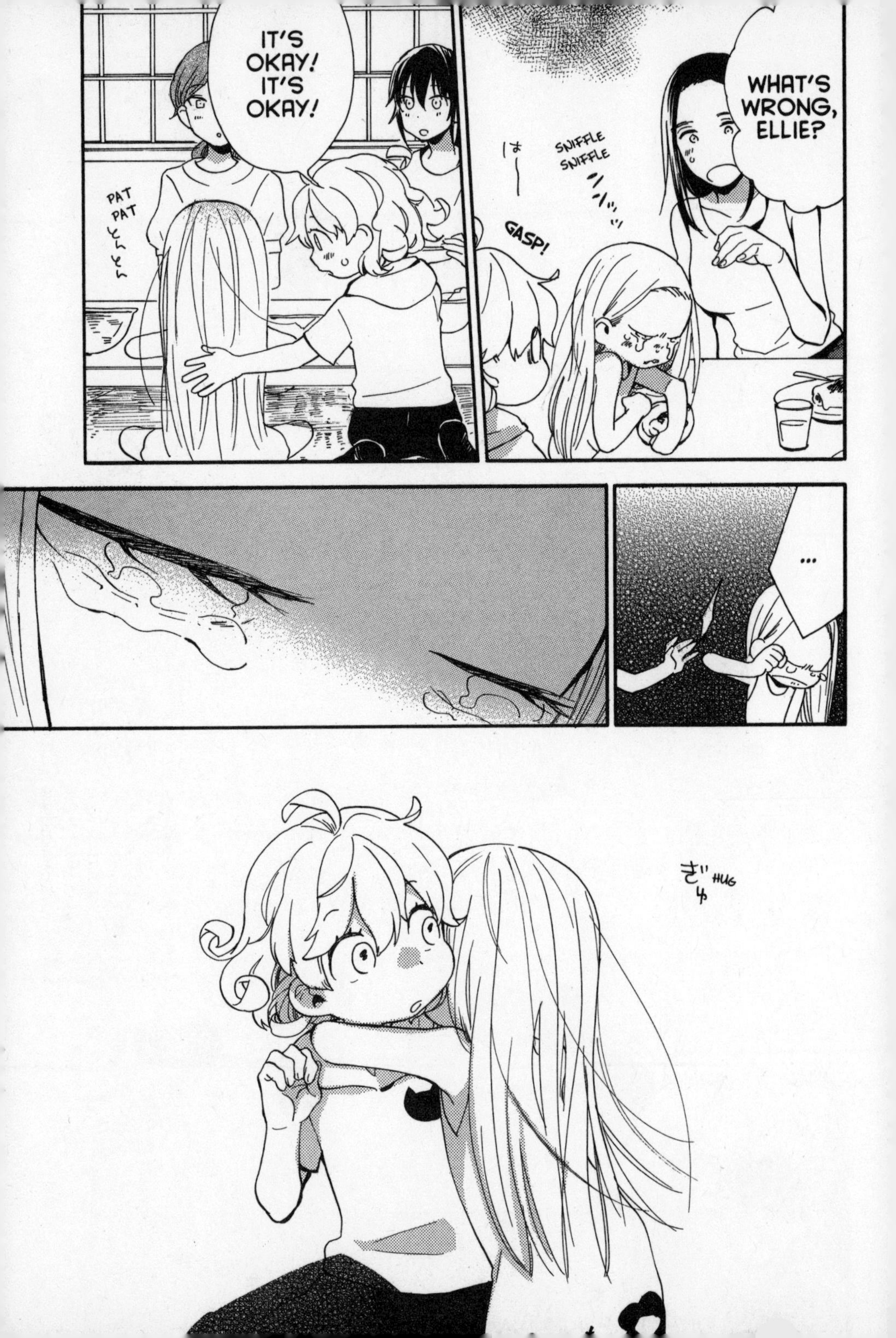
WHAT'S WRONG, ELLIE?
SNIFFLE SNIFFLE
シッ
はー
GASP!
IT'S OKAY! IT'S OKAY!
PAT PAT
とんとん
...
ぎゅ
HUG

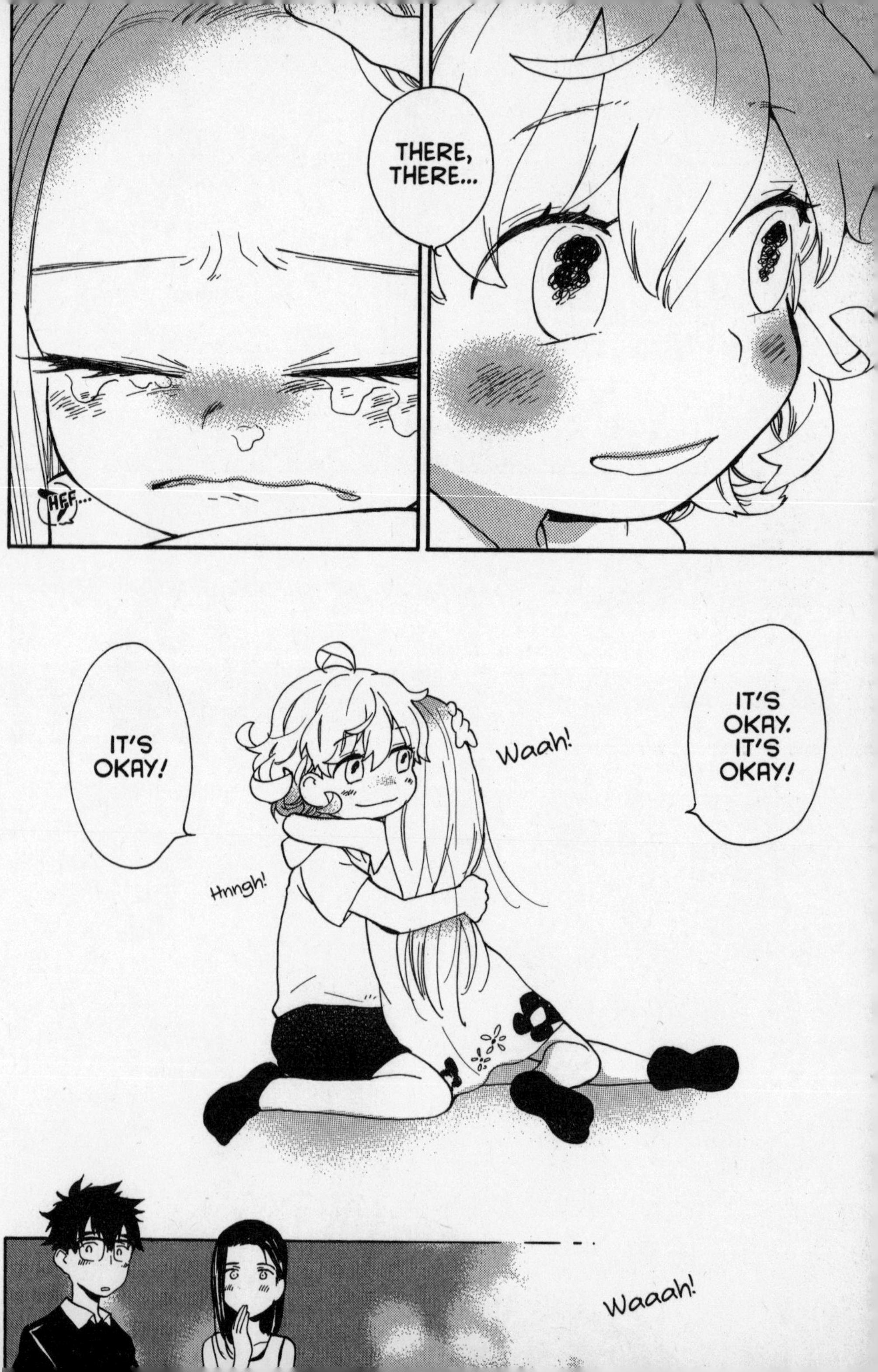
THERE, THERE...
HFF...
IT'S OKAY. IT'S OKAY!
Waah!
IT'S OKAY!
Hnngh!
Waaah!

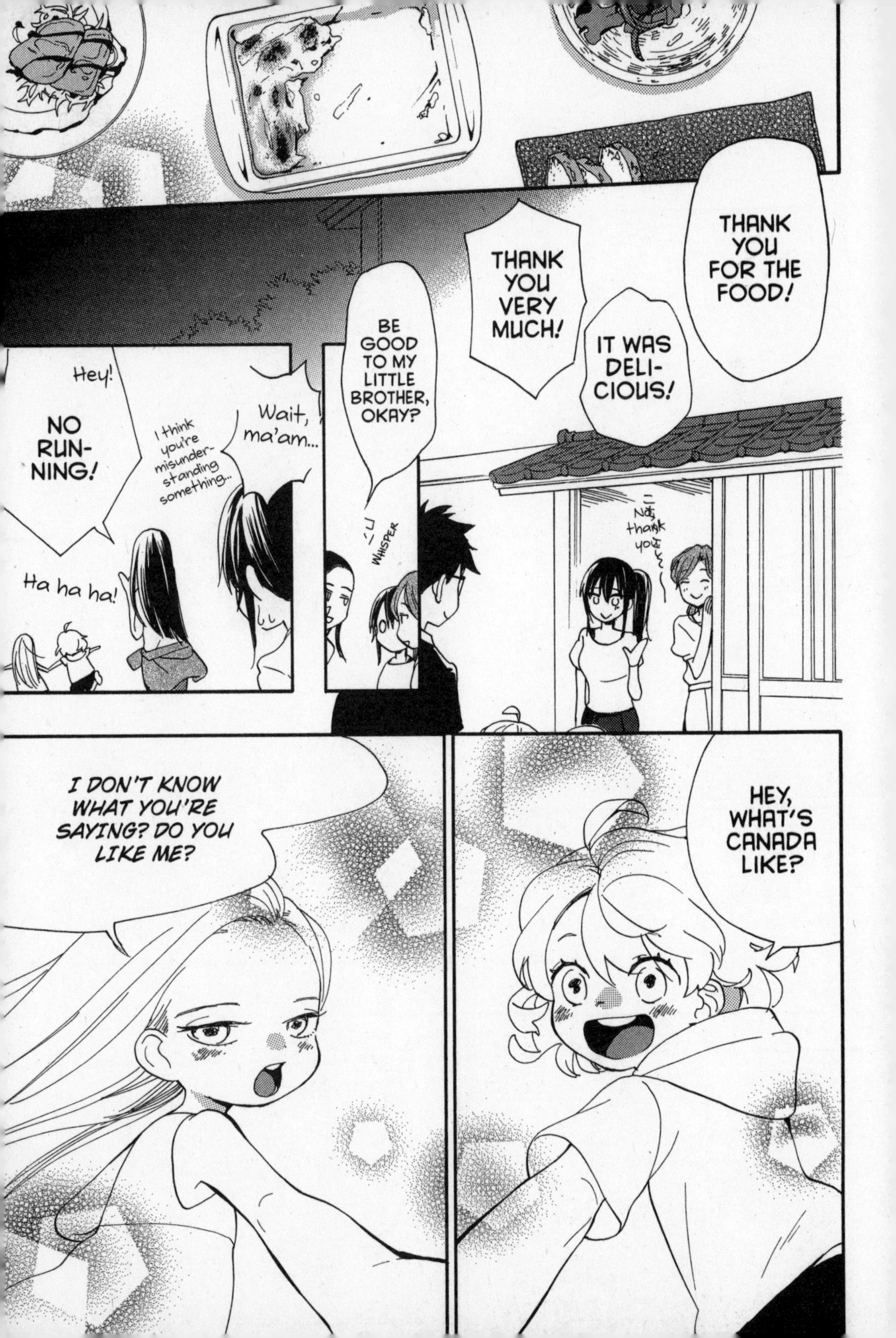
THANK YOU FOR THE FOOD!
IT WAS DELI-CIOUS!
THANK YOU VERY MUCH!
No, thank you
BE GOOD TO MY LITTLE BROTHER, OKAY?
WHISPER
Wait, ma'am...
I think you're misunder-standing something...
Hey!
NO RUN-NING!
Ha ha ha!
HEY, WHAT'S CANADA LIKE?
I DON'T KNOW WHAT YOU'RE SAYING? DO YOU LIKE ME?

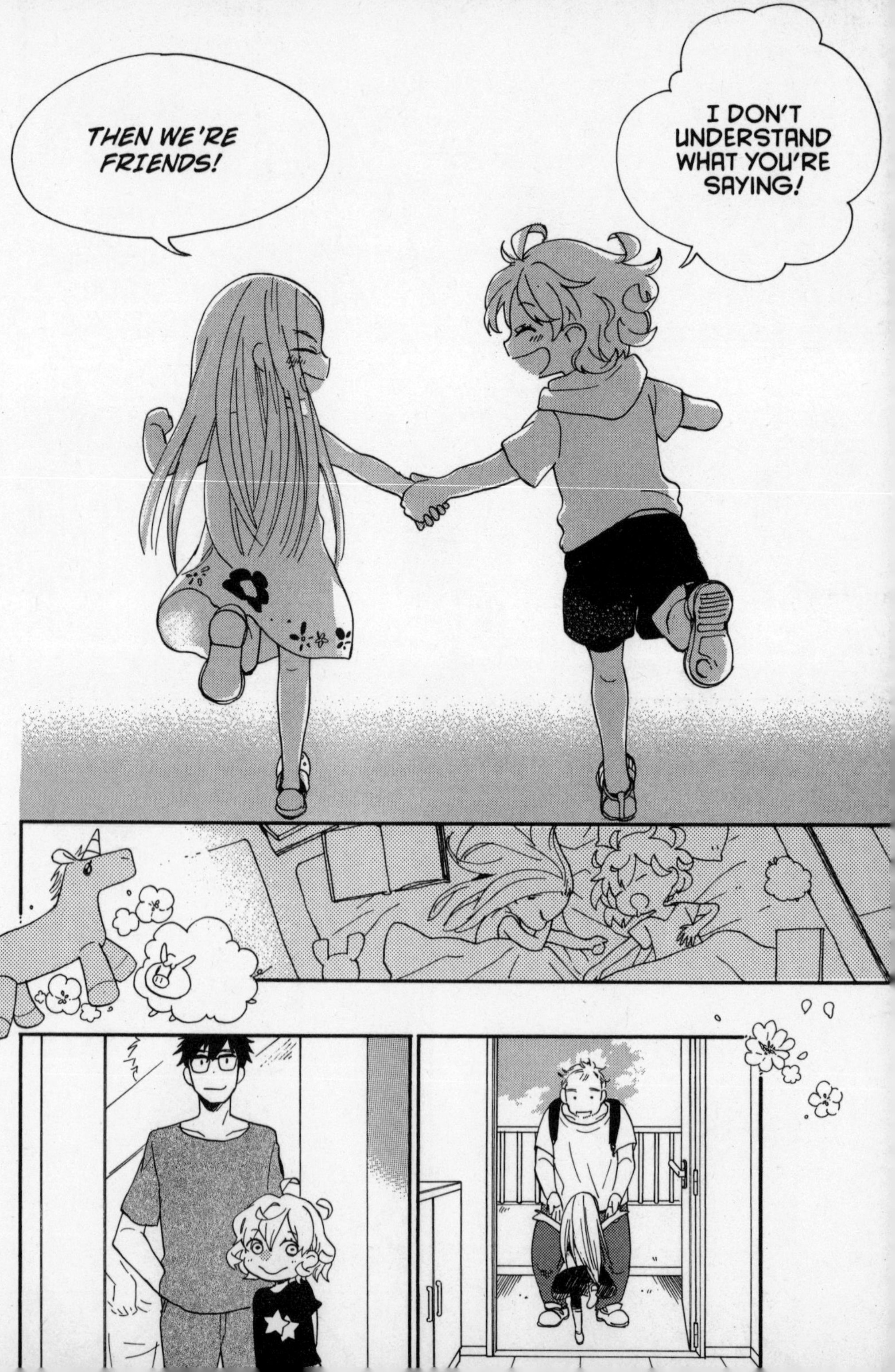
I DON'T UNDERSTAND WHAT YOU'RE SAYING!
THEN WE'RE FRIENDS!

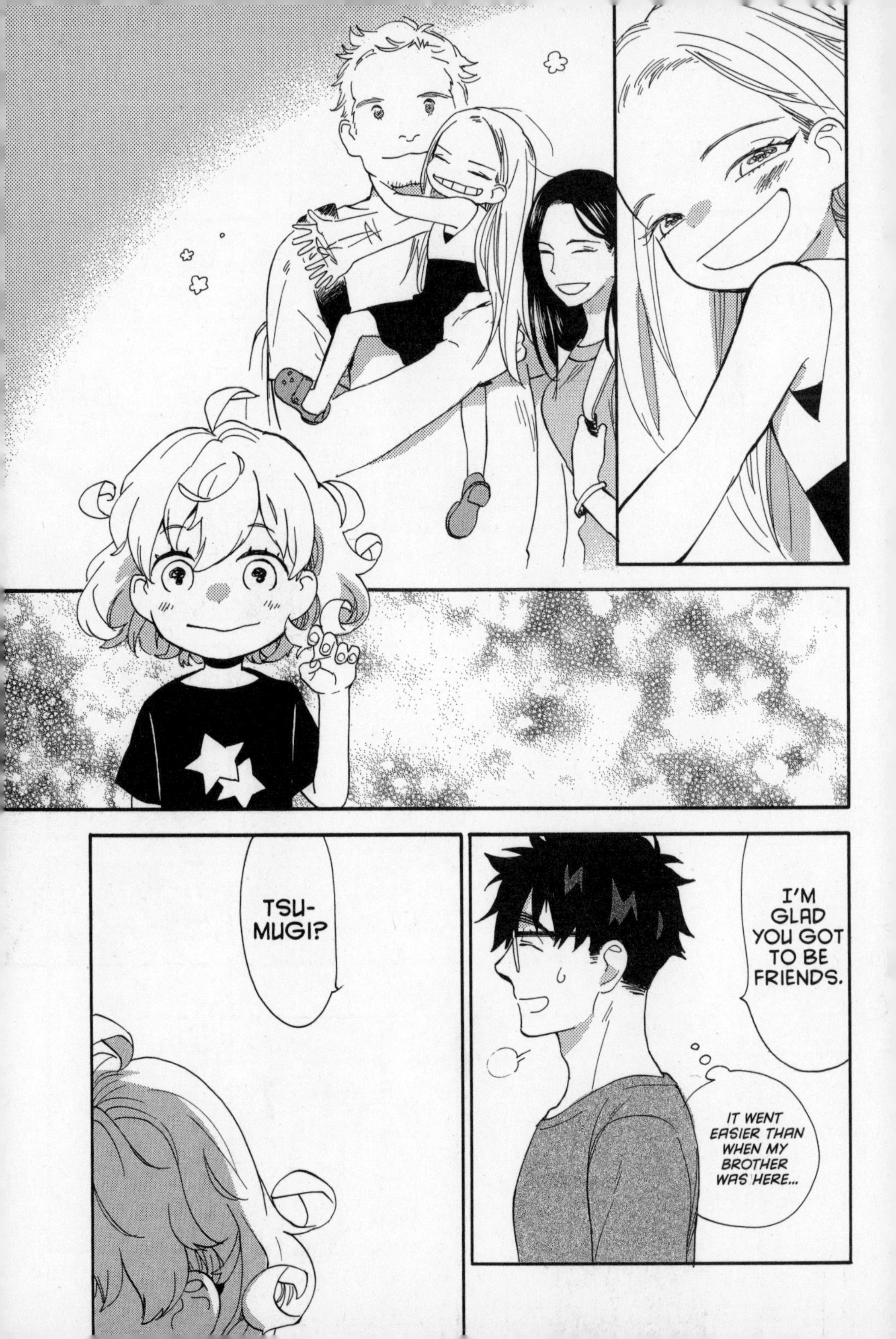
I'M GLAD YOU GOT TO BE FRIENDS.
IT WENT EASIER THAN WHEN MY BROTHER WAS HERE...
TSU-MUGI?

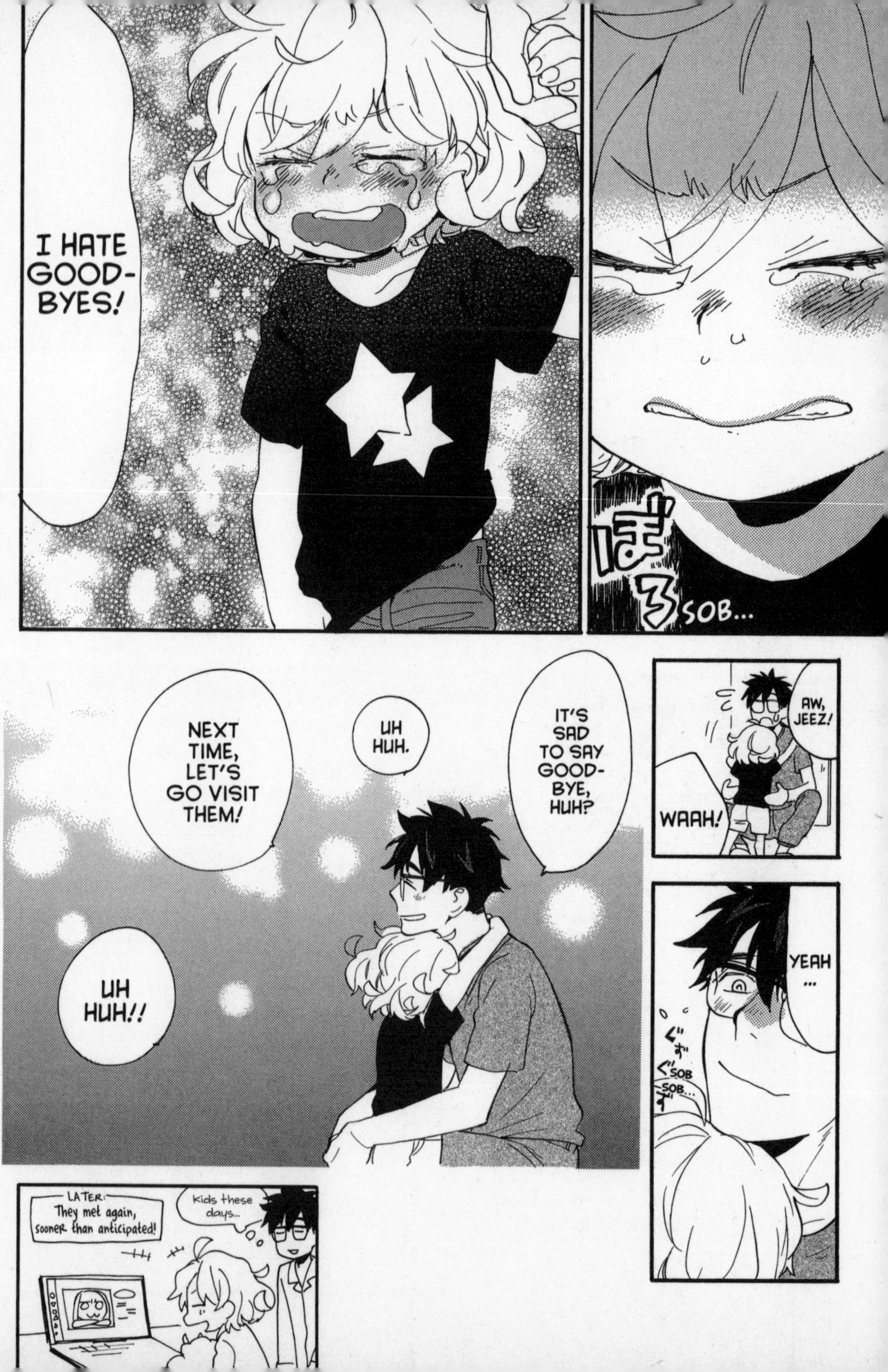
ぼろ
SOB...
I HATE GOODBYES!
AW, JEEZ!
WAAH!
YEAH...
ぐずぐず
SOB SOB...
IT'S SAD TO SAY GOODBYE, HUH?
UH HUH.
NEXT TIME, LET'S GO VISIT THEM!
UH HUH!!
LATER: They met again, sooner than anticipated!
Kids these days...

CHEESE & SPINACH CANNELLONI

☆ Ingredients (serves 3-4) ☆

- ★ 8 sticks Cannelloni (Dried)
- ★ 30g Onions
- ★ 1/2 Tablespoon Olive Oil
- ★ 1/4 scant Teaspoon Salt
- ★ A pinch of Pepper
- ★ 200g Spinach
- ★ 200g Ricotta Cheese (Cottage Cheese works as a substitute)
- ★ 40g Parmigiano Reggiano (Powdered Cheese works as a substitute)

Bechamel Sauce

500cc Cold Milk
30g Weak Flour
A Pinch of Nutmeg
30g Butter
1/4 Teaspoon Salt
A Pinch of Pepper

1. Boil the Spinach in lightly salted water, then immerse in ice water.
2. Finely mince both onion and well-squeezed 1. Take out Parmigiano Reggiano.
3. Heat olive oil in a frying pan, then place onion in it. When the onion begins to color, add spinach and reduce heat to medium. Cook for 3 minutes to reduce moisture.
4. Remove from heat. Once the pan has cooled a bit, mix in ricotta cheese.
5. Add 30g of Parmigiano Reggiano mixed with salt and pepper to 4.
6. Boil cannelloni in lightly salted water for three minutes. Once cooked, remove from water and place on a tray to cool.
7. Make the bechamel sauce. Melt the butter in a frying pan, then turn off heat and add sifted flour.
8. Mix 7 well, then place on low heat. Stir with a wooden spatula for a few minutes, then remove from heat when mixture thickens.
9. Add all the milk to 8, and mix thoroughly. Place over low heat again. Stir with a spatula or whisk and cook until smooth.
10. Add salt, pepper, and nutmeg to taste.
11. Place 5 in an icing bag, and fill cannelloni from 6.

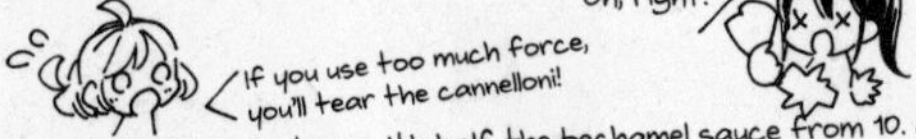
If you use too much force, you'll tear the cannelloni!
Oh, right!

12. Fill a heat-resistant baking tray with half the bechamel sauce from 10. Arrange the cannelloni in it, then cover with remaining sauce.
13. Place in an oven preheated to 425 degrees F and bake for 15 minutes, then it's done!

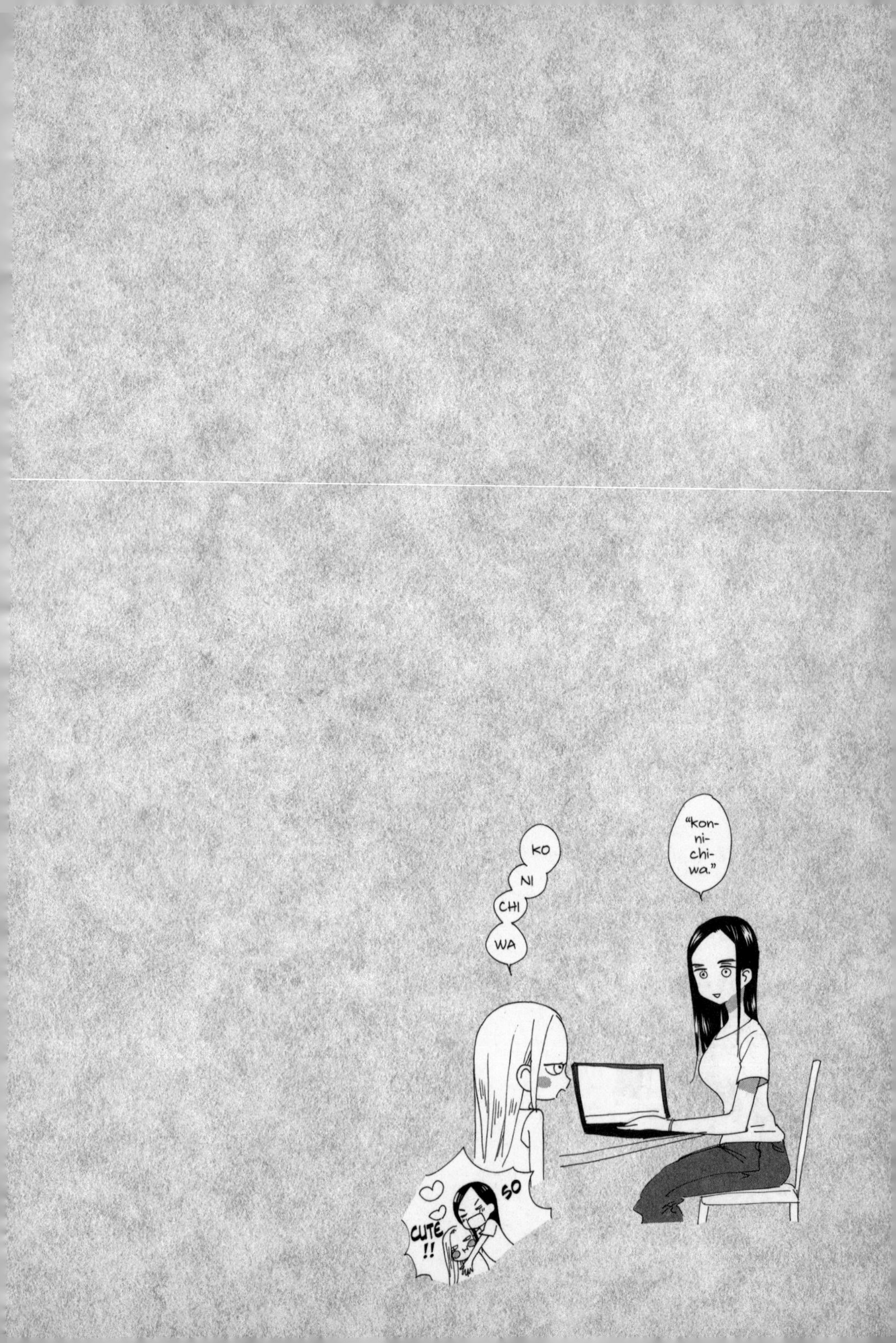
"kon-ni-chi-wa."
KO NI CHI WA
SO CUTE!!

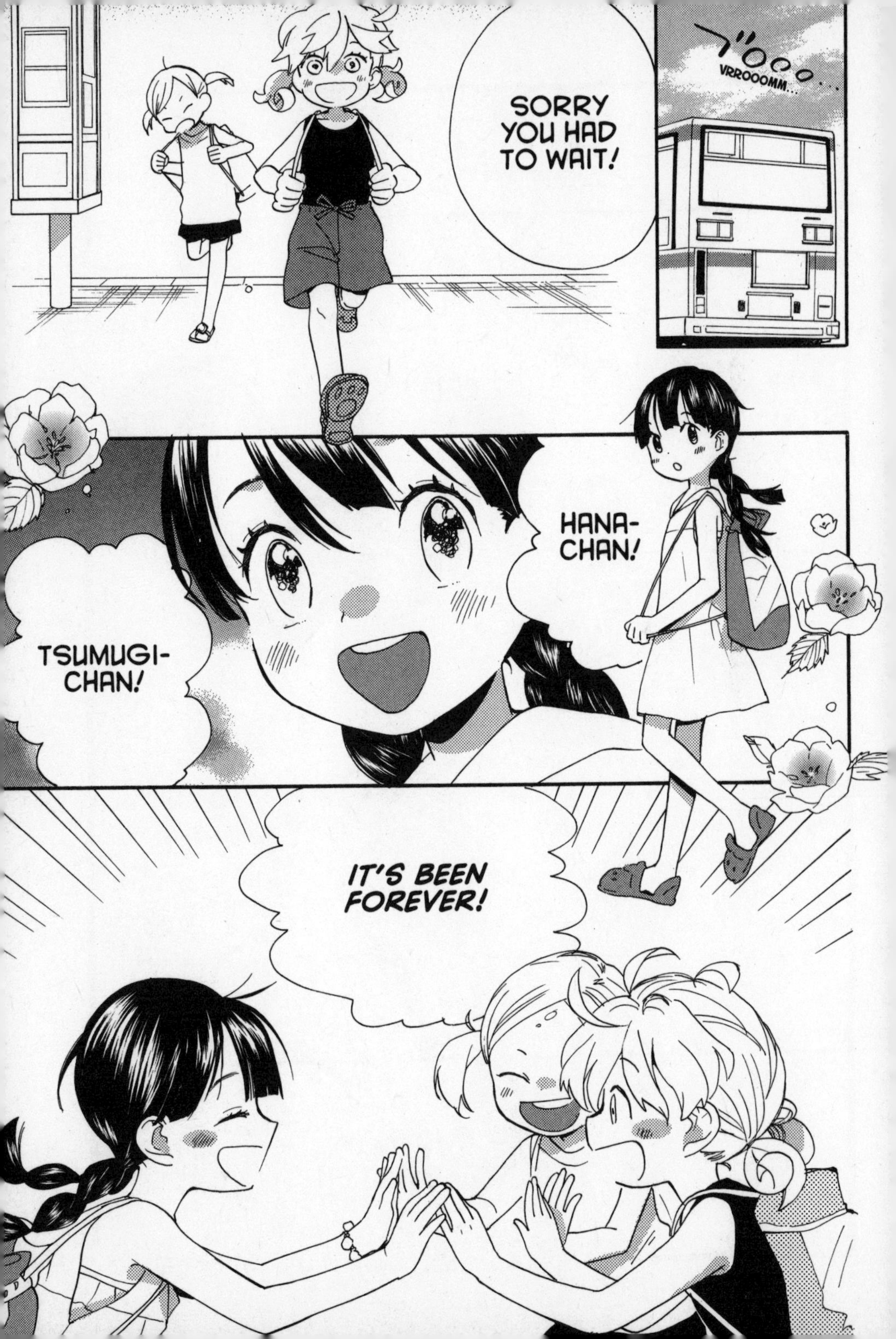
VRROOOMM...
SORRY YOU HAD TO WAIT!
HANA-CHAN!
TSUMUGI-CHAN!
IT'S BEEN FOREVER!

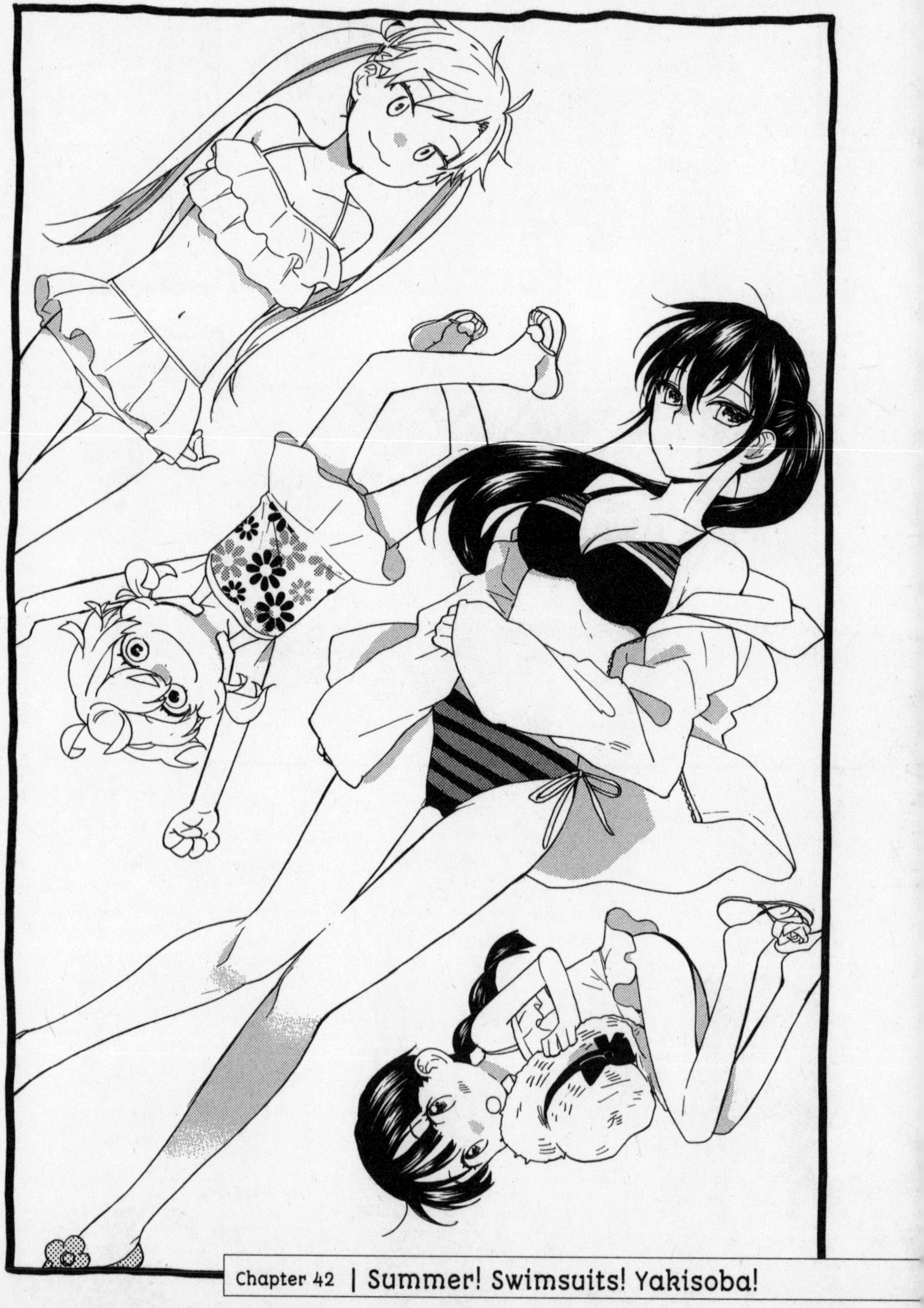

Chapter 42 | Summer! Swimsuits! Yakisoba!

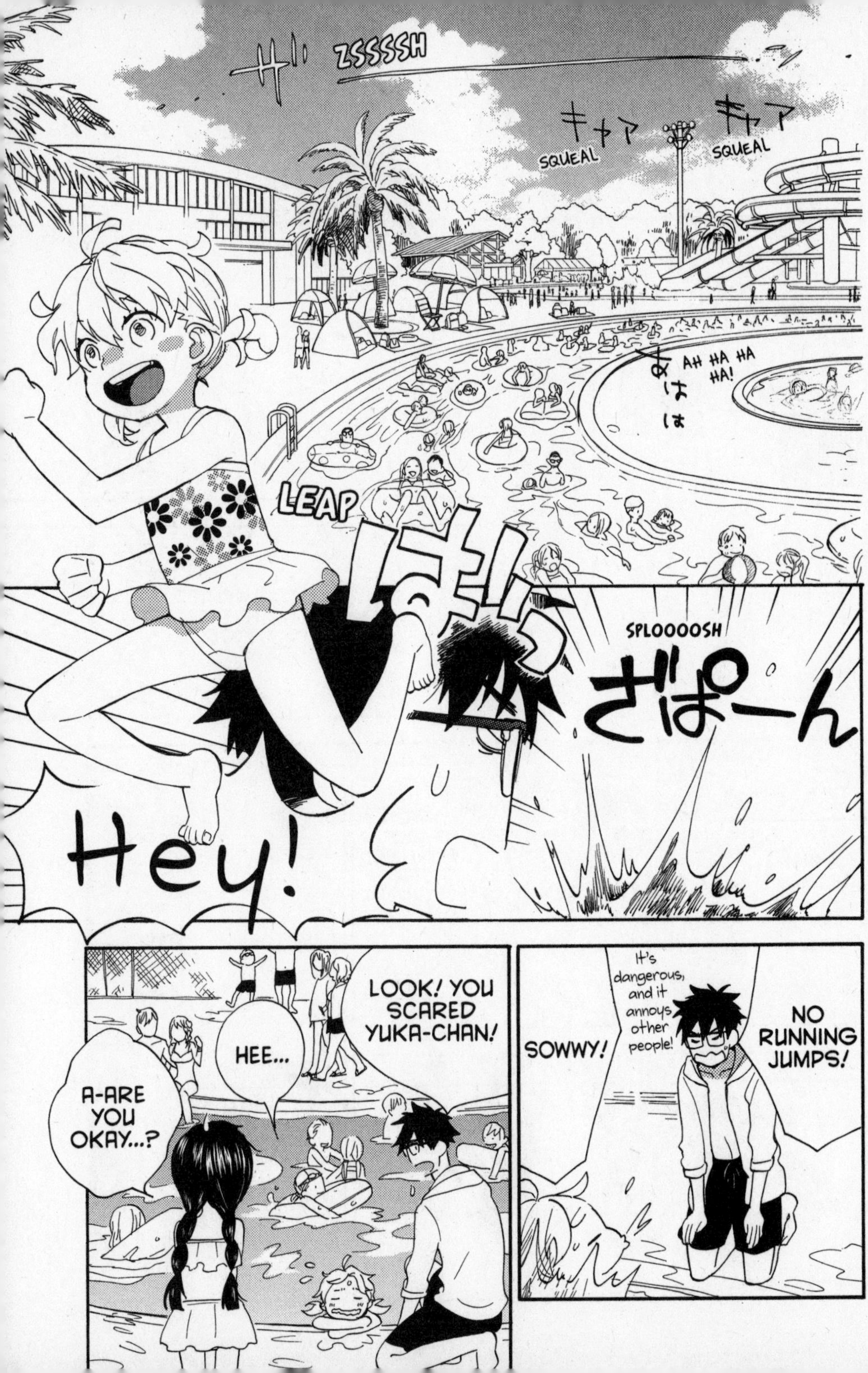
ZSSSSH
キャア
SQUEAL
キャア
SQUEAL
あはは
AH HA HA HA!
LEAP
SPLOOOOSH
ざぱーん
Hey!
NO RUNNING JUMPS!
It's dangerous, and it annoys other people!
SOWWY!
LOOK! YOU SCARED YUKA-CHAN!
HEE...
A-ARE YOU OKAY...?

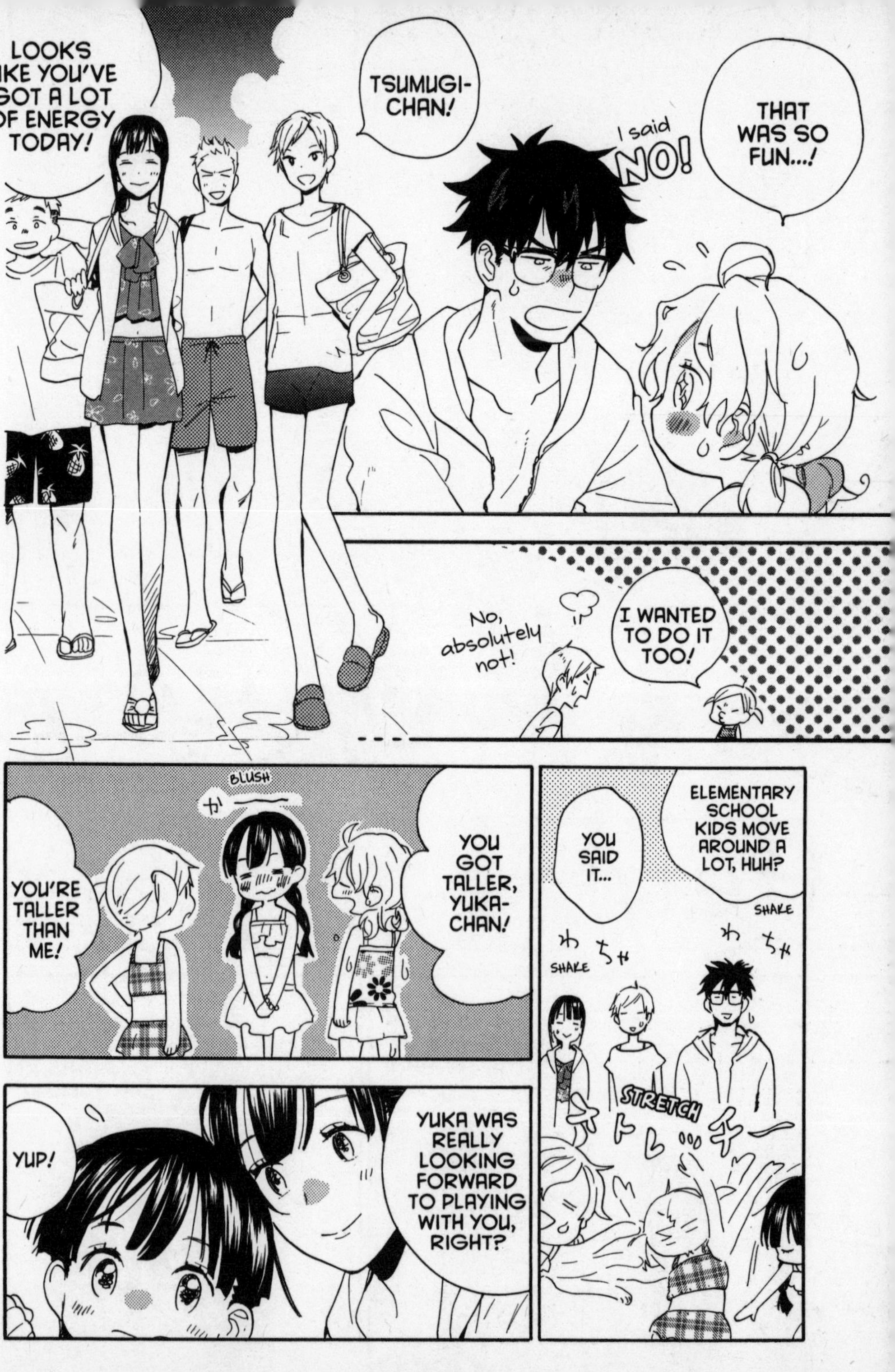
THAT WAS SO FUN...!
I said NO!
I WANTED TO DO IT TOO!
No, absolutely not!
TSUMUGI-CHAN!
LOOKS LIKE YOU'VE GOT A LOT OF ENERGY TODAY!
ELEMENTARY SCHOOL KIDS MOVE AROUND A LOT, HUH?
YOU SAID IT...
SHAKE
SHAKE
STRETCH
YOU GOT TALLER, YUKA-CHAN!
BLUSH
YOU'RE TALLER THAN ME!
YUKA WAS REALLY LOOKING FORWARD TO PLAYING WITH YOU, RIGHT?
YUP!

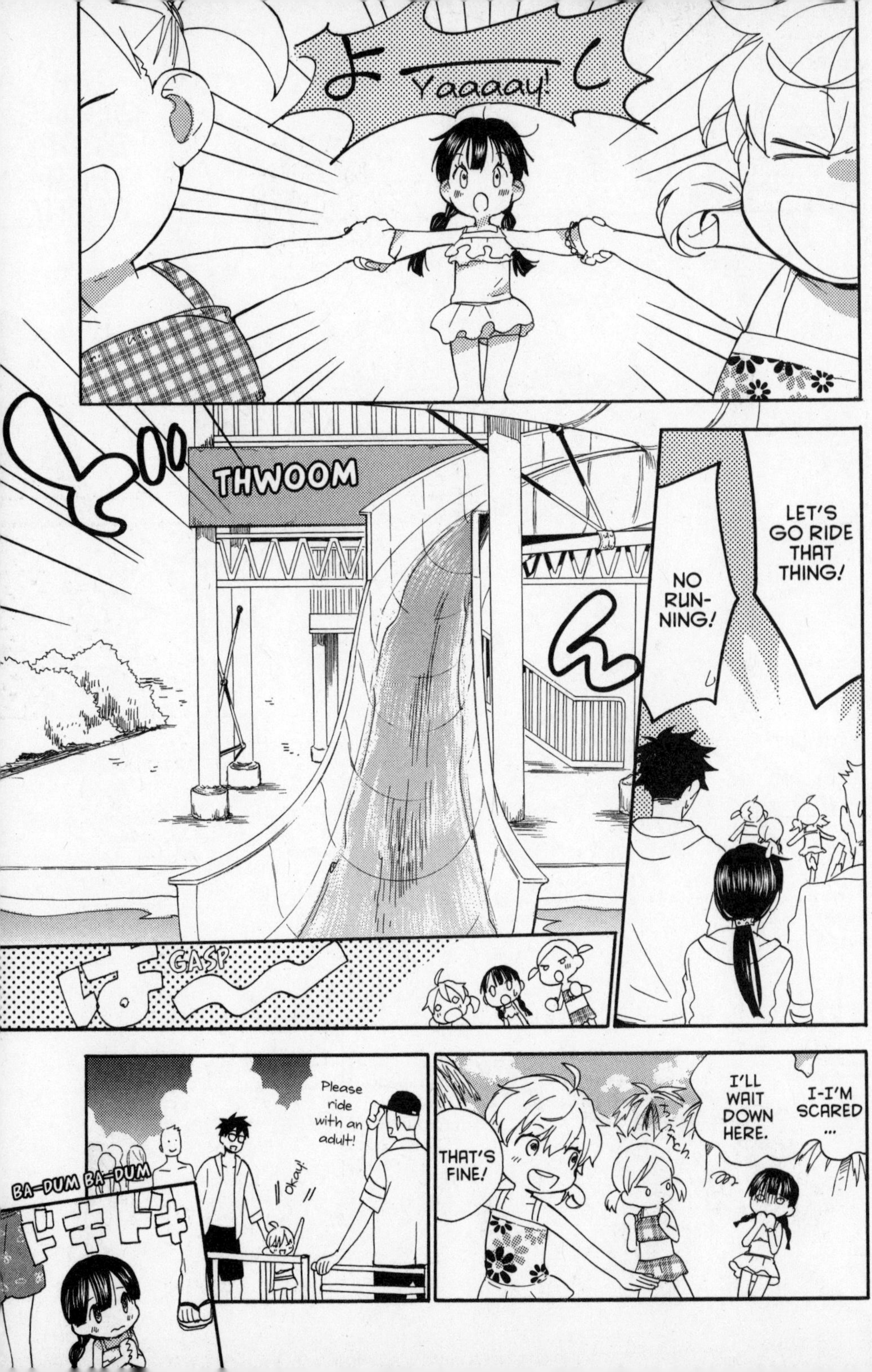
Yaaaay!
LET'S GO RIDE THAT THING!
NO RUN-NING!
THWOOM
GASP
I-I'M SCARED ...
I'LL WAIT DOWN HERE.
Tch.
THAT'S FINE!
Please ride with an adult!
Okay!
BA-DUM BA-DUM
ドキドキ

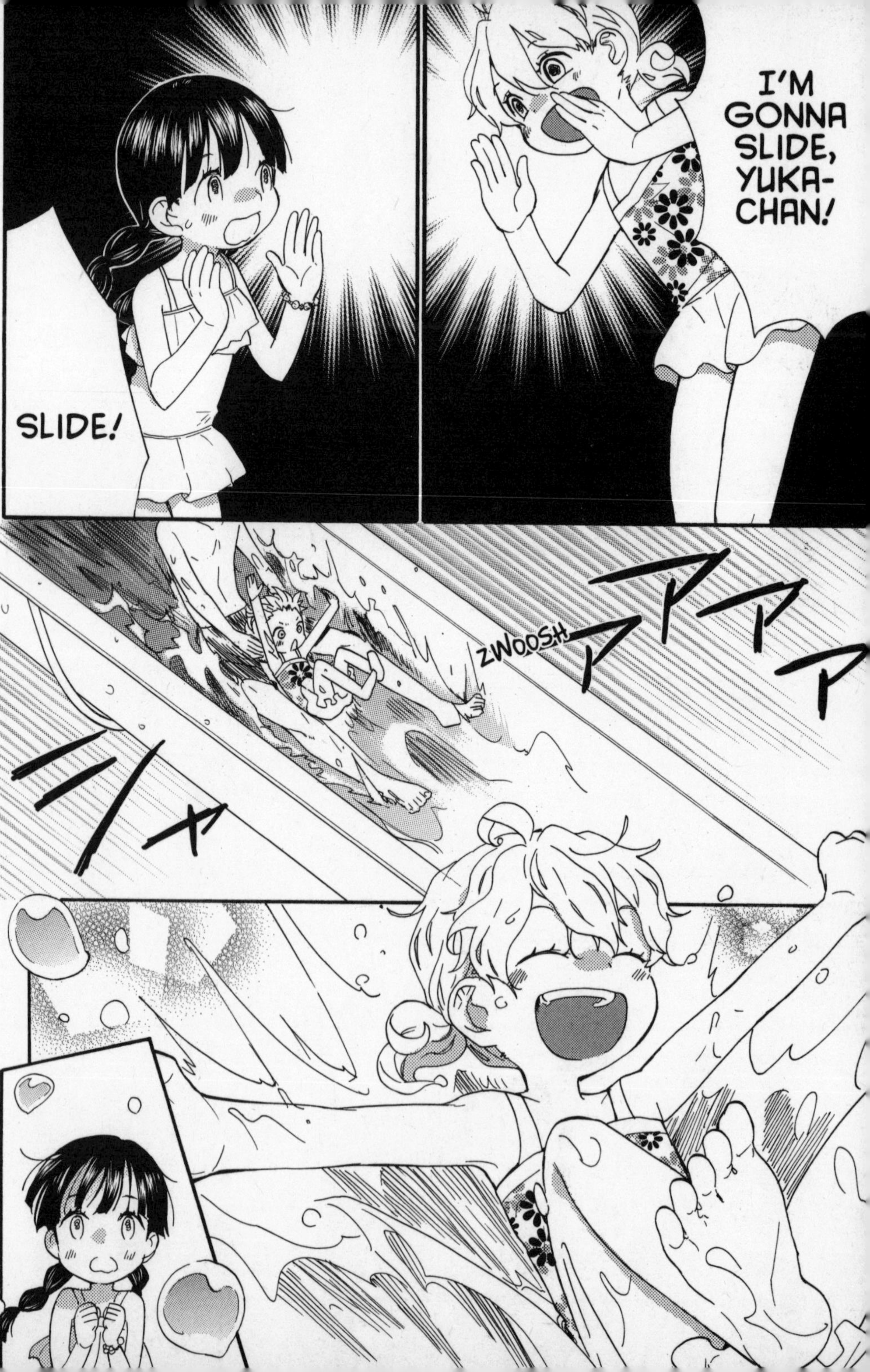
I'M GONNA SLIDE, YUKA-CHAN!
SLIDE!
アアアア
ZWOOSH
シャ

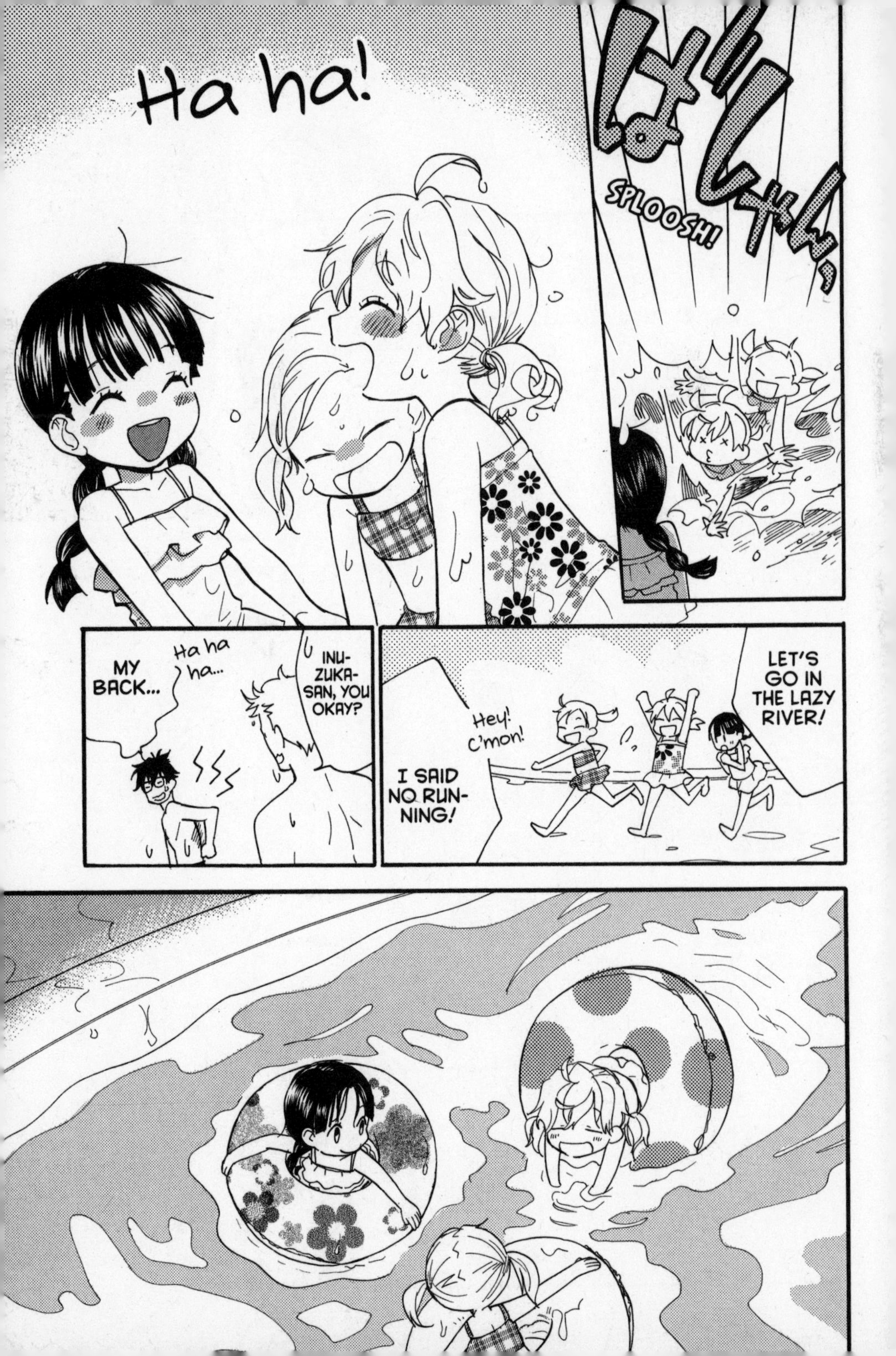
ばしゃん
SPLOOSH!
Ha ha!
LET'S GO IN THE LAZY RIVER!
Hey! C'mon!
I SAID NO RUN-NING!
INU-ZUKA-SAN, YOU OKAY?
Ha ha ha...
MY BACK...

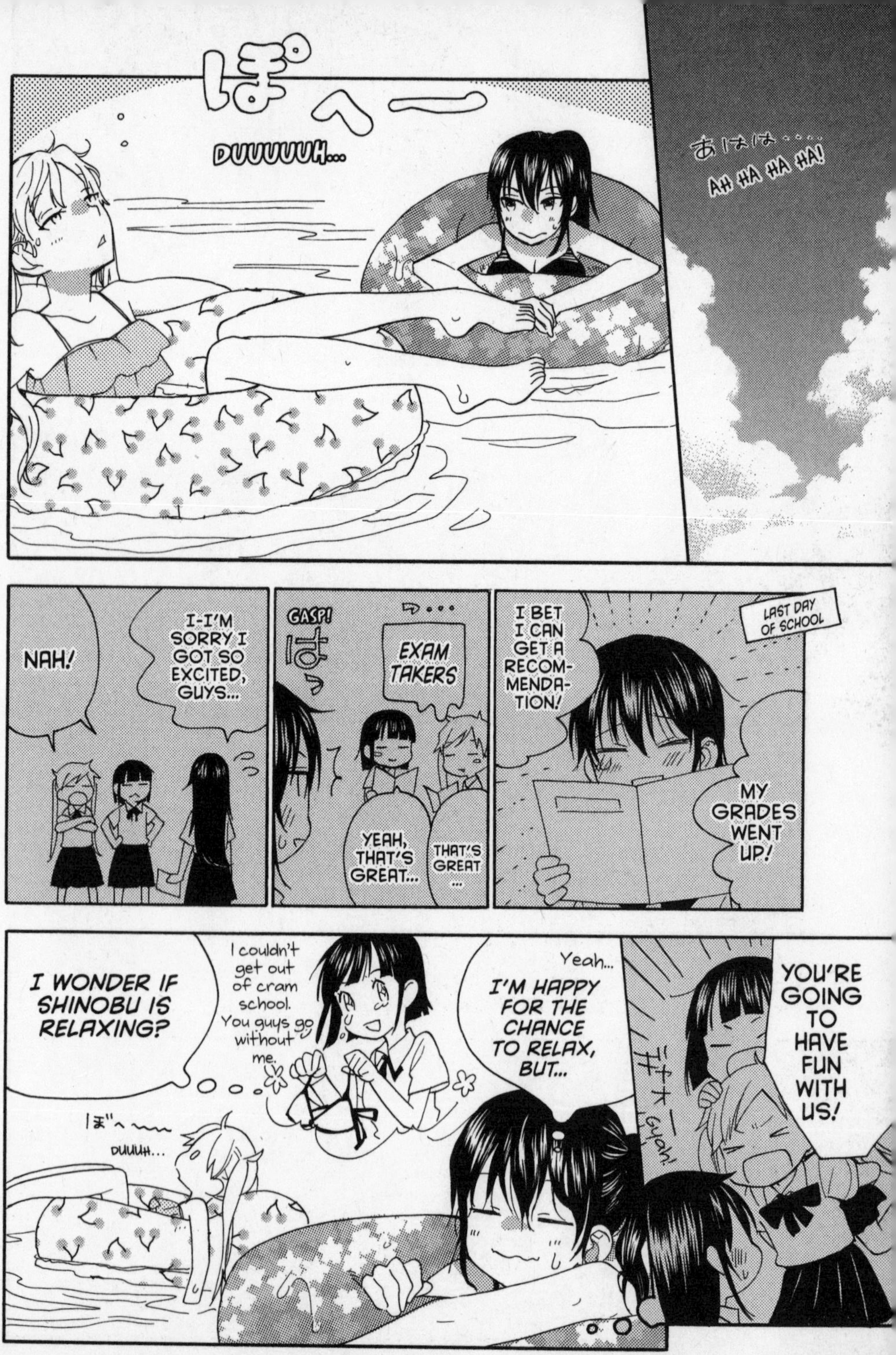
あはは……
AH HA HA HA!
ぽへー
DUUUUUH...
LAST DAY OF SCHOOL
I BET I CAN GET A RECOMMENDATION!
MY GRADES WENT UP!
EXAM TAKERS
GASP!
は
THAT'S GREAT...
YEAH, THAT'S GREAT...
I-I'M SORRY I GOT SO EXCITED, GUYS...
NAH!
YOU'RE GOING TO HAVE FUN WITH US!
ギャー
Gyah!
Yeah...
I'M HAPPY FOR THE CHANCE TO RELAX, BUT...
I couldn't get out of cram school. You guys go without me.
I WONDER IF SHINOBU IS RELAXING?
ぽ゛へ～～
DUUUH...

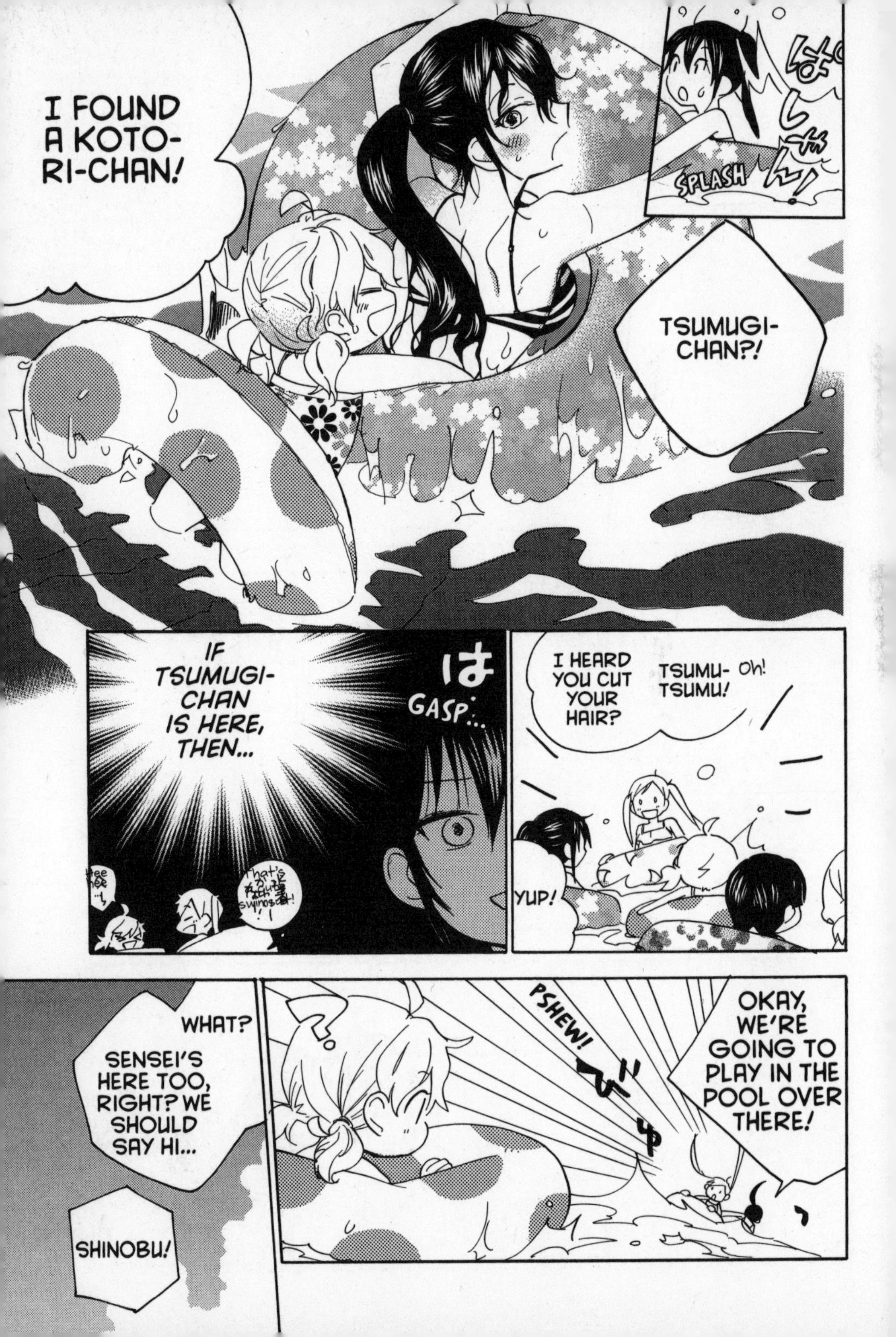

ぱしゃん!
SPLASH
I FOUND A KOTO-RI-CHAN!
TSUMUGI-CHAN?!
Oh!
TSUMU-TSUMU!
I HEARD YOU CUT YOUR HAIR?
YUP!
は
GASP...
IF TSUMUGI-CHAN IS HERE, THEN...
That's
Hee hee...!
OKAY, WE'RE GOING TO PLAY IN THE POOL OVER THERE!
PSHEW!
びゅ
WHAT?
SENSEI'S HERE TOO, RIGHT? WE SHOULD SAY HI...
SHINOBU!

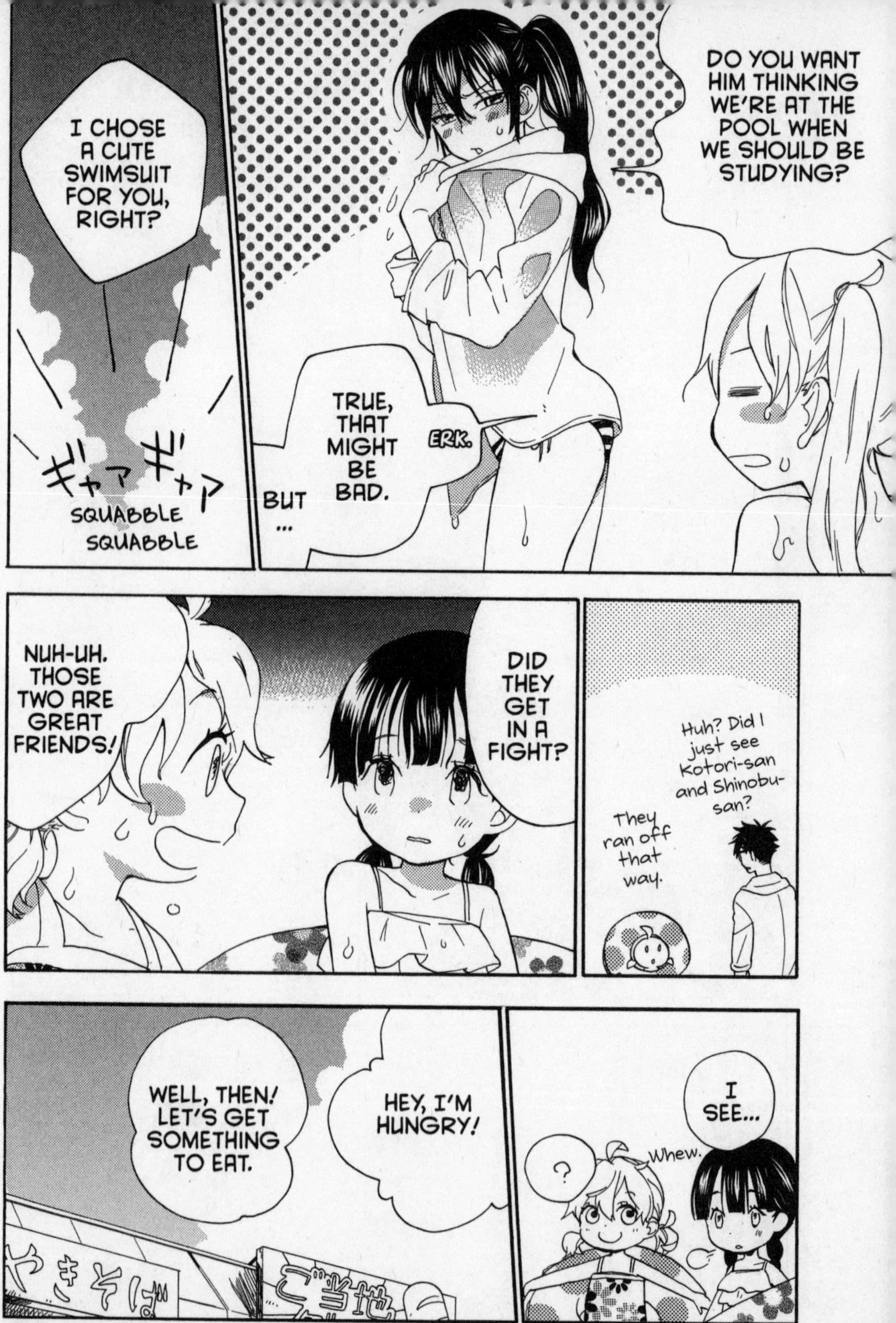
DO YOU WANT HIM THINKING WE'RE AT THE POOL WHEN WE SHOULD BE STUDYING?
ERK.
TRUE, THAT MIGHT BE BAD.
BUT ...
I CHOSE A CUTE SWIMSUIT FOR YOU, RIGHT?
ギャアギャア
SQUABBLE SQUABBLE
Huh? Did I just see Kotori-san and Shinobu-san?
They ran off that way.
DID THEY GET IN A FIGHT?
NUH-UH. THOSE TWO ARE GREAT FRIENDS!
I SEE...
Whew.
?
HEY, I'M HUNGRY!
WELL, THEN! LET'S GET SOMETHING TO EAT.
やきそば
SIGN: YAKISOBA

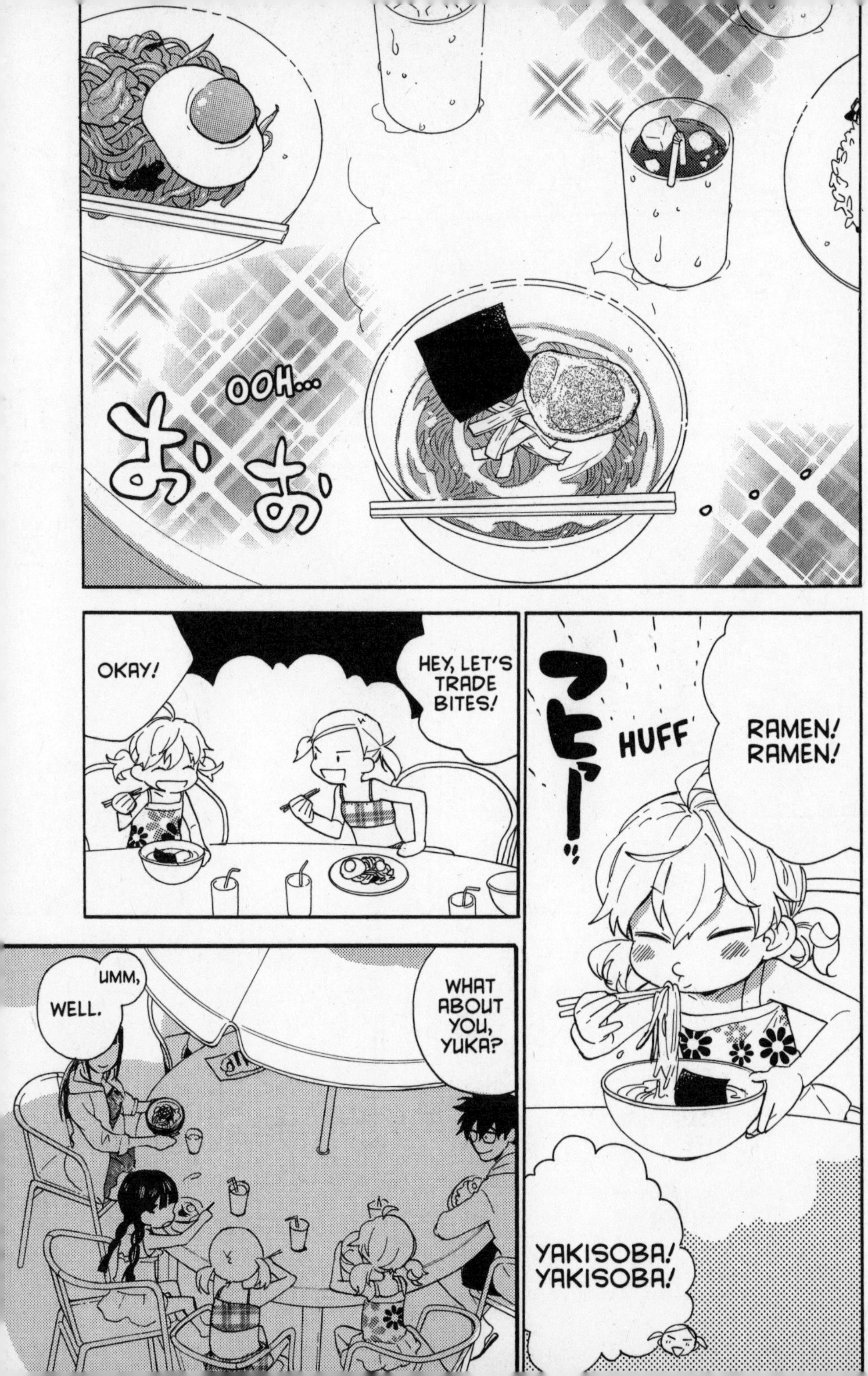

OOH...
おぉ
RAMEN! RAMEN!
フヒュー!!
HUFF
YAKISOBA! YAKISOBA!
HEY, LET'S TRADE BITES!
OKAY!
WHAT ABOUT YOU, YUKA?
UMM, WELL.

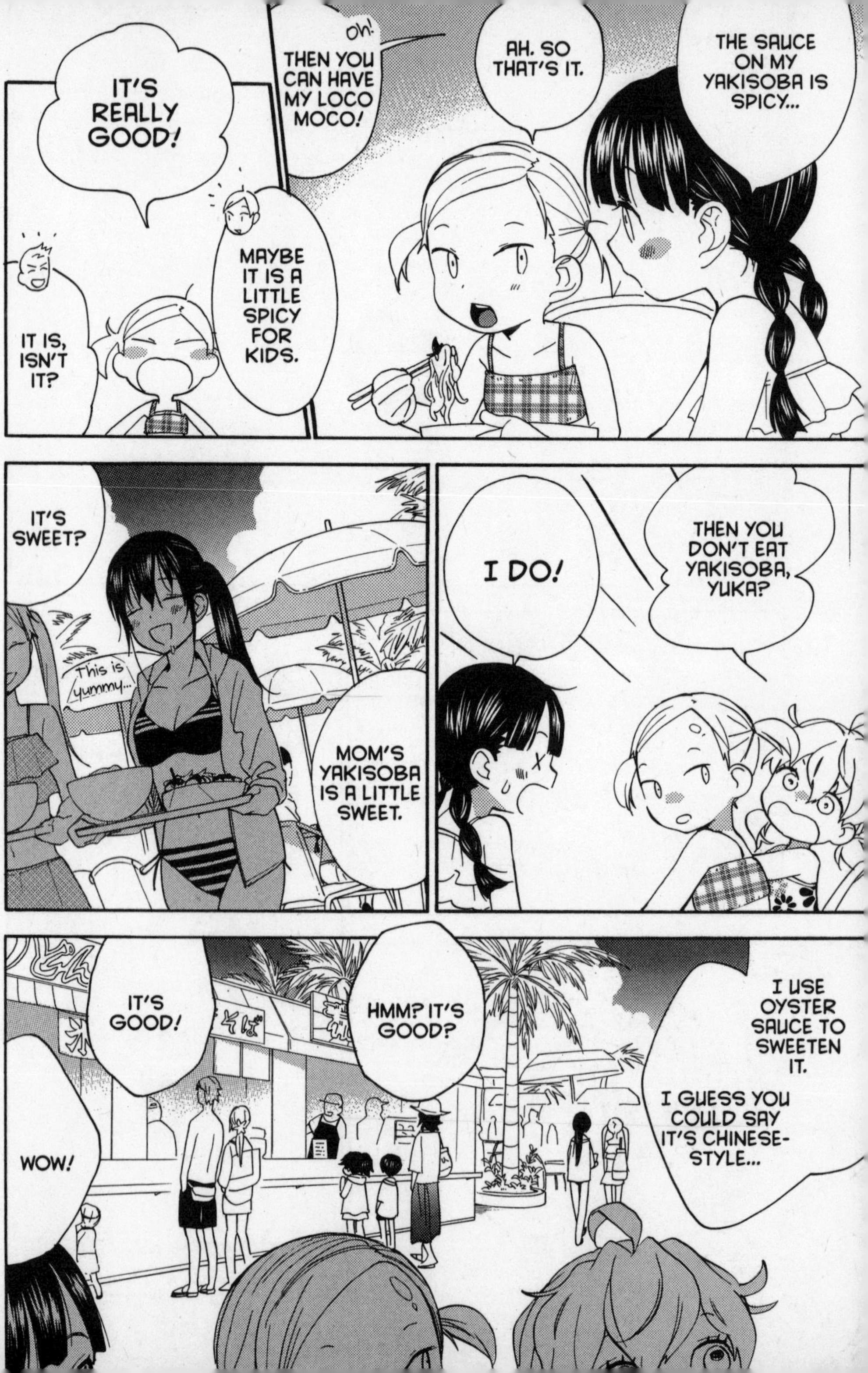
THE SAUCE ON MY YAKISOBA IS SPICY...
AH. SO THAT'S IT.
Oh!
THEN YOU CAN HAVE MY LOCO MOCO!
IT'S REALLY GOOD!
MAYBE IT IS A LITTLE SPICY FOR KIDS.
IT IS, ISN'T IT?
THEN YOU DON'T EAT YAKISOBA, YUKA?
I DO!
MOM'S YAKISOBA IS A LITTLE SWEET.
IT'S SWEET?
This is yummy...
I USE OYSTER SAUCE TO SWEETEN IT.
I GUESS YOU COULD SAY IT'S CHINESE-STYLE...
HMM? IT'S GOOD?
IT'S GOOD!
WOW!

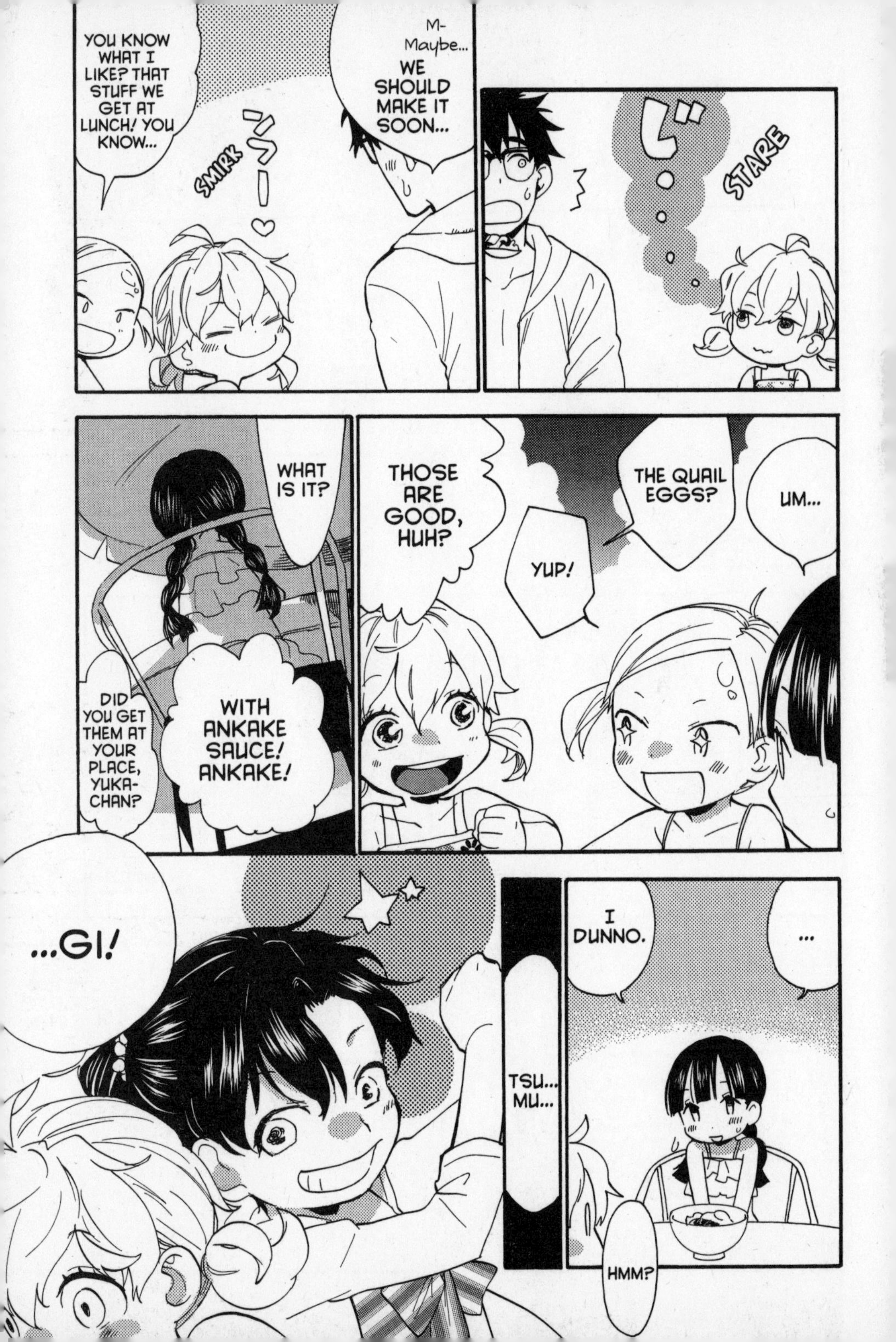
STARE
M- Maybe... WE SHOULD MAKE IT SOON...
YOU KNOW WHAT I LIKE? THAT STUFF WE GET AT LUNCH! YOU KNOW...
SMIRK
UM...
THE QUAIL EGGS?
YUP!
THOSE ARE GOOD, HUH?
WHAT IS IT?
WITH ANKAKE SAUCE! ANKAKE!
DID YOU GET THEM AT YOUR PLACE, YUKA-CHAN?
...
I DUNNO.
HMM?
TSU... MU...
...GI!

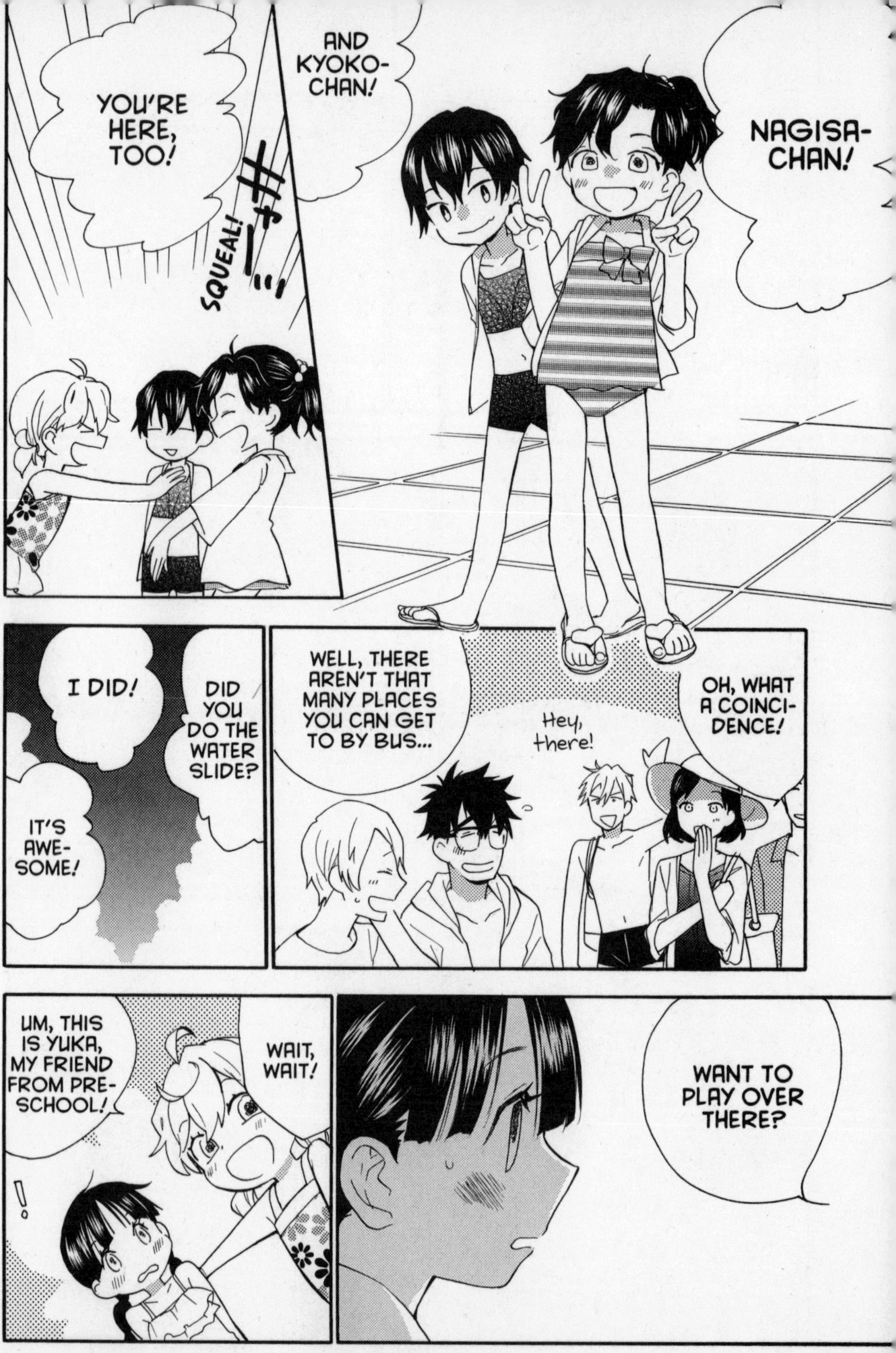
NAGISA-CHAN!
AND KYOKO-CHAN!
YOU'RE HERE, TOO!
SQUEAL!
OH, WHAT A COINCIDENCE!
Hey, there!
WELL, THERE AREN'T THAT MANY PLACES YOU CAN GET TO BY BUS...
DID YOU DO THE WATER SLIDE?
I DID!
IT'S AWESOME!
WANT TO PLAY OVER THERE?
WAIT, WAIT!
UM, THIS IS YUKA, MY FRIEND FROM PRE-SCHOOL!
!

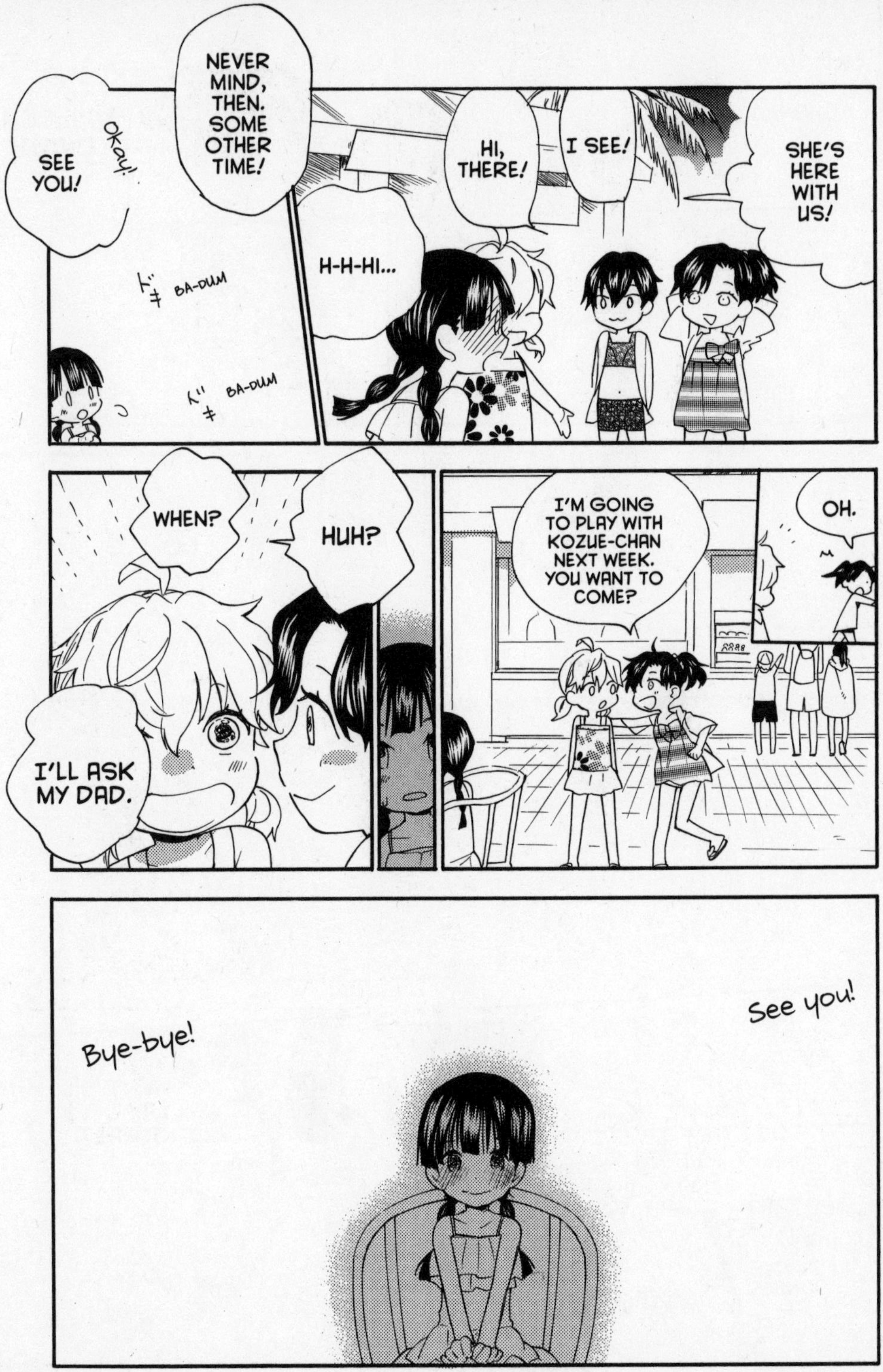

SHE'S HERE WITH US!
I SEE!
HI, THERE!
H-H-HI...
NEVER MIND, THEN. SOME OTHER TIME!
Okay!
SEE YOU!
ドキ BA-DUM
ドキ BA-DUM
I'M GOING TO PLAY WITH KOZUE-CHAN NEXT WEEK. YOU WANT TO COME?
OH.
HUH?
WHEN?
I'LL ASK MY DAD.
See you!
Bye-bye!

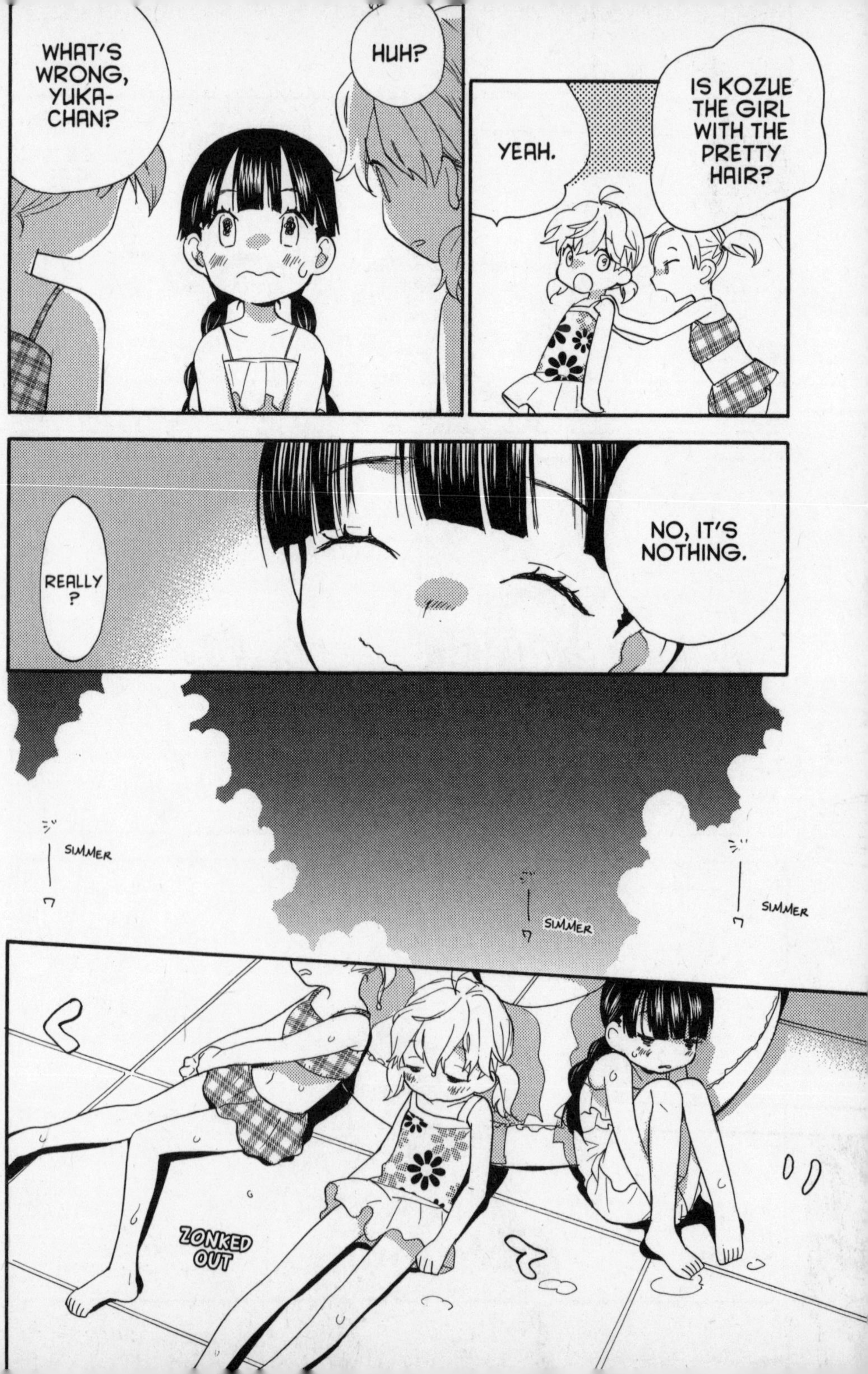
IS KOZUE THE GIRL WITH THE PRETTY HAIR?
YEAH.
WHAT'S WRONG, YUKA-CHAN?
HUH?
NO, IT'S NOTHING.
REALLY?
SIMMER
SIMMER
SIMMER
ZONKED OUT

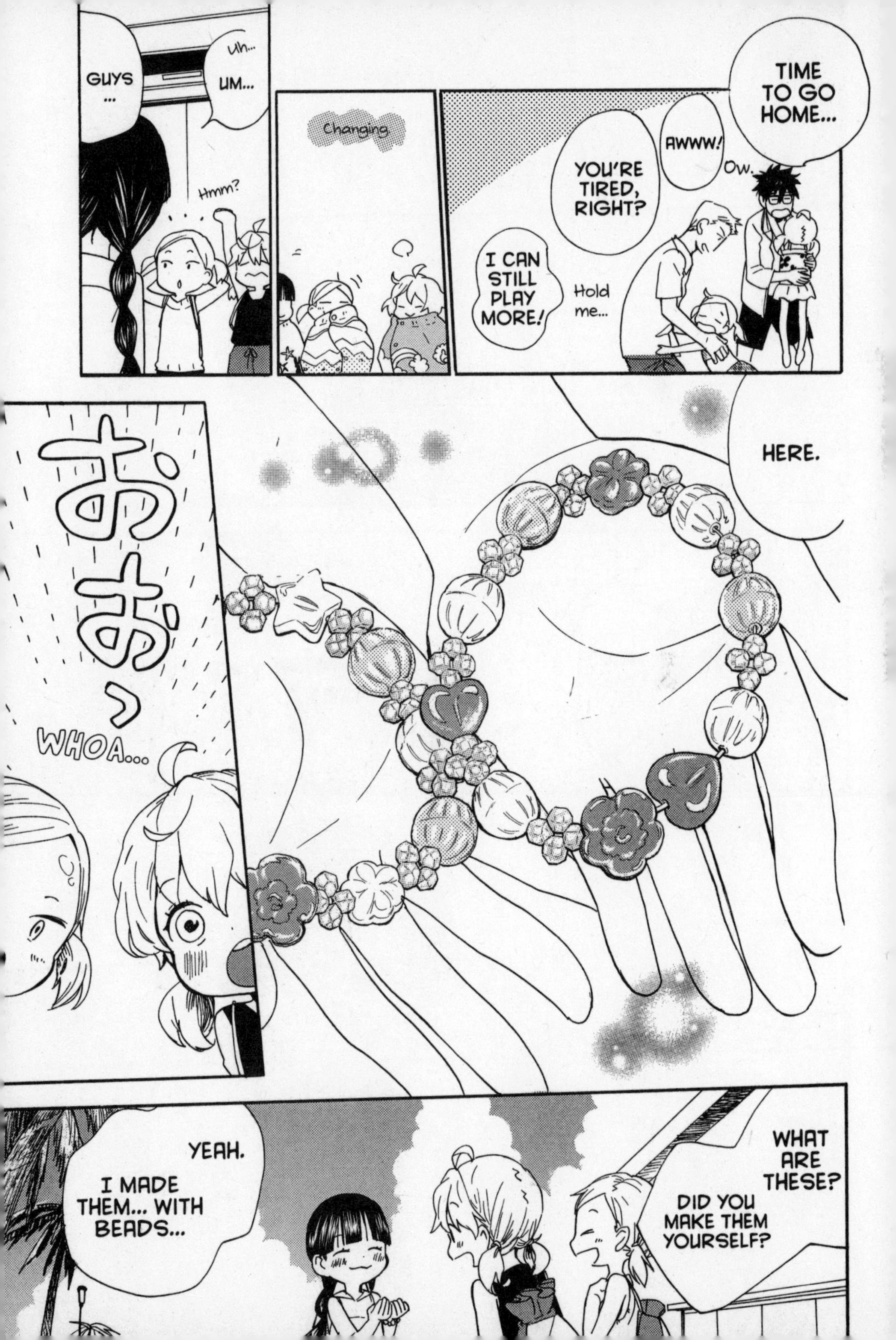
TIME TO GO HOME...
AWWW!
Ow.
YOU'RE TIRED, RIGHT?
Hold me...
I CAN STILL PLAY MORE!
Changing
Uh...
UM...
GUYS...
Hmm?
HERE.
おおっ
WHOA...
WHAT ARE THESE?
DID YOU MAKE THEM YOURSELF?
YEAH.
I MADE THEM... WITH BEADS...

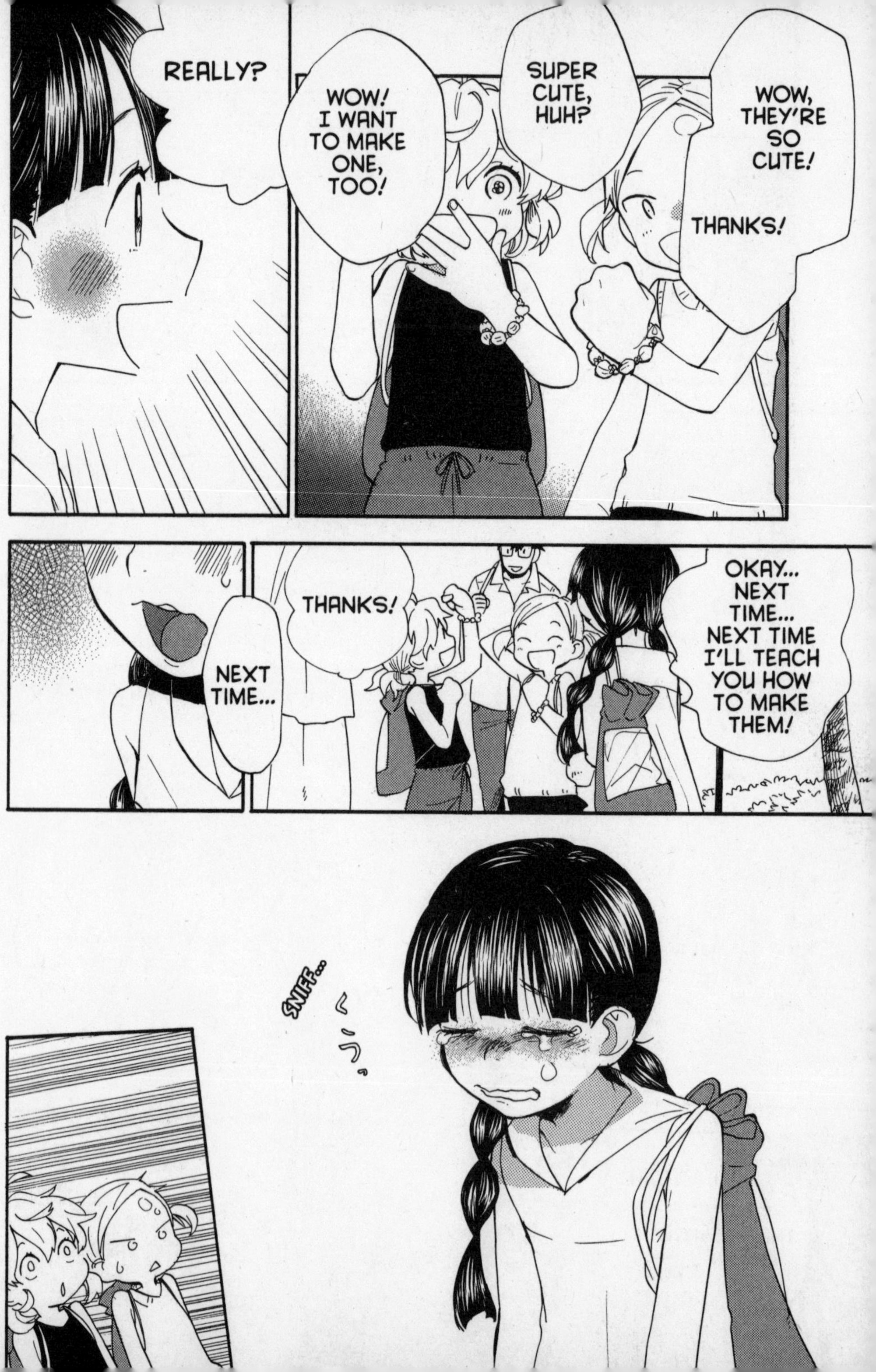
WOW, THEY'RE SO CUTE!
THANKS!
SUPER CUTE, HUH?
WOW! I WANT TO MAKE ONE, TOO!
REALLY?
OKAY... NEXT TIME... NEXT TIME I'LL TEACH YOU HOW TO MAKE THEM!
THANKS!
NEXT TIME...
SNIFF...

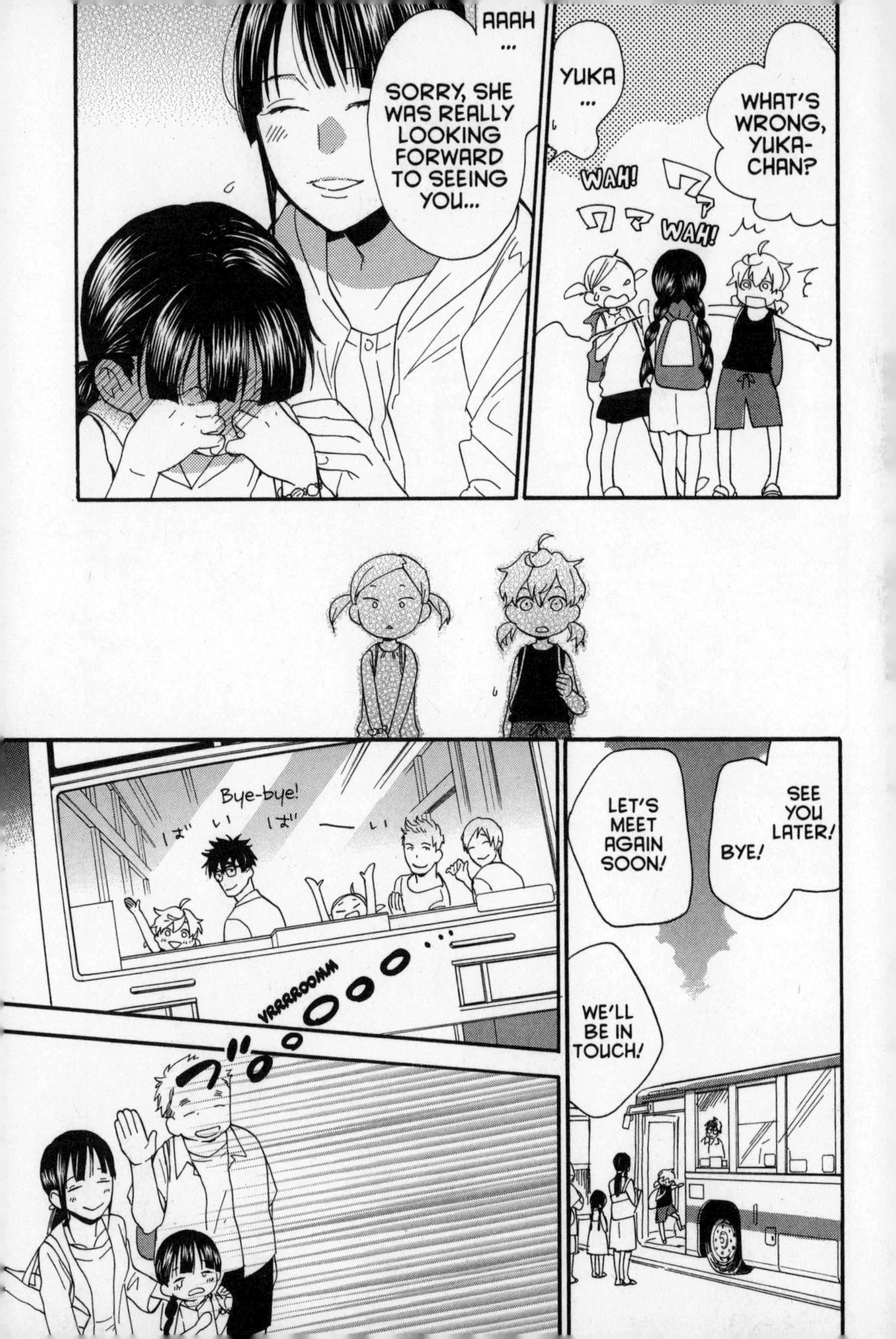
WHAT'S WRONG, YUKA-CHAN?
YUKA ...
WAH!
ワァ
WAH!
ワァ
AAAH ...
SORRY, SHE WAS REALLY LOOKING FORWARD TO SEEING YOU...
SEE YOU LATER!
BYE!
LET'S MEET AGAIN SOON!
WE'LL BE IN TOUCH!
Bye-bye!
ばいばーい
VRRRROOMM

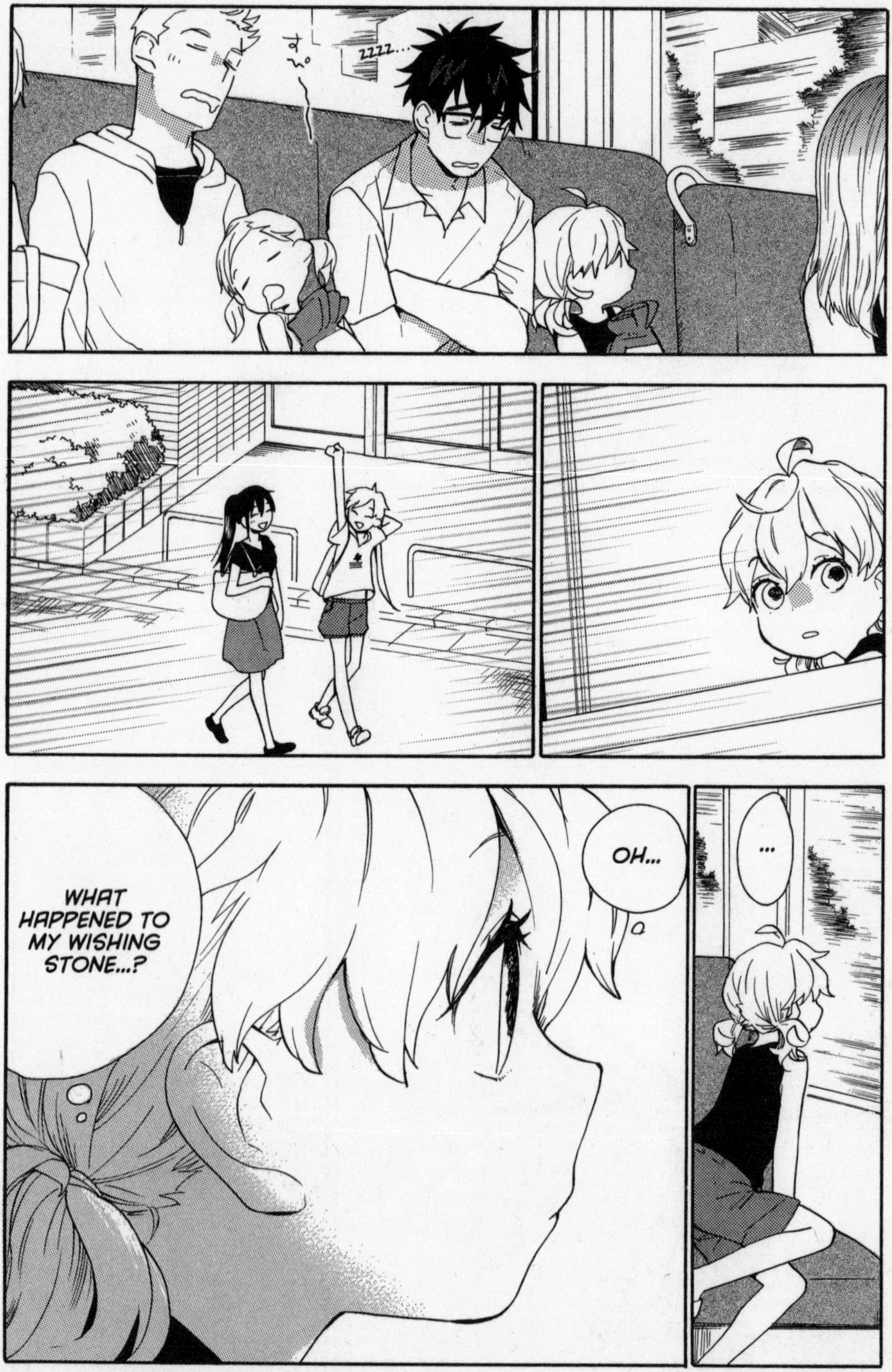
ZZZZ...
すぴ～
...
OH...
WHAT HAPPENED TO MY WISHING STONE...?

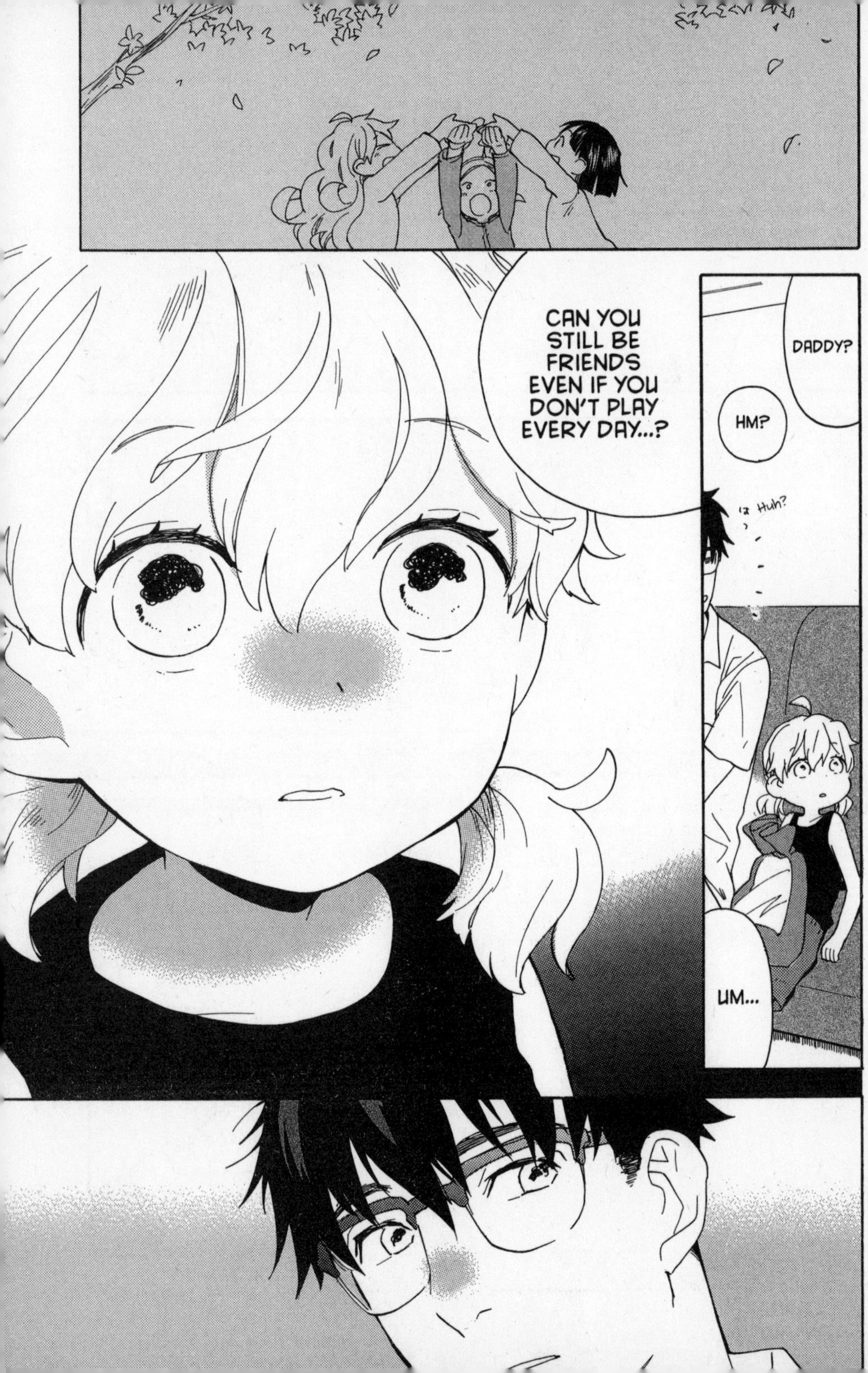
DADDY?
HM?
Huh?
UM...
CAN YOU STILL BE FRIENDS EVEN IF YOU DON'T PLAY EVERY DAY...?

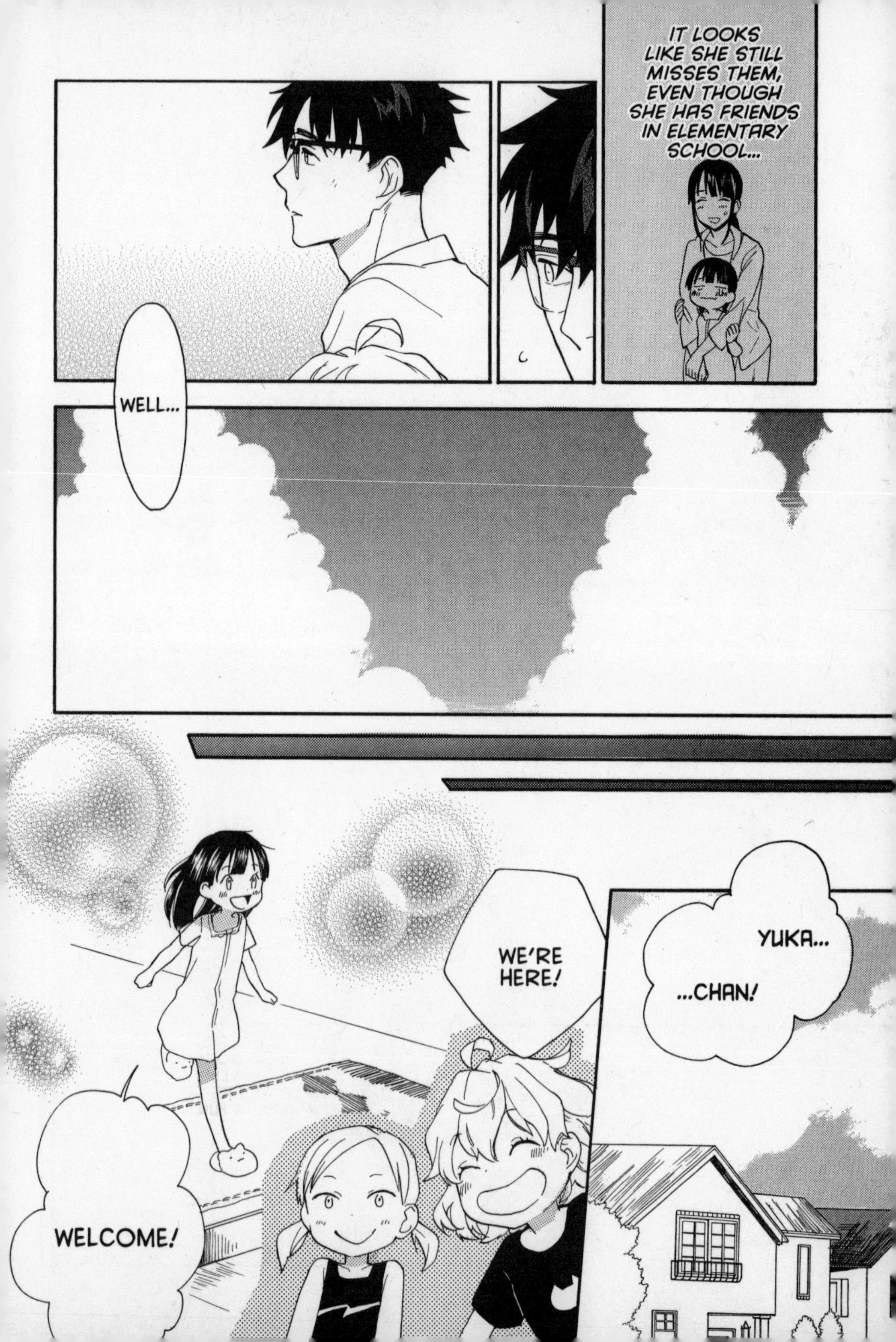
IT LOOKS LIKE SHE STILL MISSES THEM, EVEN THOUGH SHE HAS FRIENDS IN ELEMENTARY SCHOOL...
WELL...
YUKA...
...CHAN!
WE'RE HERE!
WELCOME!

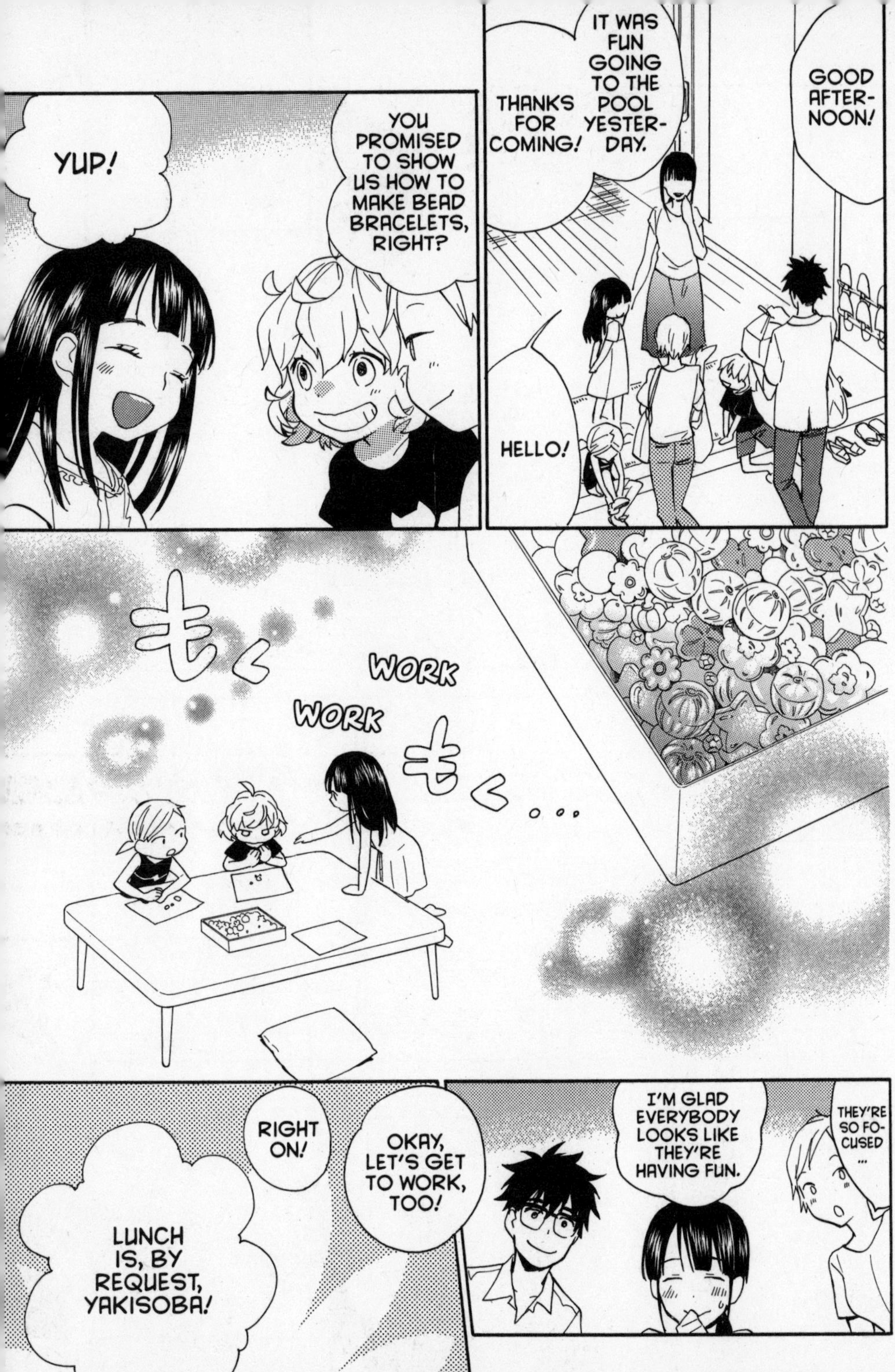
GOOD AFTER-NOON!
IT WAS FUN GOING TO THE POOL YESTER-DAY.
THANKS FOR COMING!
HELLO!
YOU PROMISED TO SHOW US HOW TO MAKE BEAD BRACELETS, RIGHT?
YUP!
もく
WORK
WORK
もく...
THEY'RE SO FO-CUSED ...
I'M GLAD EVERYBODY LOOKS LIKE THEY'RE HAVING FUN.
OKAY, LET'S GET TO WORK, TOO!
RIGHT ON!
LUNCH IS, BY REQUEST, YAKISOBA!

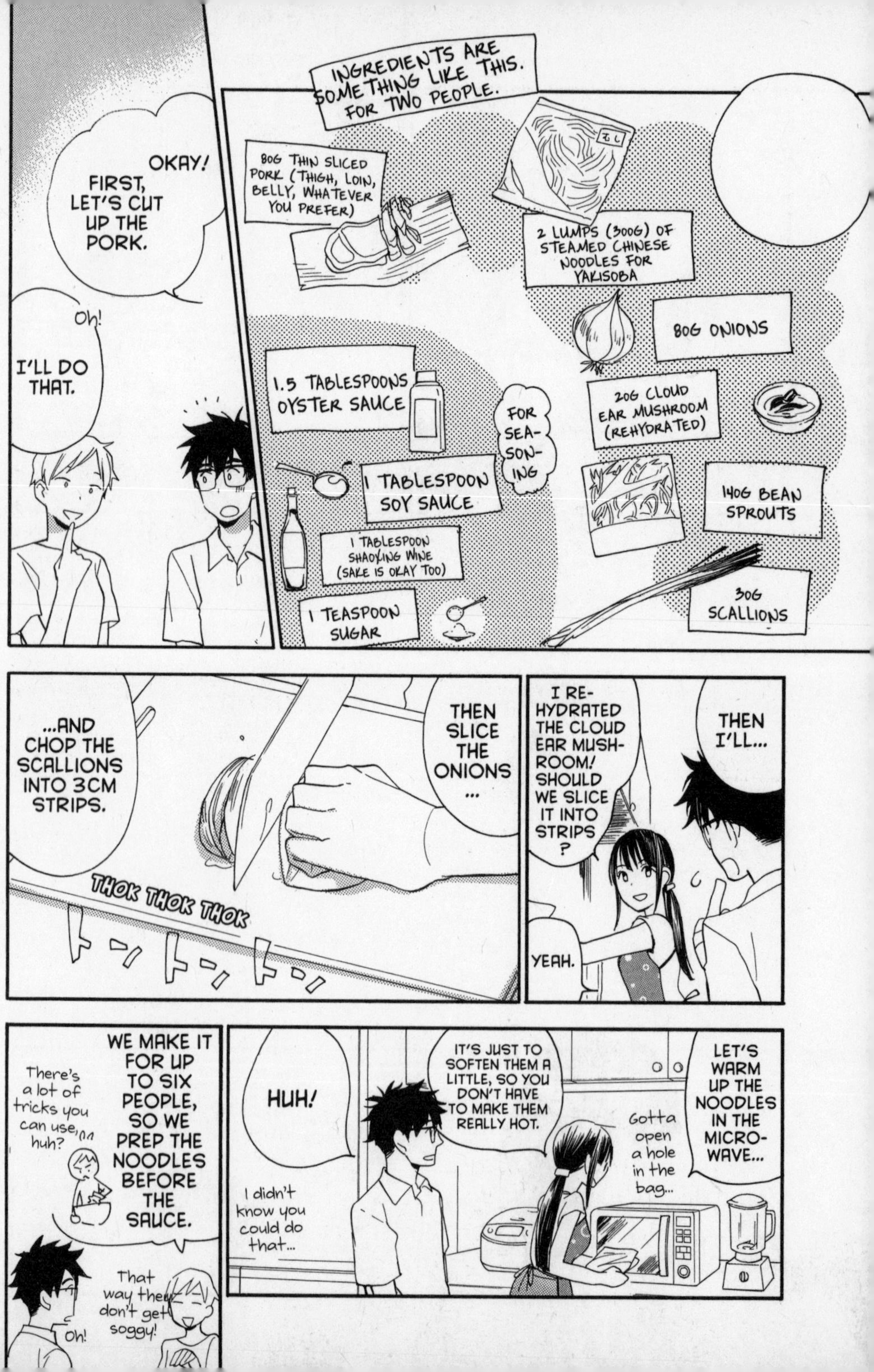

INGREDIENTS ARE SOMETHING LIKE THIS. FOR TWO PEOPLE.
2 LUMPS (300G) OF STEAMED CHINESE NOODLES FOR YAKISOBA
80G THIN SLICED PORK (THIGH, LOIN, BELLY, WHATEVER YOU PREFER)
80G ONIONS
20G CLOUD EAR MUSHROOM (REHYDRATED)
140G BEAN SPROUTS
30G SCALLIONS
FOR SEA-SON-ING
1.5 TABLESPOONS OYSTER SAUCE
1 TABLESPOON SOY SAUCE
1 TABLESPOON SHAOXING WINE (SAKE IS OKAY TOO)
1 TEASPOON SUGAR
OKAY! FIRST, LET'S CUT UP THE PORK.
Oh!
I'LL DO THAT.
THEN I'LL...
I RE-HYDRATED THE CLOUD EAR MUSH-ROOM! SHOULD WE SLICE IT INTO STRIPS?
YEAH.
THEN SLICE THE ONIONS ...
...AND CHOP THE SCALLIONS INTO 3CM STRIPS.
THOK THOK THOK
LET'S WARM UP THE NOODLES IN THE MICRO-WAVE...
Gotta open a hole in the bag...
IT'S JUST TO SOFTEN THEM A LITTLE, SO YOU DON'T HAVE TO MAKE THEM REALLY HOT.
HUH!
I didn't know you could do that...
WE MAKE IT FOR UP TO SIX PEOPLE, SO WE PREP THE NOODLES BEFORE THE SAUCE.
There's a lot of tricks you can use, huh?
That way they don't get soggy!
Oh!

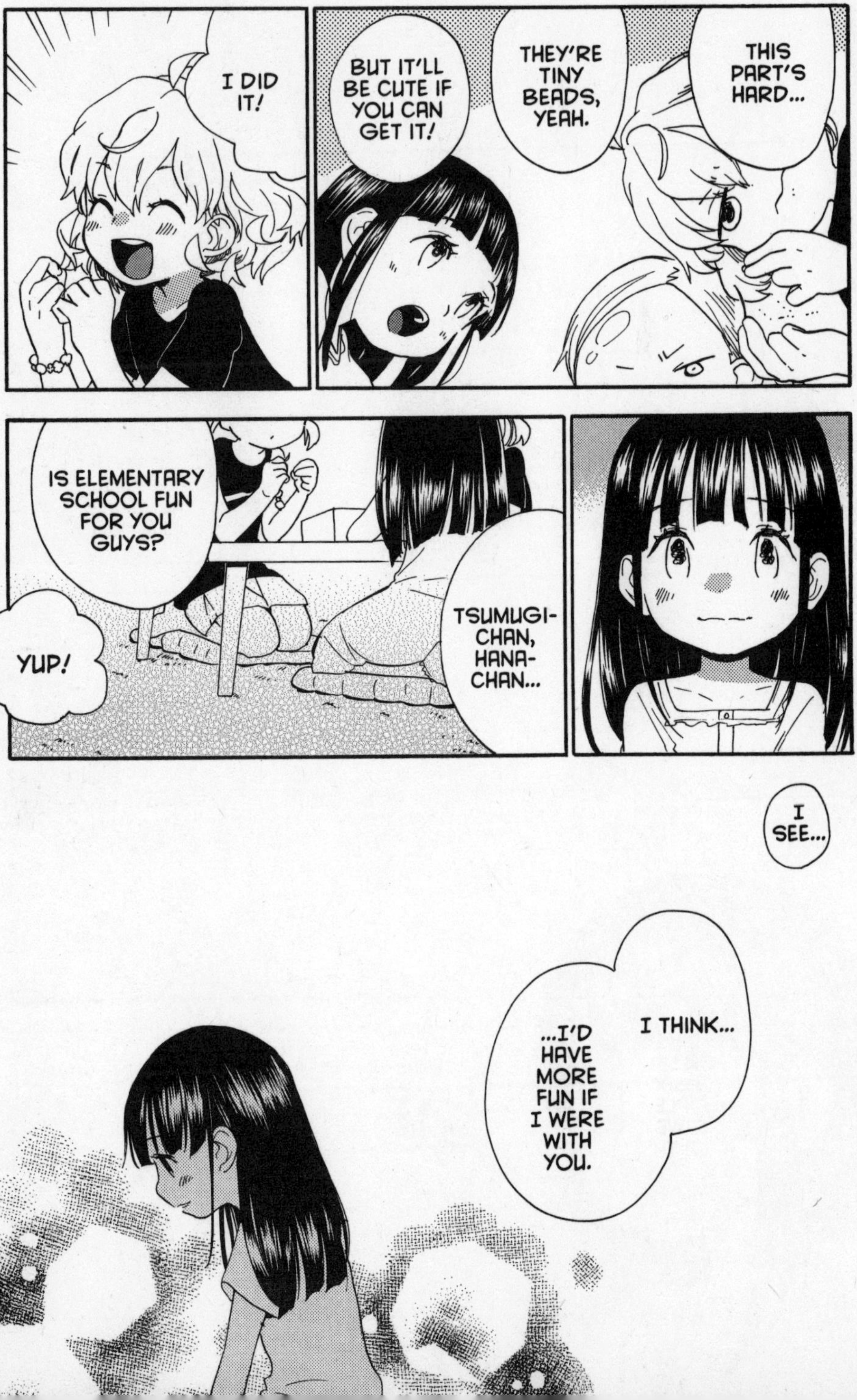
THIS PART'S HARD...
THEY'RE TINY BEADS, YEAH.
BUT IT'LL BE CUTE IF YOU CAN GET IT!
I DID IT!
TSUMUGI-CHAN, HANA-CHAN...
IS ELEMENTARY SCHOOL FUN FOR YOU GUYS?
YUP!
I SEE...
I THINK...
...I'D HAVE MORE FUN IF I WERE WITH YOU.

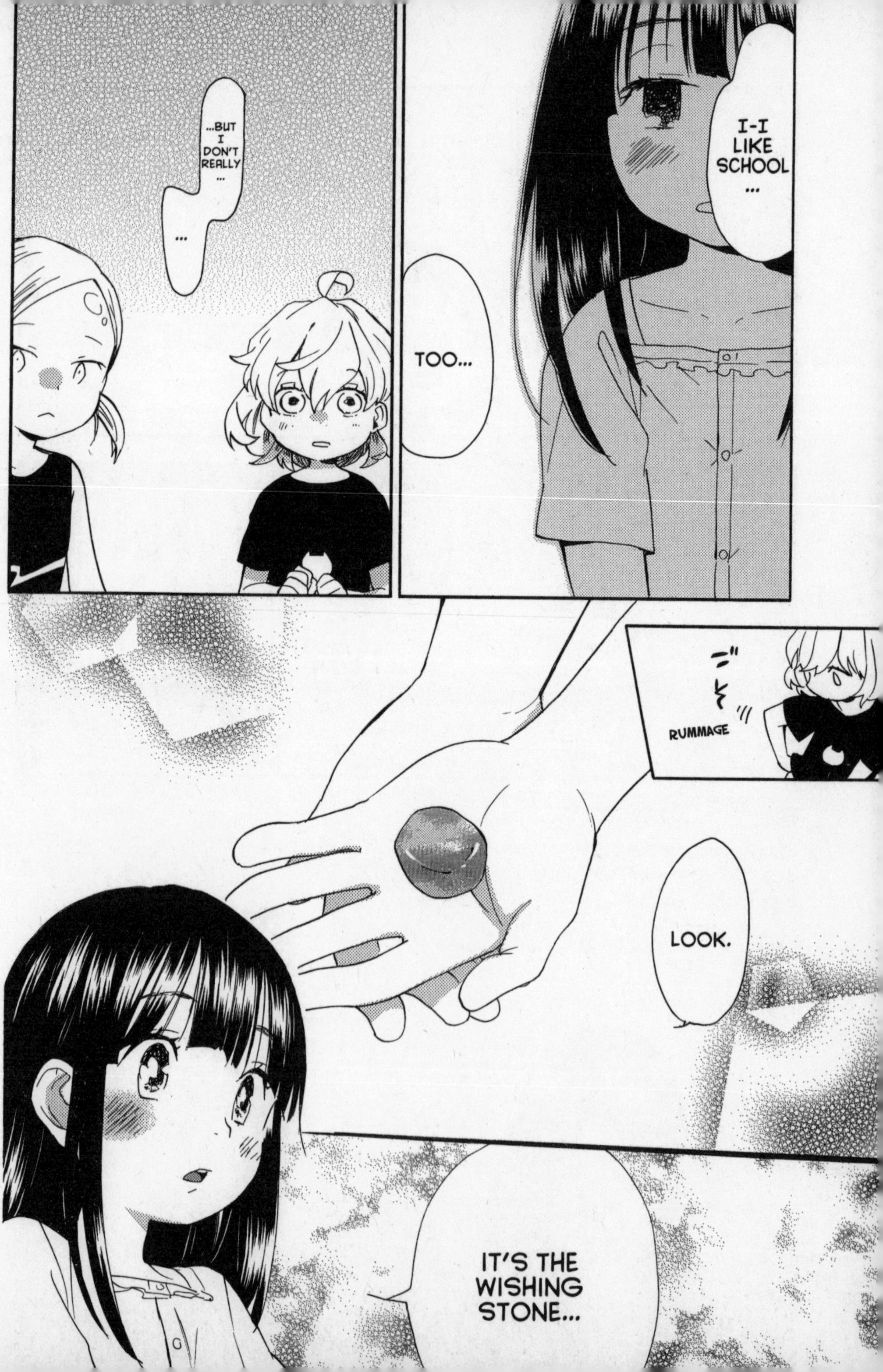
I-I LIKE SCHOOL ...
TOO...
...BUT I DON'T REALLY ...
...
RUMMAGE
LOOK.
IT'S THE WISHING STONE...

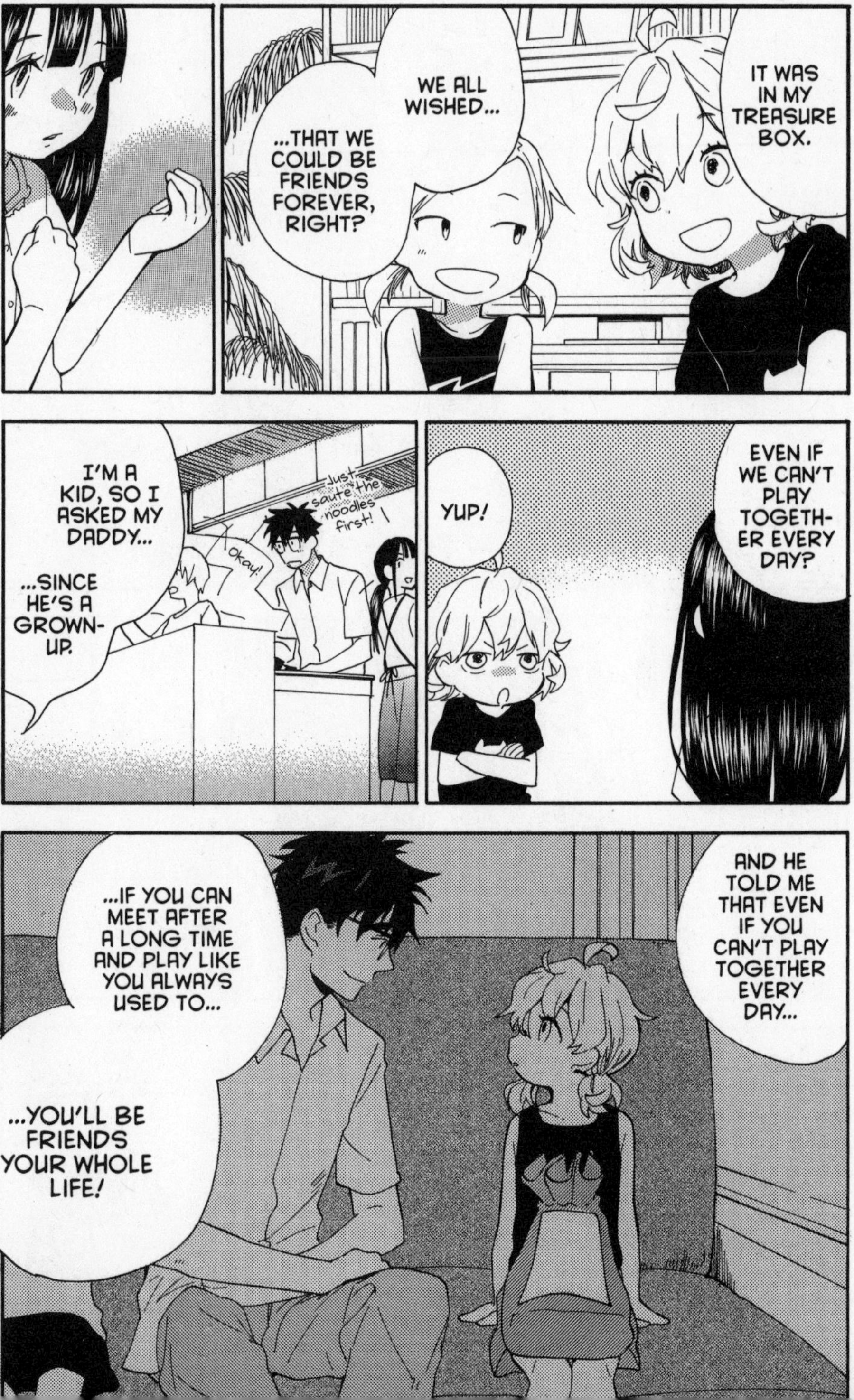
IT WAS IN MY TREASURE BOX.
WE ALL WISHED...
...THAT WE COULD BE FRIENDS FOREVER, RIGHT?
EVEN IF WE CAN'T PLAY TOGETH-ER EVERY DAY?
YUP!
Just saute the noodles first!
Okay!
I'M A KID, SO I ASKED MY DADDY...
...SINCE HE'S A GROWN-UP.
AND HE TOLD ME THAT EVEN IF YOU CAN'T PLAY TOGETHER EVERY DAY...
...IF YOU CAN MEET AFTER A LONG TIME AND PLAY LIKE YOU ALWAYS USED TO...
...YOU'LL BE FRIENDS YOUR WHOLE LIFE!

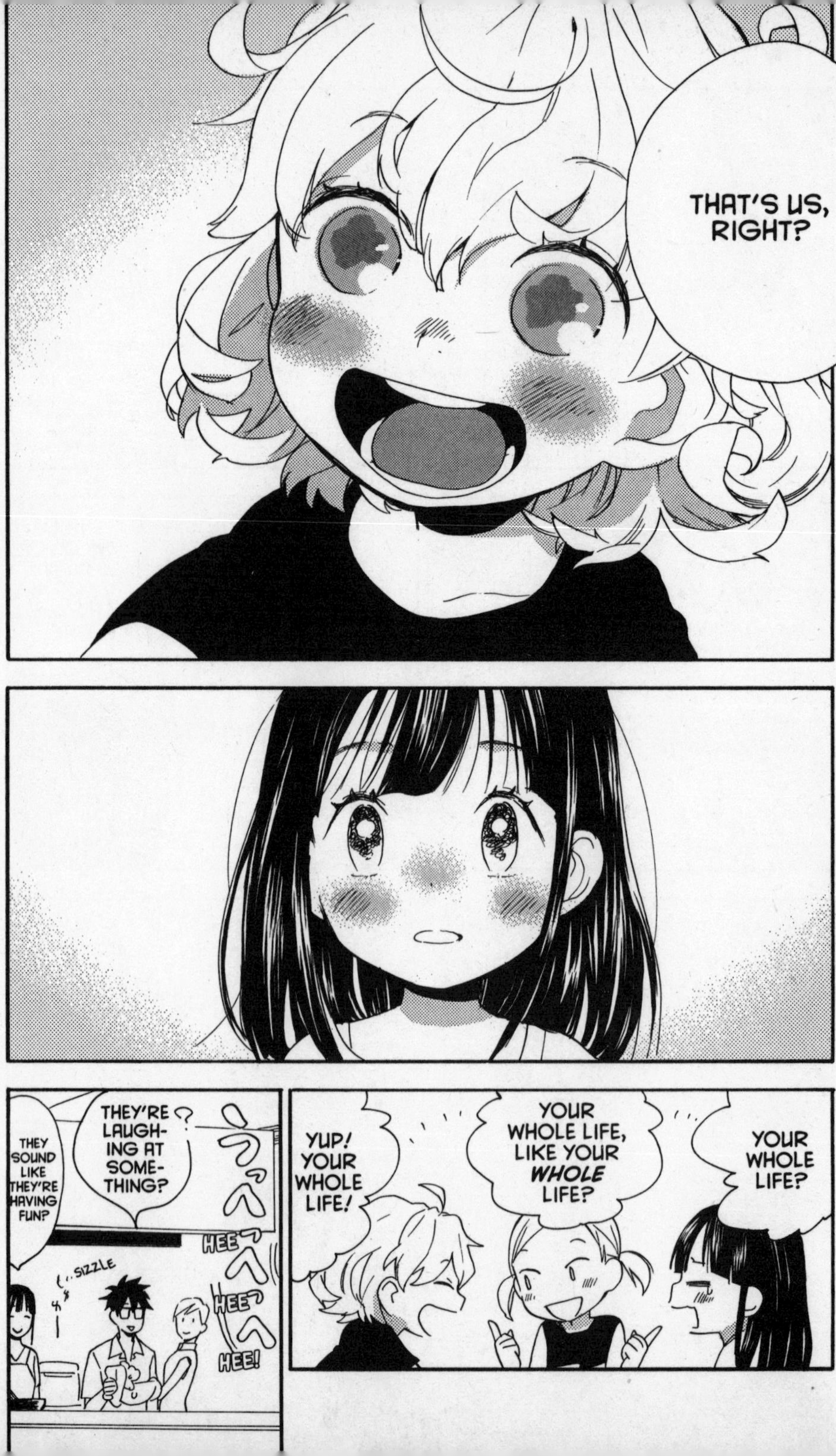
THAT'S US, RIGHT?
YOUR WHOLE LIFE?
YOUR WHOLE LIFE, LIKE YOUR *WHOLE* LIFE?
YUP! YOUR WHOLE LIFE!
THEY'RE LAUGHING AT SOMETHING?
THEY SOUND LIKE THEY'RE HAVING FUN?
HEE
HEE
HEE!
SIZZLE

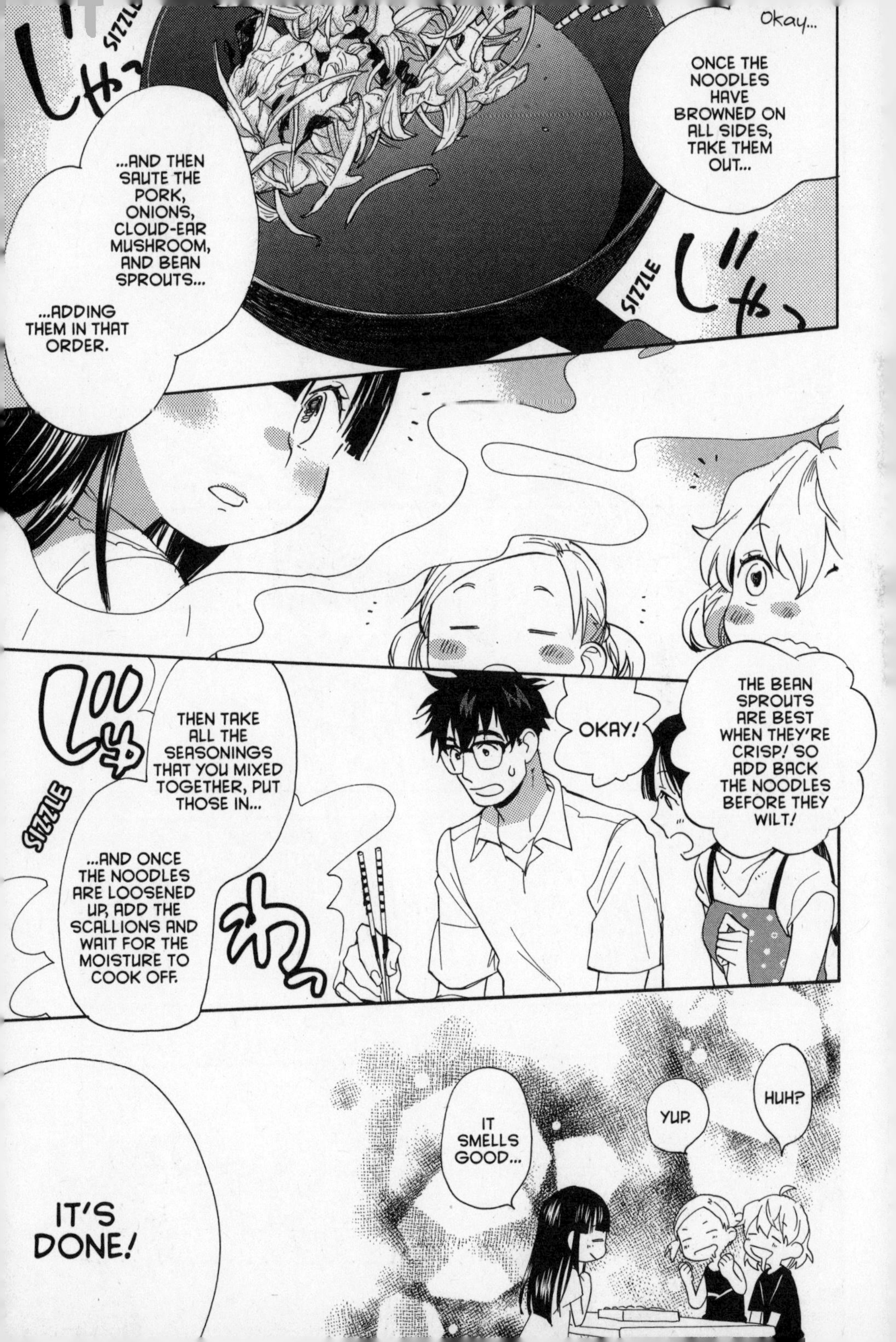
Okay...
ONCE THE NOODLES HAVE BROWNED ON ALL SIDES, TAKE THEM OUT...
SIZZLE
SIZZLE
...AND THEN SAUTE THE PORK, ONIONS, CLOUD-EAR MUSHROOM, AND BEAN SPROUTS...
...ADDING THEM IN THAT ORDER.
THE BEAN SPROUTS ARE BEST WHEN THEY'RE CRISP! SO ADD BACK THE NOODLES BEFORE THEY WILT!
OKAY!
THEN TAKE ALL THE SEASONINGS THAT YOU MIXED TOGETHER, PUT THOSE IN...
...AND ONCE THE NOODLES ARE LOOSENED UP, ADD THE SCALLIONS AND WAIT FOR THE MOISTURE TO COOK OFF.
SIZZLE
HUH?
YUP.
IT SMELLS GOOD...
IT'S DONE!

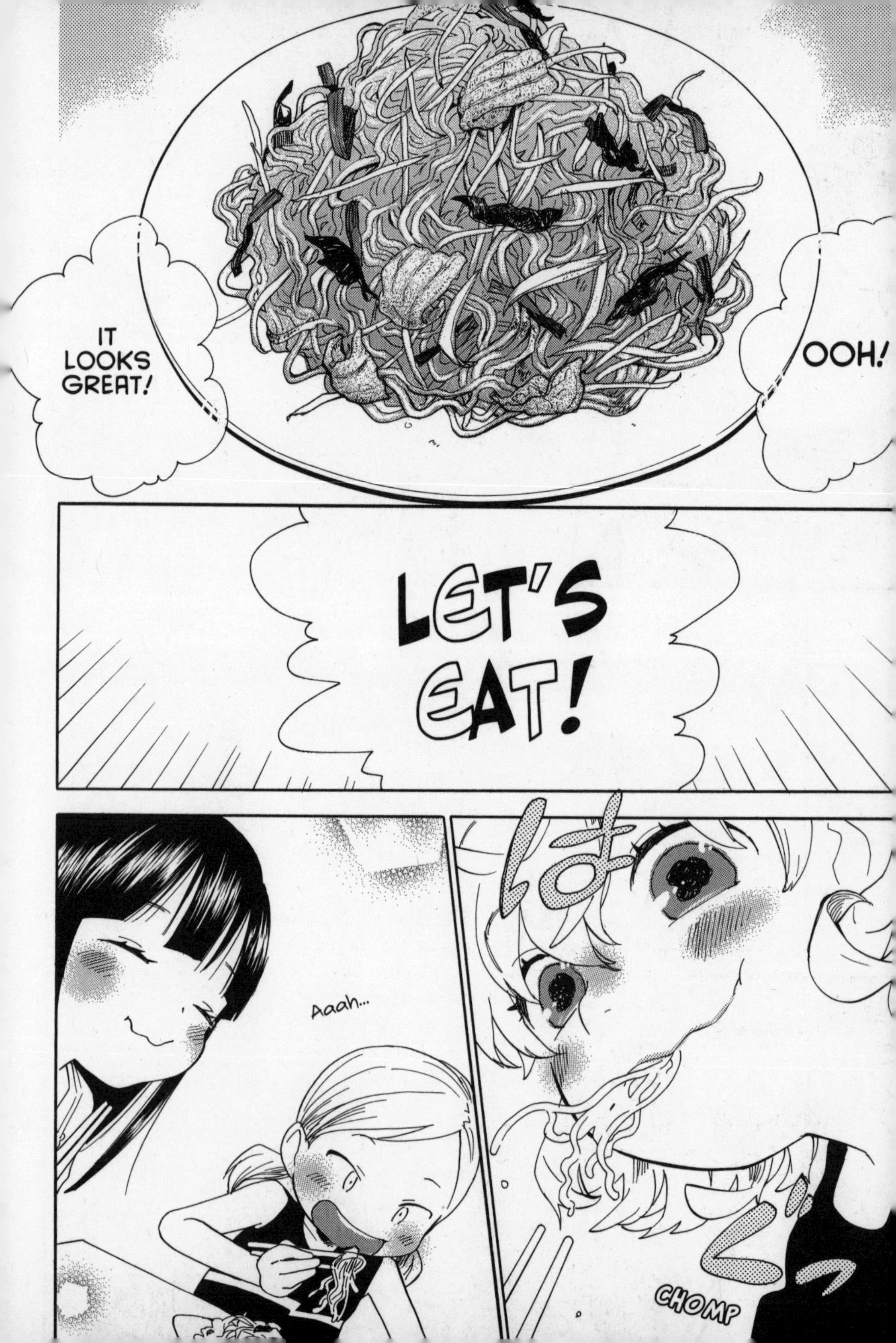
OOH!
IT LOOKS GREAT!
LET'S EAT!
CHOMP
Aaah...

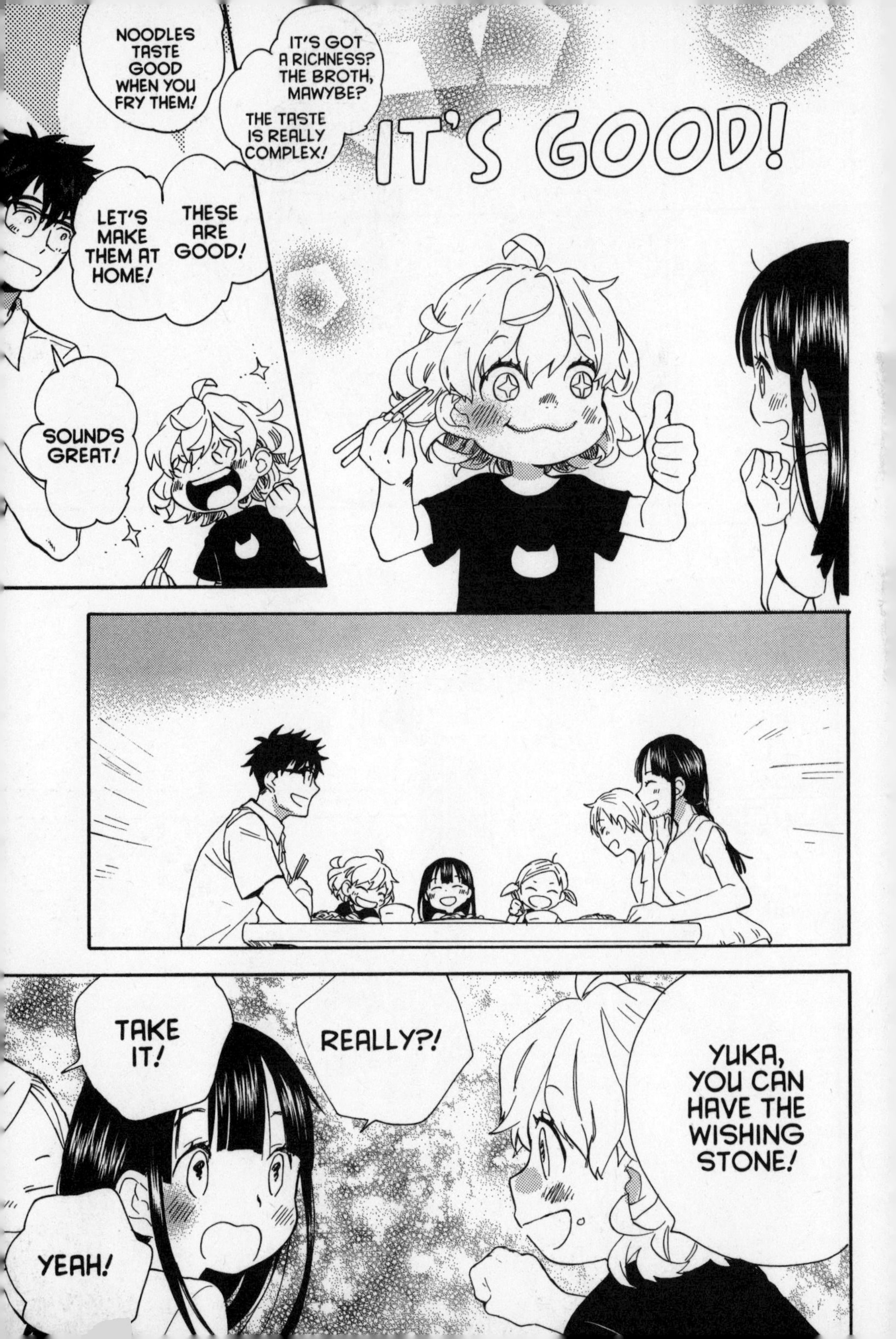
IT'S GOOD!
IT'S GOT A RICHNESS? THE BROTH, MAWYBE?
THE TASTE IS REALLY COMPLEX!
NOODLES TASTE GOOD WHEN YOU FRY THEM!
THESE ARE GOOD!
LET'S MAKE THEM AT HOME!
SOUNDS GREAT!
YUKA, YOU CAN HAVE THE WISHING STONE!
REALLY?!
TAKE IT!
YEAH!

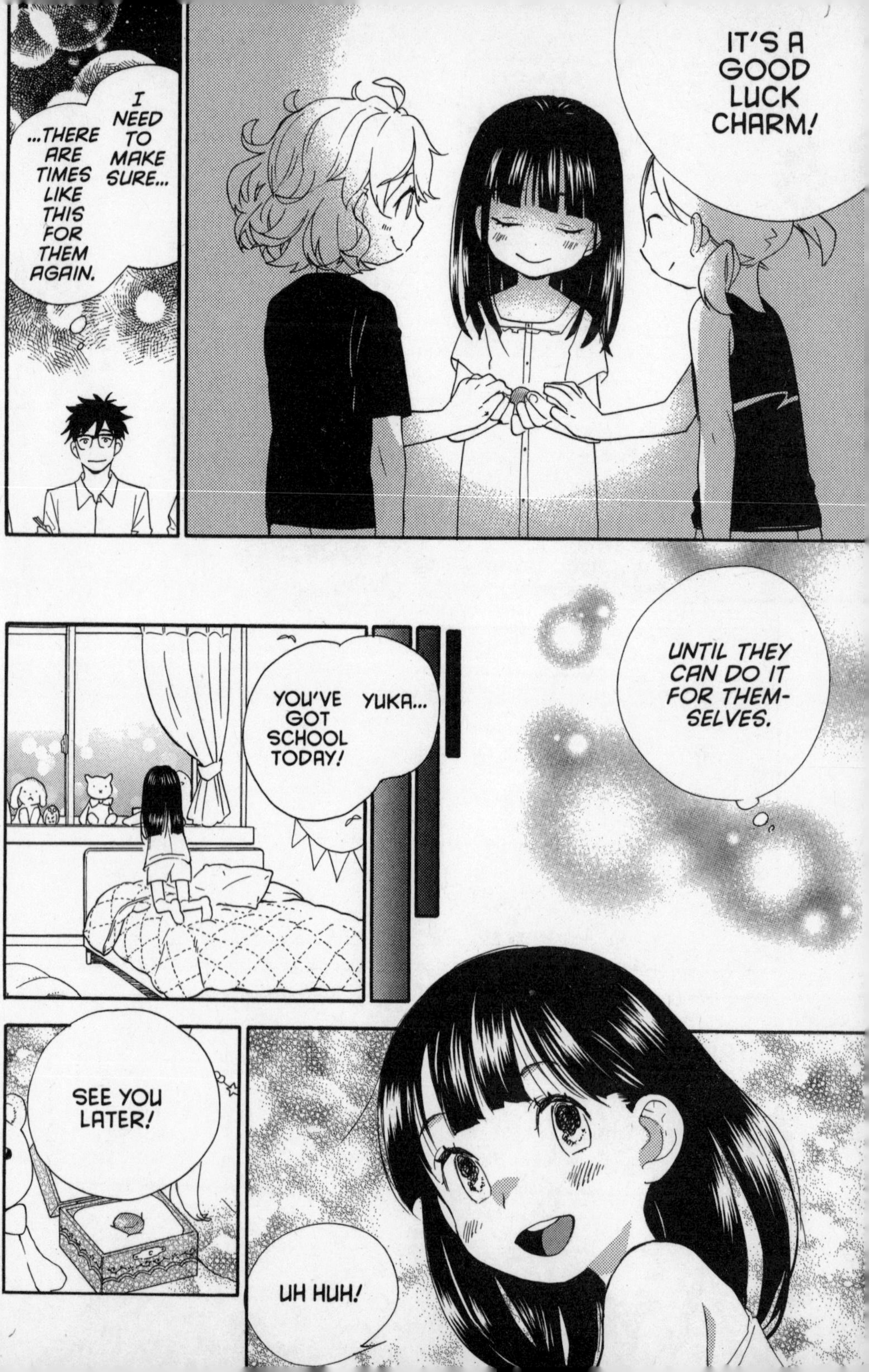
IT'S A GOOD LUCK CHARM!
I NEED TO MAKE SURE...
...THERE ARE TIMES LIKE THIS FOR THEM AGAIN.
UNTIL THEY CAN DO IT FOR THEMSELVES.
YUKA...
YOU'VE GOT SCHOOL TODAY!
UH HUH!
SEE YOU LATER!

OYSTER SAUCE YAKISOBA

☆ Ingredients (serves 2) ☆

★ 2 Balls (300g) Steamed Chinese Noodles
★ 140g Bean Sprouts
★ 30g Scallions

★ 80g Thinly Sliced Pork
★ 80g Onions
★ 20g Cloud Ear Mushrooms (rehydrated)

A:
1.5 Tablespoons Oyster Sauce
1 Tablespoon Shaoxing Wine
(Sake is okay, too)

1 Tablespoon Soy Sauce
1 Teaspoon Sugar

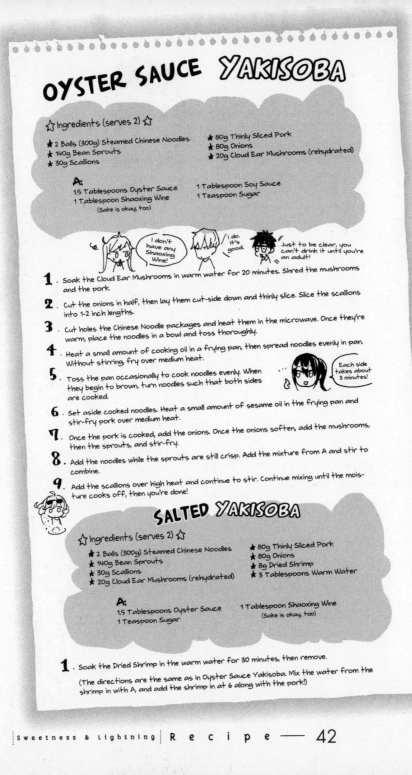

I don't have any Shaoxing Wine!

I do. It's good.

Just to be clear, you can't drink it until you're an adult!

1. Soak the Cloud Ear Mushrooms in warm water for 20 minutes. Shred the mushrooms and the pork.

2. Cut the onions in half, then lay them cut-side down and thinly slice. Slice the scallions into 1-2 inch lengths.

3. Cut holes the Chinese Noodle packages and heat them in the microwave. Once they're warm, place the noodles in a bowl and toss thoroughly.

4. Heat a small amount of cooking oil in a frying pan, then spread noodles evenly in pan. Without stirring, fry over medium heat.

5. Toss the pan occasionally to cook noodles evenly. When they begin to brown, turn noodles such that both sides are cooked.

Each side takes about 3 minutes!

6. Set aside cooked noodles. Heat a small amount of sesame oil in the frying pan and stir-fry pork over medium heat.

7. Once the pork is cooked, add the onions. Once the onions soften, add the mushrooms, then the sprouts, and stir-fry.

8. Add the noodles while the sprouts are still crisp. Add the mixture from A and stir to combine.

9. Add the scallions over high heat and continue to stir. Continue mixing until the moisture cooks off, then you're done!

SALTED YAKISOBA

☆ Ingredients (serves 2) ☆

★ 2 Balls (300g) Steamed Chinese Noodles
★ 140g Bean Sprouts
★ 30g Scallions
★ 20g Cloud Ear Mushrooms (rehydrated)

★ 80g Thinly Sliced Pork
★ 80g Onions
★ 8g Dried Shrimp
★ 3 Tablespoons Warm Water

A:
1.5 Tablespoons Oyster Sauce
1 Teaspoon Sugar

1 Tablespoon Shaoxing Wine
(Sake is okay, too)

1. Soak the Dried Shrimp in the warm water for 30 minutes, then remove.

(The directions are the same as in Oyster Sauce Yakisoba. Mix the water from the shrimp in with A, and add the shrimp in at 6 along with the pork!)

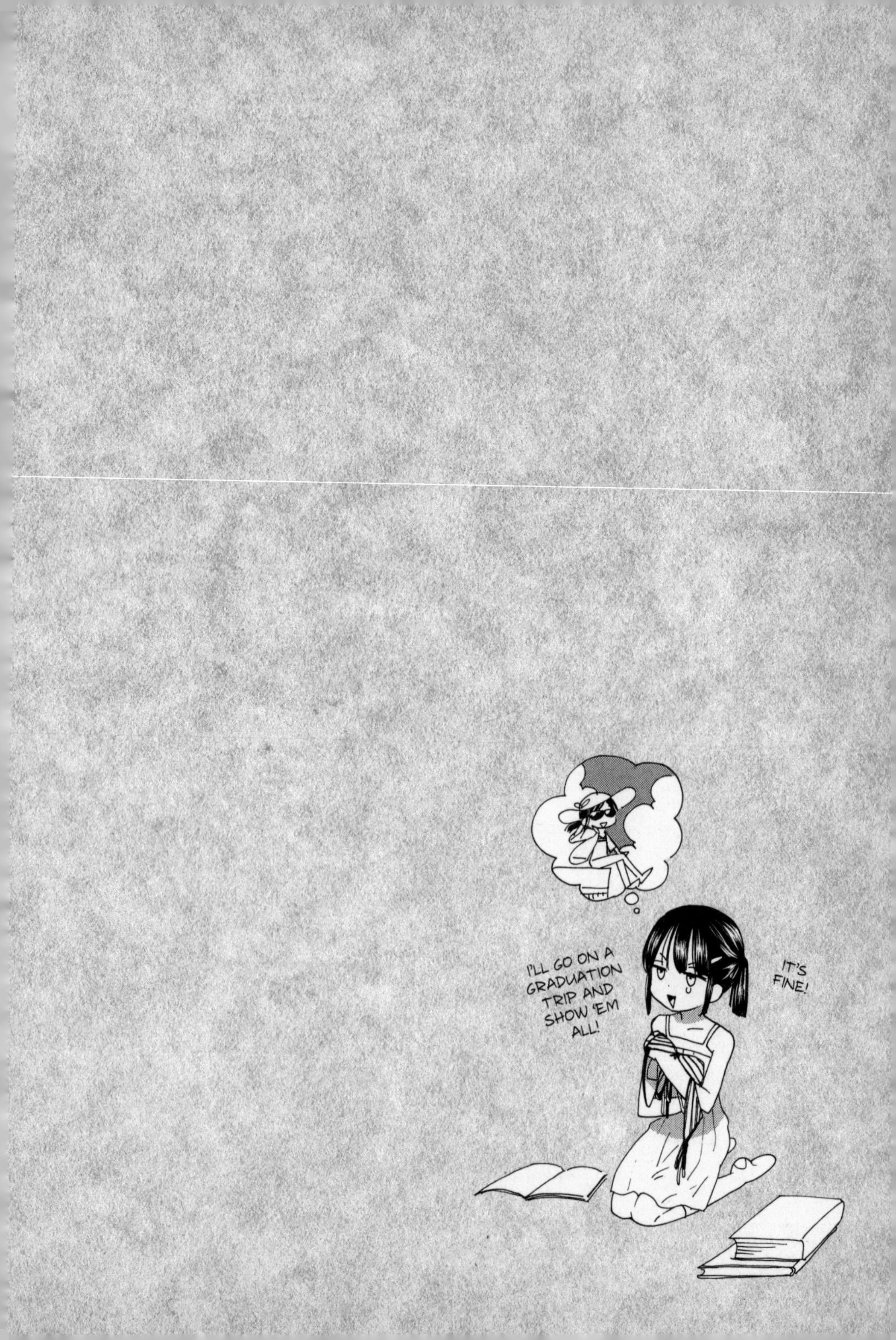
I'LL GO ON A GRADUATION TRIP AND SHOW 'EM ALL!
IT'S FINE!

Chapter 43 | My First Niku-Jaga

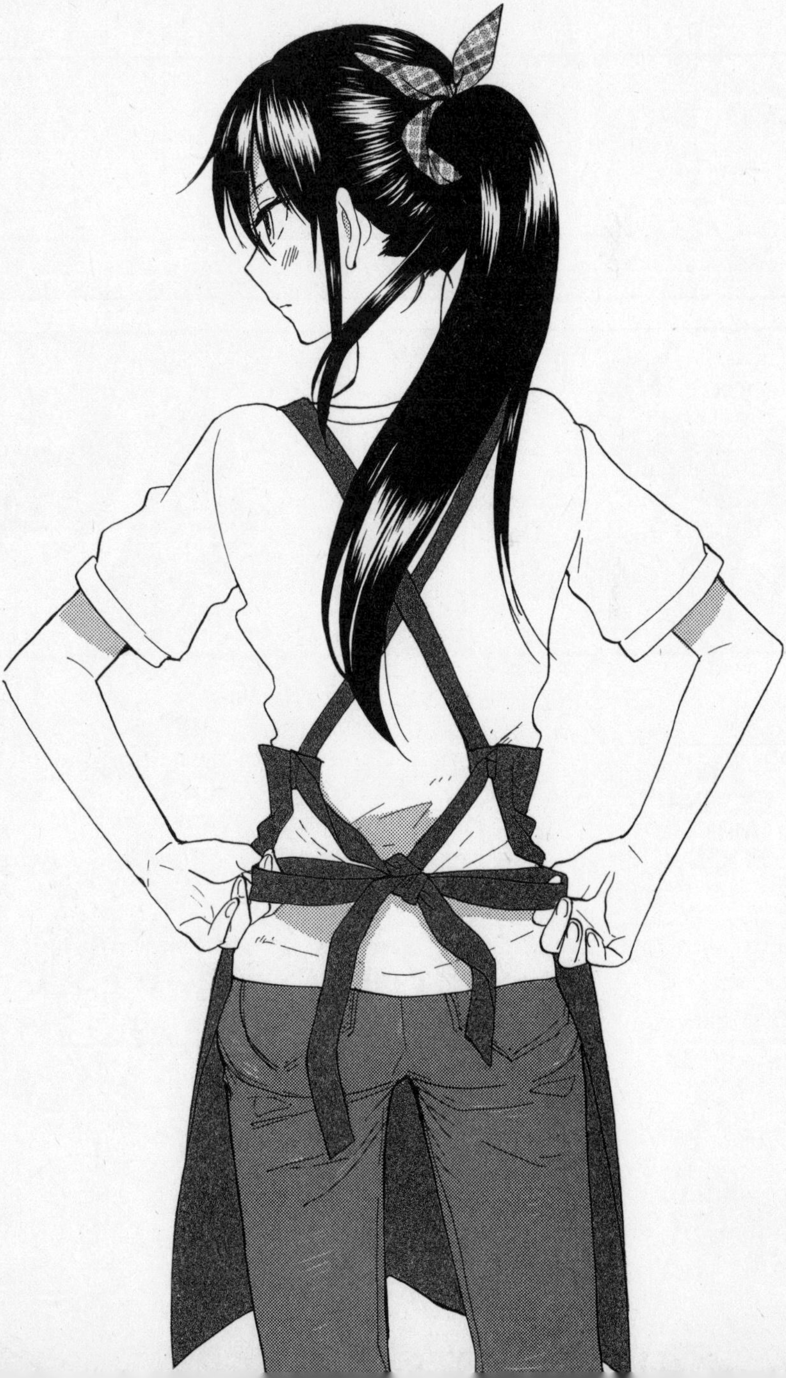

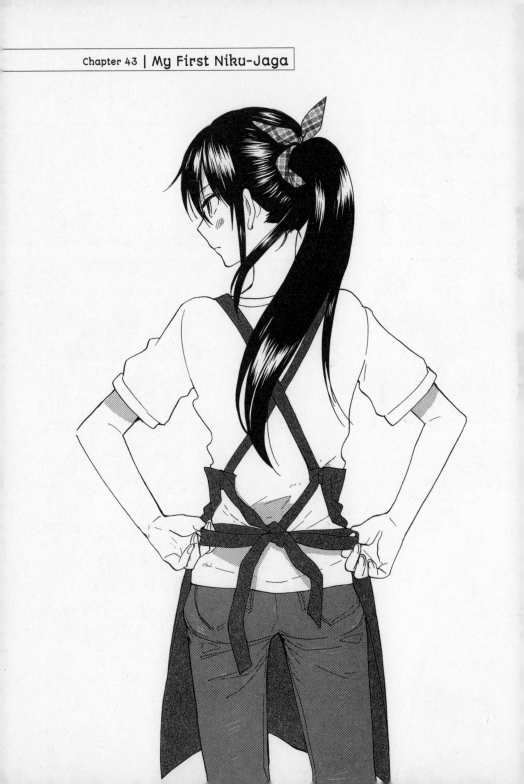

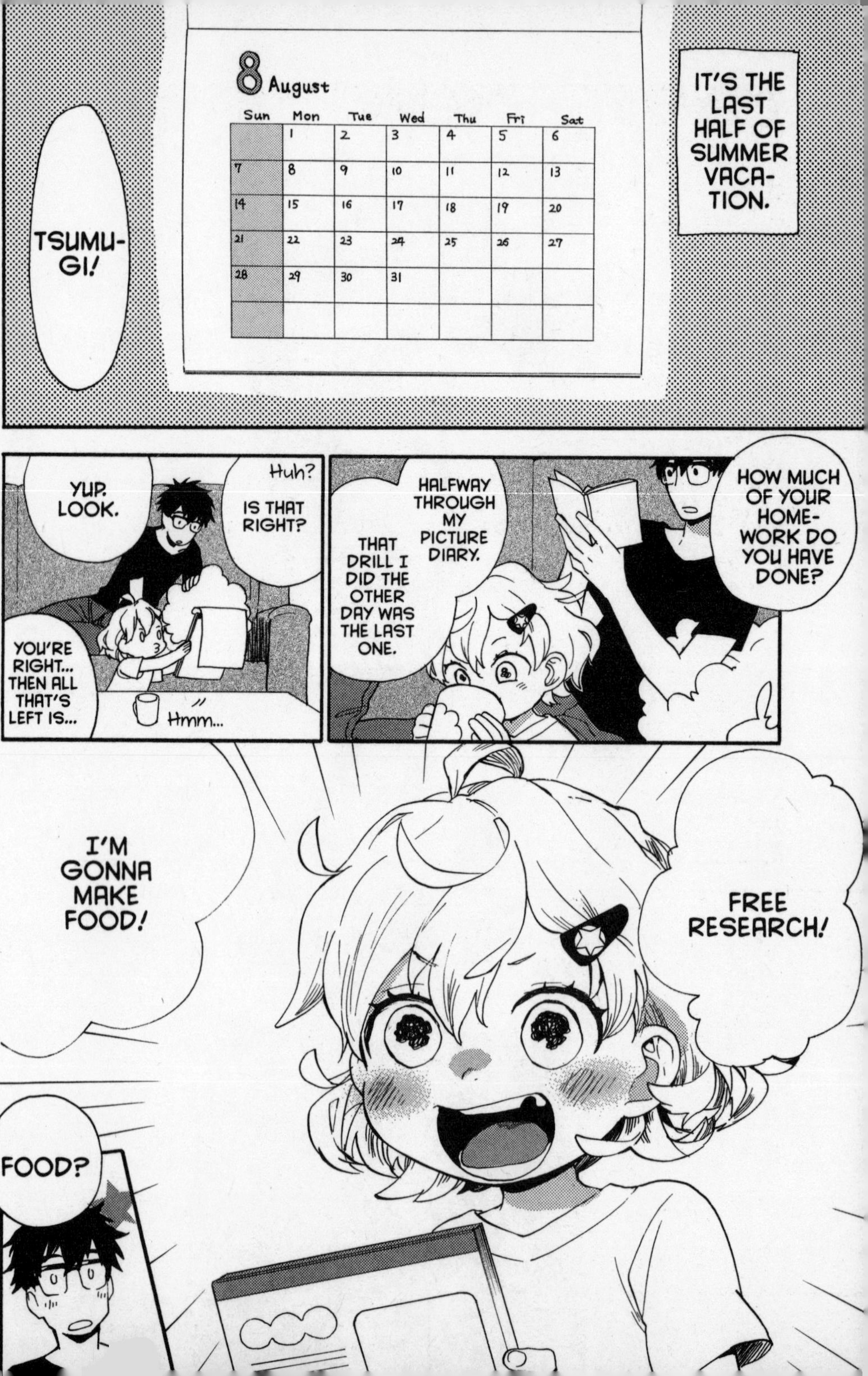
IT'S THE LAST HALF OF SUMMER VACATION.
8 August
Sun Mon Tue Wed Thu Fri Sat
1 2 3 4 5 6
7 8 9 10 11 12 13
14 15 16 17 18 19 20
21 22 23 24 25 26 27
28 29 30 31
TSUMUGI!
HOW MUCH OF YOUR HOMEWORK DO YOU HAVE DONE?
HALFWAY THROUGH MY PICTURE DIARY.
THAT DRILL I DID THE OTHER DAY WAS THE LAST ONE.
Huh?
IS THAT RIGHT?
YUP. LOOK.
YOU'RE RIGHT... THEN ALL THAT'S LEFT IS...
Hmm...
FREE RESEARCH!
I'M GONNA MAKE FOOD!
FOOD?

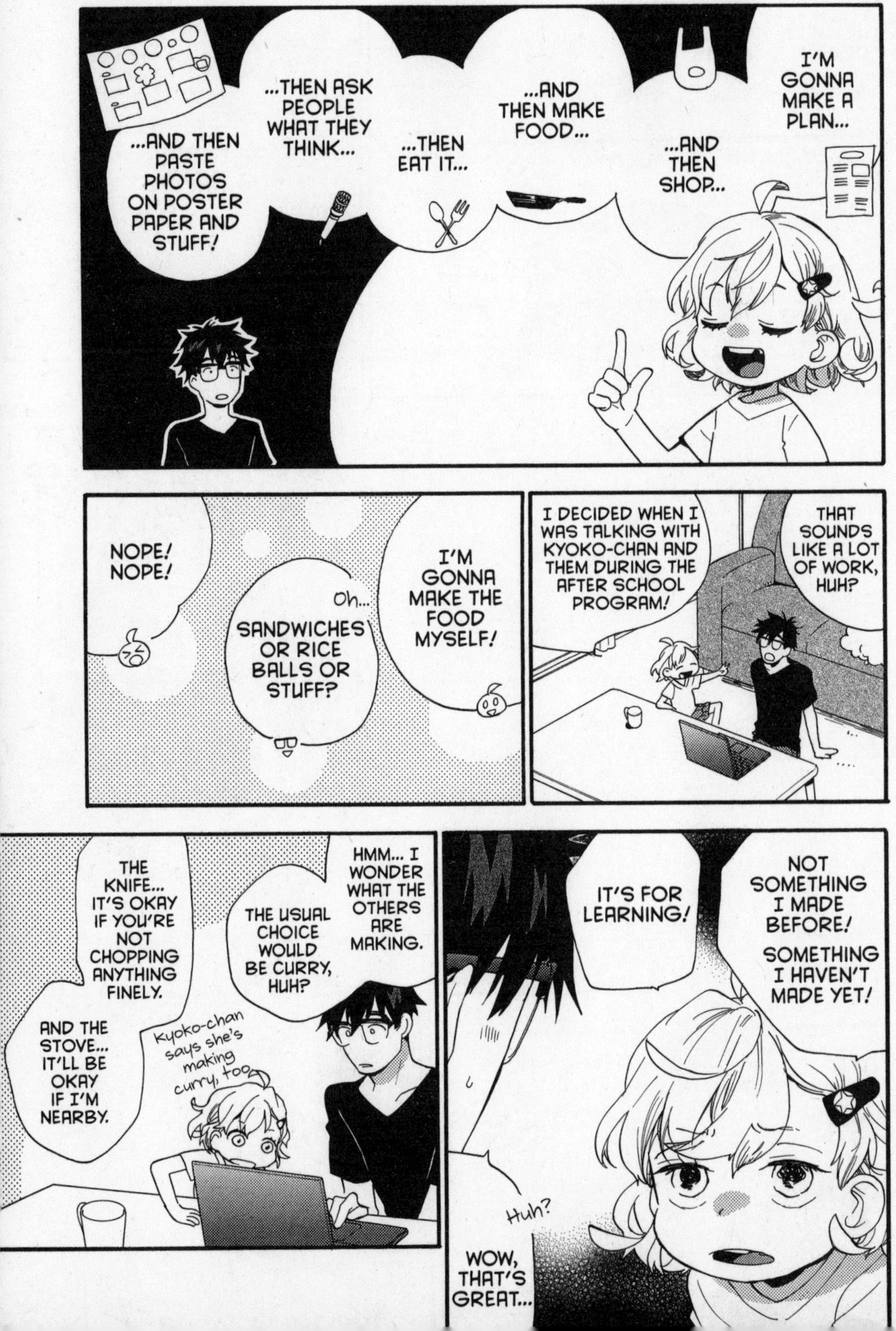
I'M GONNA MAKE A PLAN...
...AND THEN SHOP...
...AND THEN MAKE FOOD...
...THEN EAT IT...
...THEN ASK PEOPLE WHAT THEY THINK...
...AND THEN PASTE PHOTOS ON POSTER PAPER AND STUFF!
THAT SOUNDS LIKE A LOT OF WORK, HUH?
I DECIDED WHEN I WAS TALKING WITH KYOKO-CHAN AND THEM DURING THE AFTER SCHOOL PROGRAM!
I'M GONNA MAKE THE FOOD MYSELF!
Oh...
SANDWICHES OR RICE BALLS OR STUFF?
NOPE! NOPE!
NOT SOMETHING I MADE BEFORE!
SOMETHING I HAVEN'T MADE YET!
IT'S FOR LEARNING!
Huh?
WOW, THAT'S GREAT...
HMM... I WONDER WHAT THE OTHERS ARE MAKING.
THE USUAL CHOICE WOULD BE CURRY, HUH?
Kyoko-chan says she's making curry, too
THE KNIFE... IT'S OKAY IF YOU'RE NOT CHOPPING ANYTHING FINELY.
AND THE STOVE... IT'LL BE OKAY IF I'M NEARBY.

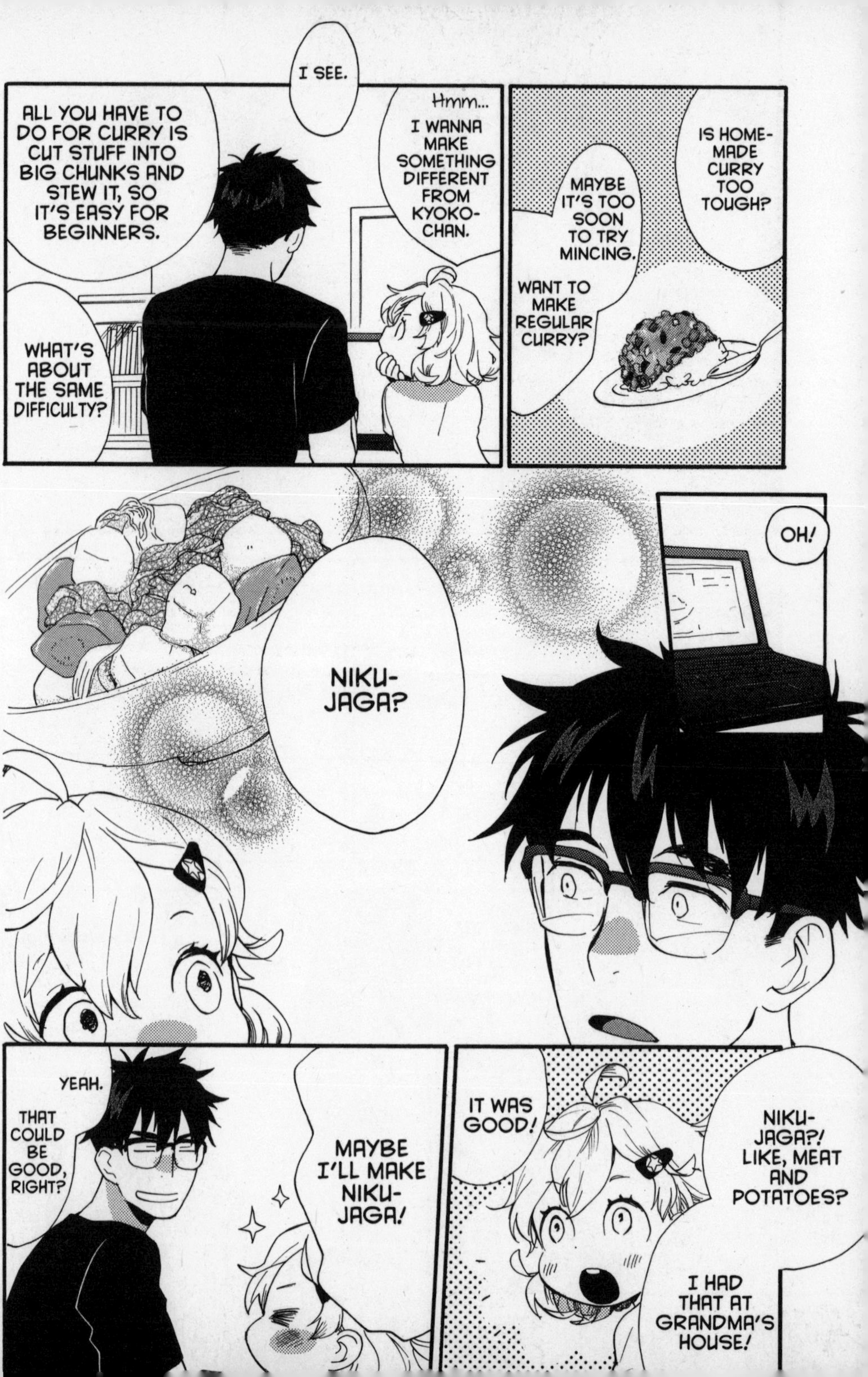
IS HOME-MADE CURRY TOO TOUGH?
MAYBE IT'S TOO SOON TO TRY MINCING.
WANT TO MAKE REGULAR CURRY?
Hmm... I WANNA MAKE SOMETHING DIFFERENT FROM KYOKO-CHAN.
I SEE.
ALL YOU HAVE TO DO FOR CURRY IS CUT STUFF INTO BIG CHUNKS AND STEW IT, SO IT'S EASY FOR BEGINNERS.
WHAT'S ABOUT THE SAME DIFFICULTY?
OH!
NIKU-JAGA?
NIKU-JAGA?! LIKE, MEAT AND POTATOES?
I HAD THAT AT GRANDMA'S HOUSE!
IT WAS GOOD!
MAYBE I'LL MAKE NIKU-JAGA!
YEAH.
THAT COULD BE GOOD, RIGHT?

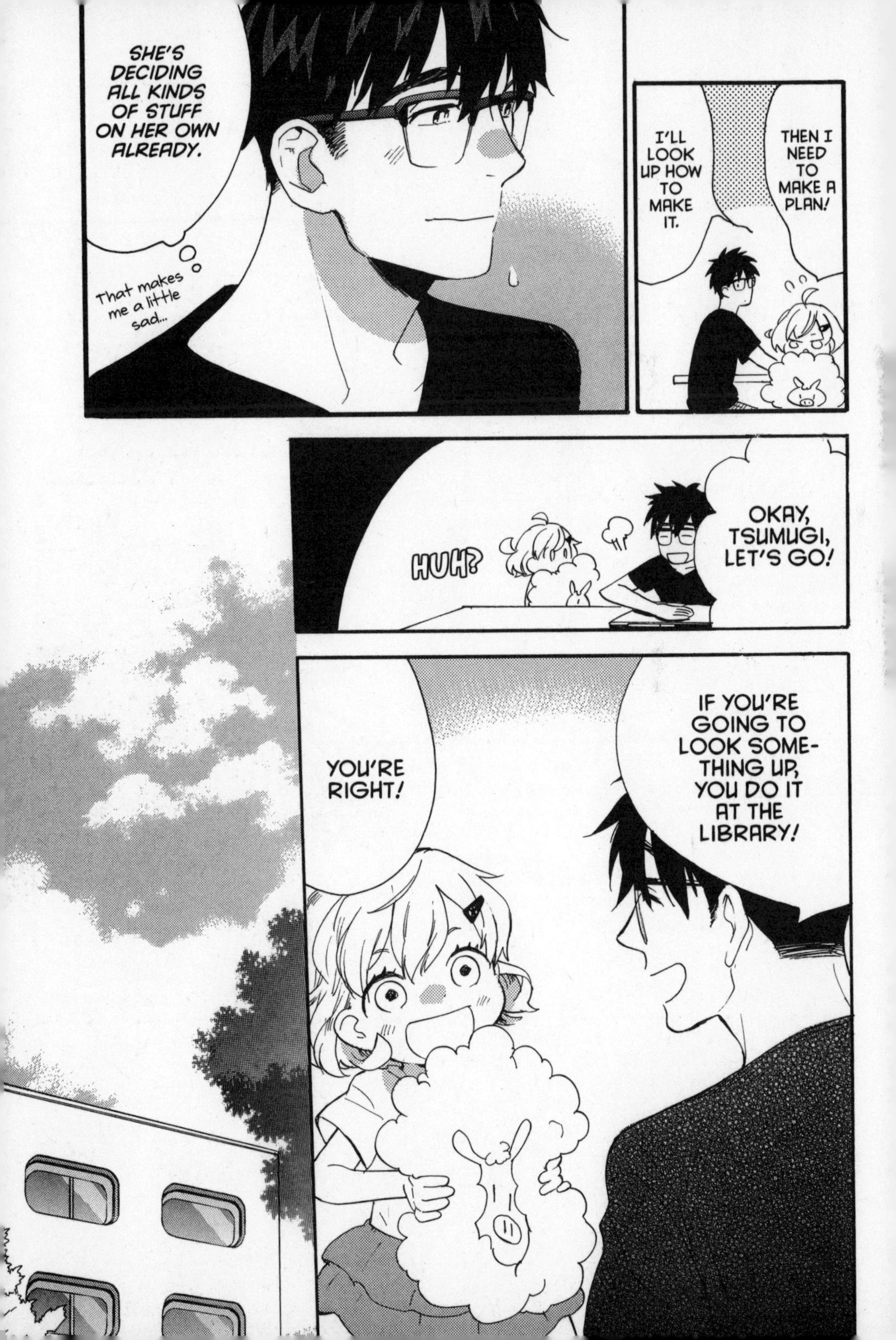
THEN I NEED TO MAKE A PLAN!
I'LL LOOK UP HOW TO MAKE IT.
SHE'S DECIDING ALL KINDS OF STUFF ON HER OWN ALREADY.
That makes me a little sad...
OKAY, TSUMUGI, LET'S GO!
HUH?
IF YOU'RE GOING TO LOOK SOME-THING UP, YOU DO IT AT THE LIBRARY!
YOU'RE RIGHT!

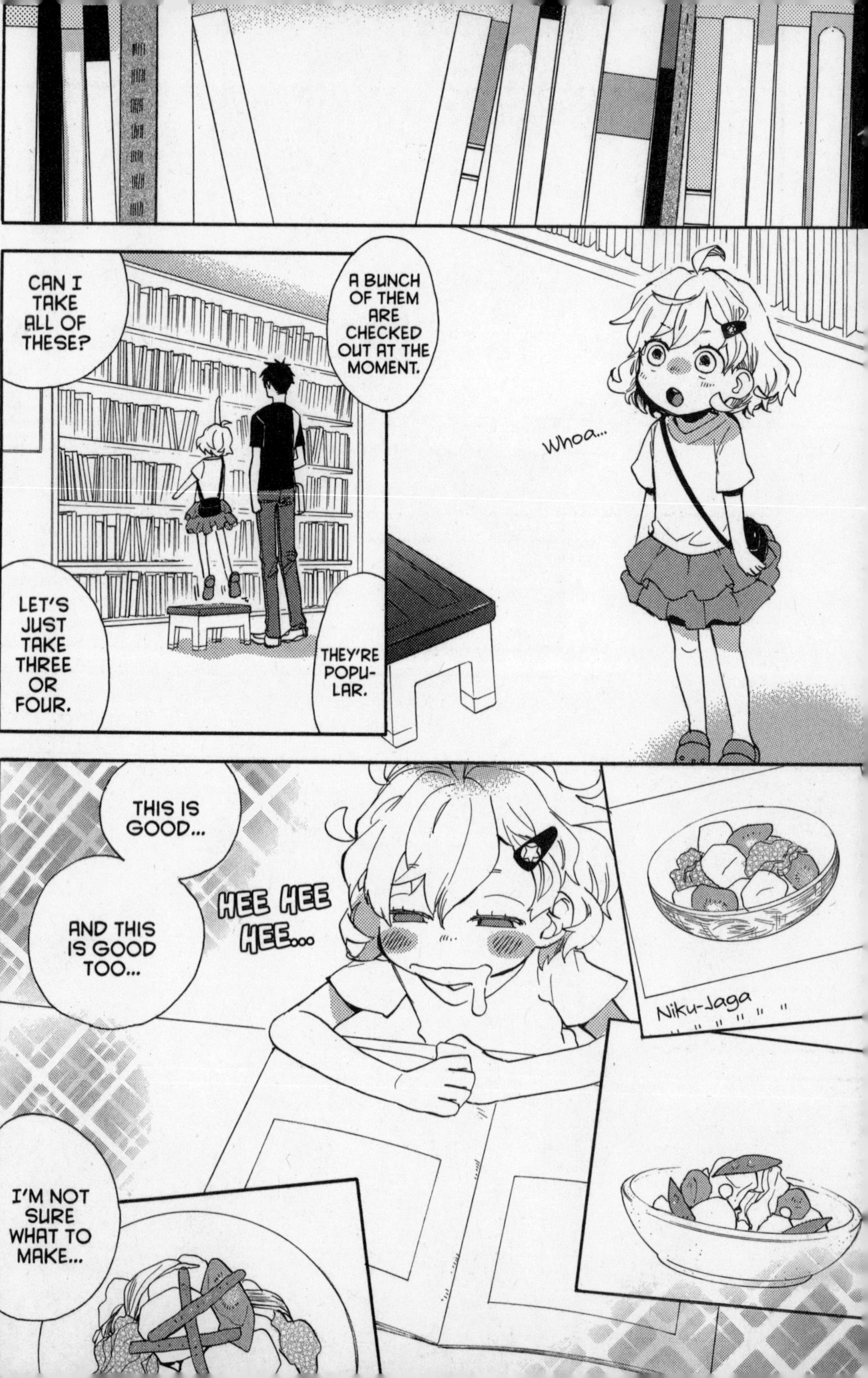
Whoa...
A BUNCH OF THEM ARE CHECKED OUT AT THE MOMENT.
CAN I TAKE ALL OF THESE?
THEY'RE POPU-LAR.
LET'S JUST TAKE THREE OR FOUR.
THIS IS GOOD...
AND THIS IS GOOD TOO...
HEE HEE HEE...
Niku-Jaga
I'M NOT SURE WHAT TO MAKE...

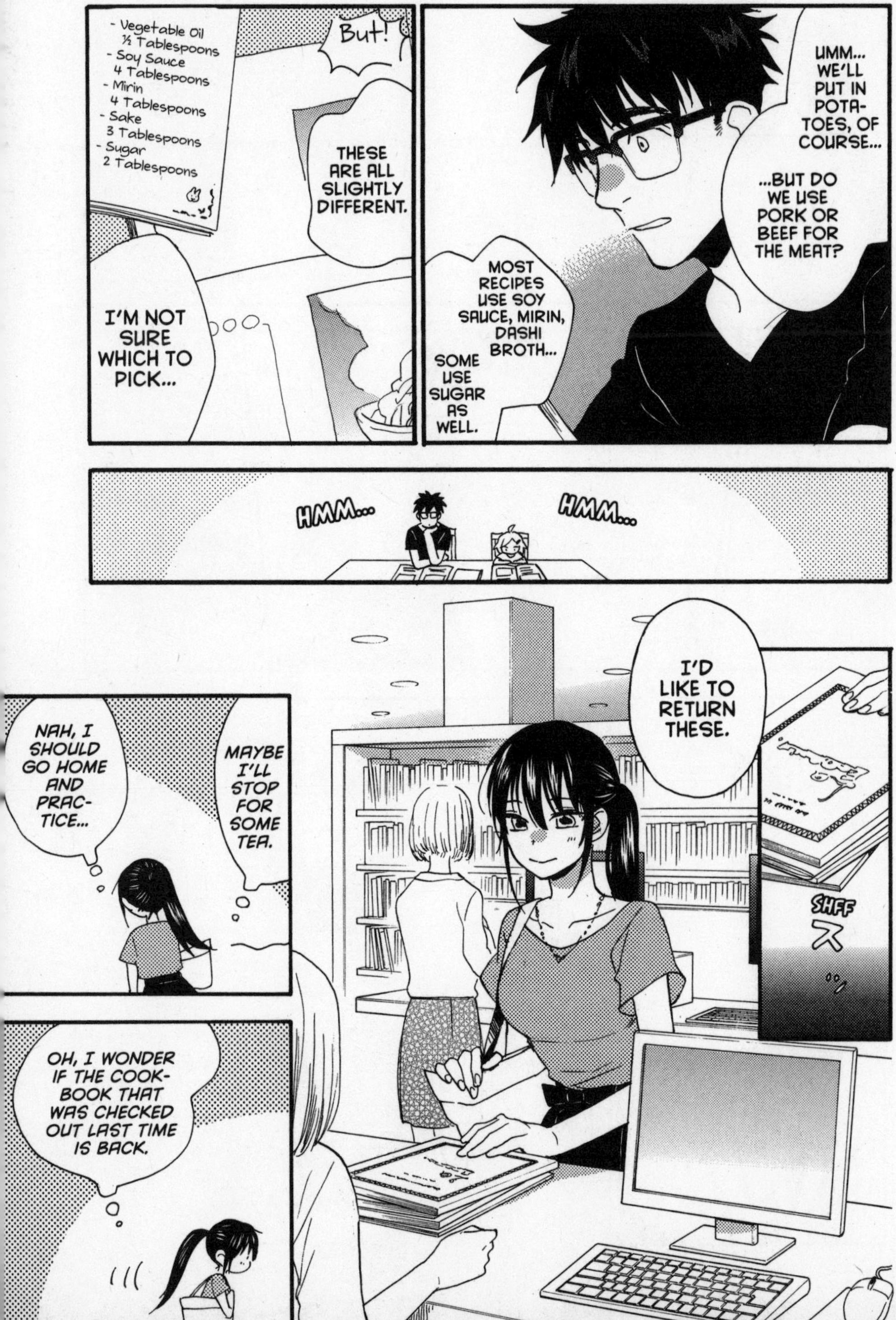
UMM... WE'LL PUT IN POTATOES, OF COURSE...
...BUT DO WE USE PORK OR BEEF FOR THE MEAT?
MOST RECIPES USE SOY SAUCE, MIRIN, DASHI BROTH...
SOME USE SUGAR AS WELL.
- Vegetable Oil ½ Tablespoons
- Soy Sauce 4 Tablespoons
- Mirin 4 Tablespoons
- Sake 3 Tablespoons
- Sugar 2 Tablespoons
But!
THESE ARE ALL SLIGHTLY DIFFERENT.
I'M NOT SURE WHICH TO PICK...
HMM...
HMM...
I'D LIKE TO RETURN THESE.
SHFF
ス
MAYBE I'LL STOP FOR SOME TEA.
NAH, I SHOULD GO HOME AND PRACTICE...
OH, I WONDER IF THE COOKBOOK THAT WAS CHECKED OUT LAST TIME IS BACK.

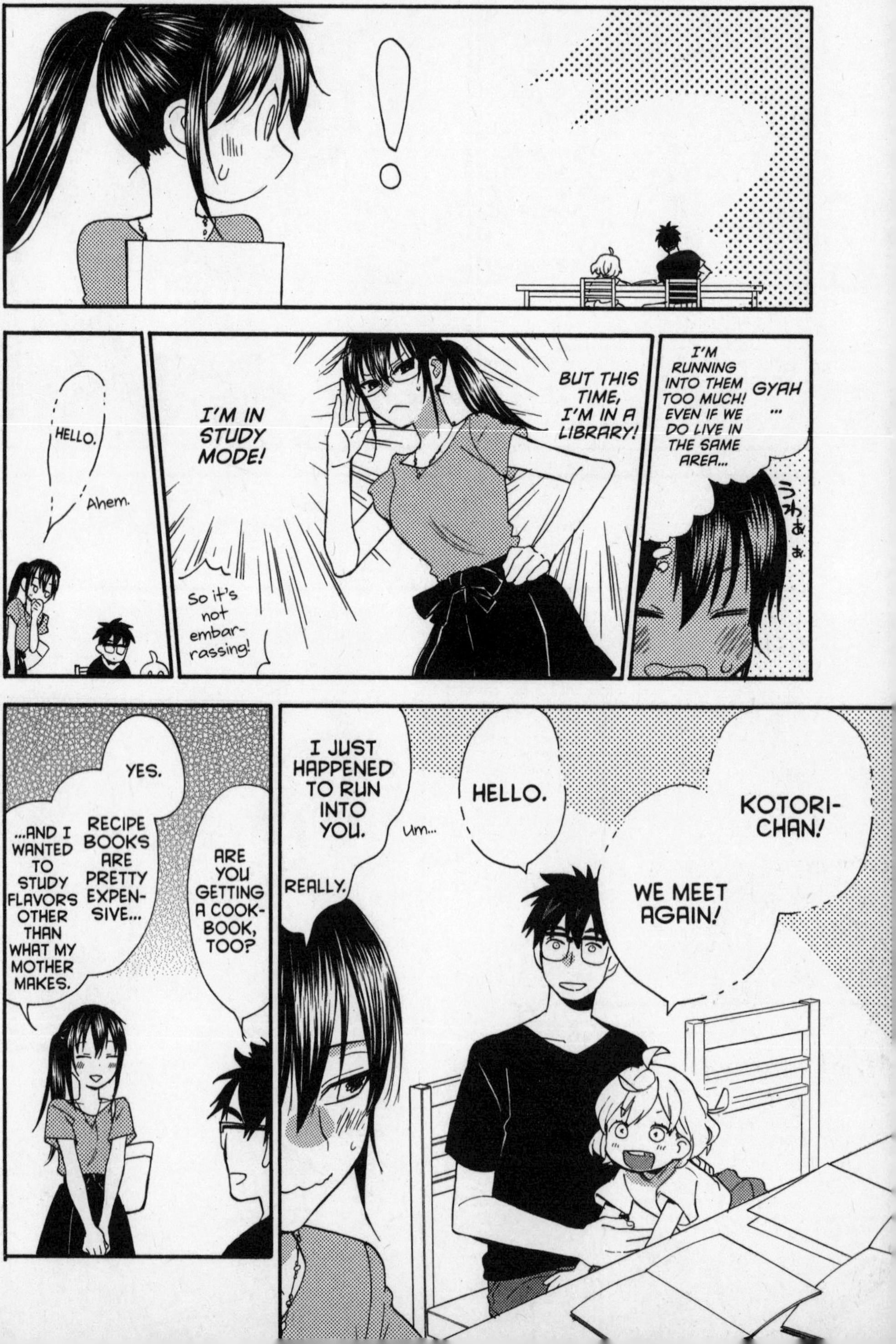
!
GYAH...
I'M RUNNING INTO THEM TOO MUCH! EVEN IF WE DO LIVE IN THE SAME AREA...
うわぁぁ
BUT THIS TIME, I'M IN A LIBRARY!
I'M IN STUDY MODE!
So it's not embarrassing!
HELLO.
Ahem.
KOTORI-CHAN!
WE MEET AGAIN!
HELLO.
I JUST HAPPENED TO RUN INTO YOU.
um...
REALLY.
ARE YOU GETTING A COOKBOOK, TOO?
YES.
RECIPE BOOKS ARE PRETTY EXPENSIVE...
...AND I WANTED TO STUDY FLAVORS OTHER THAN WHAT MY MOTHER MAKES.

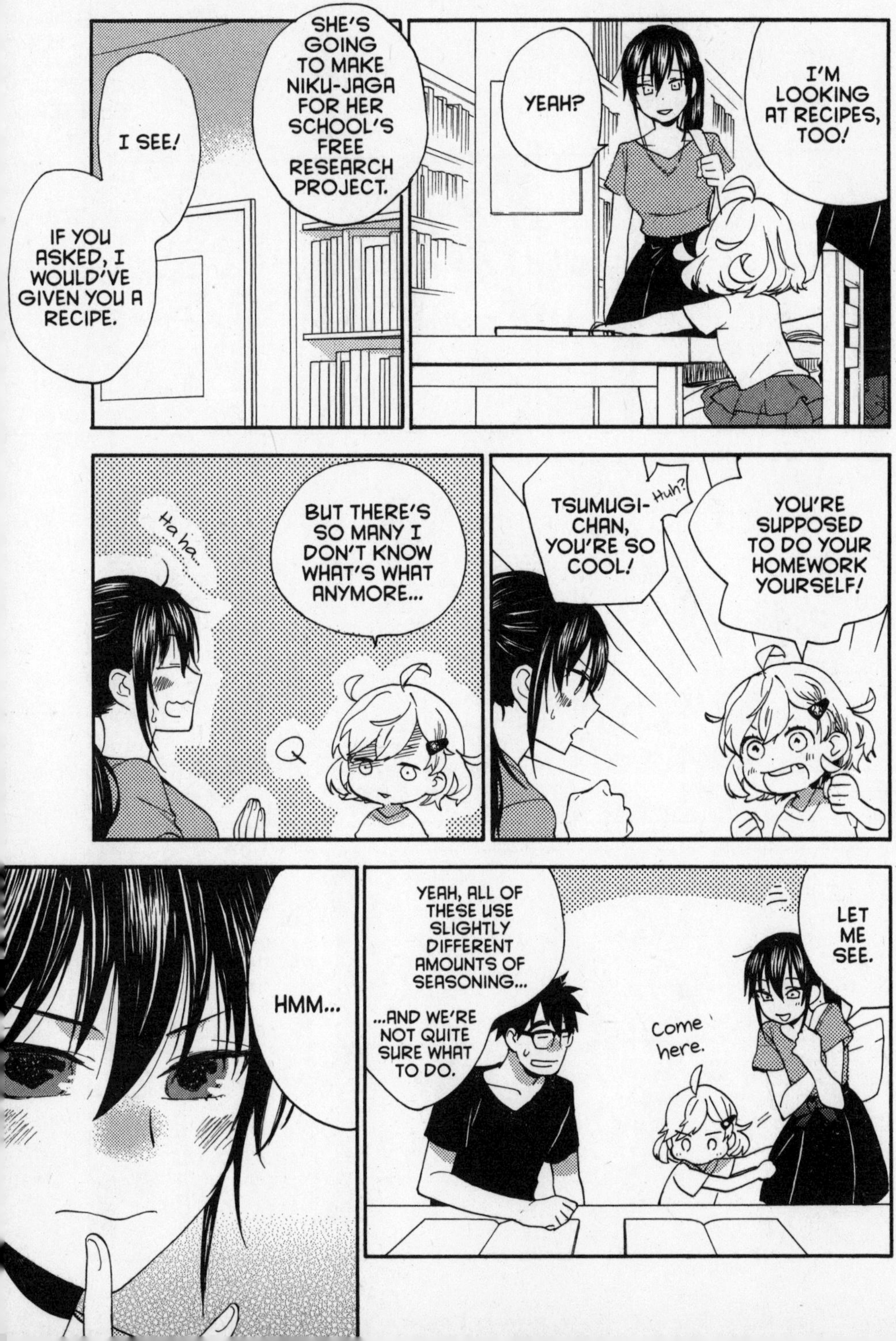
I'M LOOKING AT RECIPES, TOO!
YEAH?
SHE'S GOING TO MAKE NIKU-JAGA FOR HER SCHOOL'S FREE RESEARCH PROJECT.
I SEE!
IF YOU ASKED, I WOULD'VE GIVEN YOU A RECIPE.
YOU'RE SUPPOSED TO DO YOUR HOMEWORK YOURSELF!
TSUMUGI-CHAN, YOU'RE SO COOL!
Huh?
BUT THERE'S SO MANY I DON'T KNOW WHAT'S WHAT ANYMORE...
Ha ha...
LET ME SEE.
Come here.
YEAH, ALL OF THESE USE SLIGHTLY DIFFERENT AMOUNTS OF SEASONING...
...AND WE'RE NOT QUITE SURE WHAT TO DO.
HMM...

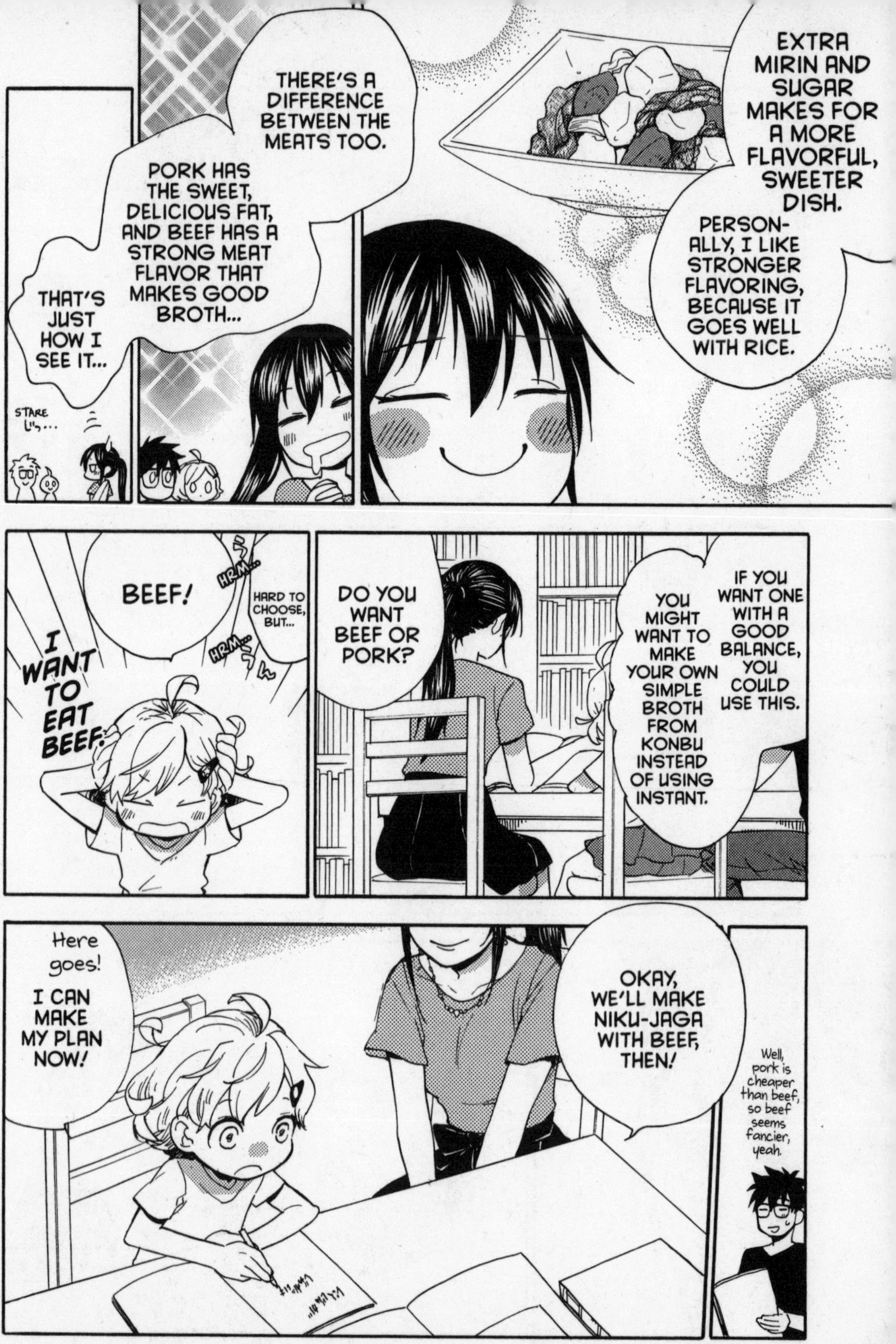

EXTRA MIRIN AND SUGAR MAKES FOR A MORE FLAVORFUL, SWEETER DISH.
PERSON-ALLY, I LIKE STRONGER FLAVORING, BECAUSE IT GOES WELL WITH RICE.
THERE'S A DIFFERENCE BETWEEN THE MEATS TOO.
PORK HAS THE SWEET, DELICIOUS FAT, AND BEEF HAS A STRONG MEAT FLAVOR THAT MAKES GOOD BROTH...
THAT'S JUST HOW I SEE IT...
STARE じぃ...
IF YOU WANT ONE WITH A GOOD BALANCE, YOU COULD USE THIS.
YOU MIGHT WANT TO MAKE YOUR OWN SIMPLE BROTH FROM KONBU INSTEAD OF USING INSTANT.
DO YOU WANT BEEF OR PORK?
HRM...
HARD TO CHOOSE, BUT...
HRM...
BEEF!
I WANT TO EAT BEEF!
Well, pork is cheaper than beef, so beef seems fancier, yeah.
OKAY, WE'LL MAKE NIKU-JAGA WITH BEEF, THEN!
Here goes!
I CAN MAKE MY PLAN NOW!

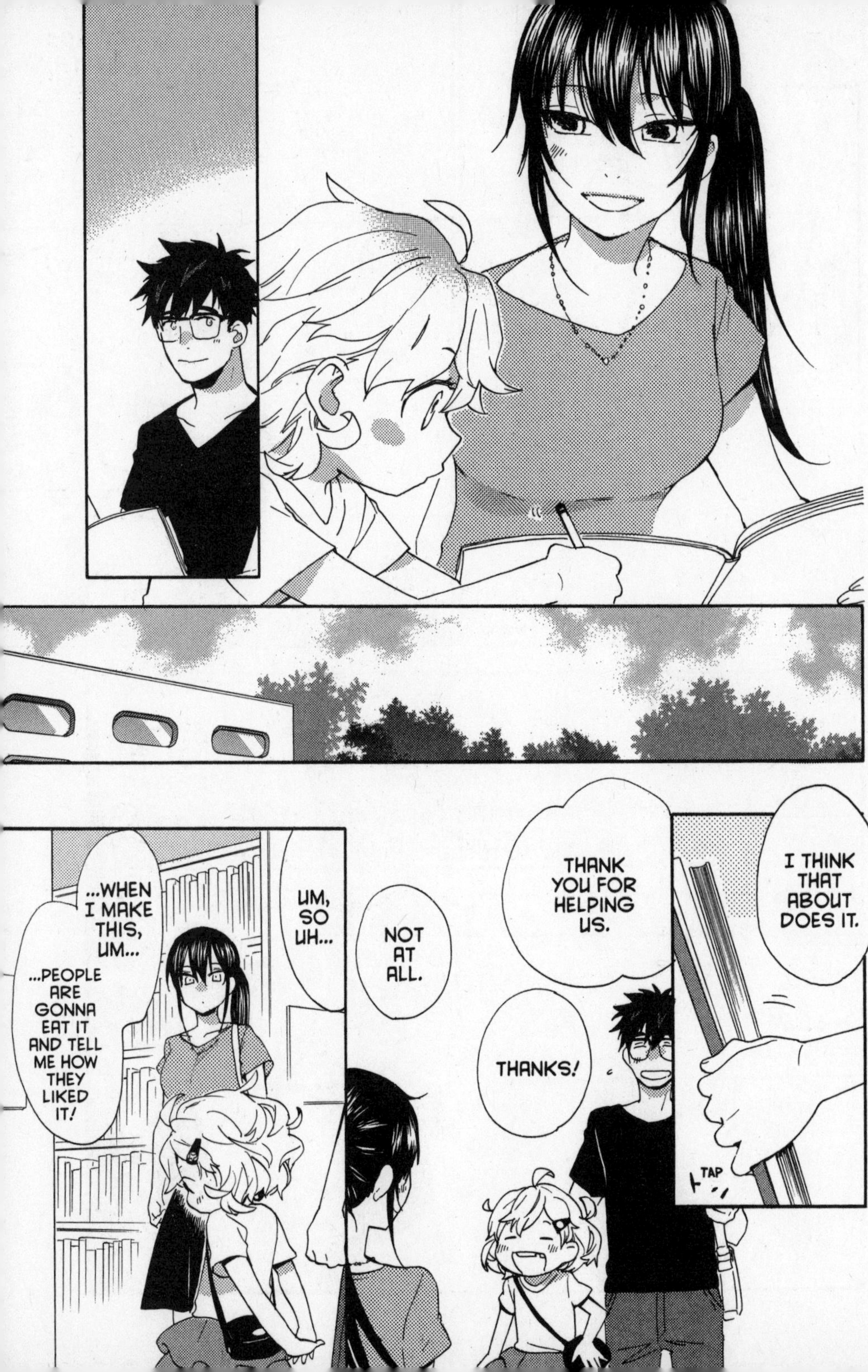
I THINK THAT ABOUT DOES IT.
TAP
THANK YOU FOR HELPING US.
THANKS!
NOT AT ALL.
UM, SO UH...
...WHEN I MAKE THIS, UM...
...PEOPLE ARE GONNA EAT IT AND TELL ME HOW THEY LIKED IT!

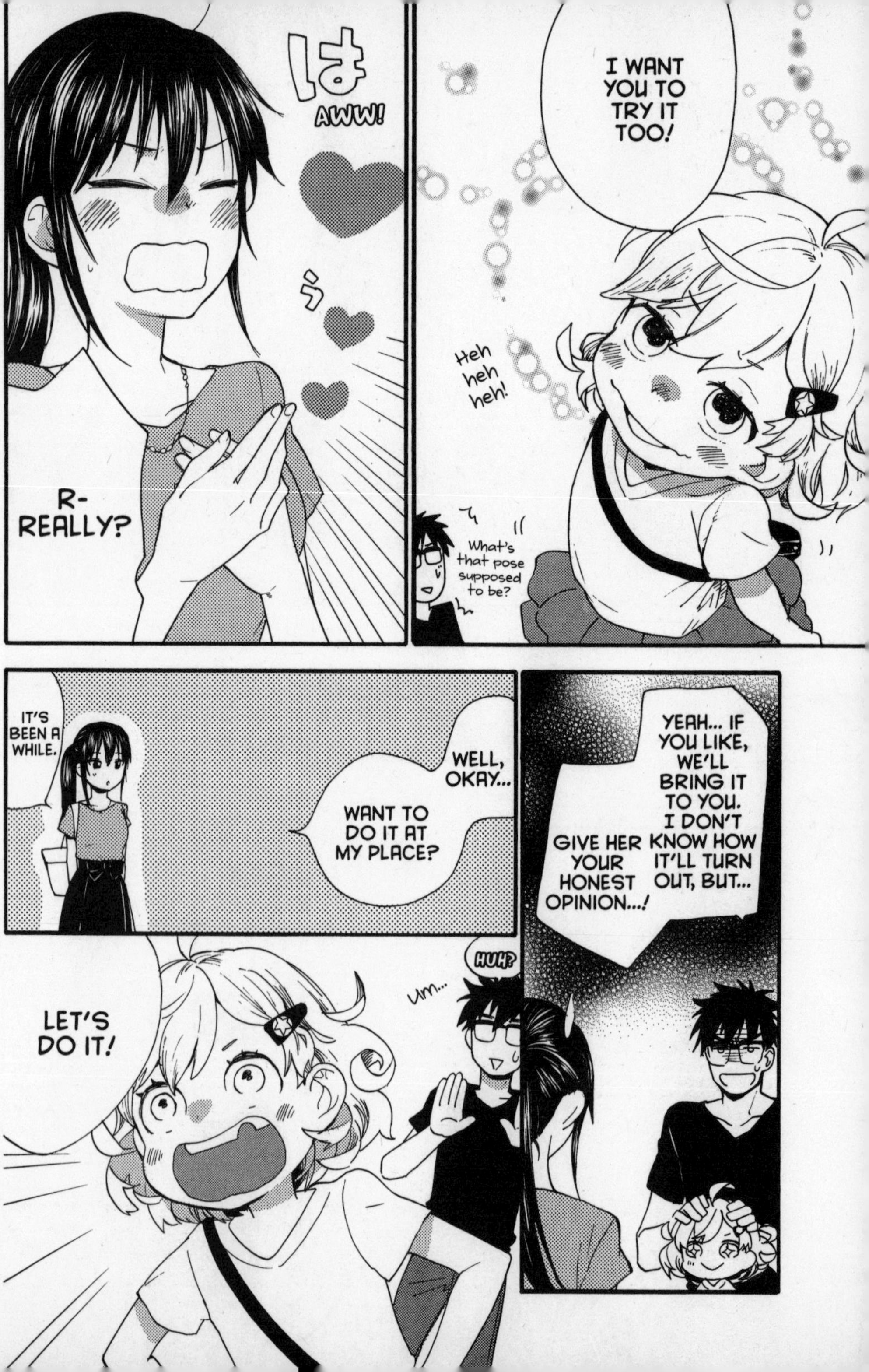
I WANT YOU TO TRY IT TOO!
Heh heh heh!
What's that pose supposed to be?
は
AWW!
う
R-REALLY?
YEAH... IF YOU LIKE, WE'LL BRING IT TO YOU. I DON'T KNOW HOW IT'LL TURN OUT, BUT...
GIVE HER YOUR HONEST OPINION...!
WELL, OKAY...
WANT TO DO IT AT MY PLACE?
IT'S BEEN A WHILE.
HUH?
Um...
LET'S DO IT!

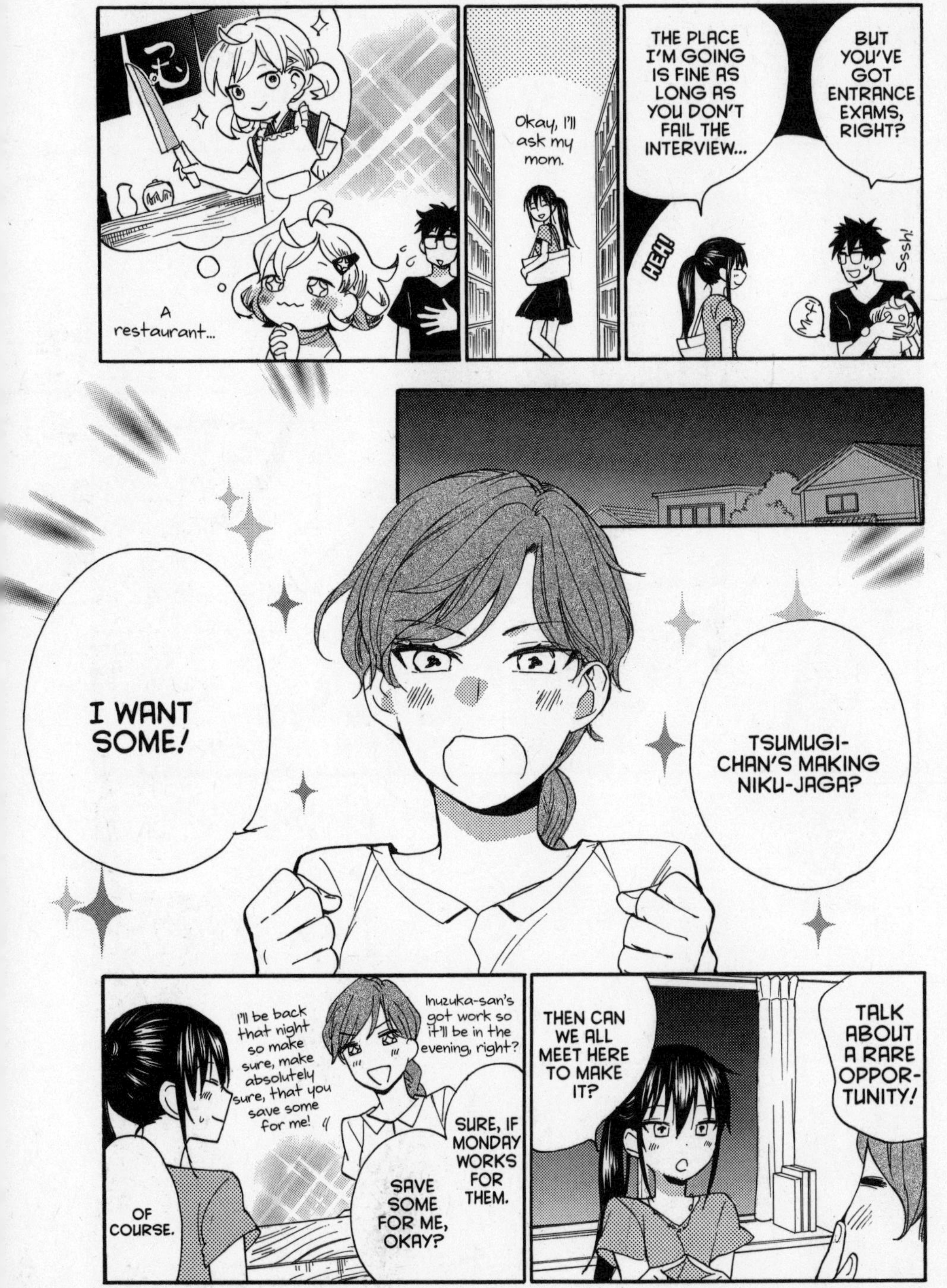

BUT YOU'VE GOT ENTRANCE EXAMS, RIGHT?
THE PLACE I'M GOING IS FINE AS LONG AS YOU DON'T FAIL THE INTERVIEW...
Sssh!
HEH!
Mrf!
Okay, I'll ask my mom.
A restaurant...
TSUMUGI-CHAN'S MAKING NIKU-JAGA?
I WANT SOME!
TALK ABOUT A RARE OPPORTUNITY!
THEN CAN WE ALL MEET HERE TO MAKE IT?
Inuzuka-san's got work so it'll be in the evening, right?
SURE, IF MONDAY WORKS FOR THEM.
I'll be back that night so make sure, make absolutely sure, that you save some for me!
SAVE SOME FOR ME, OKAY?
OF COURSE.

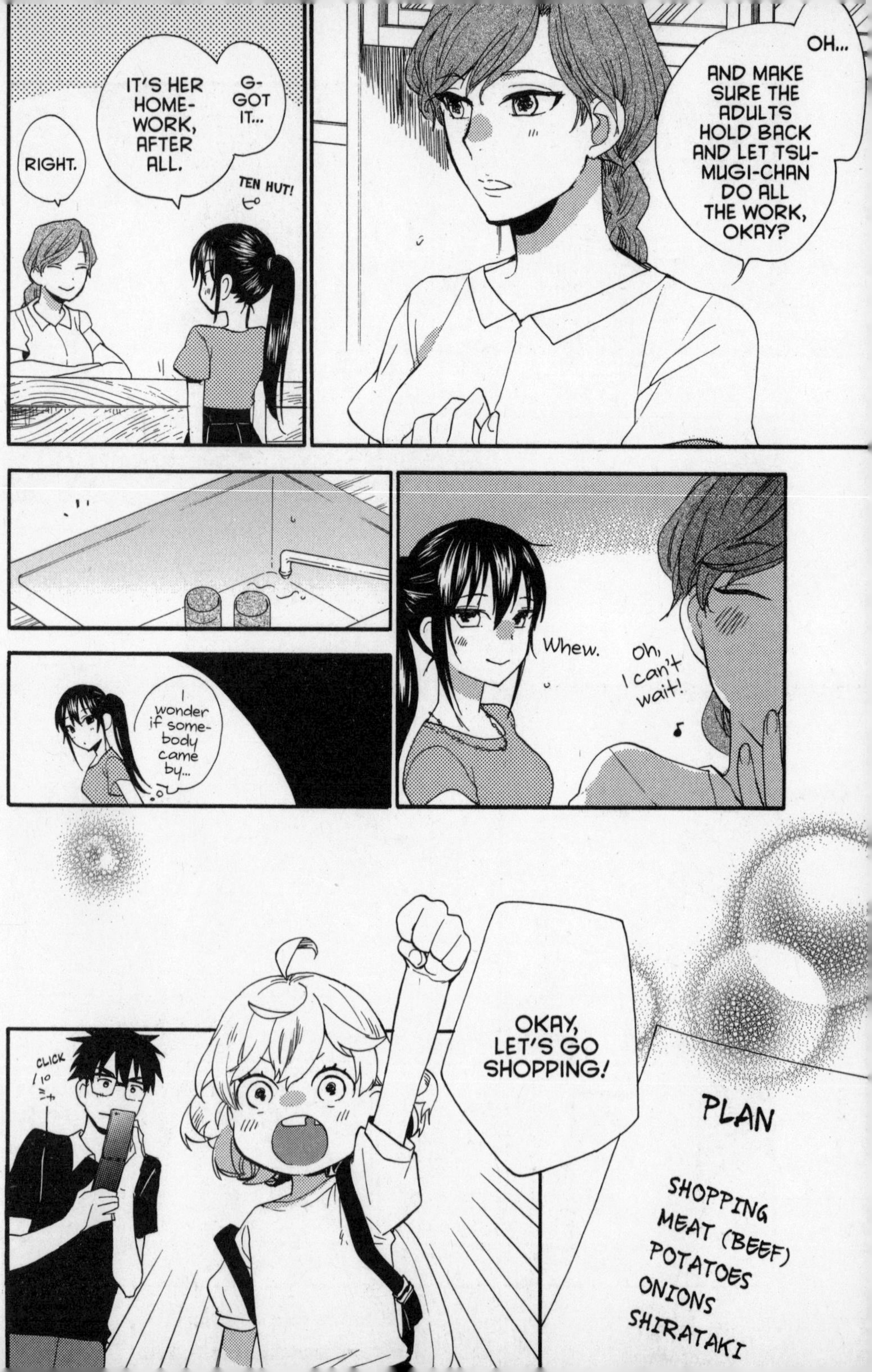
OH... AND MAKE SURE THE ADULTS HOLD BACK AND LET TSU-MUGI-CHAN DO ALL THE WORK, OKAY?
G-GOT IT...
IT'S HER HOME-WORK, AFTER ALL.
TEN HUT!
RIGHT.
Oh, I can't wait!
Whew.
I wonder if some-body came by...
PLAN
SHOPPING
MEAT (BEEF)
POTATOES
ONIONS
SHIRATAKI
OKAY, LET'S GO SHOPPING!
CLICK

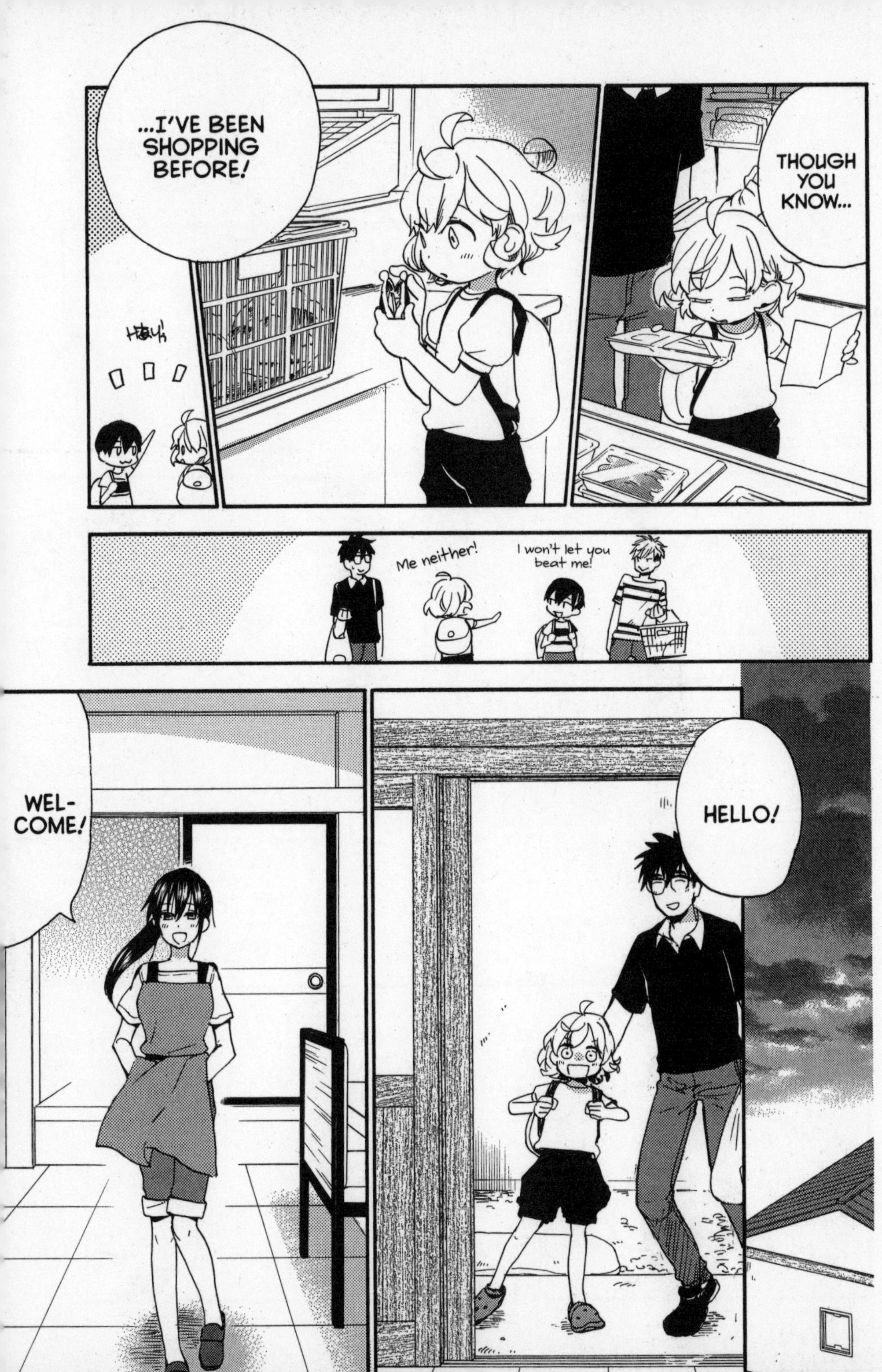
THOUGH YOU KNOW...
...I'VE BEEN SHOPPING BEFORE!
I won't let you beat me!
Me neither!
HELLO!
WEL-COME!

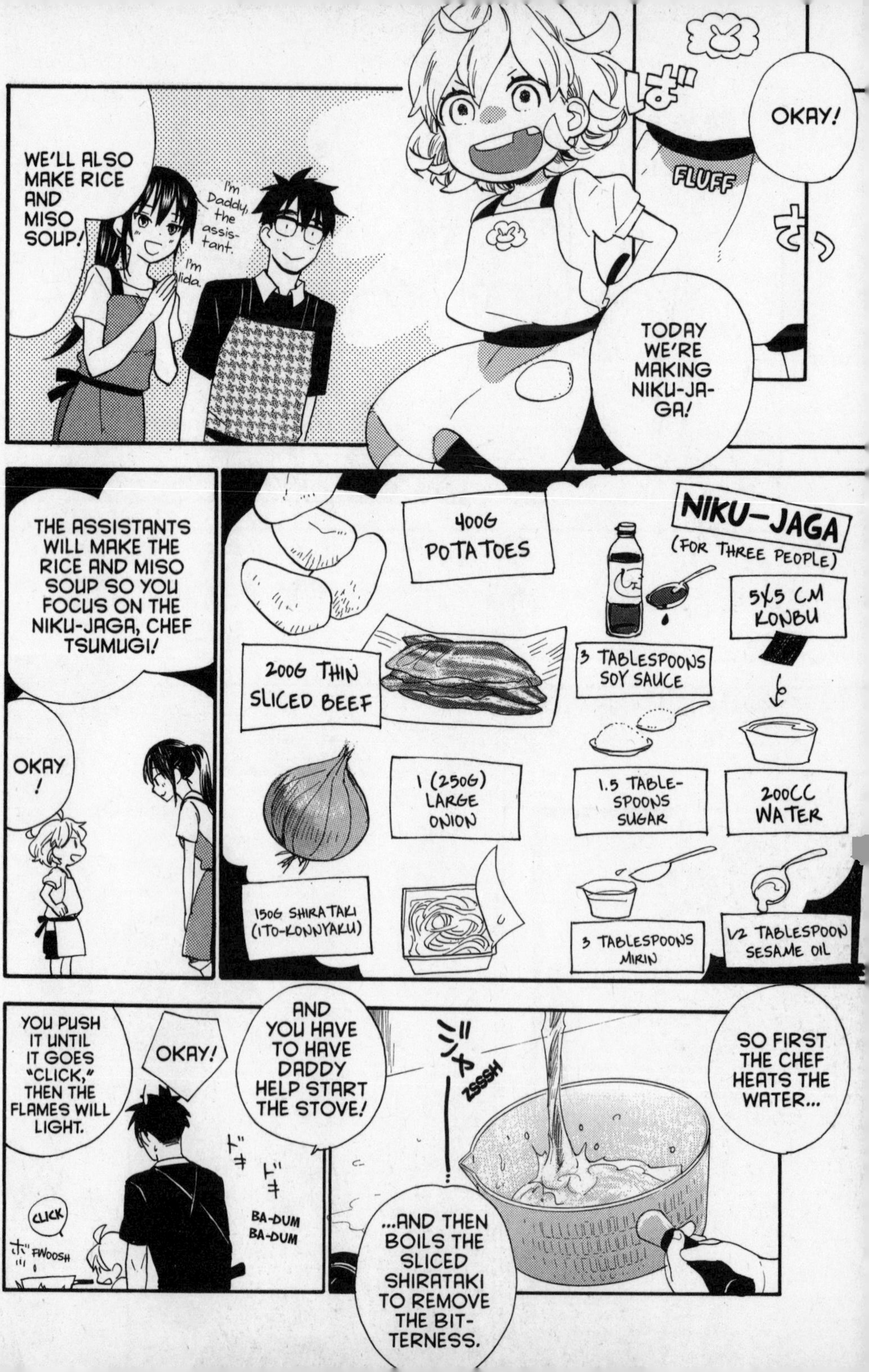
ば
OKAY!
FLUFF
さっ
TODAY WE'RE MAKING NIKU-JAGA!
WE'LL ALSO MAKE RICE AND MISO SOUP!
I'm Daddy, the assis- tant.
I'm Iida.
NIKU-JAGA
(FOR THREE PEOPLE)
5X5 CM KONBU
3 TABLESPOONS SOY SAUCE
400G POTATOES
200G THIN SLICED BEEF
200CC WATER
1.5 TABLE- SPOONS SUGAR
1 (250G) LARGE ONION
1/2 TABLESPOON SESAME OIL
3 TABLESPOONS MIRIN
150G SHIRATAKI (ITO-KONNYAKU)
THE ASSISTANTS WILL MAKE THE RICE AND MISO SOUP SO YOU FOCUS ON THE NIKU-JAGA, CHEF TSUMUGI!
OKAY!
SO FIRST THE CHEF HEATS THE WATER...
ジャー!
ZSSSH
...AND THEN BOILS THE SLICED SHIRATAKI TO REMOVE THE BIT- TERNESS.
AND YOU HAVE TO HAVE DADDY HELP START THE STOVE!
OKAY!
YOU PUSH IT UNTIL IT GOES "CLICK," THEN THE FLAMES WILL LIGHT.
ドキ ドキ
BA-DUM BA-DUM
CLICK
ボッ
FWOOSH

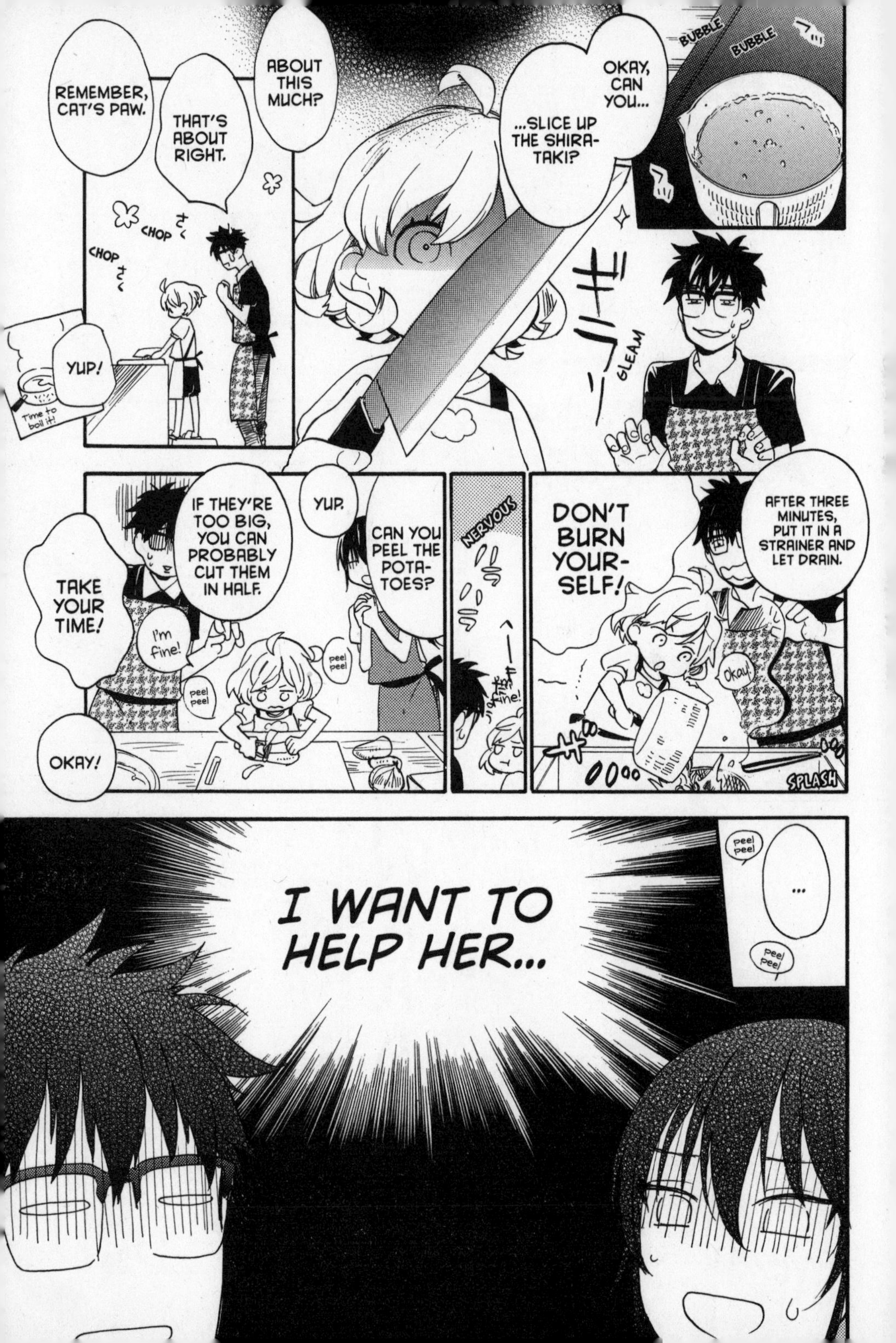
BUBBLE
BUBBLE
OKAY, CAN YOU...
...SLICE UP THE SHIRA-TAKI?
GLEAM
ABOUT THIS MUCH?
THAT'S ABOUT RIGHT.
REMEMBER, CAT'S PAW.
CHOP
CHOP
YUP!
Time to boil it!
AFTER THREE MINUTES, PUT IT IN A STRAINER AND LET DRAIN.
DON'T BURN YOUR-SELF!
Okay!
SPLASH
NERVOUS
fine!
CAN YOU PEEL THE POTA-TOES?
YUP.
IF THEY'RE TOO BIG, YOU CAN PROBABLY CUT THEM IN HALF.
TAKE YOUR TIME!
I'm fine!
peel peel
peel peel
OKAY!
peel peel
...
peel peel
I WANT TO HELP HER...

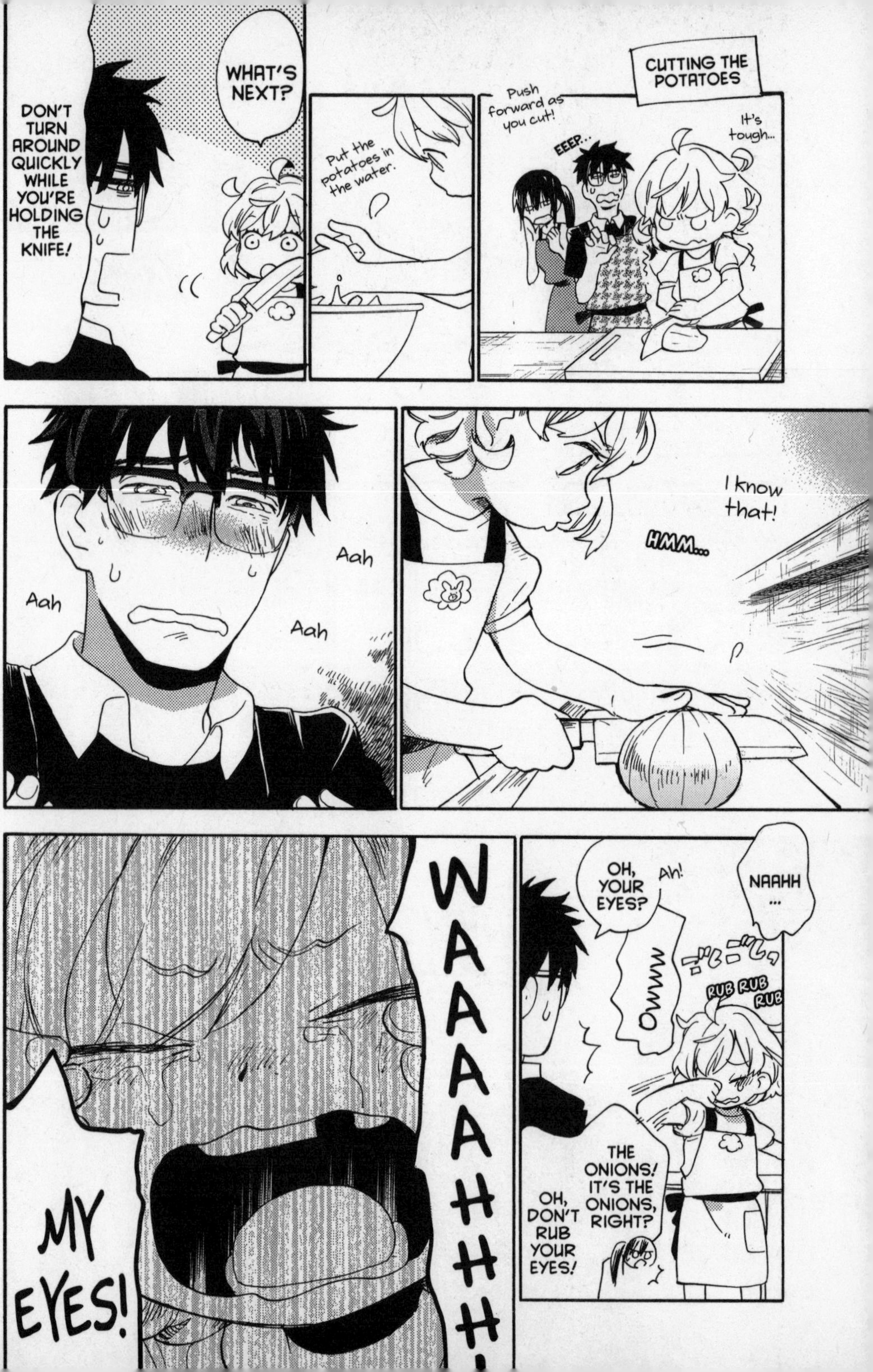
CUTTING THE POTATOES
Push forward as you cut!
EEEP...
It's tough...
Put the potatoes in the water.
WHAT'S NEXT?
DON'T TURN AROUND QUICKLY WHILE YOU'RE HOLDING THE KNIFE!
I know that!
HMM...
Aah
Aah
Aah
NAAHH ...
Ah!
OH, YOUR EYES?
OWWW
RUB RUB RUB
THE ONIONS! IT'S THE ONIONS, RIGHT?
OH, DON'T RUB YOUR EYES!
WAAAAHHH!
MY EYES!

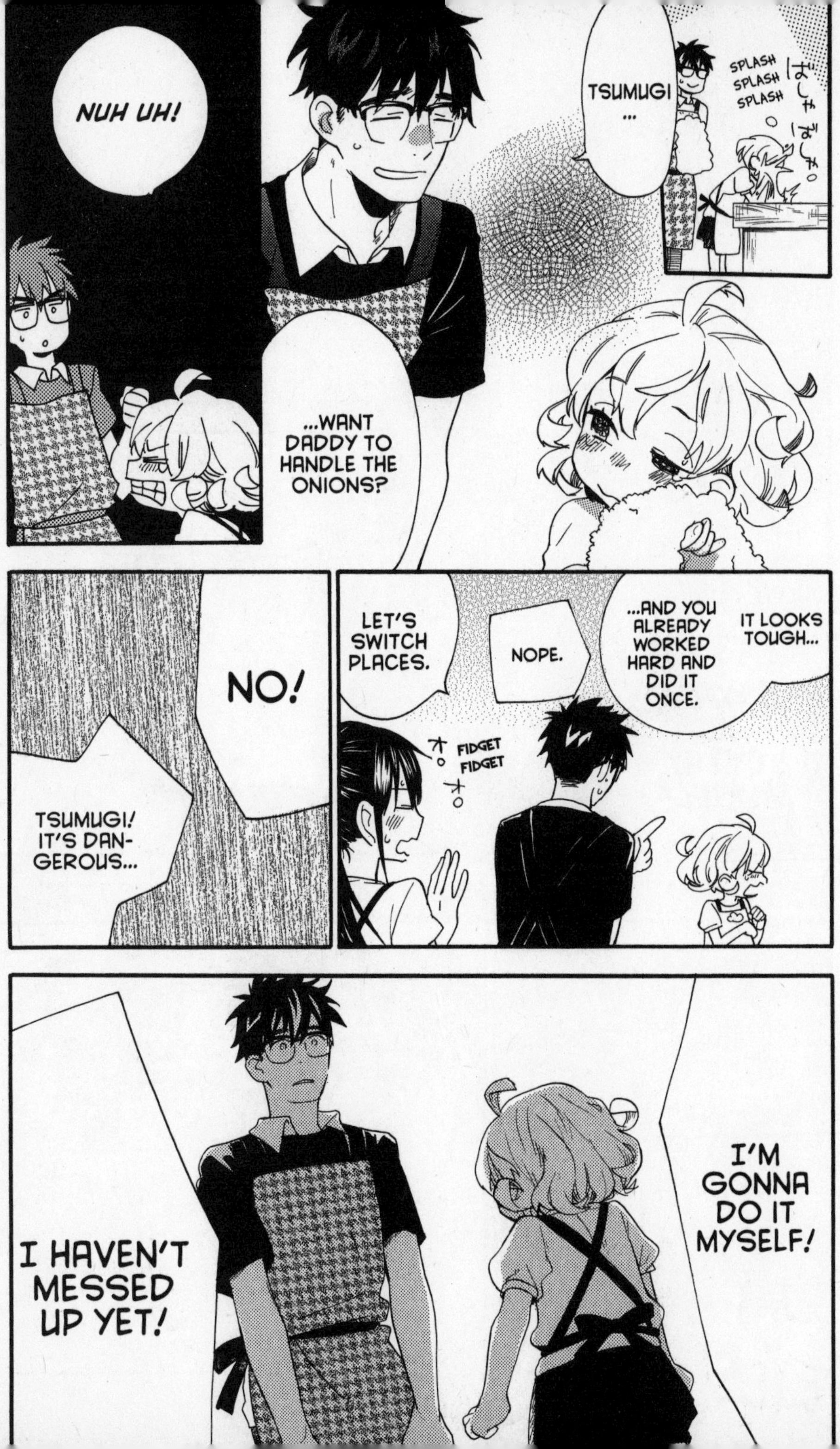

TSUMUGI ...
SPLASH SPLASH SPLASH
ばしゃ ばしゃ
...WANT DADDY TO HANDLE THE ONIONS?
NUH UH!
IT LOOKS TOUGH...
...AND YOU ALREADY WORKED HARD AND DID IT ONCE.
NOPE.
LET'S SWITCH PLACES.
FIDGET FIDGET
NO!
TSUMUGI! IT'S DAN-GEROUS...
I'M GONNA DO IT MYSELF!
I HAVEN'T MESSED UP YET!

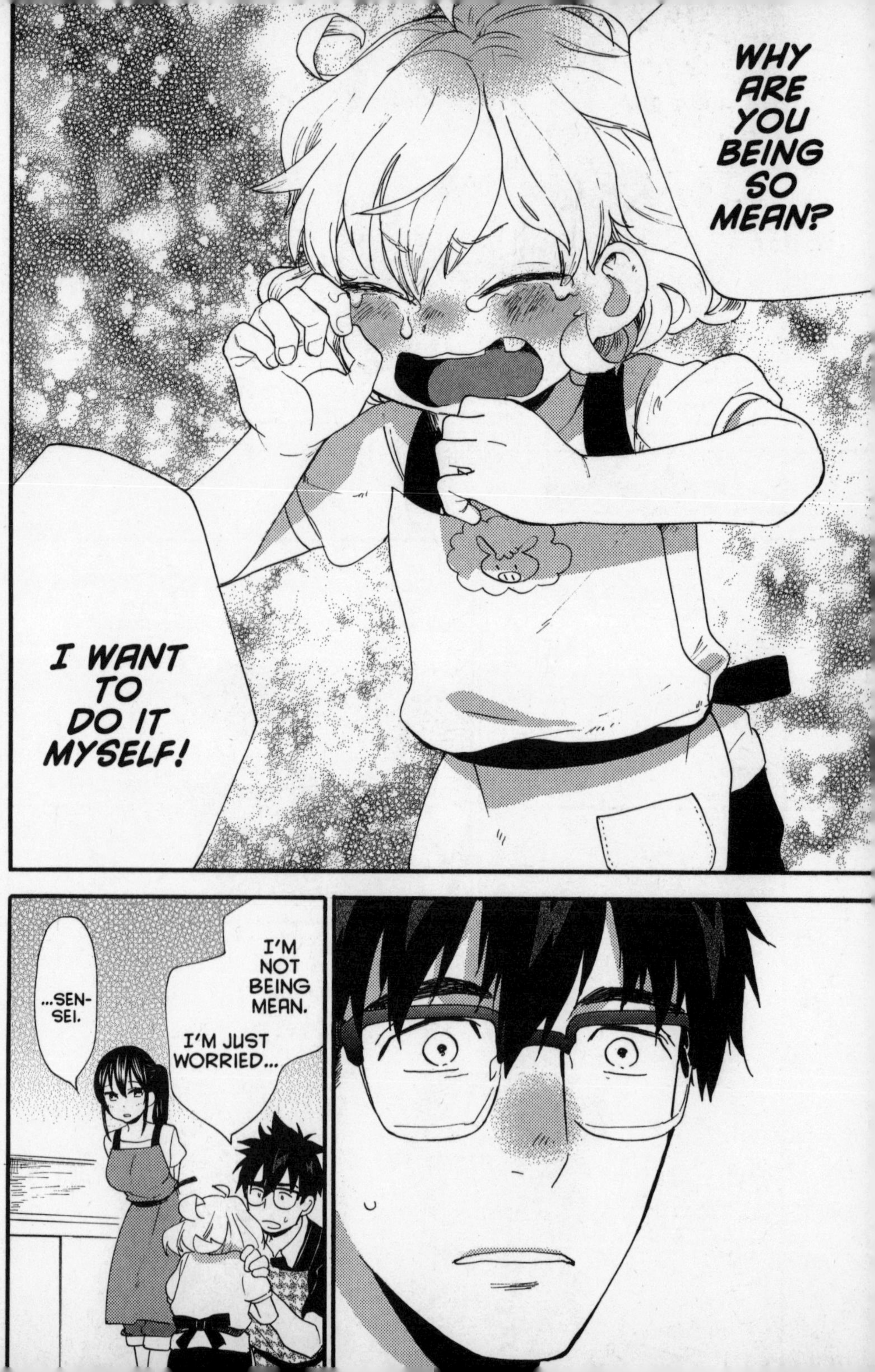
WHY ARE YOU BEING SO MEAN?
I WANT TO DO IT MYSELF!
I'M NOT BEING MEAN.
I'M JUST WORRIED...
...SEN-SEI.

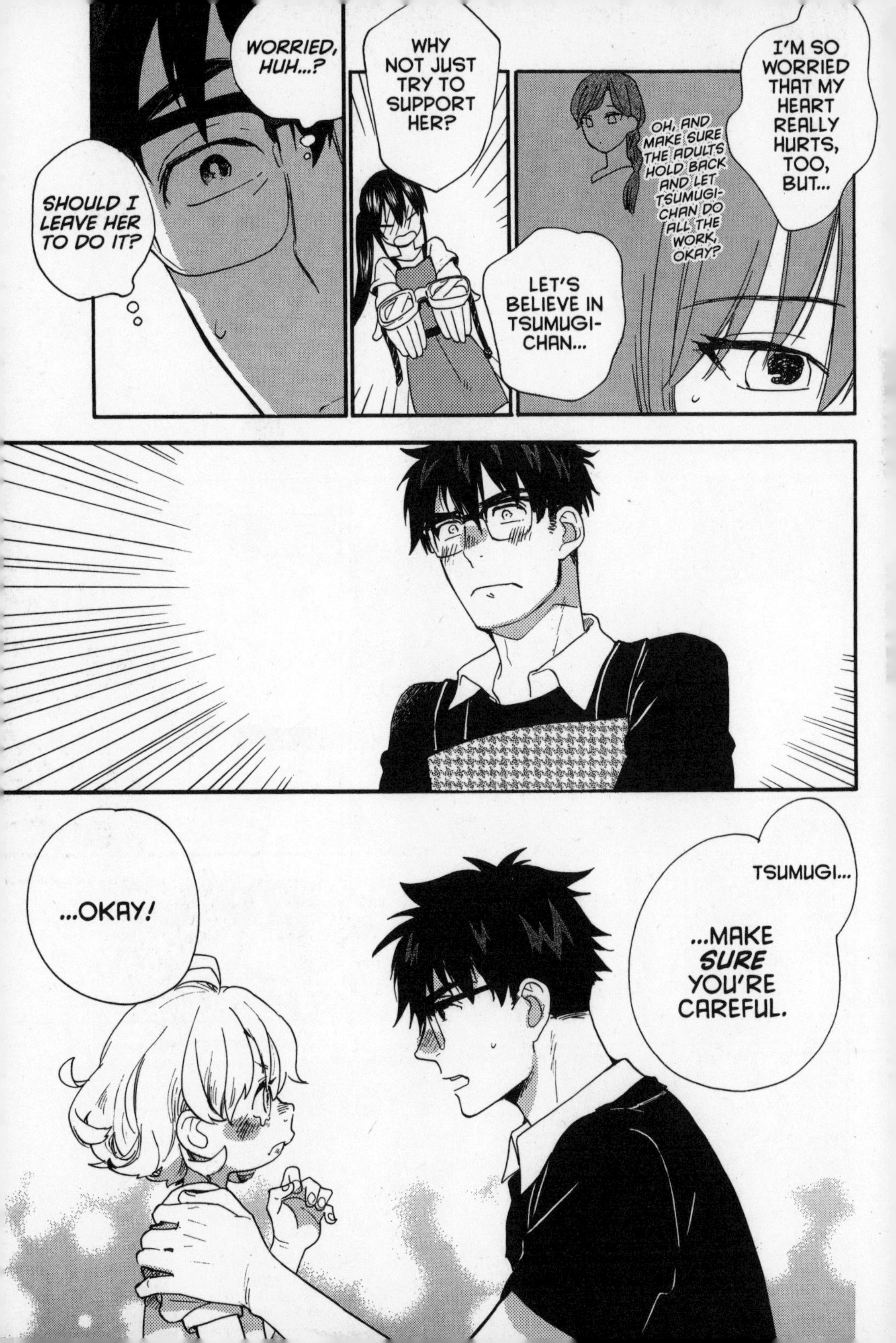
I'M SO WORRIED THAT MY HEART REALLY HURTS, TOO, BUT...
OH, AND MAKE SURE THE ADULTS HOLD BACK AND LET TSUMUGI-CHAN DO ALL THE WORK, OKAY?
LET'S BELIEVE IN TSUMUGI-CHAN...
WHY NOT JUST TRY TO SUPPORT HER?
WORRIED, HUH...?
SHOULD I LEAVE HER TO DO IT?
TSUMUGI...
...MAKE *SURE* YOU'RE CAREFUL.
...OKAY!

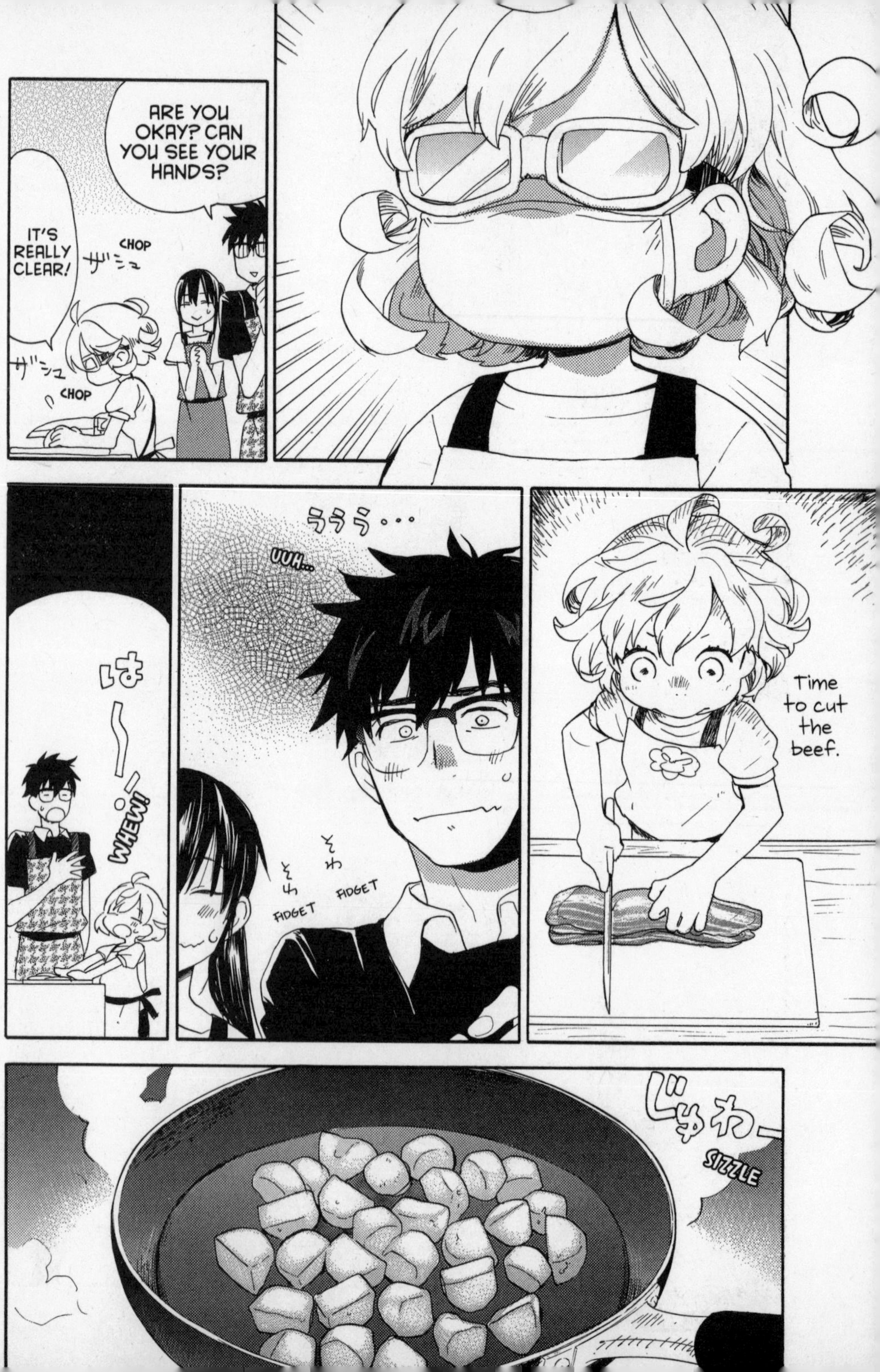
ARE YOU OKAY? CAN YOU SEE YOUR HANDS?
IT'S REALLY CLEAR!
ザシュ
CHOP
ザシュ
CHOP
Time to cut the beef.
ううう…
UUH…
そわ
FIDGET
そわ
FIDGET
はぁ～～！
WHEW!
じゅわー
SIZZLE

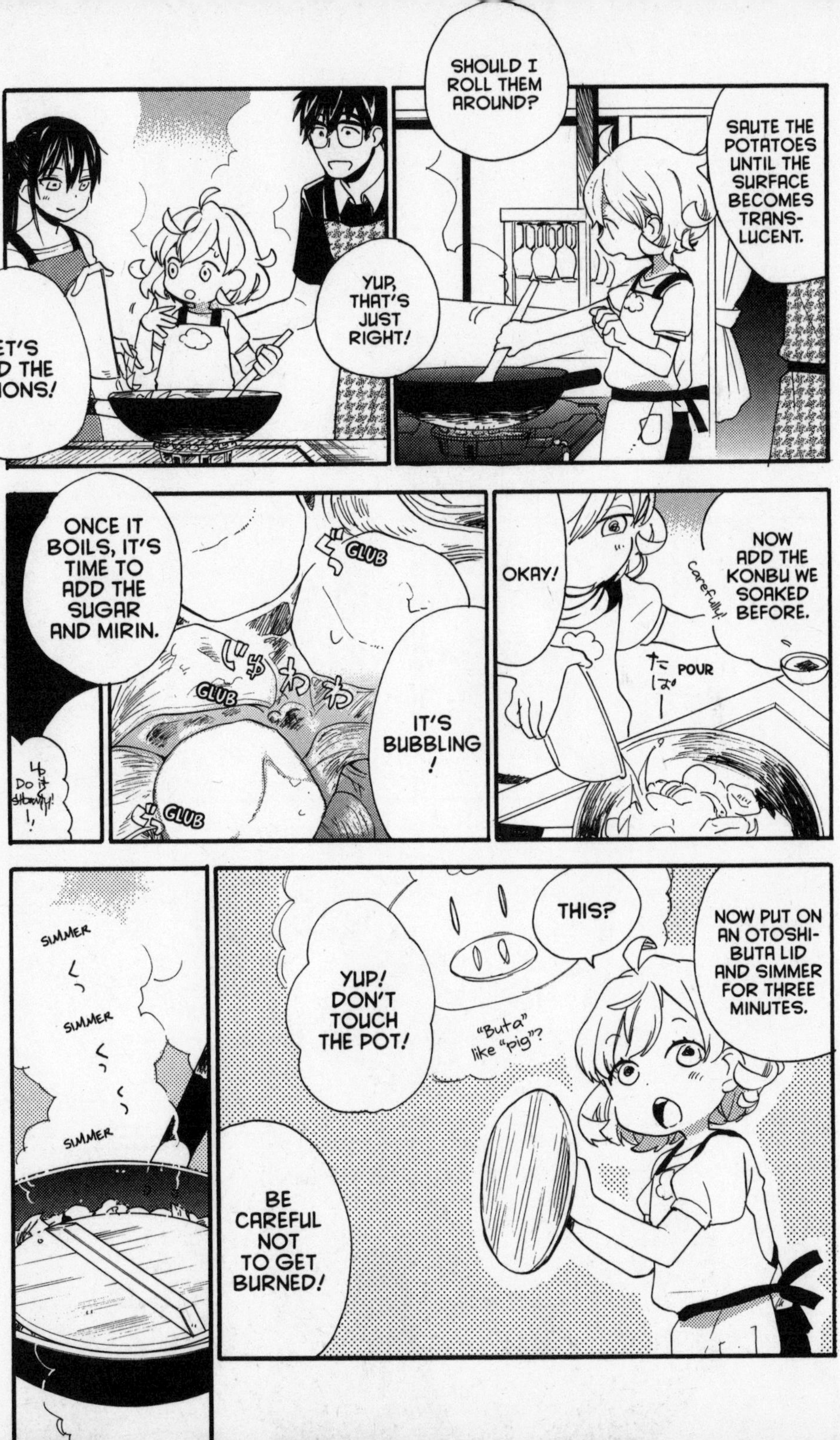
SAUTE THE POTATOES UNTIL THE SURFACE BECOMES TRANS-LUCENT.
SHOULD I ROLL THEM AROUND?
YUP, THAT'S JUST RIGHT!
LET'S ADD THE ONIONS!
NOW ADD THE KONBU WE SOAKED BEFORE.
Carefully!
OKAY!
POUR
IT'S BUBBLING!
GLUB
ONCE IT BOILS, IT'S TIME TO ADD THE SUGAR AND MIRIN.
GLUB
GLUB
Do it slowly!!
NOW PUT ON AN OTOSHI-BUTA LID AND SIMMER FOR THREE MINUTES.
THIS?
"Buta" like "pig"?
YUP! DON'T TOUCH THE POT!
BE CAREFUL NOT TO GET BURNED!
SIMMER
SIMMER
SIMMER

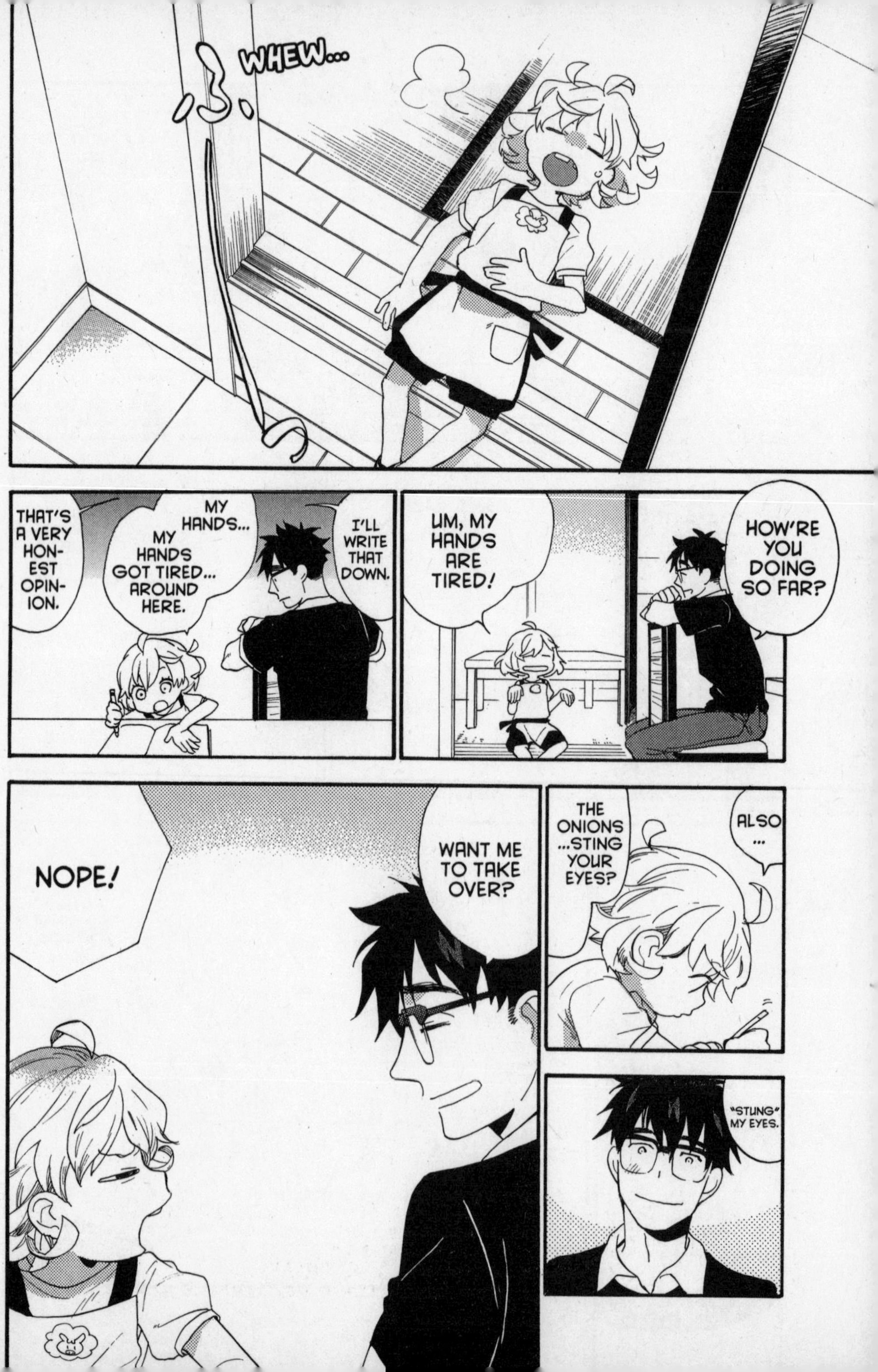
WHEW...
HOW'RE YOU DOING SO FAR?
UM, MY HANDS ARE TIRED!
I'LL WRITE THAT DOWN.
MY HANDS... MY HANDS GOT TIRED... AROUND HERE.
THAT'S A VERY HON-EST OPIN-ION.
ALSO...
THE ONIONS ...STING YOUR EYES?
"STUNG" MY EYES.
WANT ME TO TAKE OVER?
NOPE!

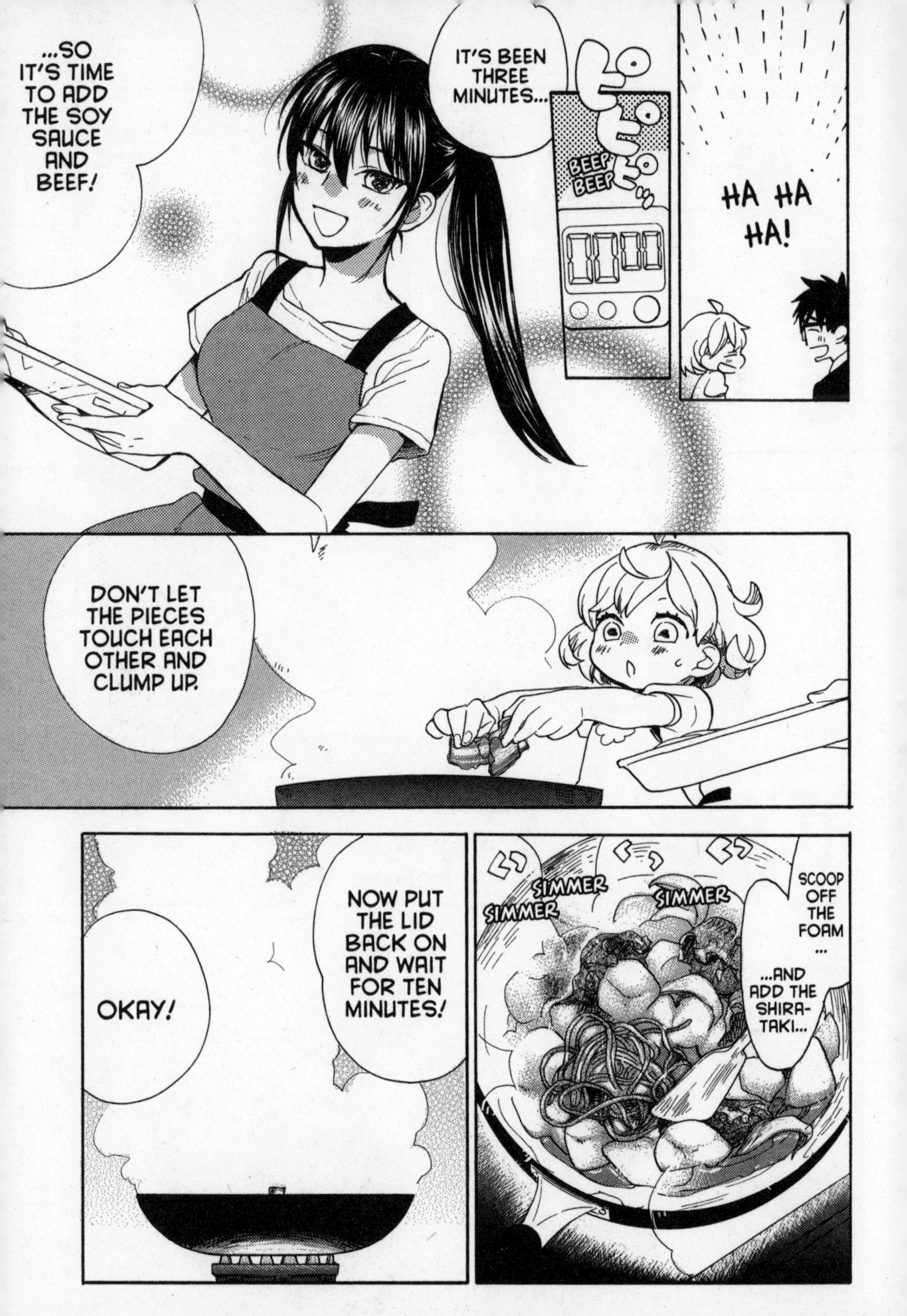
HA HA HA!
IT'S BEEN THREE MINUTES...
BEEP BEEP
...SO IT'S TIME TO ADD THE SOY SAUCE AND BEEF!
DON'T LET THE PIECES TOUCH EACH OTHER AND CLUMP UP.
SCOOP OFF THE FOAM...
...AND ADD THE SHIRA-TAKI...
SIMMER
SIMMER
SIMMER
NOW PUT THE LID BACK ON AND WAIT FOR TEN MINUTES!
OKAY!

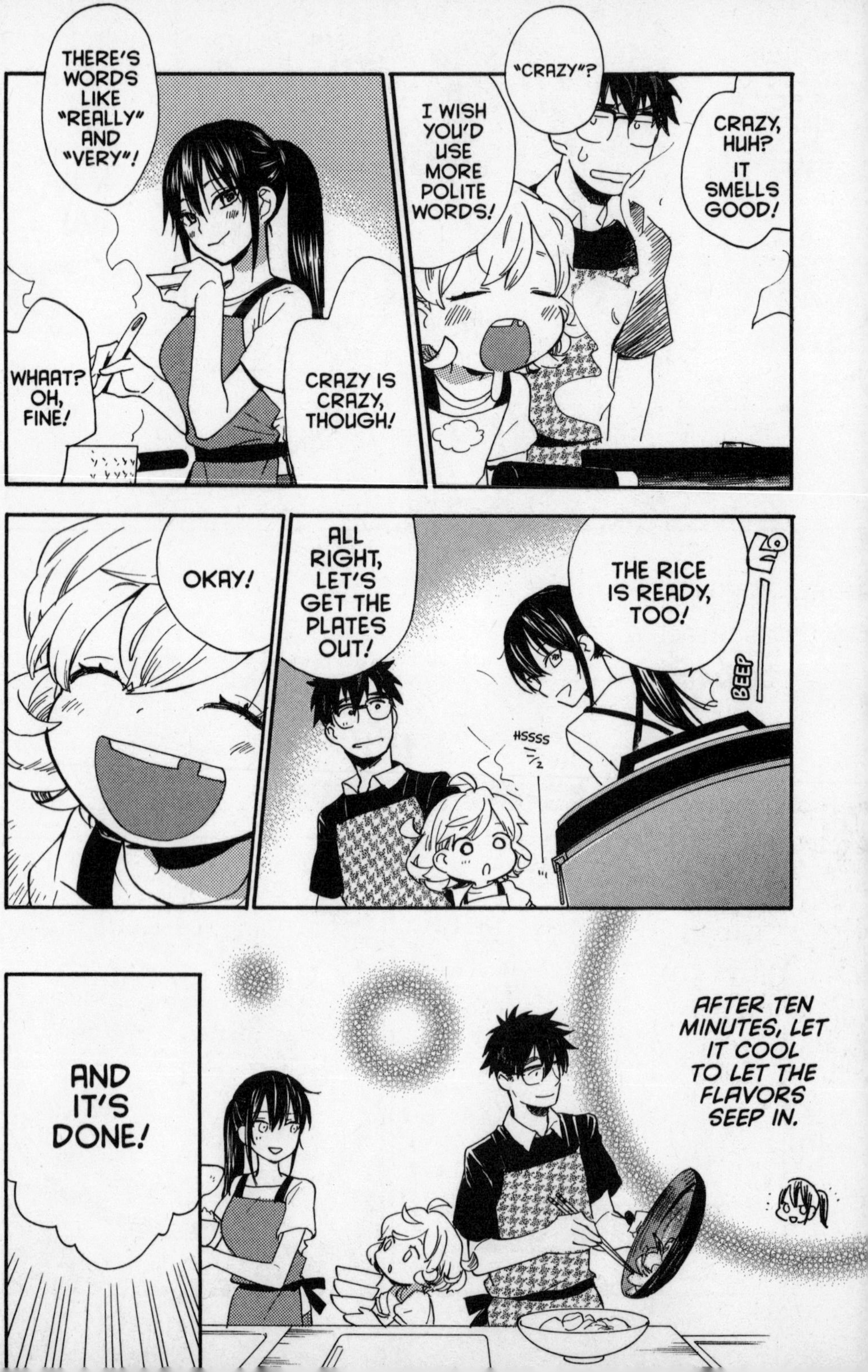
CRAZY, HUH? IT SMELLS GOOD!
"CRAZY"?
I WISH YOU'D USE MORE POLITE WORDS!
CRAZY IS CRAZY, THOUGH!
THERE'S WORDS LIKE "REALLY" AND "VERY"!
WHAAT? OH, FINE!
THE RICE IS READY, TOO!
BEEP
HSSSS
ALL RIGHT, LET'S GET THE PLATES OUT!
OKAY!
AFTER TEN MINUTES, LET IT COOL TO LET THE FLAVORS SEEP IN.
AND IT'S DONE!

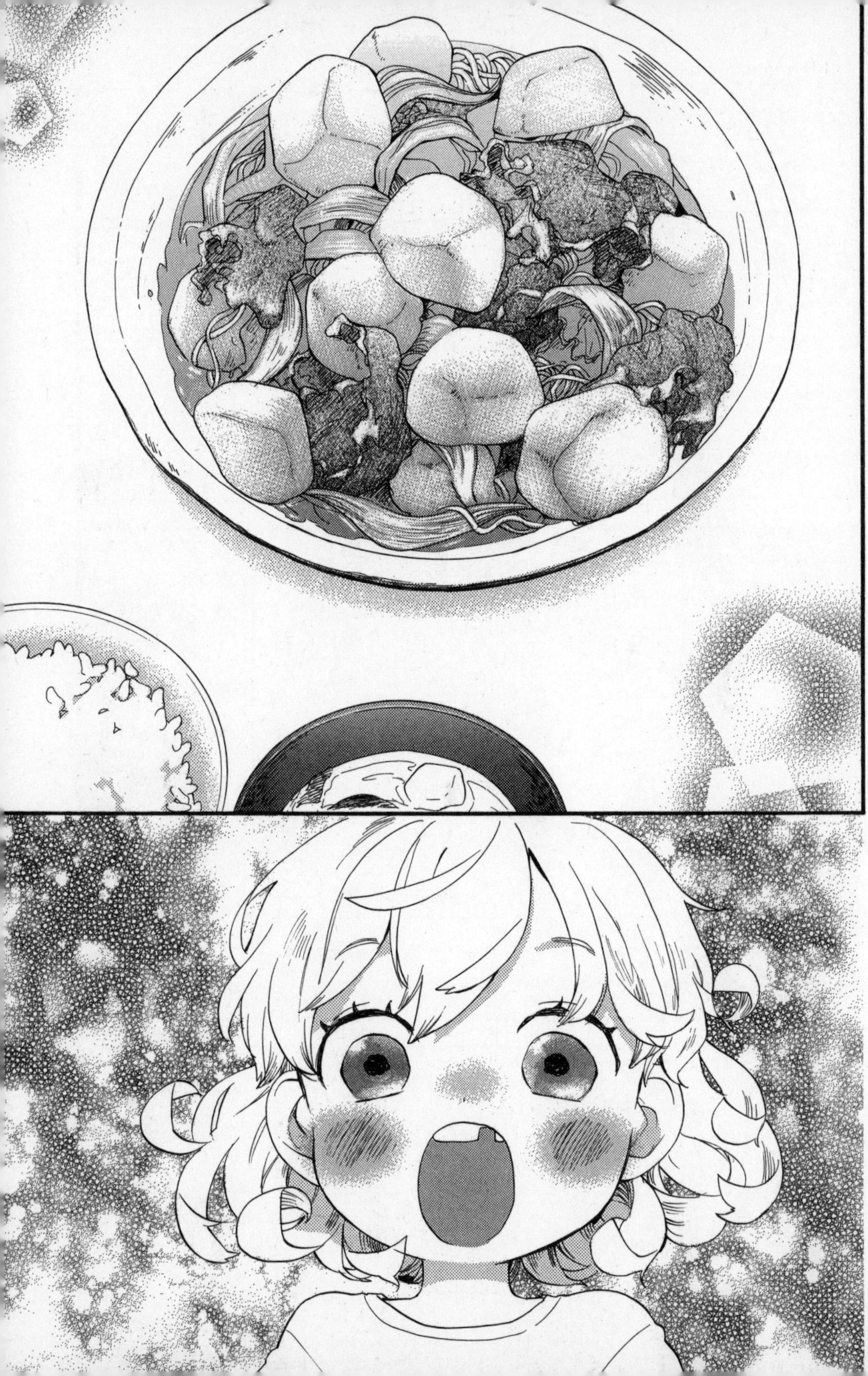

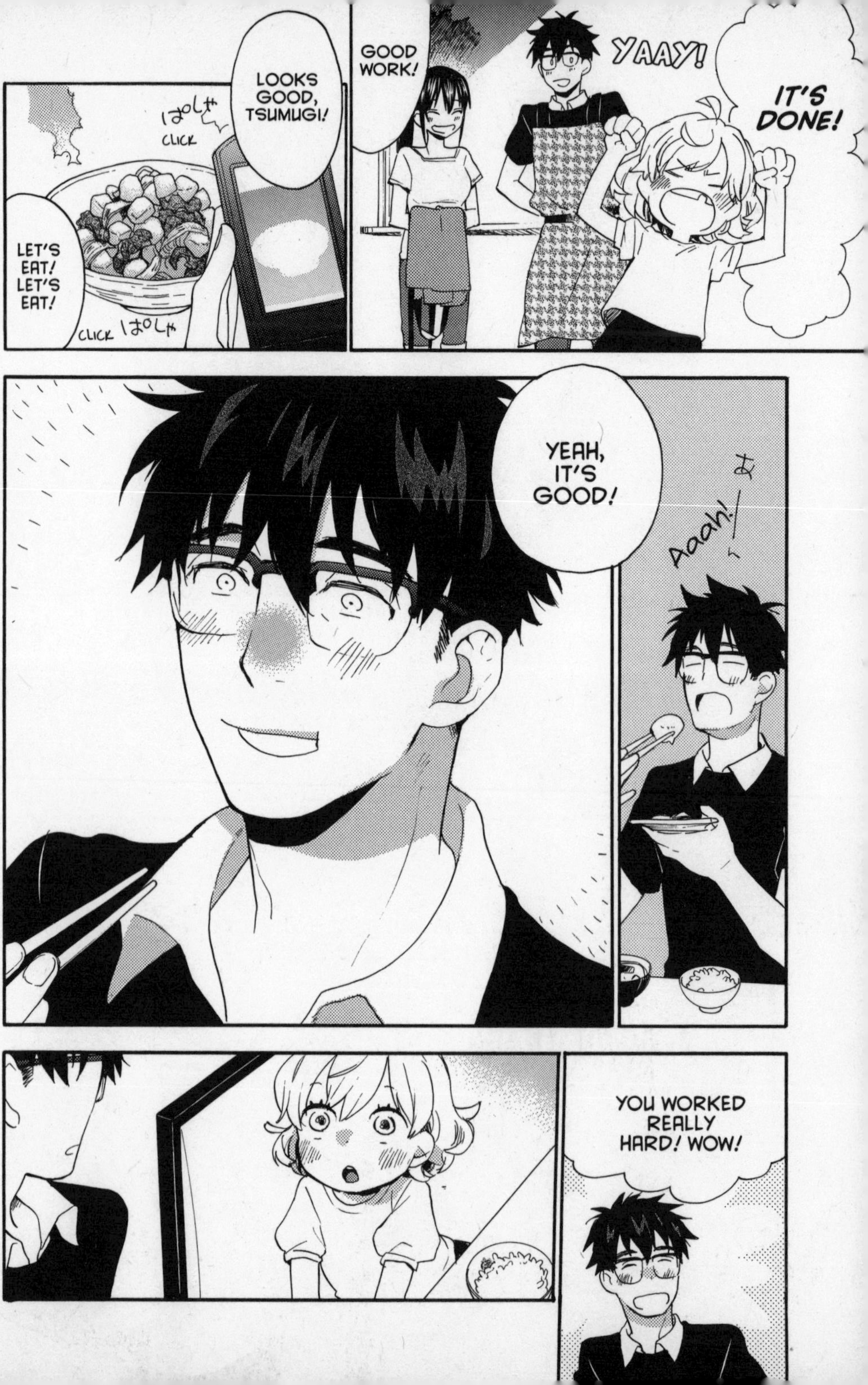
IT'S DONE!
YAAY!
GOOD WORK!
LOOKS GOOD, TSUMUGI!
ぱしゃ
CLICK
LET'S EAT! LET'S EAT!
CLICK ぱしゃ
あー
Aaah!
YEAH, IT'S GOOD!
YOU WORKED REALLY HARD! WOW!

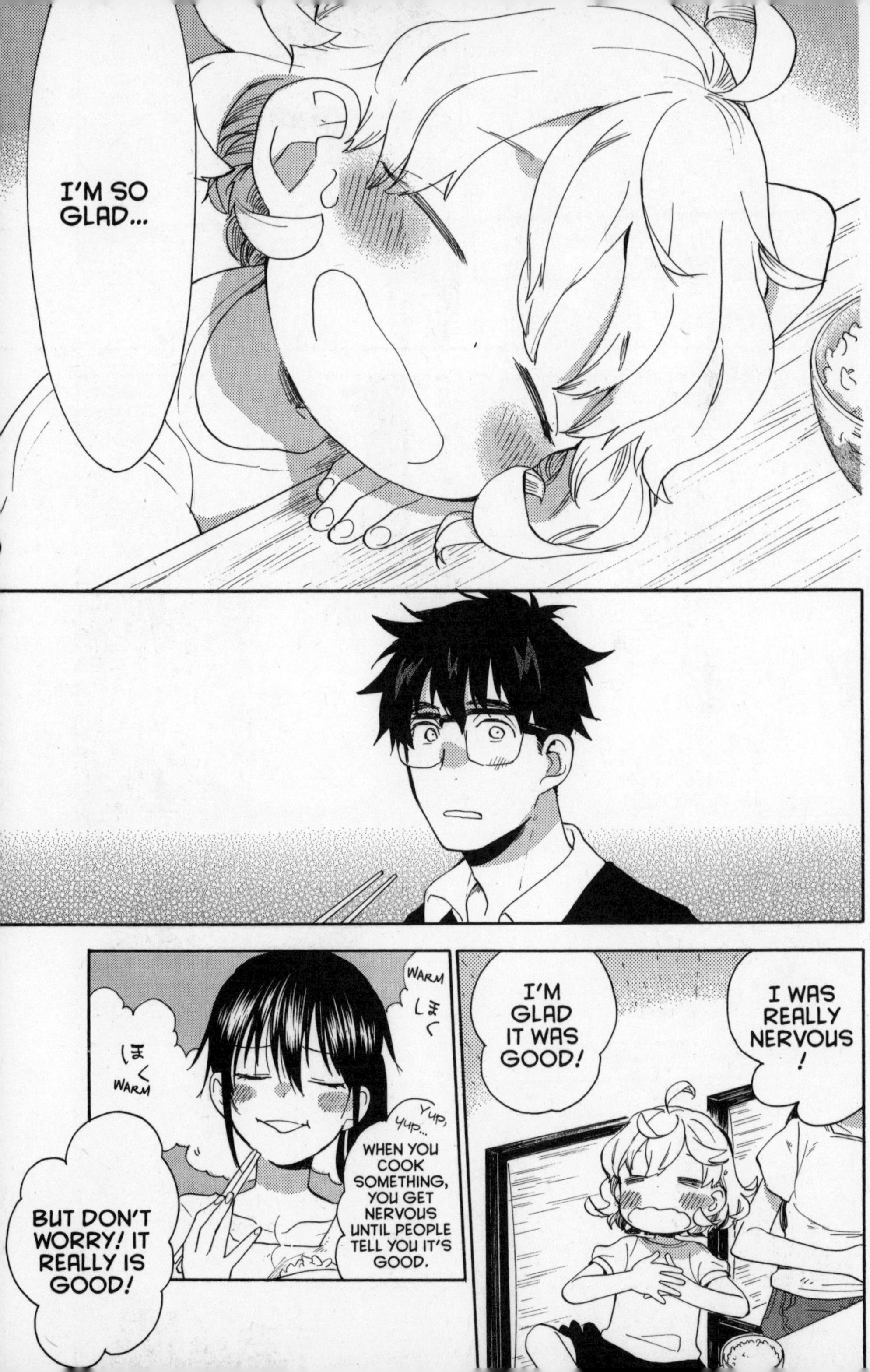
I'M SO GLAD...
I WAS REALLY NERVOUS!
I'M GLAD IT WAS GOOD!
WARM ほく
ほく WARM
Yup, yup...
WHEN YOU COOK SOMETHING, YOU GET NERVOUS UNTIL PEOPLE TELL YOU IT'S GOOD.
BUT DON'T WORRY! IT REALLY IS GOOD!

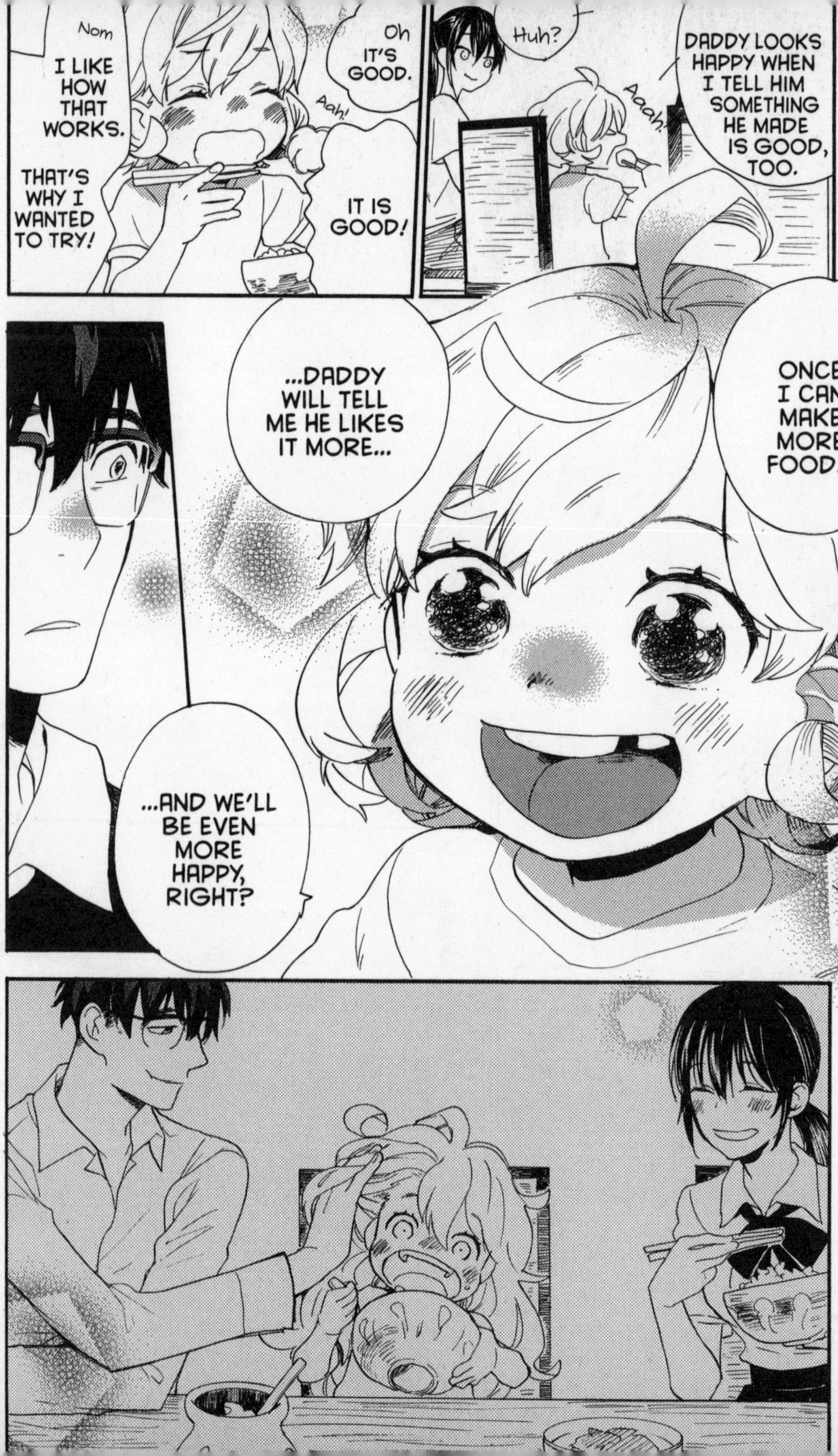
DADDY LOOKS HAPPY WHEN I TELL HIM SOMETHING HE MADE IS GOOD, TOO.
Huh?
Aaah!
Oh IT'S GOOD.
Nom
I LIKE HOW THAT WORKS.
Aah!
IT IS GOOD!
THAT'S WHY I WANTED TO TRY!
ONCE I CAN MAKE MORE FOOD...
...DADDY WILL TELL ME HE LIKES IT MORE...
...AND WE'LL BE EVEN MORE HAPPY, RIGHT?

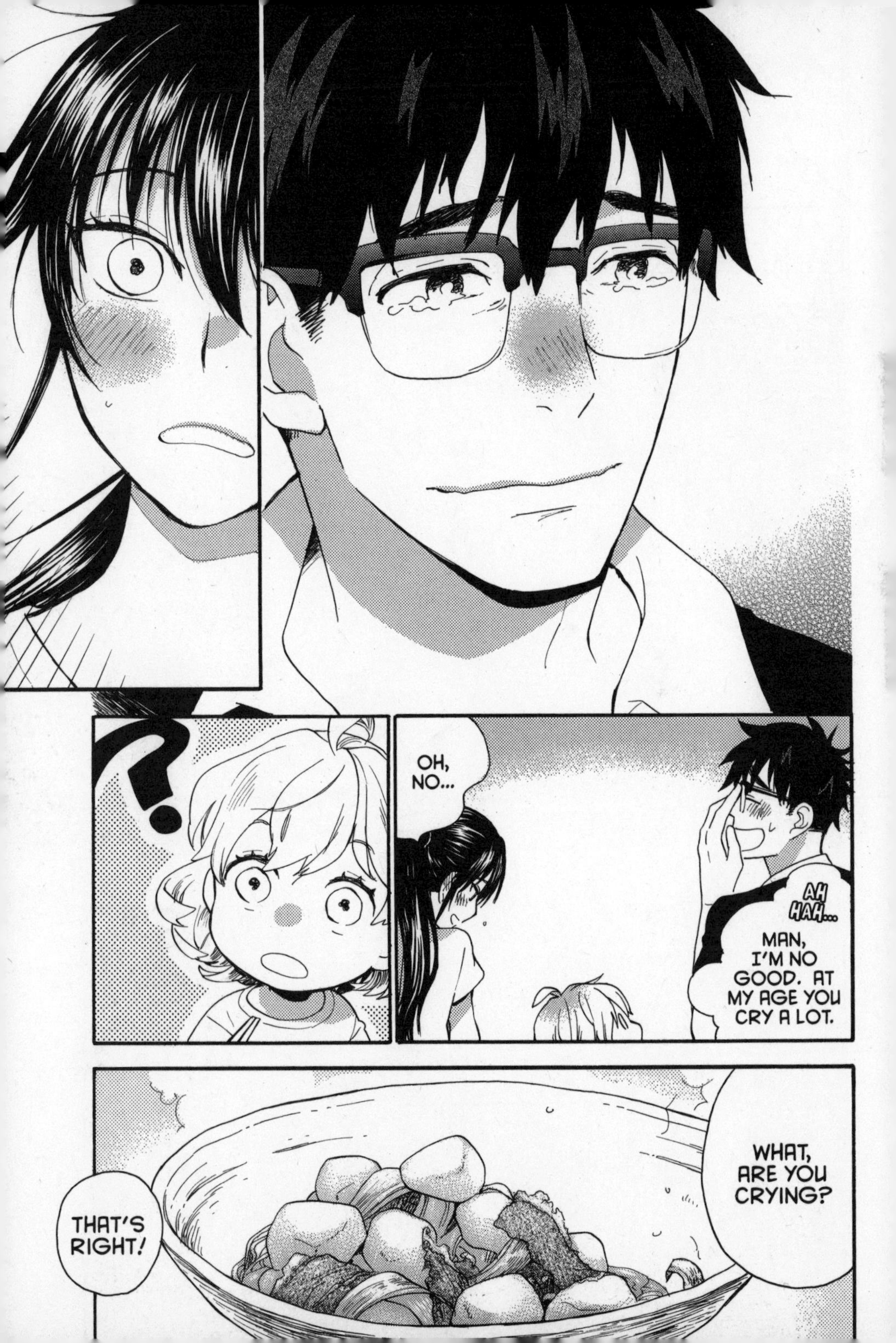
OH, NO...
AH HAH...
MAN, I'M NO GOOD. AT MY AGE YOU CRY A LOT.
?
WHAT, ARE YOU CRYING?
THAT'S RIGHT!

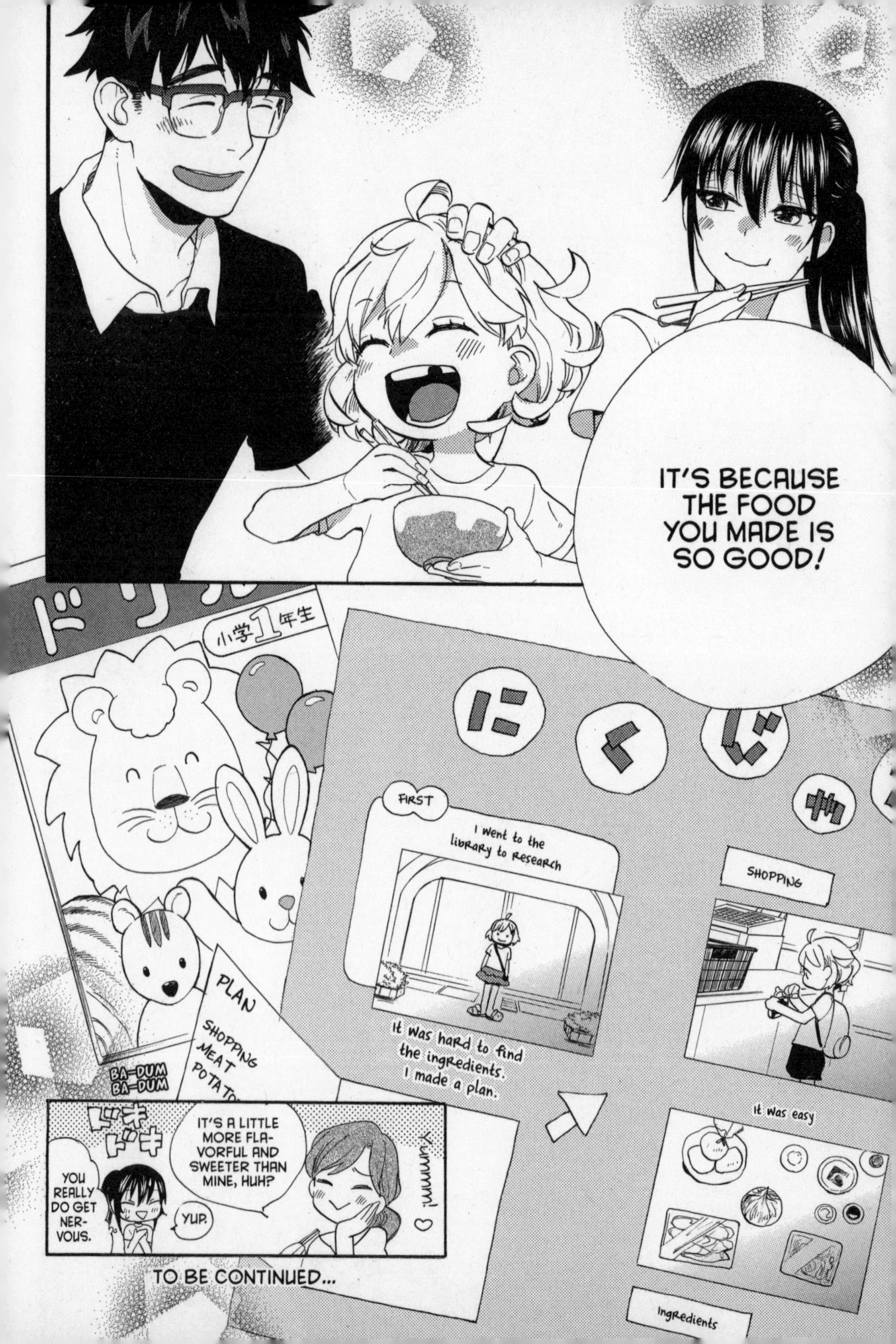

IT'S BECAUSE THE FOOD YOU MADE IS SO GOOD!
にくじゃ
SHOPPING
It was easy
Ingredients
FIRST
I went to the library to research
It was hard to find the ingredients. I made a plan.
小学1年生
ドリ
PLAN
SHOPPING
MEAT
POTATO
BA-DUM BA-DUM
Yummm!
IT'S A LITTLE MORE FLAVORFUL AND SWEETER THAN MINE, HUH?
YUP.
ドキドキ
YOU REALLY DO GET NERVOUS.
TO BE CONTINUED...

Tsumugi's NIKU - JAGA

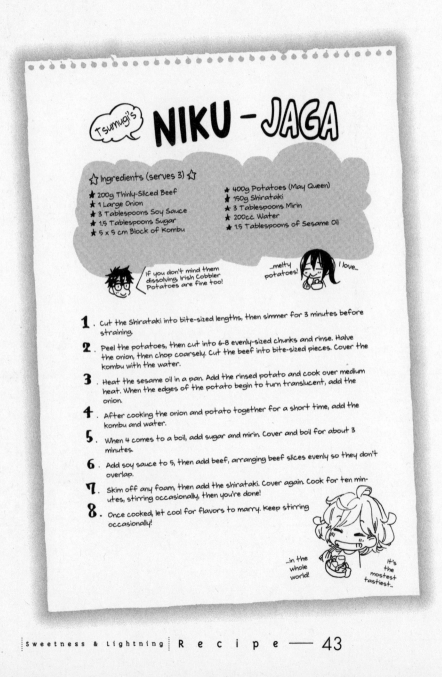

☆ Ingredients (serves 3) ☆

- ★ 200g Thinly-Sliced Beef
- ★ 1 Large Onion
- ★ 3 Tablespoons Soy Sauce
- ★ 1.5 Tablespoons Sugar
- ★ 5 x 5 cm Block of Kombu
- ★ 400g Potatoes (May Queen)
- ★ 150g Shirataki
- ★ 3 Tablespoons Mirin
- ★ 200cc Water
- ★ 1.5 Tablespoons of Sesame Oil

If you don't mind them dissolving, Irish Cobbler Potatoes are fine too!

I love...
...melty potatoes!

1. Cut the Shirataki into bite-sized lengths, then simmer for 3 minutes before straining.
2. Peel the potatoes, then cut into 6-8 evenly-sized chunks and rinse. Halve the onion, then chop coarsely. Cut the beef into bite-sized pieces. Cover the kombu with the water.
3. Heat the sesame oil in a pan. Add the rinsed potato and cook over medium heat. When the edges of the potato begin to turn translucent, add the onion.
4. After cooking the onion and potato together for a short time, add the kombu and water.
5. When 4 comes to a boil, add sugar and mirin. Cover and boil for about 3 minutes.
6. Add soy sauce to 5, then add beef, arranging beef slices evenly so they don't overlap.
7. Skim off any foam, then add the shirataki. Cover again. Cook for ten minutes, stirring occasionally, then you're done!
8. Once cooked, let cool for flavors to marry. Keep stirring occasionally!

It's the mostest tastiest...
...in the whole world!

KYOKO AND NAGISA
GO THE SAME PRESCHOOL

It's
okay.

Sorry
I was mean
to you...

Chapter 44 | It's Yummy! It's New! It's Fish Curry!

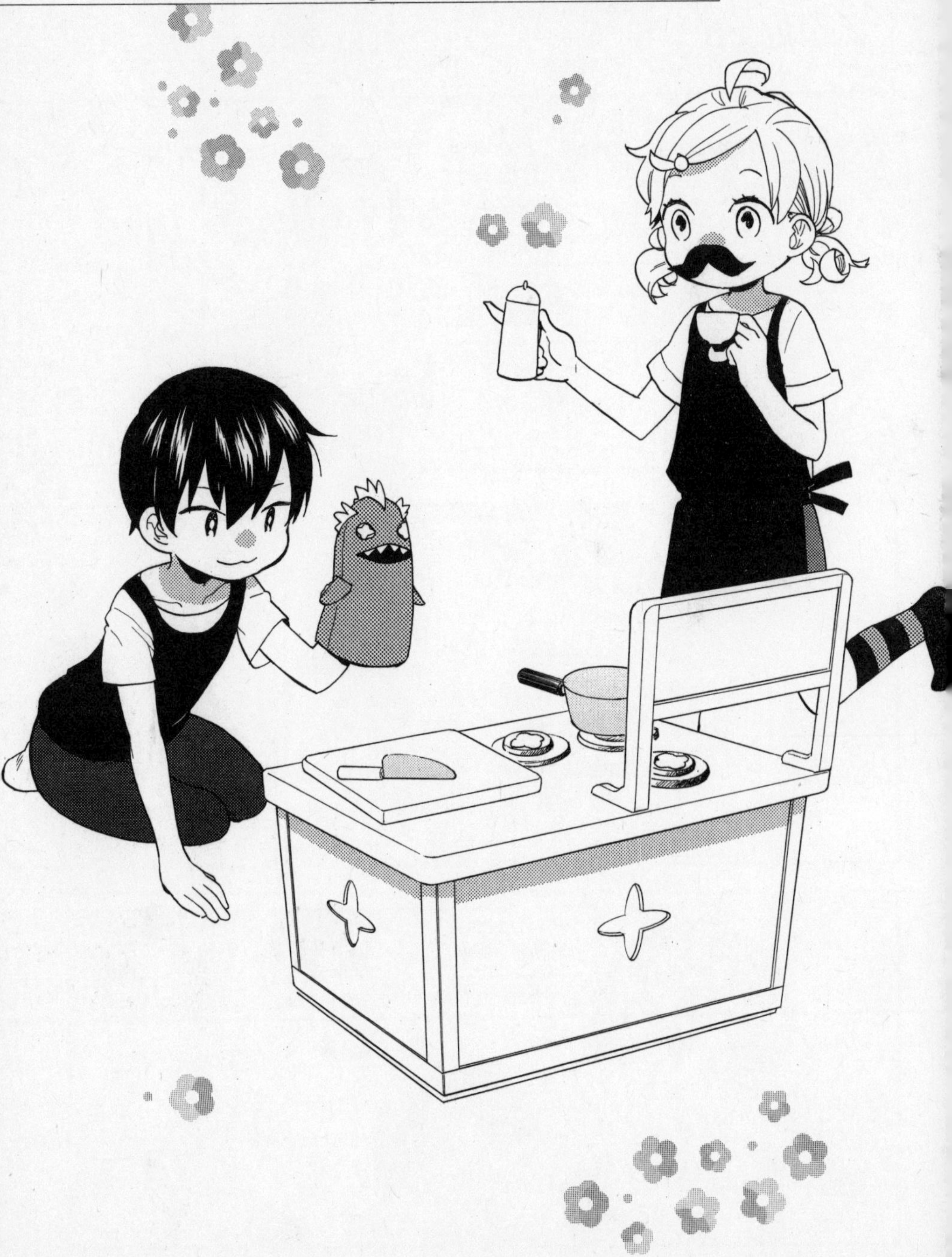

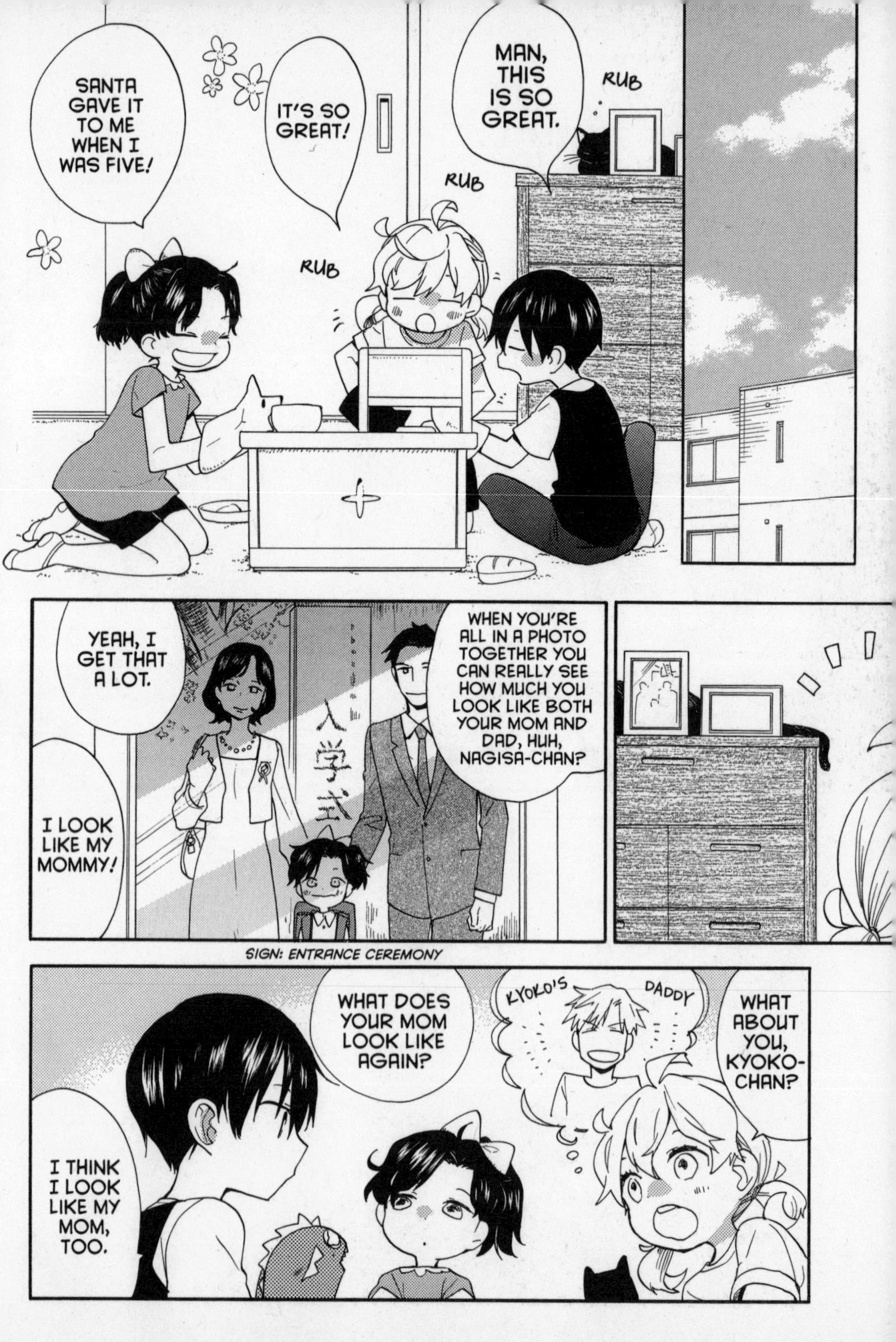
MAN, THIS IS SO GREAT.
RUB
IT'S SO GREAT!
RUB
SANTA GAVE IT TO ME WHEN I WAS FIVE!
RUB
WHEN YOU'RE ALL IN A PHOTO TOGETHER YOU CAN REALLY SEE HOW MUCH YOU LOOK LIKE BOTH YOUR MOM AND DAD, HUH, NAGISA-CHAN?
YEAH, I GET THAT A LOT.
I LOOK LIKE MY MOMMY!
入学式
SIGN: ENTRANCE CEREMONY
WHAT ABOUT YOU, KYOKO-CHAN?
KYOKO'S DADDY
WHAT DOES YOUR MOM LOOK LIKE AGAIN?
I THINK I LOOK LIKE MY MOM, TOO.

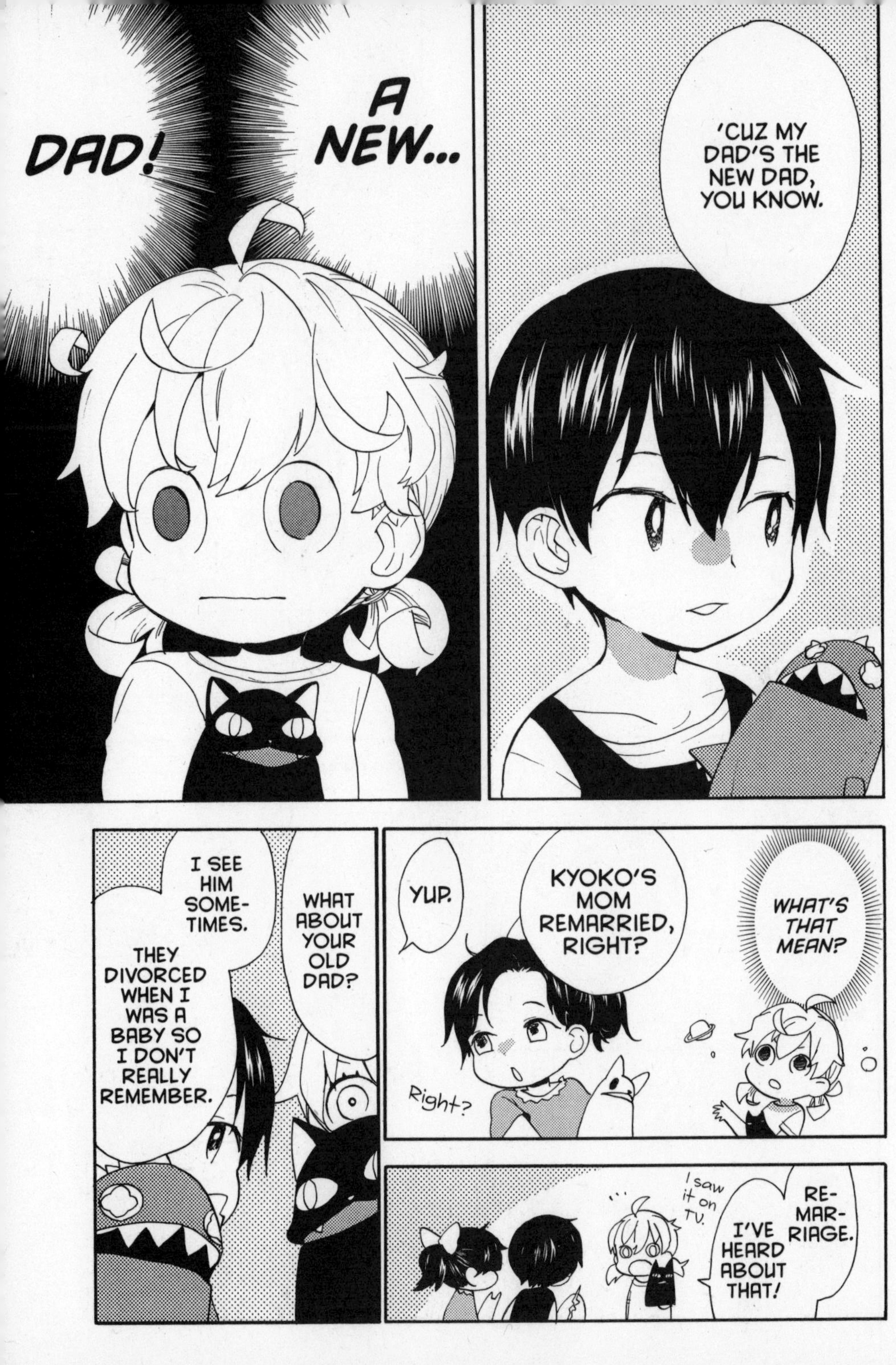
'CUZ MY DAD'S THE NEW DAD, YOU KNOW.
A NEW...
DAD!
WHAT'S THAT MEAN?
KYOKO'S MOM REMARRIED, RIGHT?
YUP.
Right?
RE-MAR-RIAGE.
I'VE HEARD ABOUT THAT!
I saw it on TV.
WHAT ABOUT YOUR OLD DAD?
I SEE HIM SOMETIMES.
THEY DIVORCED WHEN I WAS A BABY SO I DON'T REALLY REMEMBER.

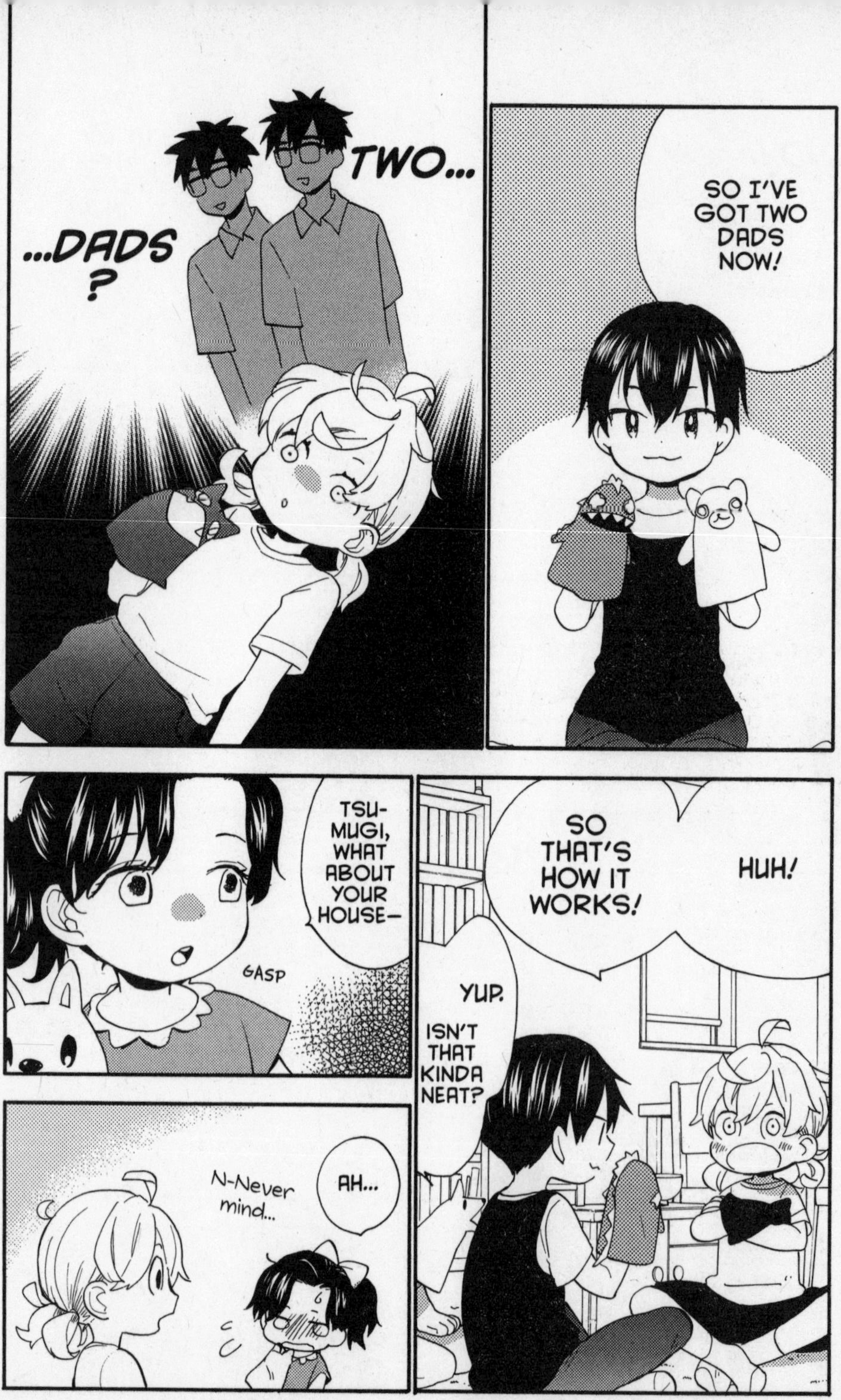

SO I'VE GOT TWO DADS NOW!
TWO...
...DADS ?
HUH!
SO THAT'S HOW IT WORKS!
YUP.
ISN'T THAT KINDA NEAT?
TSU-MUGI, WHAT ABOUT YOUR HOUSE—
GASP
AH...
N-Never mind...

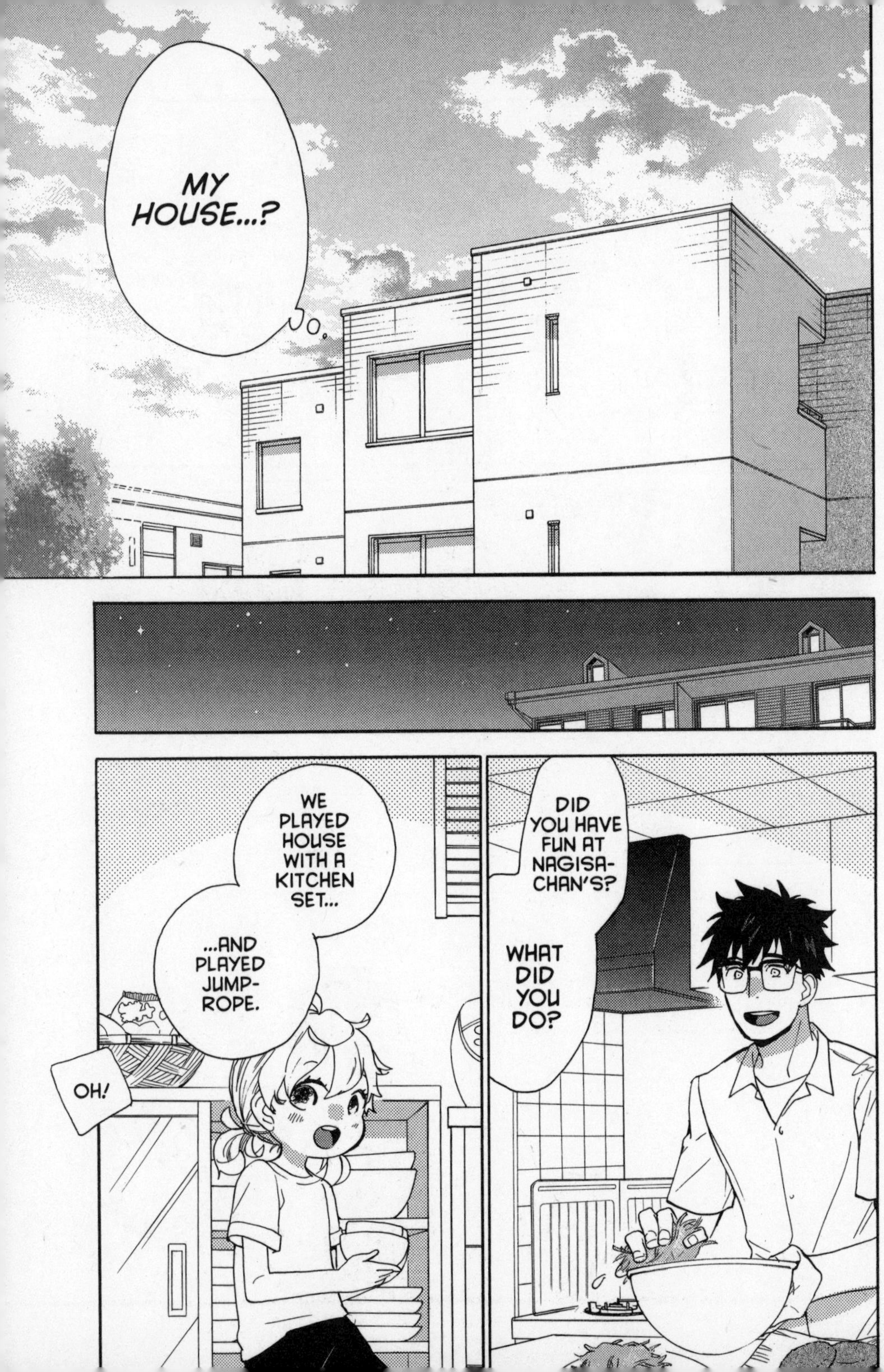
MY HOUSE...?
DID YOU HAVE FUN AT NAGISA-CHAN'S?
WHAT DID YOU DO?
WE PLAYED HOUSE WITH A KITCHEN SET...
...AND PLAYED JUMP-ROPE.
OH!

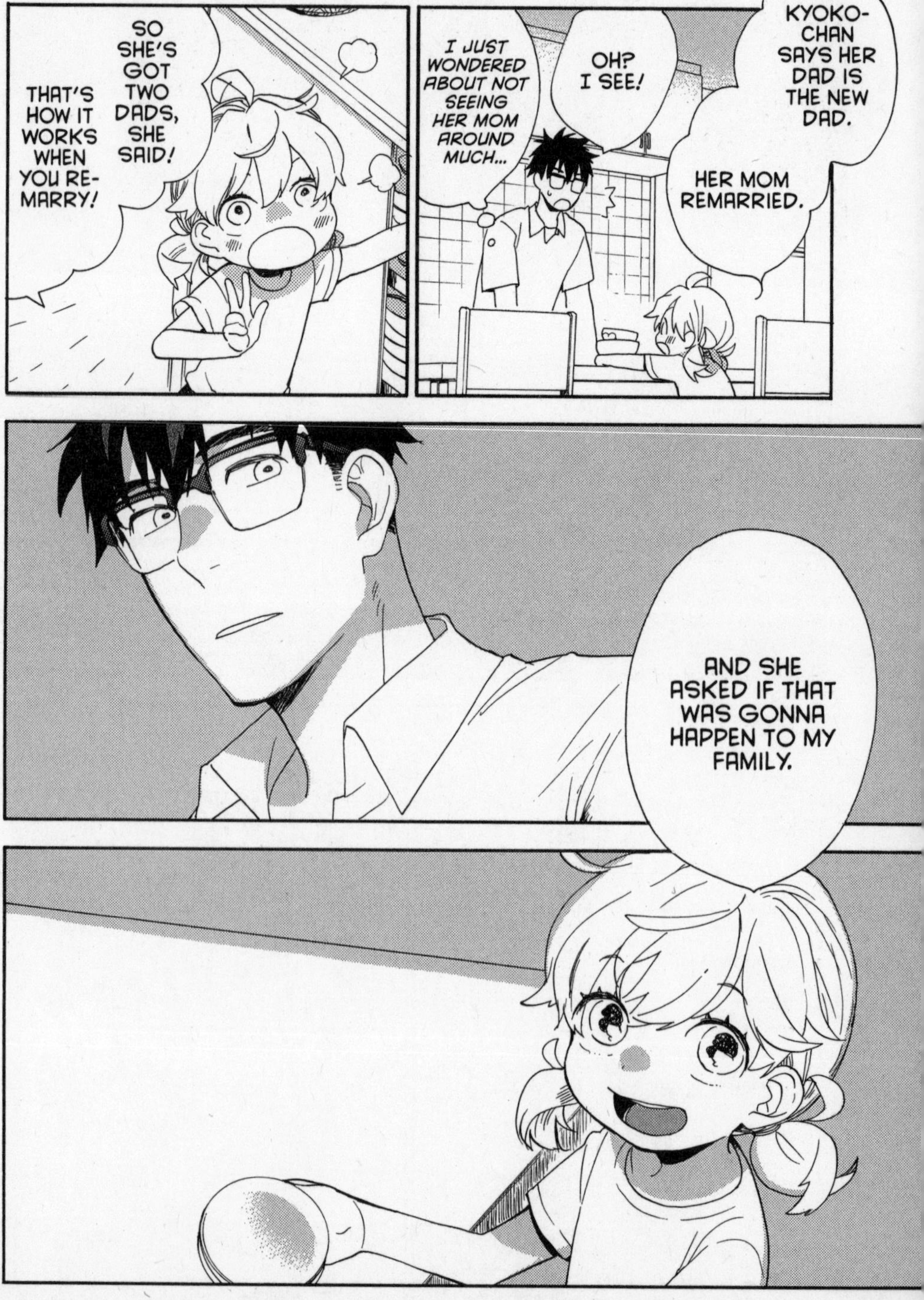
KYOKO-CHAN SAYS HER DAD IS THE NEW DAD.
HER MOM REMARRIED.
OH? I SEE!
I JUST WONDERED ABOUT NOT SEEING HER MOM AROUND MUCH...
SO SHE'S GOT TWO DADS, SHE SAID!
THAT'S HOW IT WORKS WHEN YOU RE-MARRY!
AND SHE ASKED IF THAT WAS GONNA HAPPEN TO MY FAMILY.

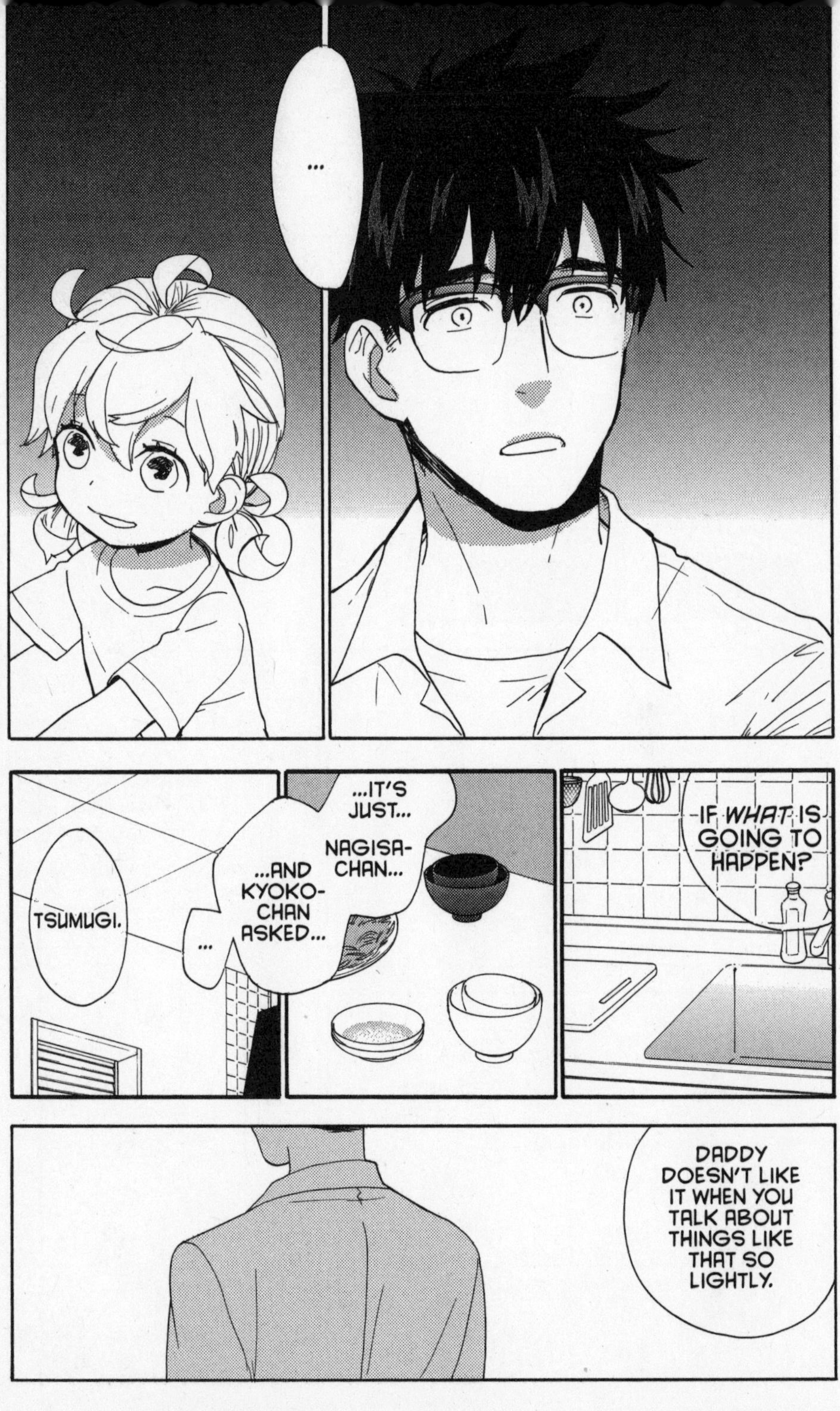
...
IF *WHAT* IS GOING TO HAPPEN?
...IT'S JUST...
NAGISA-CHAN...
...AND KYOKO-CHAN ASKED...
...
TSUMUGI.
DADDY DOESN'T LIKE IT WHEN YOU TALK ABOUT THINGS LIKE THAT SO LIGHTLY.

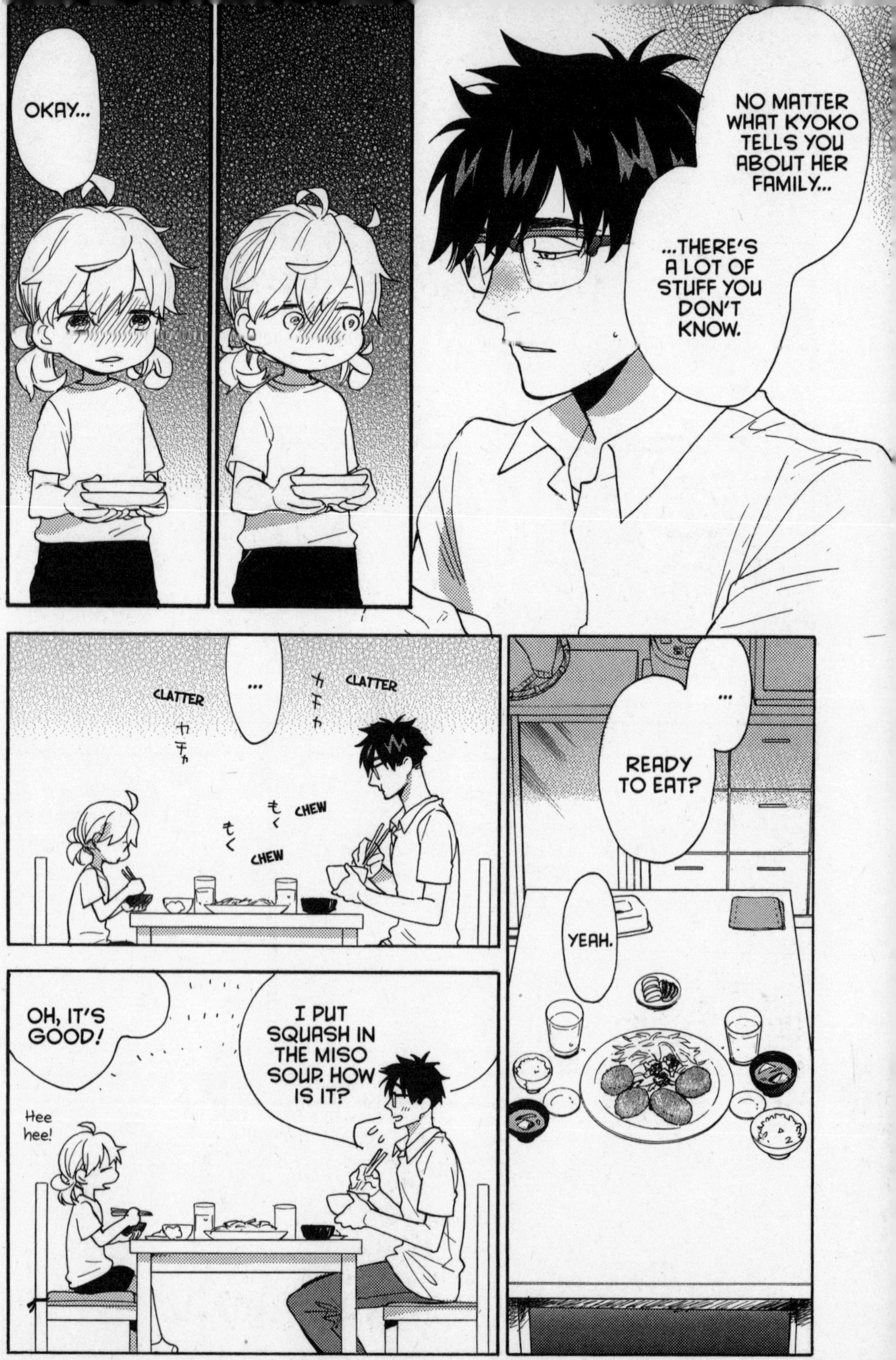
NO MATTER WHAT KYOKO TELLS YOU ABOUT HER FAMILY...
...THERE'S A LOT OF STUFF YOU DON'T KNOW.
OKAY...
...
READY TO EAT?
YEAH.
CLATTER
カチャ
...
CLATTER
カチャ
CHEW
もく
CHEW
もく
I PUT SQUASH IN THE MISO SOUP. HOW IS IT?
OH, IT'S GOOD!
Hee hee!

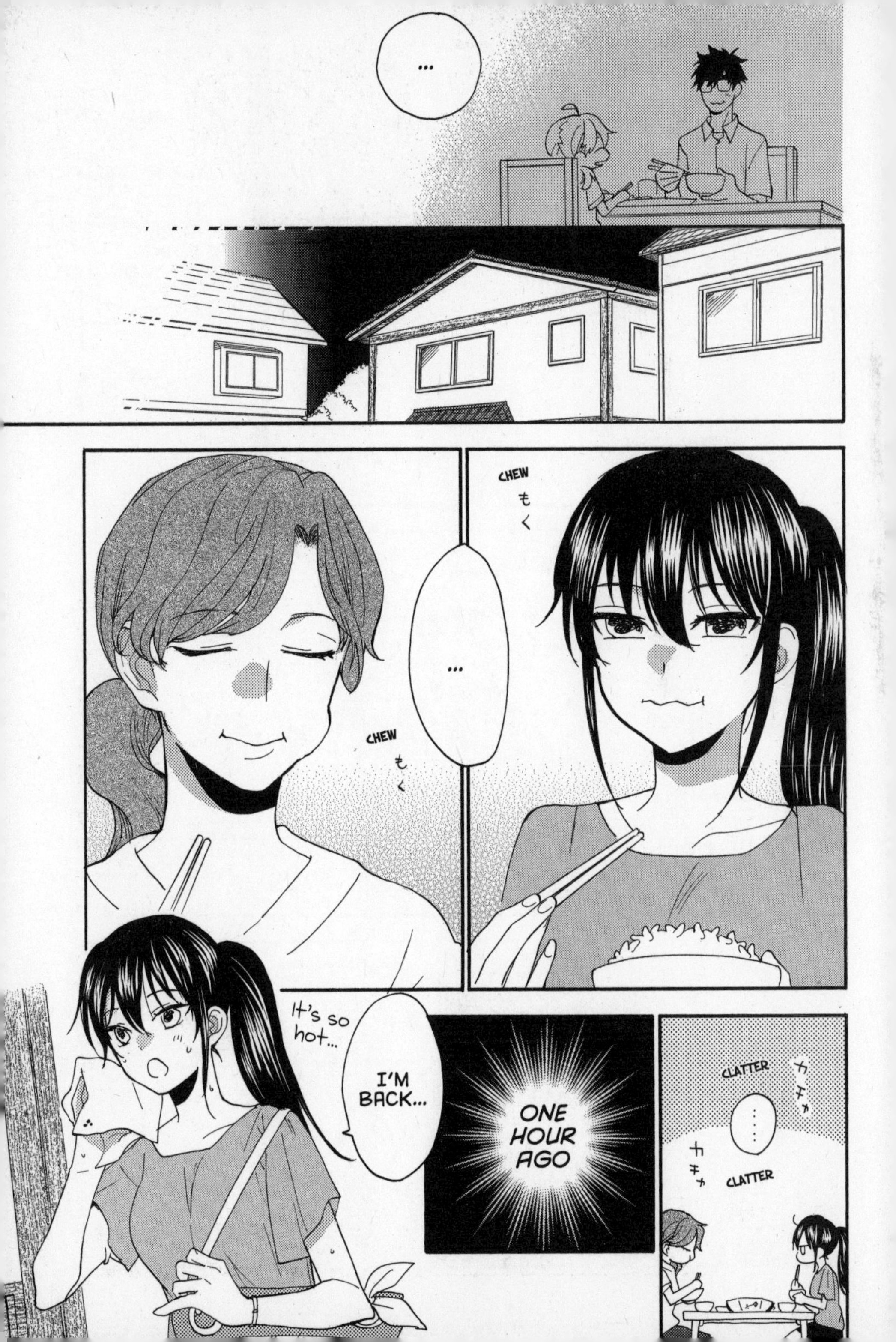
...
CHEW
もく
...
CHEW
もく
CLATTER
カチャ
......
カチャ
CLATTER
ONE HOUR AGO
I'M BACK...
It's so hot...

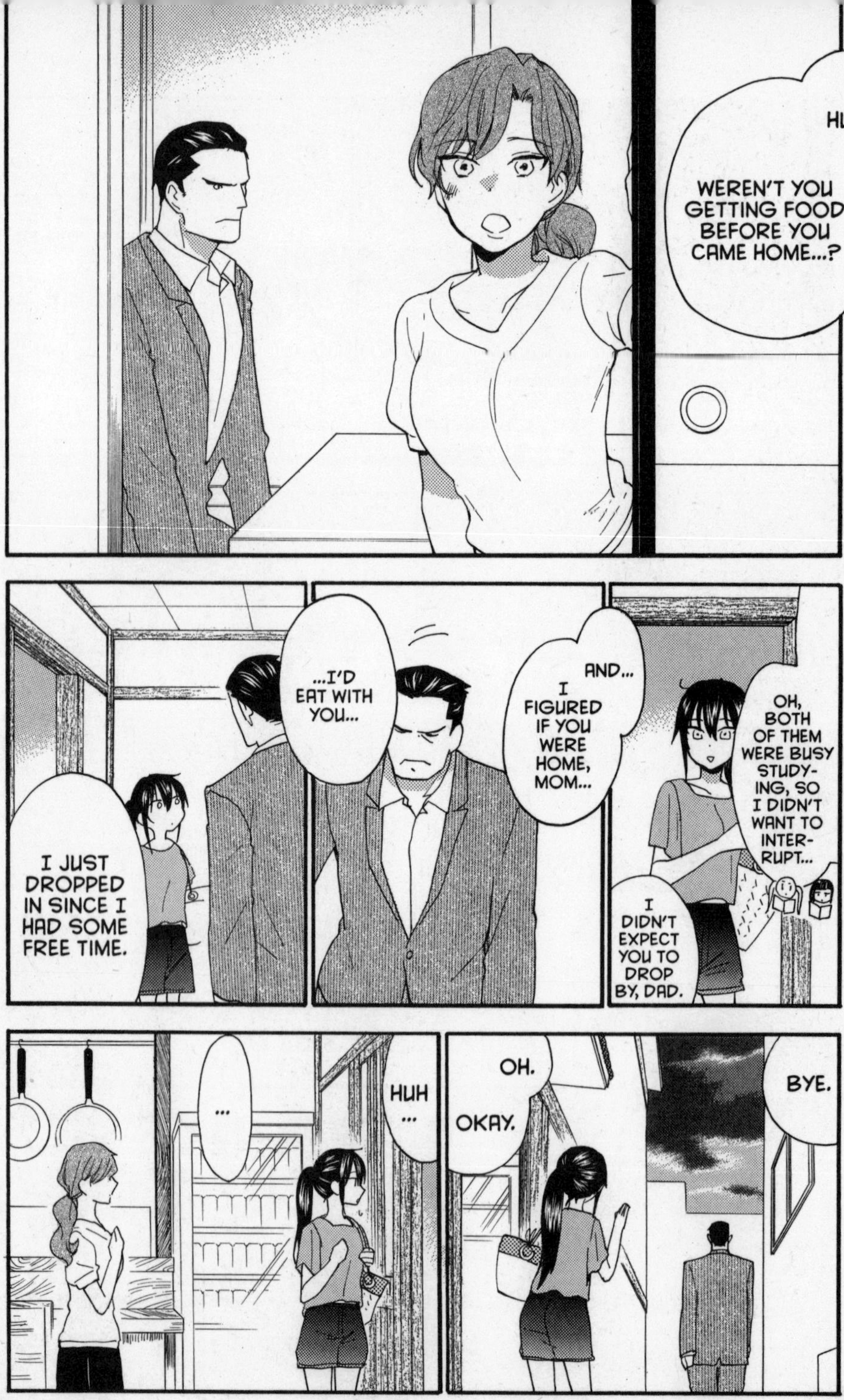
HUH?
WEREN'T YOU GETTING FOOD BEFORE YOU CAME HOME...?
OH, BOTH OF THEM WERE BUSY STUDYING, SO I DIDN'T WANT TO INTERRUPT...
I DIDN'T EXPECT YOU TO DROP BY, DAD.
AND... I FIGURED IF YOU WERE HOME, MOM...
...I'D EAT WITH YOU...
I JUST DROPPED IN SINCE I HAD SOME FREE TIME.
BYE.
OH.
OKAY.
HUH ...
...

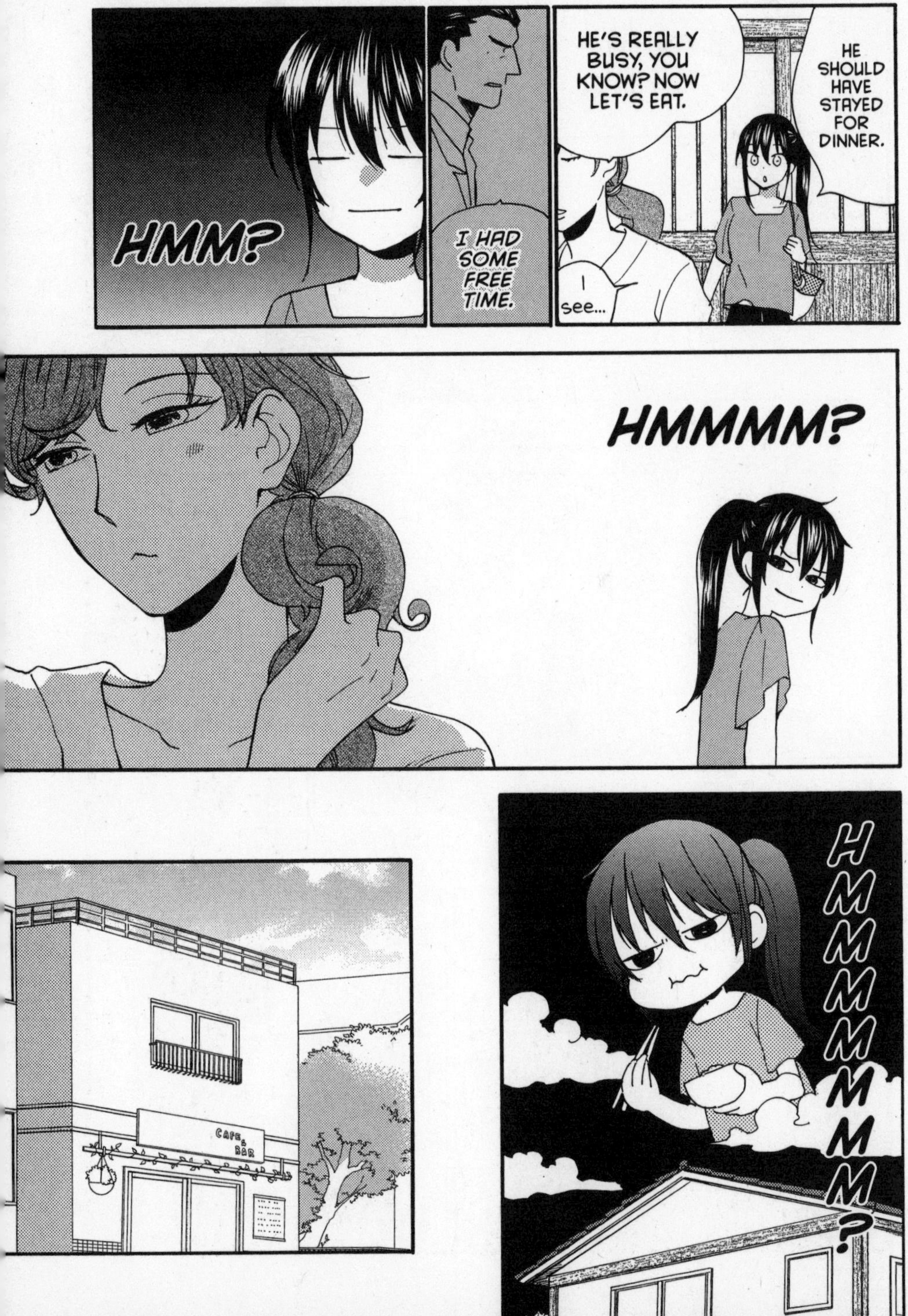
HE SHOULD HAVE STAYED FOR DINNER.
HE'S REALLY BUSY, YOU KNOW? NOW LET'S EAT.
I see...
I HAD SOME FREE TIME.
HMM?
HMMMM?
HMMMMMMM?
CAFE & BAR

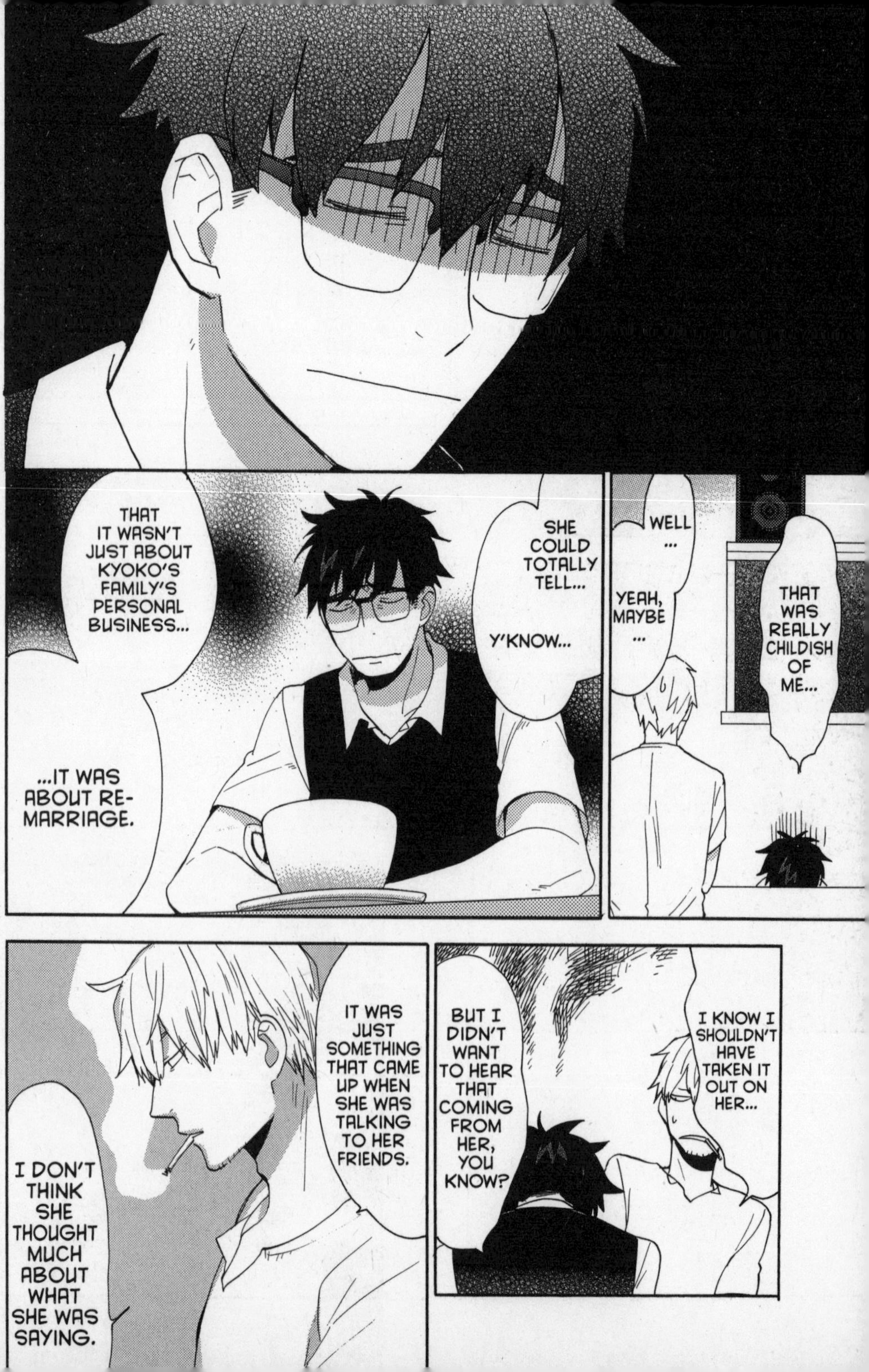
WELL...
YEAH, MAYBE...
THAT WAS REALLY CHILDISH OF ME...
SHE COULD TOTALLY TELL... Y'KNOW...
THAT IT WASN'T JUST ABOUT KYOKO'S FAMILY'S PERSONAL BUSINESS...
...IT WAS ABOUT RE-MARRIAGE.
I KNOW I SHOULDN'T HAVE TAKEN IT OUT ON HER...
BUT I DIDN'T WANT TO HEAR THAT COMING FROM HER, YOU KNOW?
IT WAS JUST SOMETHING THAT CAME UP WHEN SHE WAS TALKING TO HER FRIENDS.
I DON'T THINK SHE THOUGHT MUCH ABOUT WHAT SHE WAS SAYING.

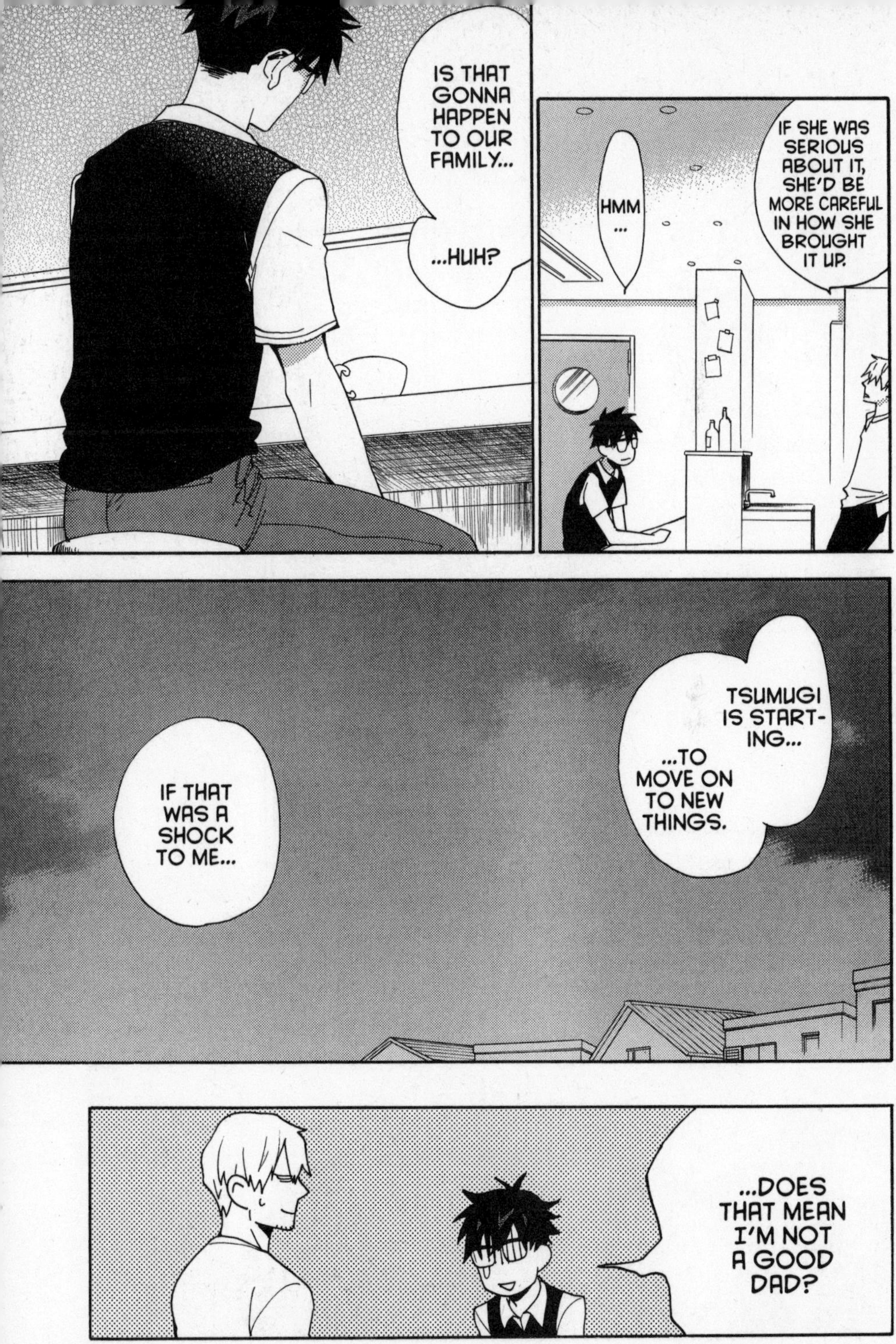
IF SHE WAS SERIOUS ABOUT IT, SHE'D BE MORE CAREFUL IN HOW SHE BROUGHT IT UP.
HMM...
IS THAT GONNA HAPPEN TO OUR FAMILY...
...HUH?
TSUMUGI IS START-ING...
...TO MOVE ON TO NEW THINGS.
IF THAT WAS A SHOCK TO ME...
...DOES THAT MEAN I'M NOT A GOOD DAD?

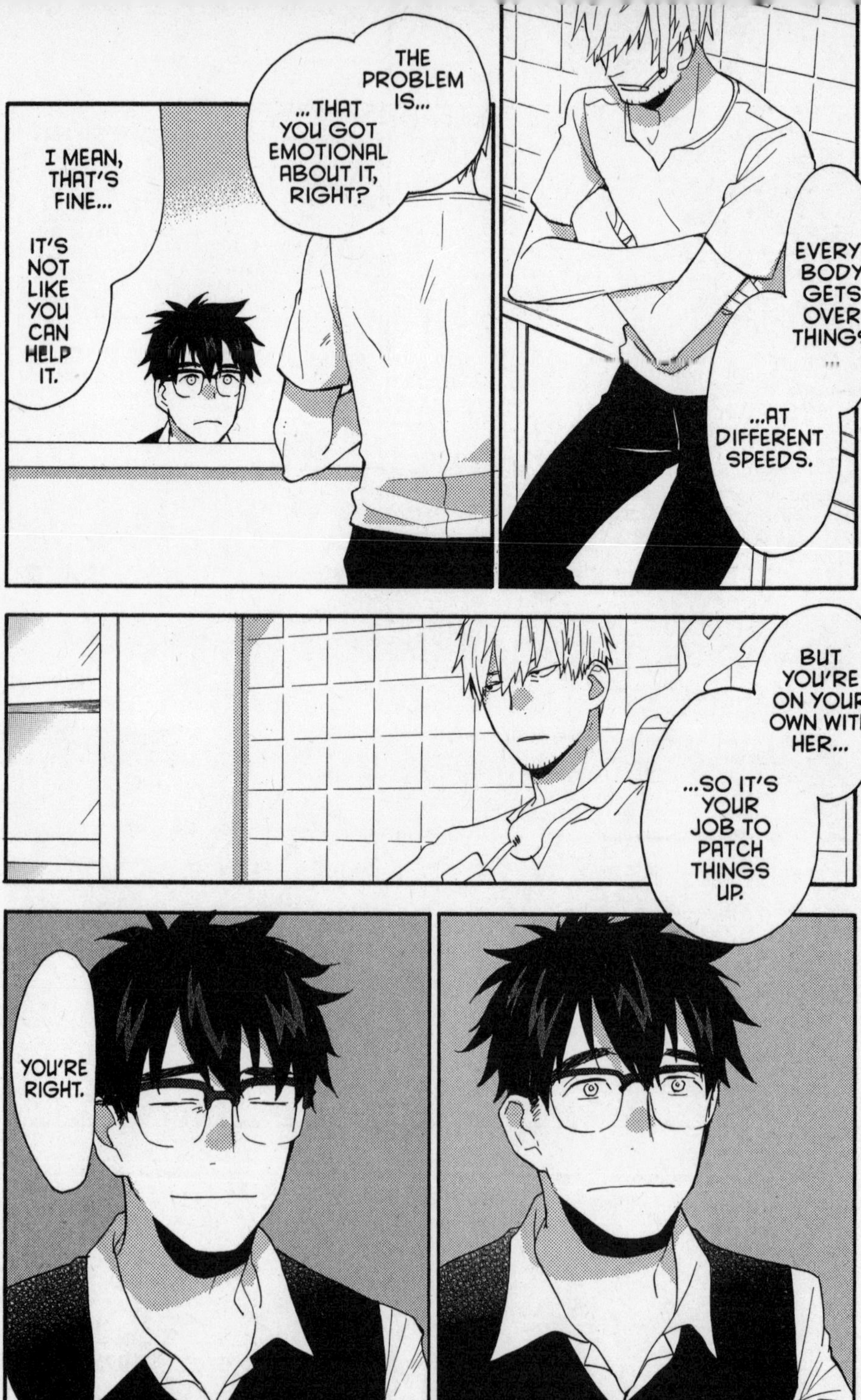
THE PROBLEM IS...
...THAT YOU GOT EMOTIONAL ABOUT IT, RIGHT?
I MEAN, THAT'S FINE...
IT'S NOT LIKE YOU CAN HELP IT.
EVERYBODY GETS OVER THINGS ...
...AT DIFFERENT SPEEDS.
BUT YOU'RE ON YOUR OWN WITH HER...
...SO IT'S YOUR JOB TO PATCH THINGS UP.
YOU'RE RIGHT.

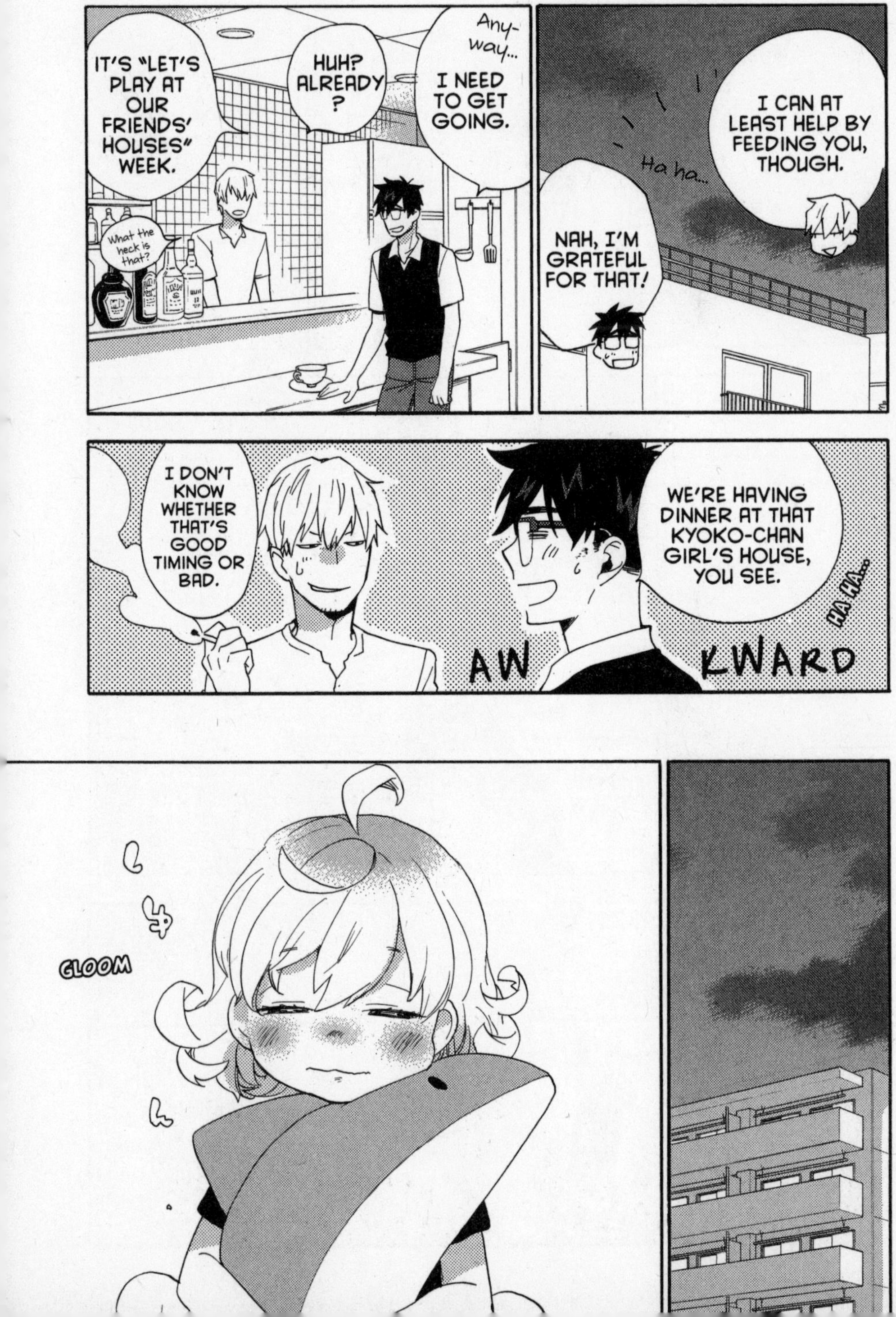
I CAN AT LEAST HELP BY FEEDING YOU, THOUGH.
Ha ha...
NAH, I'M GRATEFUL FOR THAT!
Any-way...
I NEED TO GET GOING.
HUH? ALREADY?
IT'S "LET'S PLAY AT OUR FRIENDS' HOUSES" WEEK.
What the heck is that?
WE'RE HAVING DINNER AT THAT KYOKO-CHAN GIRL'S HOUSE, YOU SEE.
HA HA...
AWKWARD
I DON'T KNOW WHETHER THAT'S GOOD TIMING OR BAD.
GLOOM

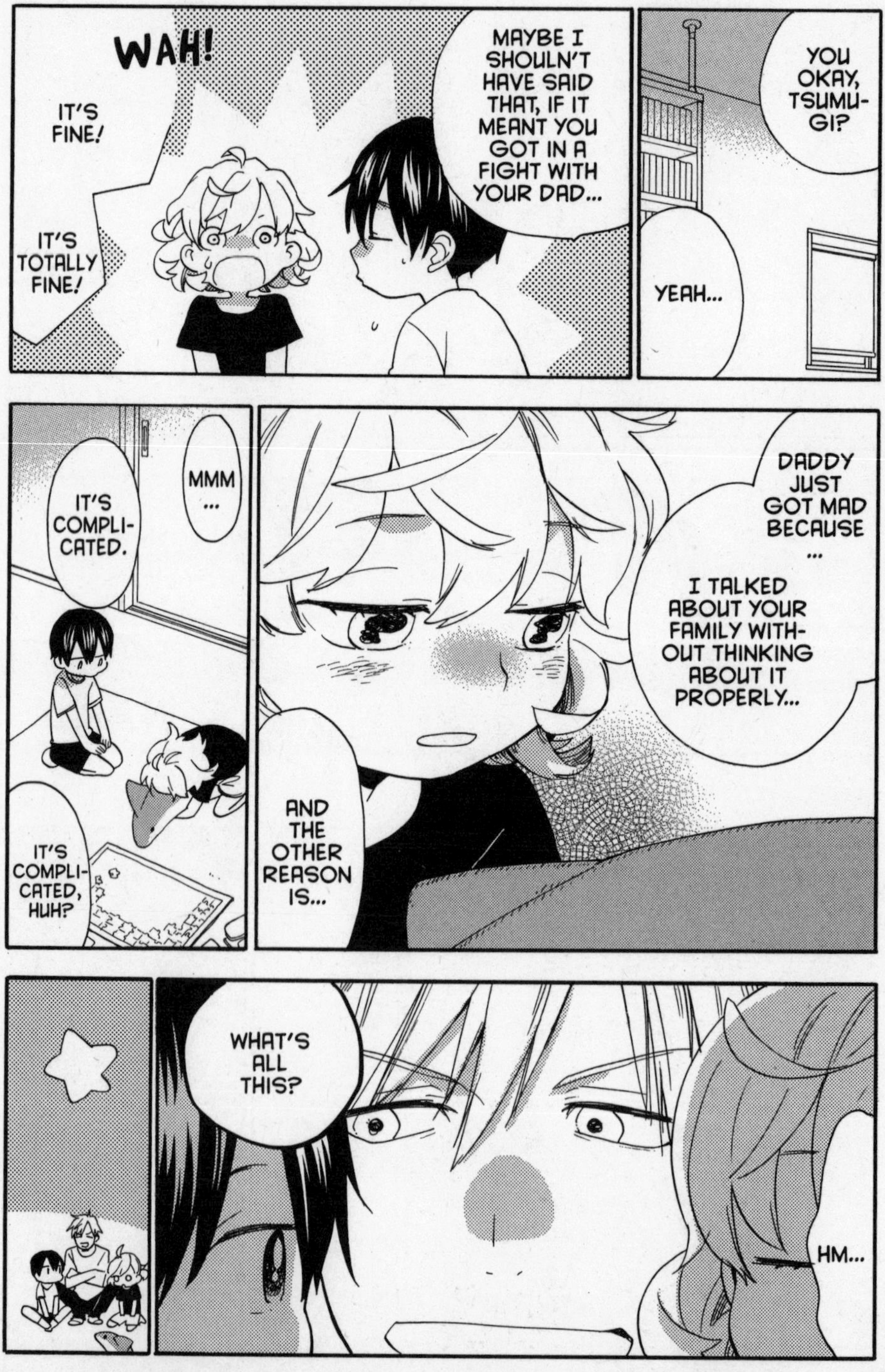
YOU OKAY, TSUMUGI?
YEAH...
MAYBE I SHOULN'T HAVE SAID THAT, IF IT MEANT YOU GOT IN A FIGHT WITH YOUR DAD...
WAH!
IT'S FINE!
IT'S TOTALLY FINE!
DADDY JUST GOT MAD BECAUSE ...
I TALKED ABOUT YOUR FAMILY WITHOUT THINKING ABOUT IT PROPERLY...
AND THE OTHER REASON IS...
MMM ...
IT'S COMPLICATED.
IT'S COMPLICATED, HUH?
WHAT'S ALL THIS?
HM...

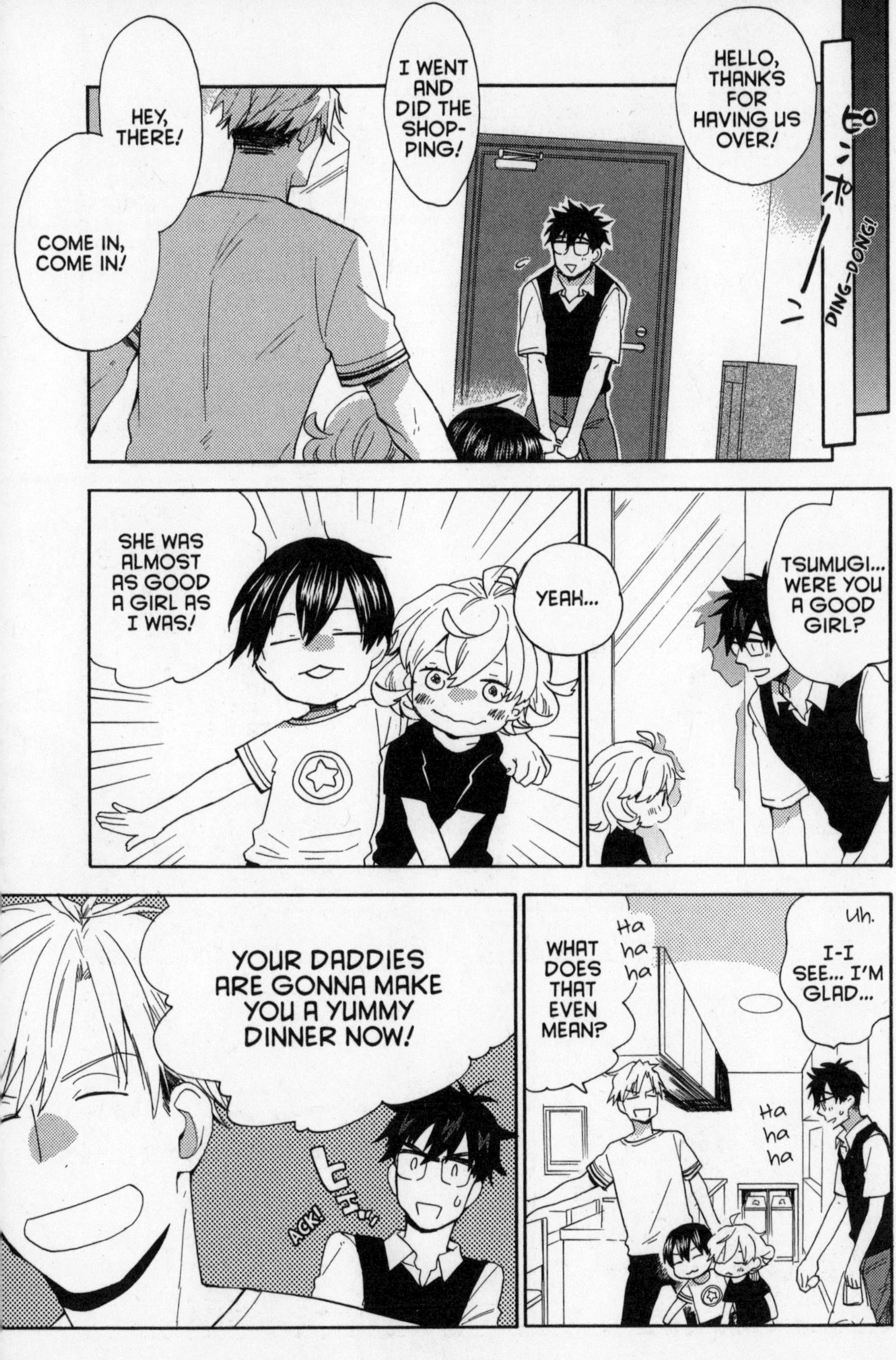
DING-DONG!
HELLO, THANKS FOR HAVING US OVER!
I WENT AND DID THE SHOP-PING!
HEY, THERE!
COME IN, COME IN!
TSUMUGI... WERE YOU A GOOD GIRL?
YEAH...
SHE WAS ALMOST AS GOOD A GIRL AS I WAS!
Uh.
I-I SEE... I'M GLAD...
Ha ha ha
WHAT DOES THAT EVEN MEAN?
Ha ha ha
YOUR DADDIES ARE GONNA MAKE YOU A YUMMY DINNER NOW!
ACK!

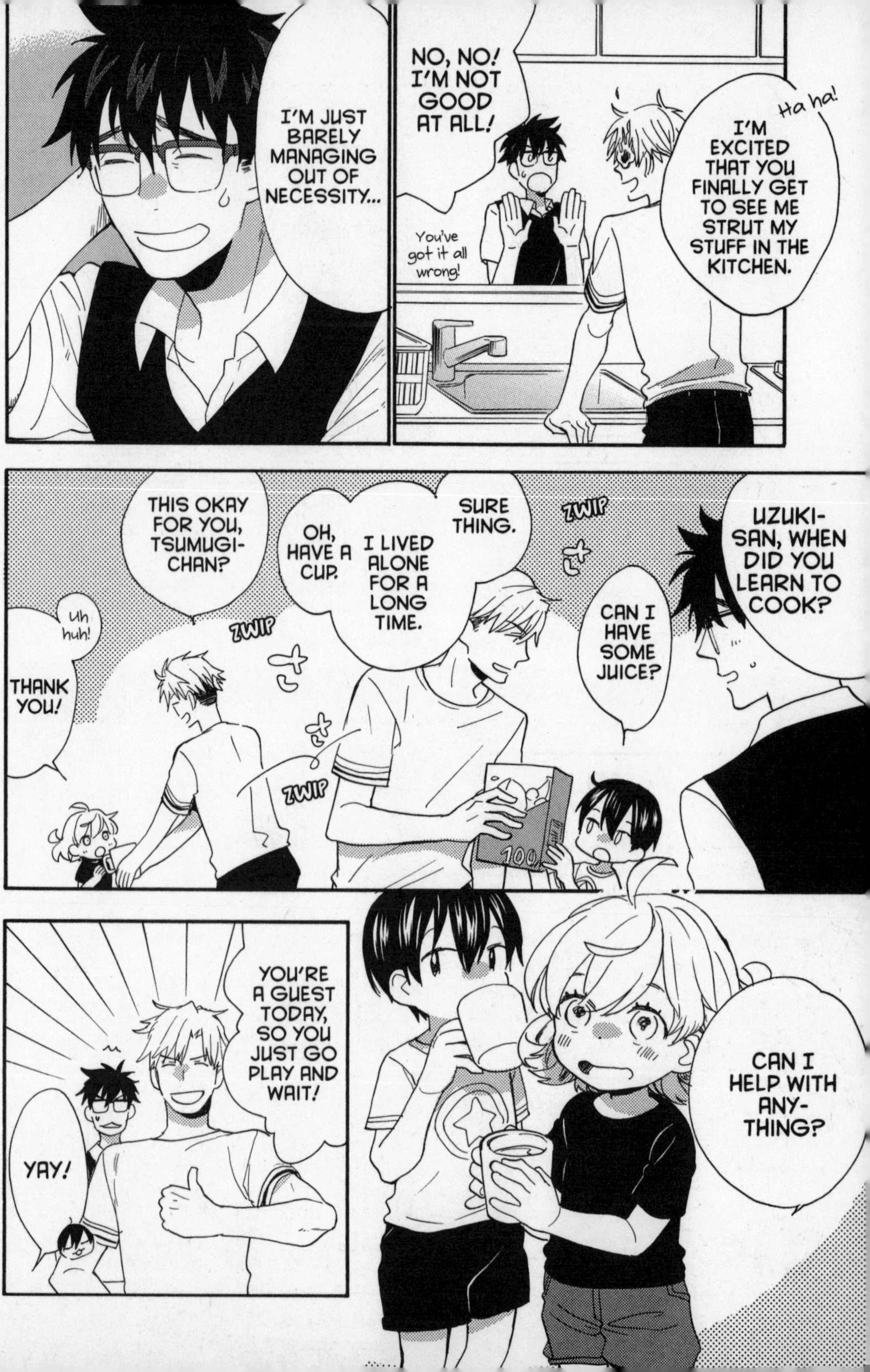
Ha ha!
I'M EXCITED THAT YOU FINALLY GET TO SEE ME STRUT MY STUFF IN THE KITCHEN.
NO, NO! I'M NOT GOOD AT ALL!
You've got it all wrong!
I'M JUST BARELY MANAGING OUT OF NECESSITY...
UZUKI-SAN, WHEN DID YOU LEARN TO COOK?
ZWIP
SURE THING.
CAN I HAVE SOME JUICE?
I LIVED ALONE FOR A LONG TIME.
OH, HAVE A CUP.
THIS OKAY FOR YOU, TSUMUGI-CHAN?
ZWIP
Uh huh!
THANK YOU!
ZWIP
CAN I HELP WITH ANY-THING?
YOU'RE A GUEST TODAY, SO YOU JUST GO PLAY AND WAIT!
YAY!

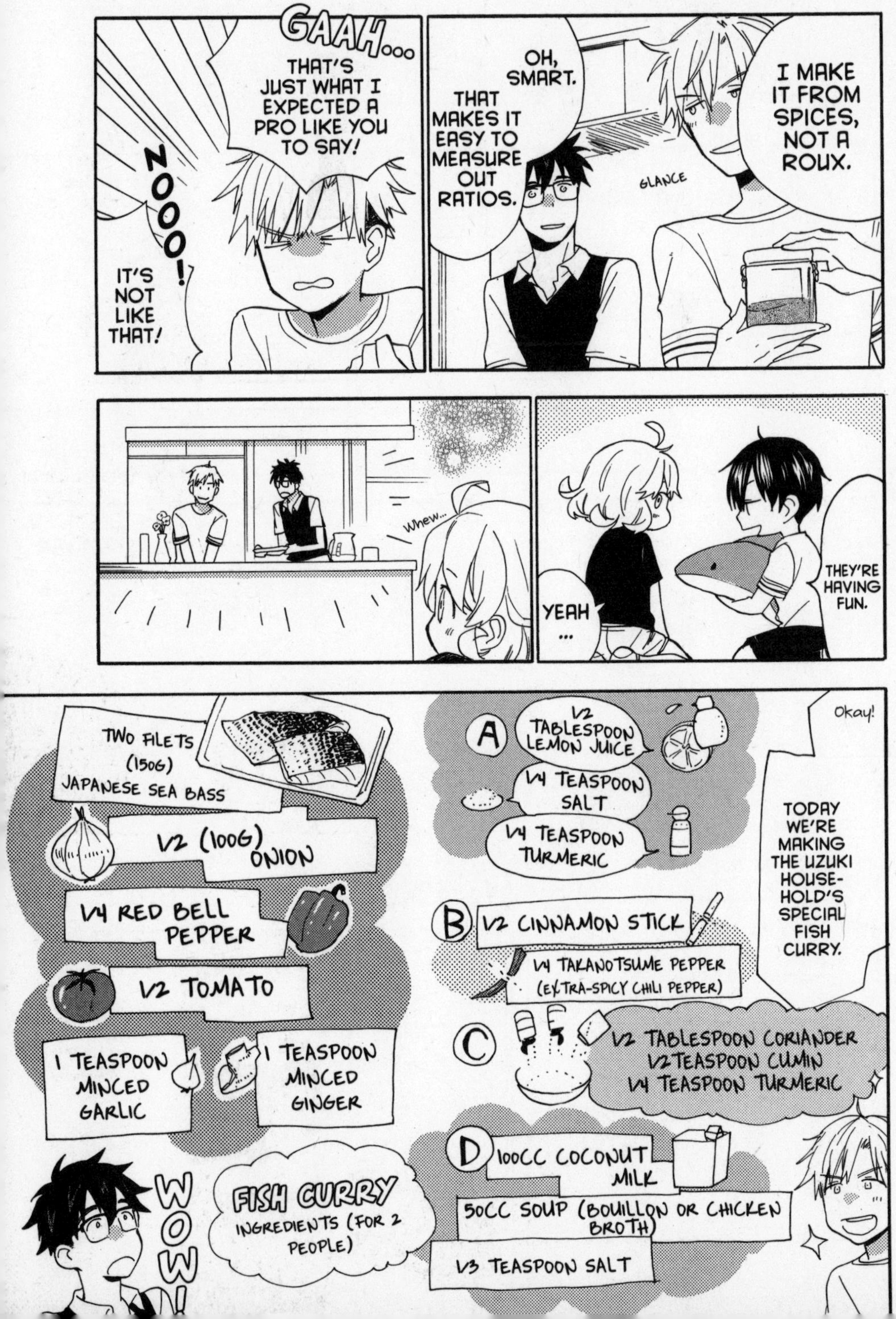
I MAKE IT FROM SPICES, NOT A ROUX.
GLANCE
OH, SMART.
THAT MAKES IT EASY TO MEASURE OUT RATIOS.
GAAH...
THAT'S JUST WHAT I EXPECTED A PRO LIKE YOU TO SAY!
NOOOO!
IT'S NOT LIKE THAT!
THEY'RE HAVING FUN.
YEAH...
Whew...
Okay!
TODAY WE'RE MAKING THE UZUKI HOUSE-HOLD'S SPECIAL FISH CURRY.
FISH CURRY
INGREDIENTS (FOR 2 PEOPLE)
WOW!
TWO FILETS (150G) JAPANESE SEA BASS
1/2 (100G) ONION
1/4 RED BELL PEPPER
1/2 TOMATO
1 TEASPOON MINCED GARLIC
1 TEASPOON MINCED GINGER
A
1/2 TABLESPOON LEMON JUICE
1/4 TEASPOON SALT
1/4 TEASPOON TURMERIC
B
1/2 CINNAMON STICK
1/4 TAKANOTSUME PEPPER (EXTRA-SPICY CHILI PEPPER)
C
1/2 TABLESPOON CORIANDER
1/2 TEASPOON CUMIN
1/4 TEASPOON TURMERIC
D
100CC COCONUT MILK
50CC SOUP (BOUILLON OR CHICKEN BROTH)
1/3 TEASPOON SALT

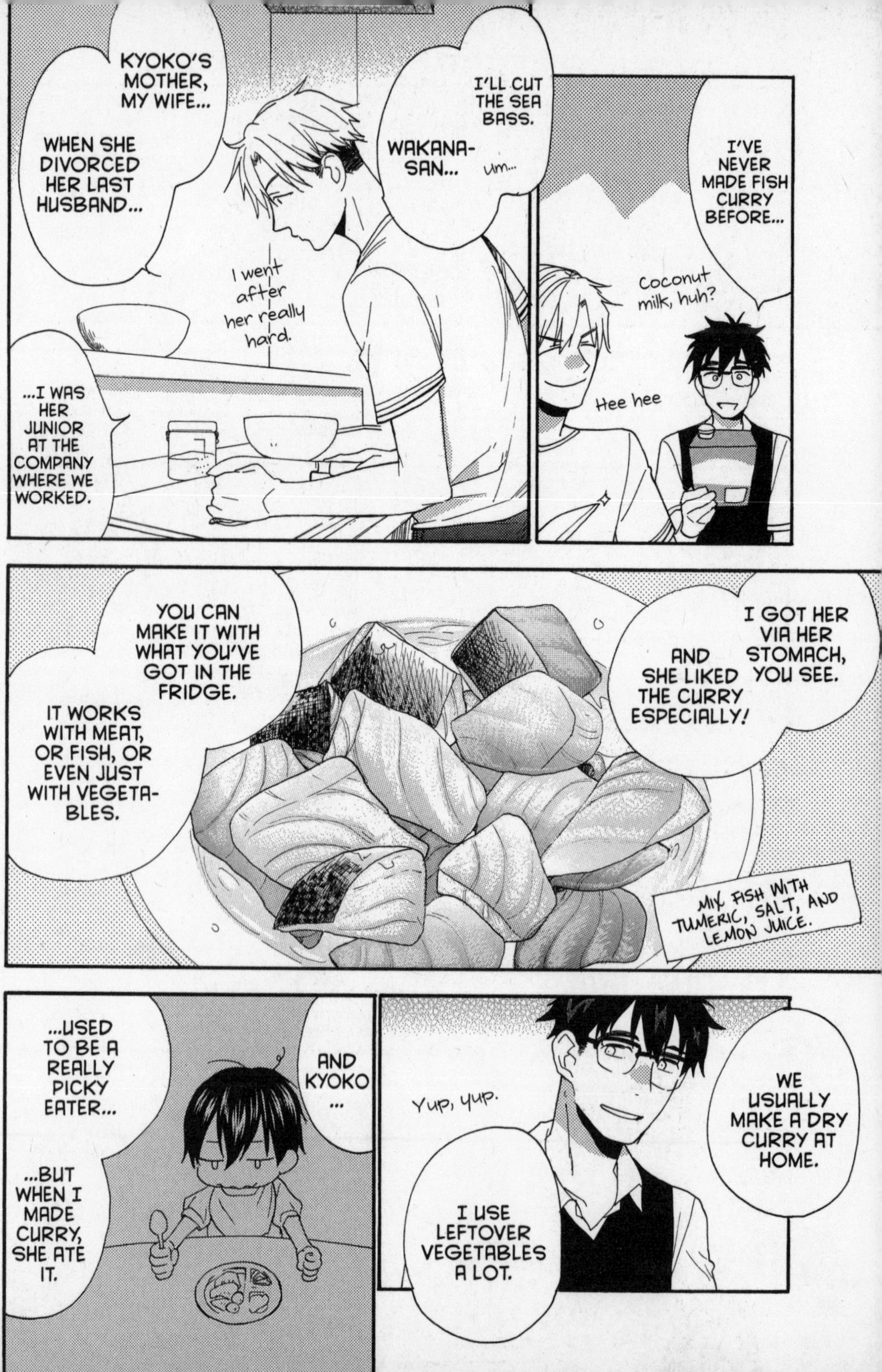
I'VE NEVER MADE FISH CURRY BEFORE...
Coconut milk, huh?
Hee hee
I'LL CUT THE SEA BASS.
WAKANA-SAN...
um...
KYOKO'S MOTHER, MY WIFE...
WHEN SHE DIVORCED HER LAST HUSBAND...
I went after her really hard.
...I WAS HER JUNIOR AT THE COMPANY WHERE WE WORKED.
I GOT HER VIA HER STOMACH, YOU SEE.
AND SHE LIKED THE CURRY ESPECIALLY!
YOU CAN MAKE IT WITH WHAT YOU'VE GOT IN THE FRIDGE.
IT WORKS WITH MEAT, OR FISH, OR EVEN JUST WITH VEGETA-BLES.
MIX FISH WITH TUMERIC, SALT, AND LEMON JUICE.
WE USUALLY MAKE A DRY CURRY AT HOME.
Yup, yup.
I USE LEFTOVER VEGETABLES A LOT.
AND KYOKO...
...USED TO BE A REALLY PICKY EATER...
...BUT WHEN I MADE CURRY, SHE ATE IT.

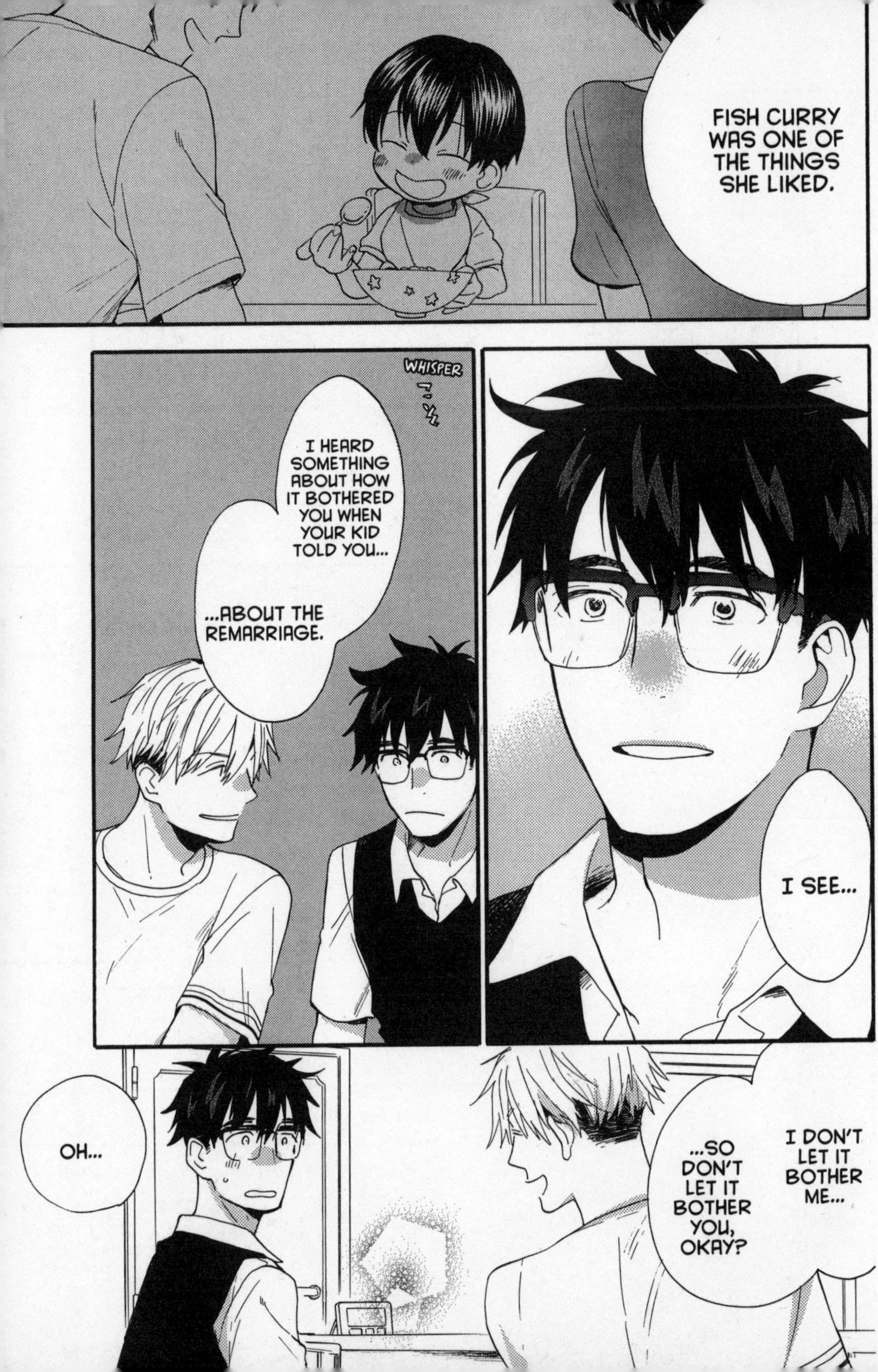
FISH CURRY WAS ONE OF THE THINGS SHE LIKED.
I SEE...
WHISPER
I HEARD SOMETHING ABOUT HOW IT BOTHERED YOU WHEN YOUR KID TOLD YOU...
...ABOUT THE REMARRIAGE.
I DON'T LET IT BOTHER ME...
...SO DON'T LET IT BOTHER YOU, OKAY?
OH...

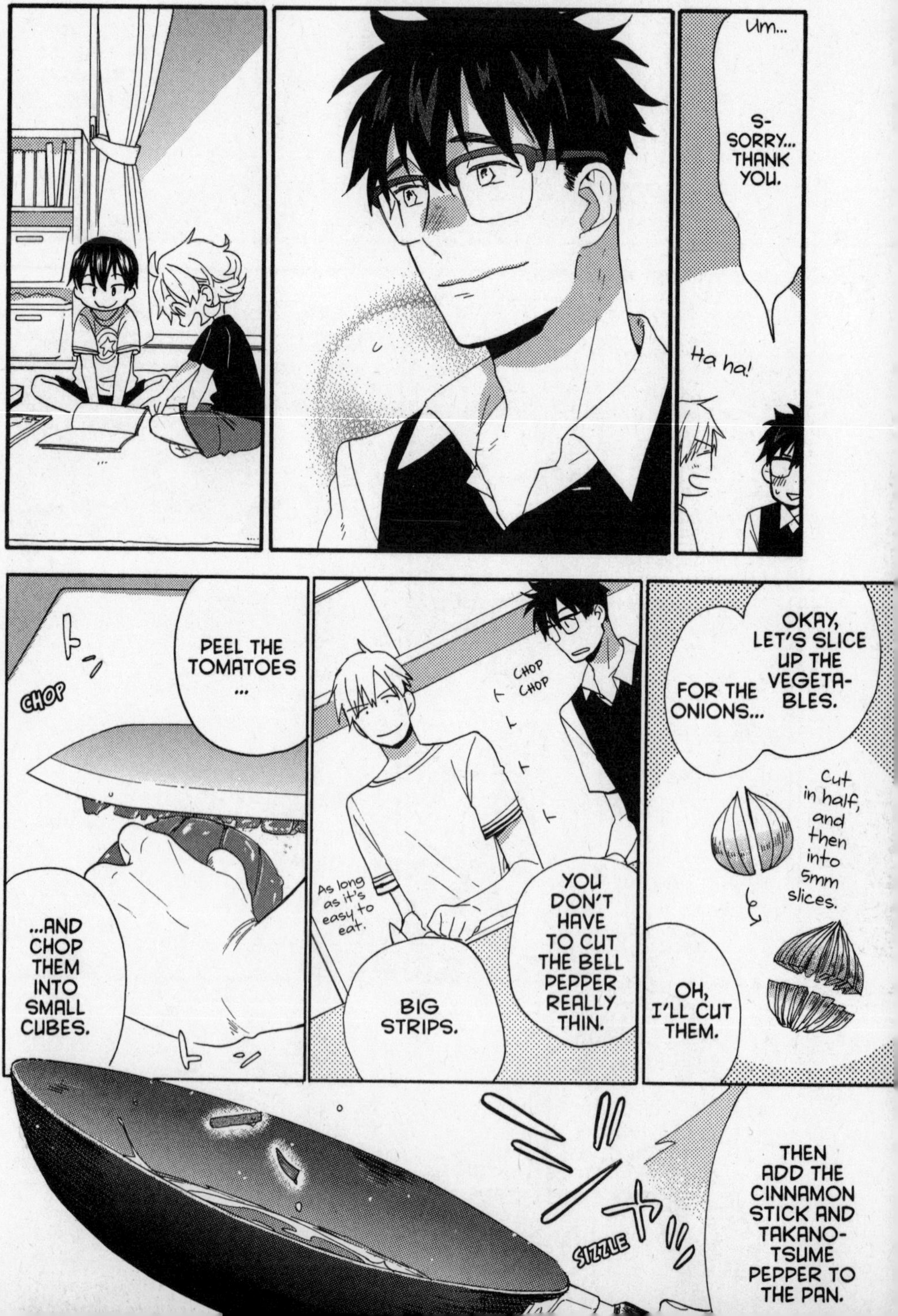
Um...
S-SORRY... THANK YOU.
Ha ha!
OKAY, LET'S SLICE UP THE VEGETABLES.
FOR THE ONIONS...
Cut in half, and then into 5mm slices.
OH, I'LL CUT THEM.
CHOP CHOP
YOU DON'T HAVE TO CUT THE BELL PEPPER REALLY THIN.
BIG STRIPS.
As long as it's easy to eat.
PEEL THE TOMATOES...
CHOP
...AND CHOP THEM INTO SMALL CUBES.
THEN ADD THE CINNAMON STICK AND TAKANO-TSUME PEPPER TO THE PAN.
SIZZLE

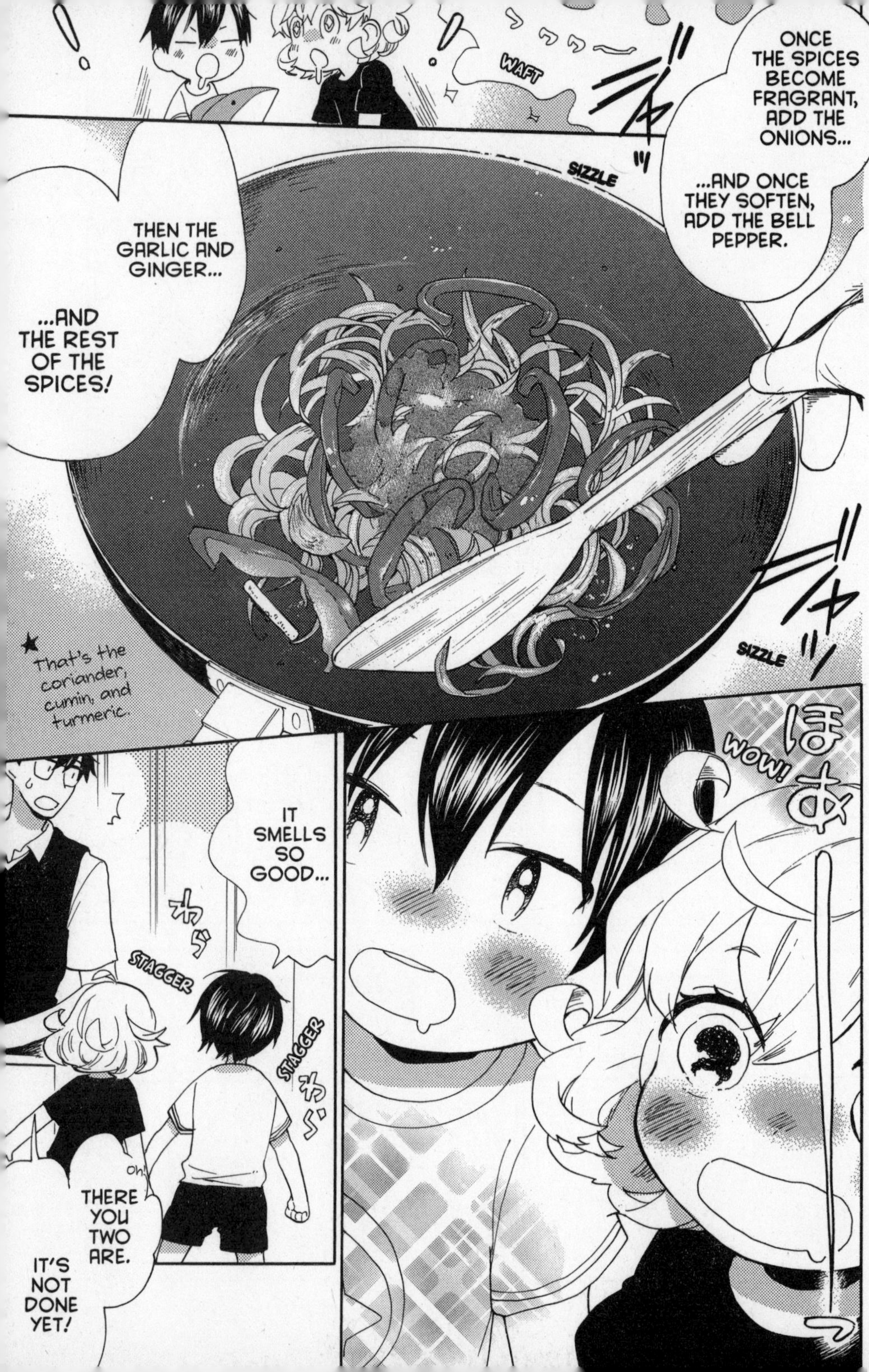
WAFT
ONCE THE SPICES BECOME FRAGRANT, ADD THE ONIONS...
...AND ONCE THEY SOFTEN, ADD THE BELL PEPPER.
SIZZLE
THEN THE GARLIC AND GINGER...
...AND THE REST OF THE SPICES!
SIZZLE
★ That's the coriander, cumin, and turmeric.
WOW!
IT SMELLS SO GOOD...
STAGGER
STAGGER
Oh!
THERE YOU TWO ARE.
IT'S NOT DONE YET!

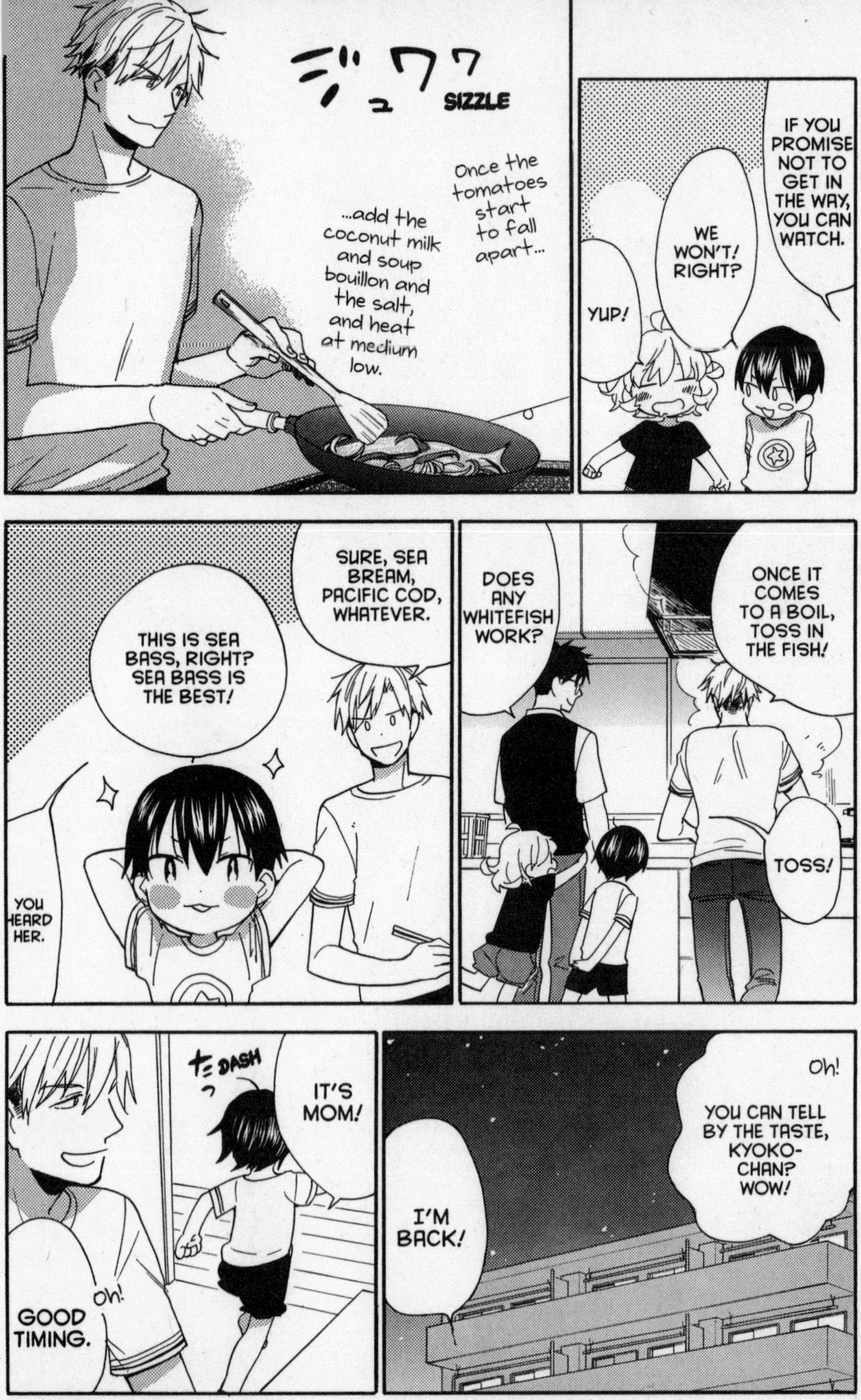
IF YOU PROMISE NOT TO GET IN THE WAY, YOU CAN WATCH.
WE WON'T! RIGHT?
YUP!
ジュワワ
SIZZLE
Once the tomatoes start to fall apart...
...add the coconut milk and soup bouillon and the salt, and heat at medium low.
ONCE IT COMES TO A BOIL, TOSS IN THE FISH!
DOES ANY WHITEFISH WORK?
TOSS!
SURE, SEA BREAM, PACIFIC COD, WHATEVER.
THIS IS SEA BASS, RIGHT? SEA BASS IS THE BEST!
YOU HEARD HER.
Oh!
YOU CAN TELL BY THE TASTE, KYOKO-CHAN? WOW!
I'M BACK!
IT'S MOM!
DASH
Oh!
GOOD TIMING.

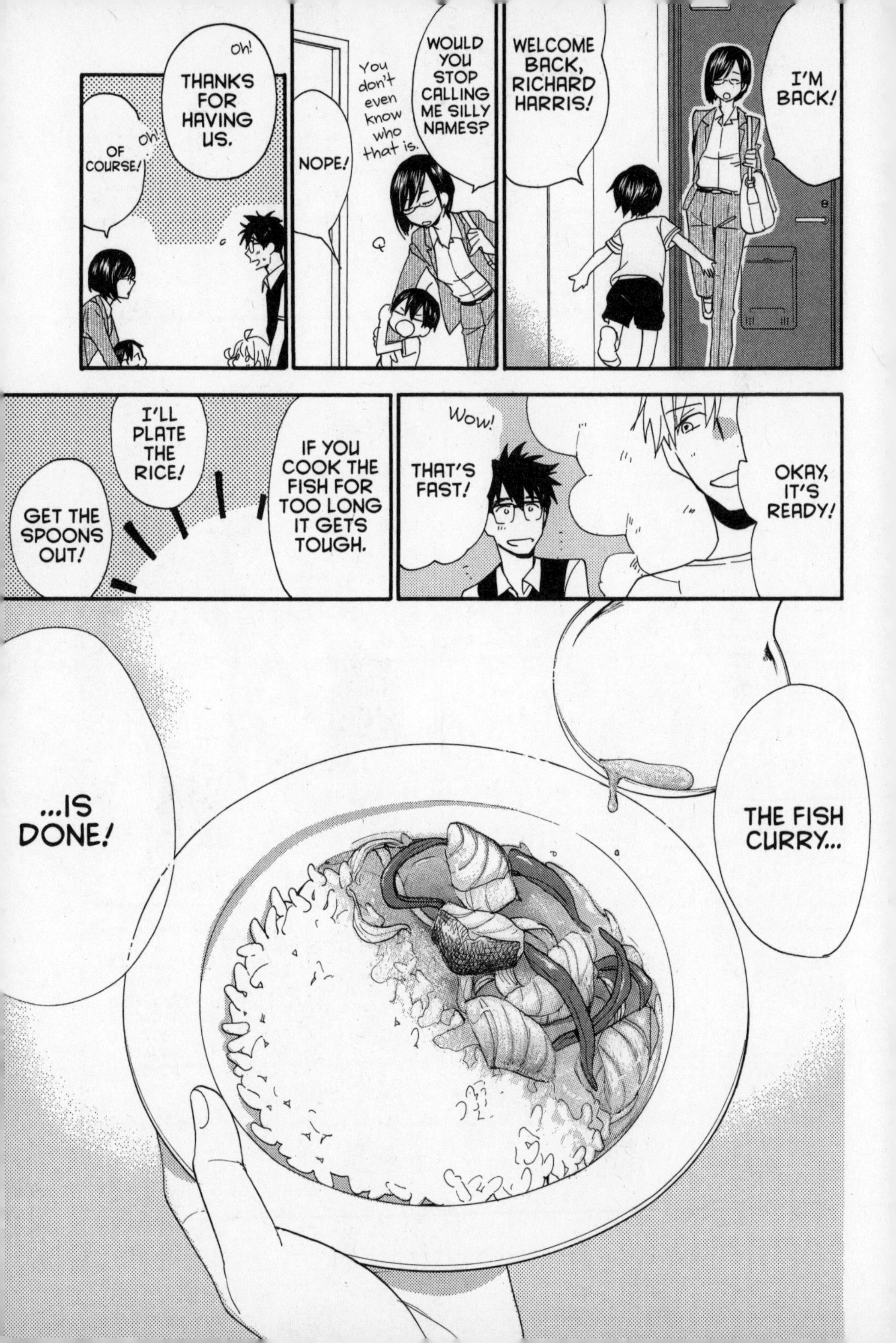
I'M BACK!
WELCOME BACK, RICHARD HARRIS!
WOULD YOU STOP CALLING ME SILLY NAMES?
You don't even know who that is.
NOPE!
Oh!
THANKS FOR HAVING US.
Oh!
OF COURSE!
OKAY, IT'S READY!
Wow!
THAT'S FAST!
IF YOU COOK THE FISH FOR TOO LONG IT GETS TOUGH.
I'LL PLATE THE RICE!
GET THE SPOONS OUT!
THE FISH CURRY...
...IS DONE!

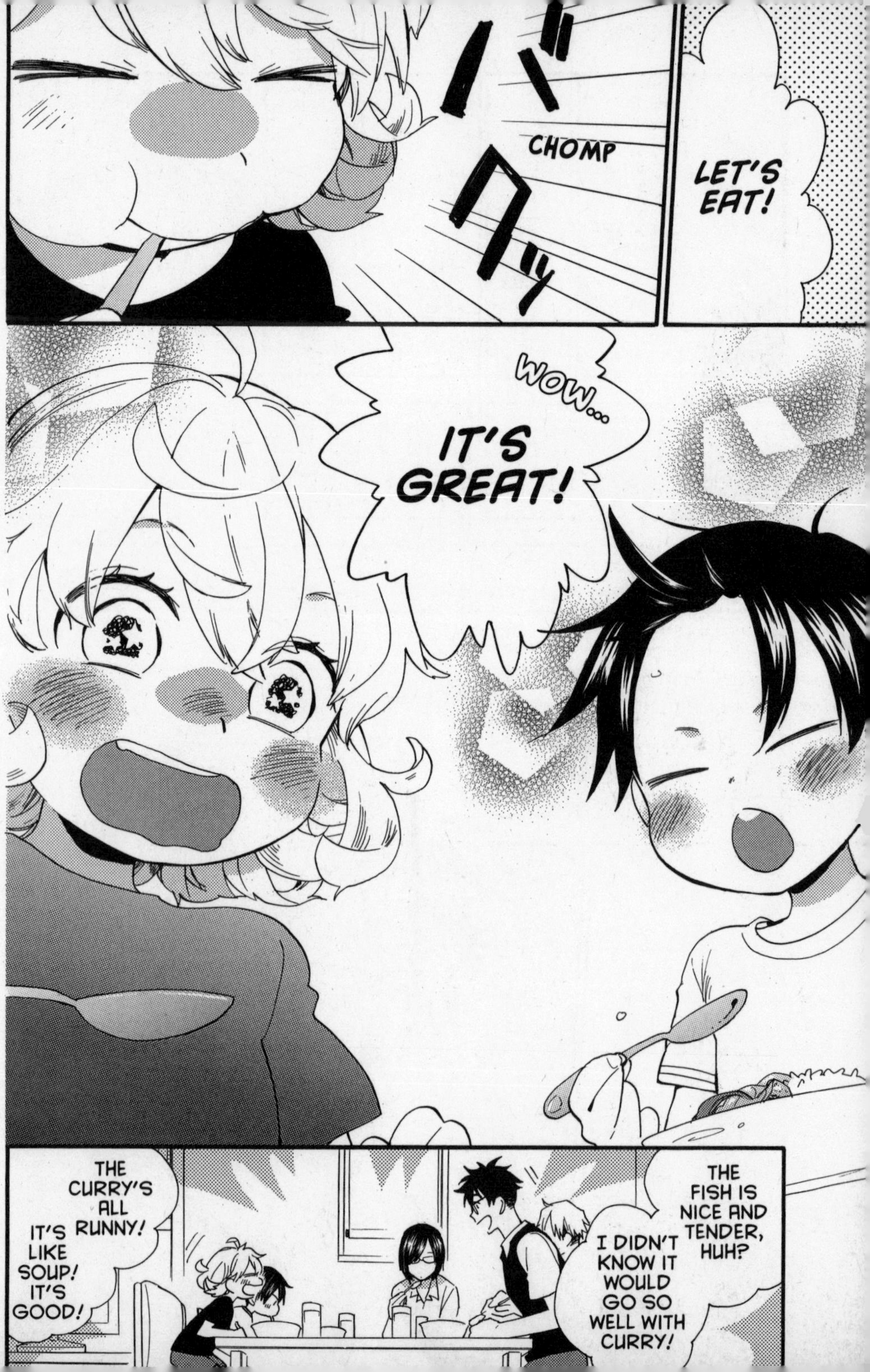
LET'S EAT!
バクッ
CHOMP
WOW... IT'S GREAT!
THE FISH IS NICE AND TENDER, HUH?
I DIDN'T KNOW IT WOULD GO SO WELL WITH CURRY!
THE CURRY'S ALL RUNNY!
IT'S LIKE SOUP! IT'S GOOD!

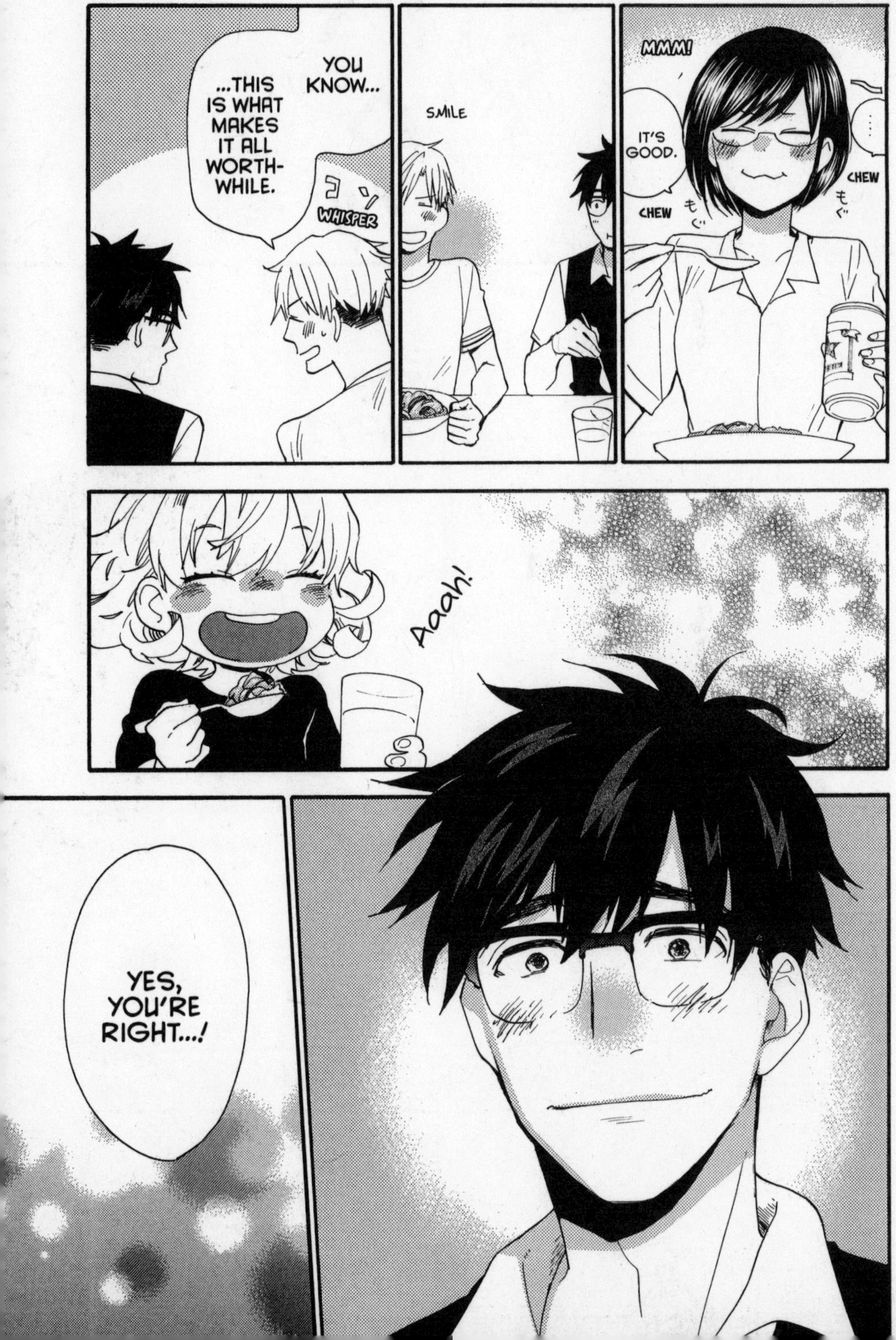
MMM!
…
IT'S GOOD.
CHEW もぐ
CHEW もぐ
SMILE
YOU KNOW...
...THIS IS WHAT MAKES IT ALL WORTH-WHILE.
コソ WHISPER
Aaah!
YES, YOU'RE RIGHT...!

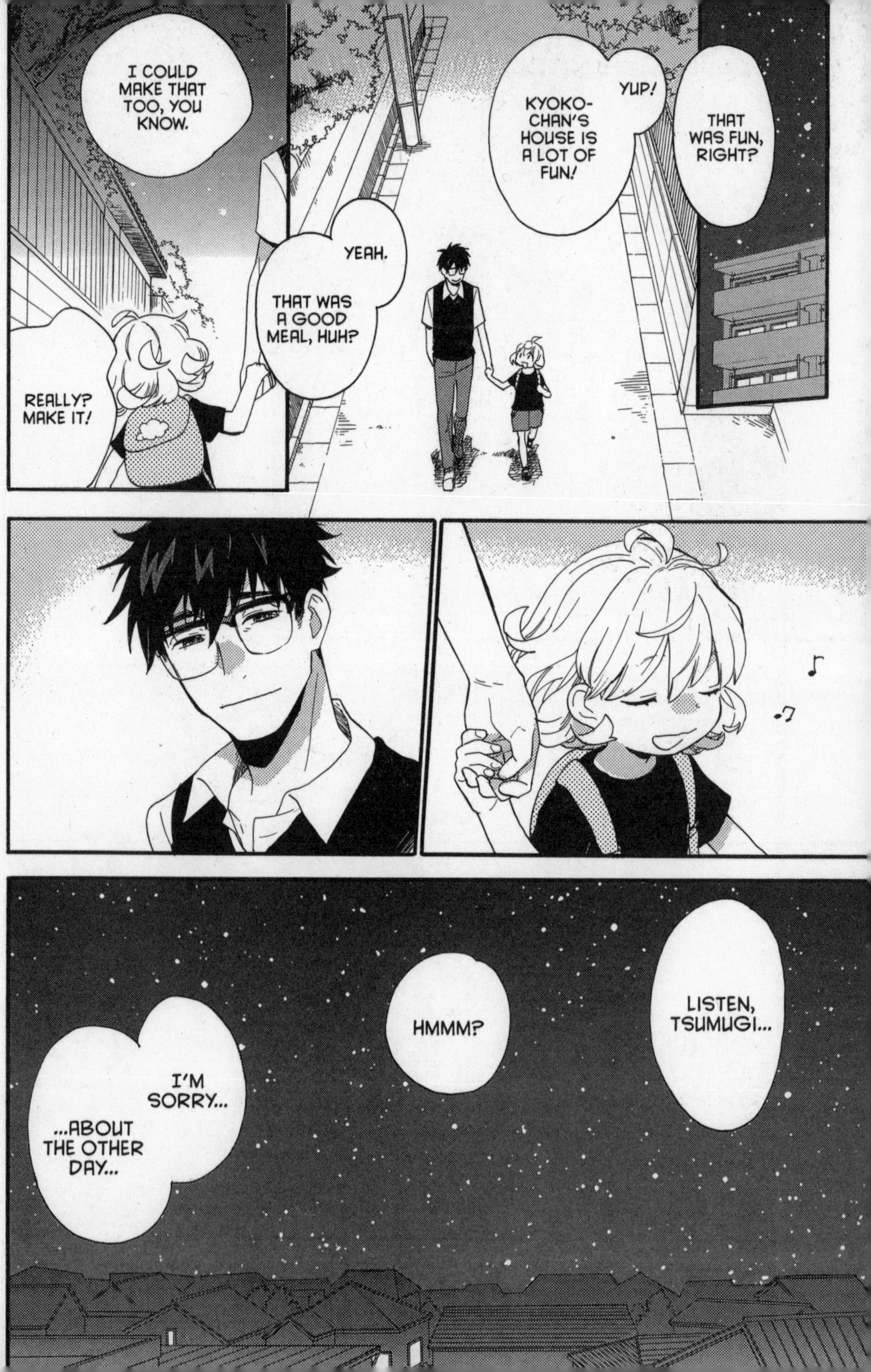
THAT WAS FUN, RIGHT?
YUP!
KYOKO-CHAN'S HOUSE IS A LOT OF FUN!
YEAH.
THAT WAS A GOOD MEAL, HUH?
I COULD MAKE THAT TOO, YOU KNOW.
REALLY? MAKE IT!
LISTEN, TSUMUGI...
HMMM?
I'M SORRY...
...ABOUT THE OTHER DAY...

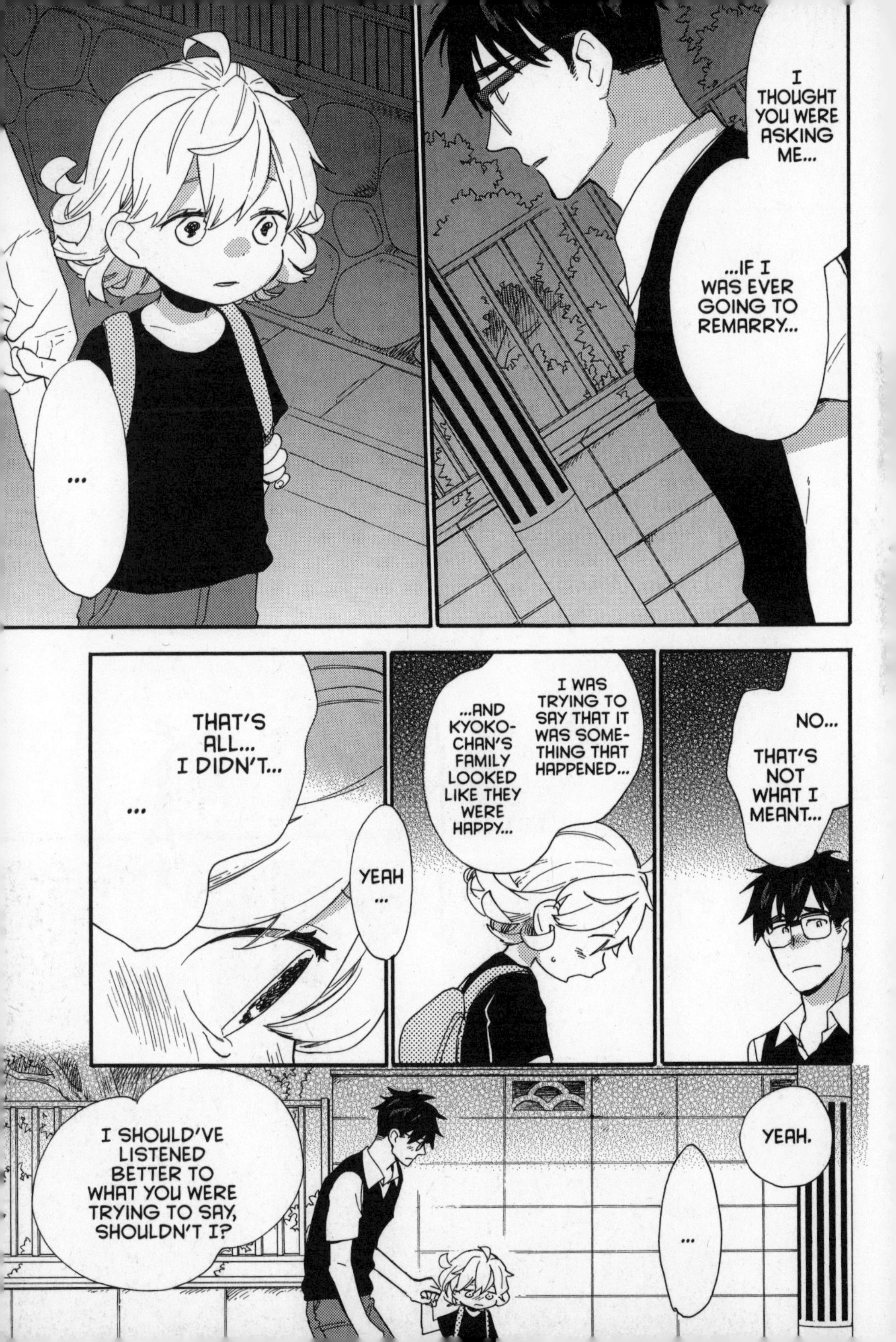

I THOUGHT YOU WERE ASKING ME...
...IF I WAS EVER GOING TO REMARRY...
...
NO...
THAT'S NOT WHAT I MEANT...
I WAS TRYING TO SAY THAT IT WAS SOME-THING THAT HAPPENED...
...AND KYOKO-CHAN'S FAMILY LOOKED LIKE THEY WERE HAPPY...
THAT'S ALL... I DIDN'T...
...
YEAH ...
YEAH.
...
I SHOULD'VE LISTENED BETTER TO WHAT YOU WERE TRYING TO SAY, SHOULDN'T I?

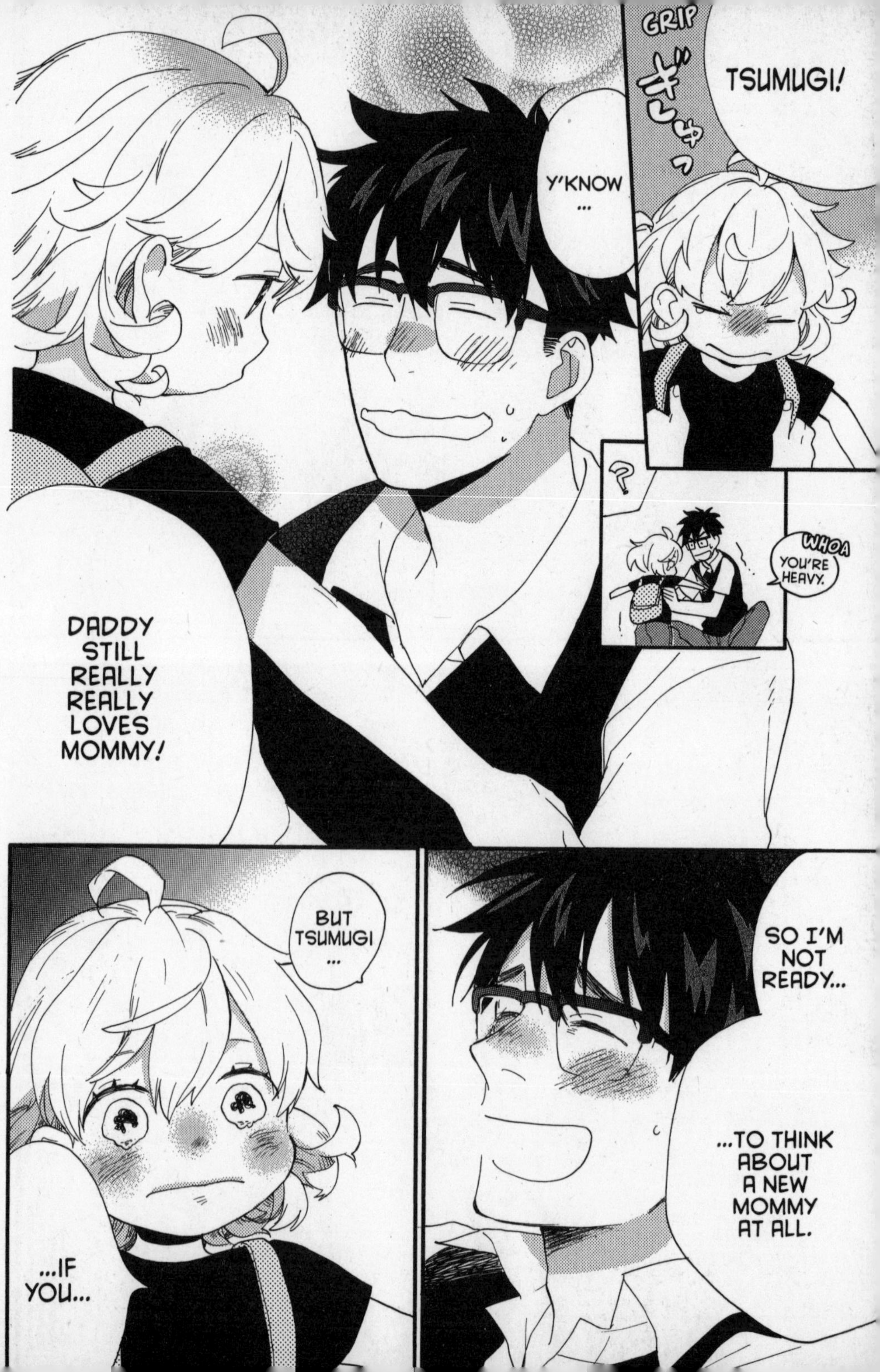
GRIP
ぎゅっ
TSUMUGI!
?
WHOA
YOU'RE HEAVY.
Y'KNOW...
DADDY STILL REALLY REALLY LOVES MOMMY!
SO I'M NOT READY...
...TO THINK ABOUT A NEW MOMMY AT ALL.
BUT TSUMUGI...
...IF YOU...

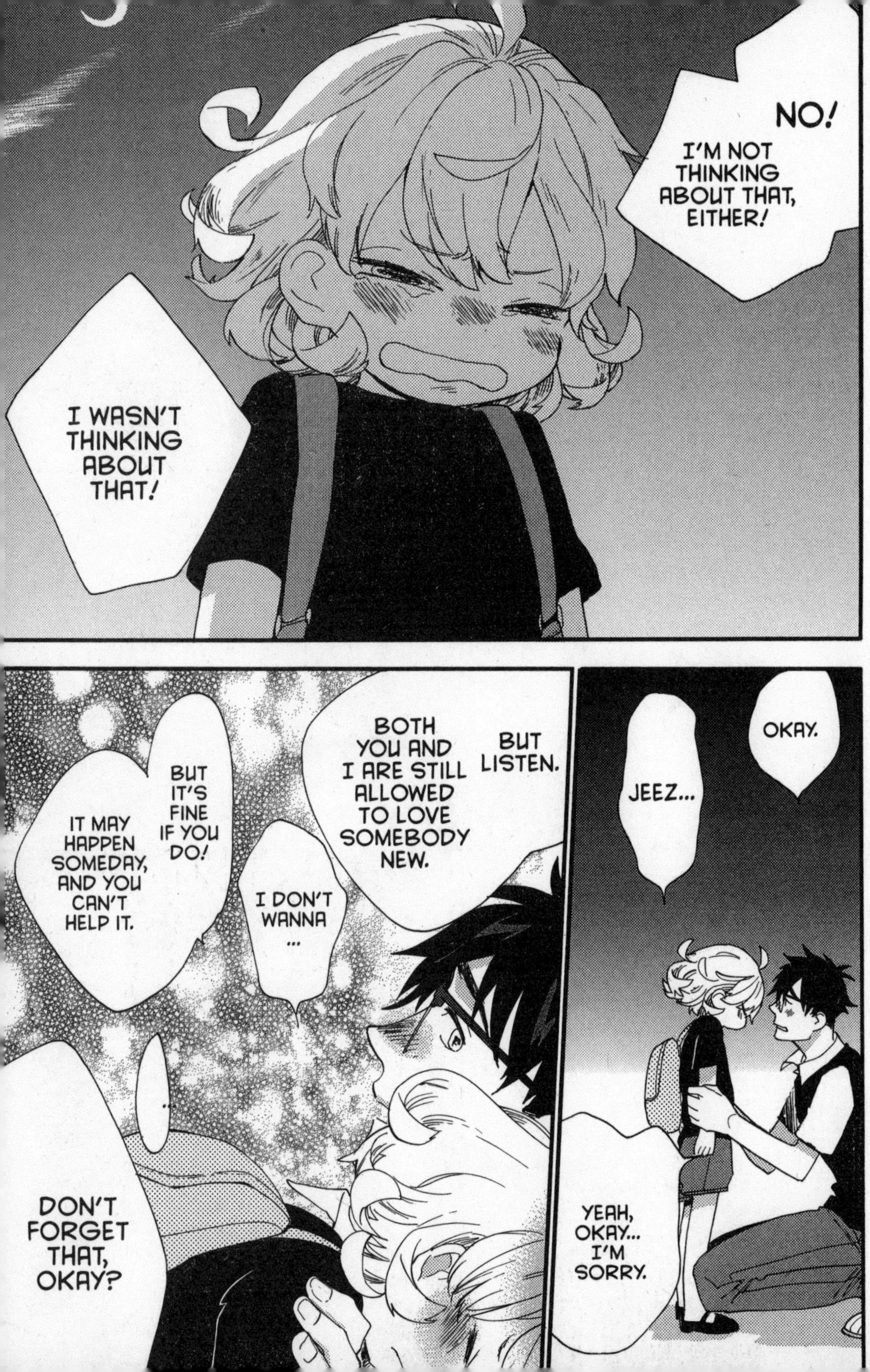
NO! I'M NOT THINKING ABOUT THAT, EITHER!
I WASN'T THINKING ABOUT THAT!
OKAY.
JEEZ...
YEAH, OKAY... I'M SORRY.
BUT LISTEN.
BOTH YOU AND I ARE STILL ALLOWED TO LOVE SOMEBODY NEW.
I DON'T WANNA ...
BUT IT'S FINE IF YOU DO!
IT MAY HAPPEN SOMEDAY, AND YOU CAN'T HELP IT.
...
DON'T FORGET THAT, OKAY?

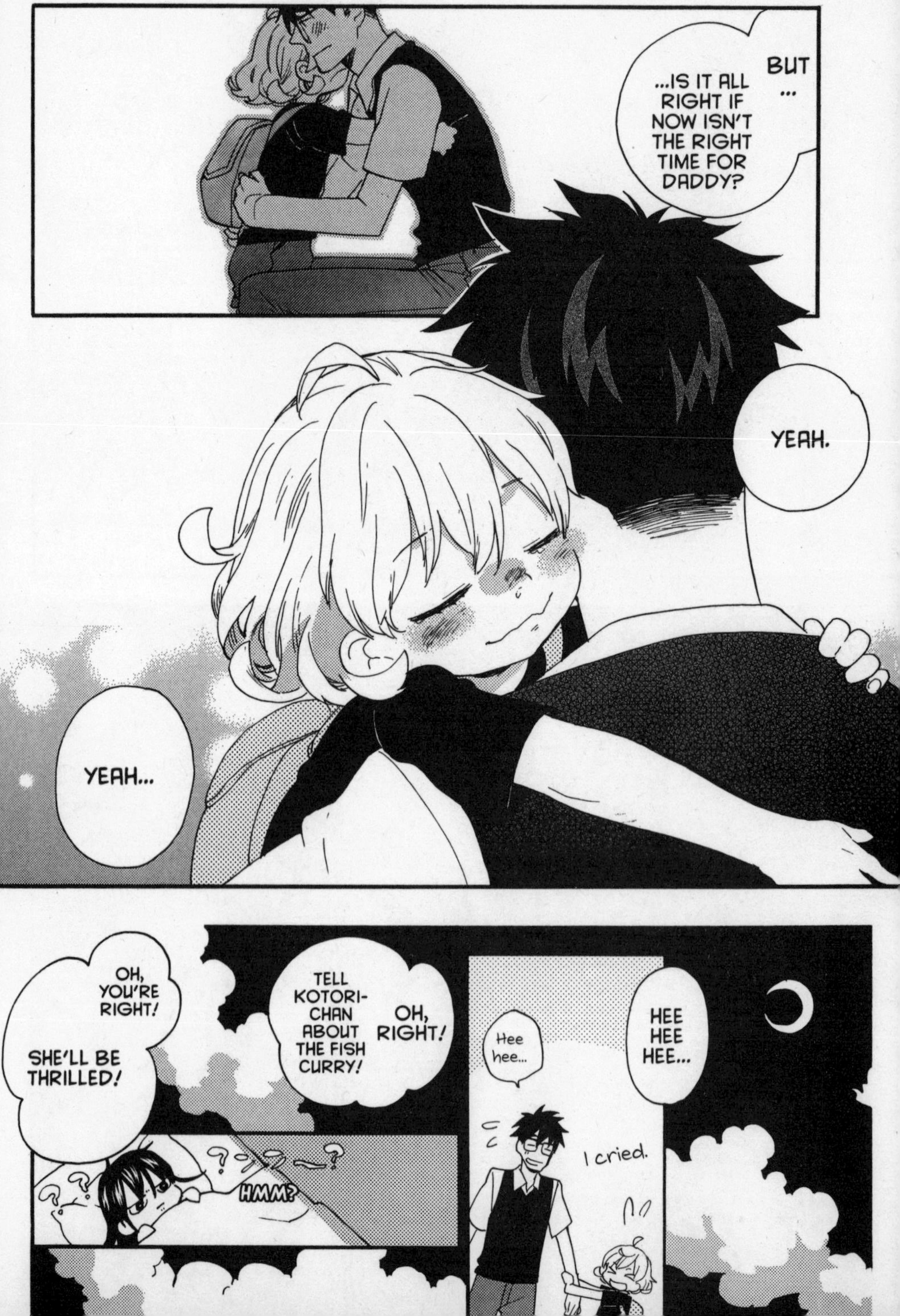
BUT...
...IS IT ALL RIGHT IF NOW ISN'T THE RIGHT TIME FOR DADDY?
YEAH.
YEAH...
HEE HEE HEE...
Hee hee...
I cried.
OH, RIGHT!
TELL KOTORI-CHAN ABOUT THE FISH CURRY!
OH, YOU'RE RIGHT!
SHE'LL BE THRILLED!
HMM?

FISH CURRY

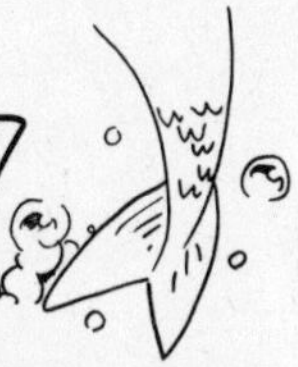

☆Ingredients (serves 2)☆

★2 Fillets (150g) Sea Bass
★Paprika Pepper (Red)
★1 Scant Teaspoon Garlic
★Half an Onion (150g)
★1/2 Tomato
★1 Scant Teaspoon Ginger

A:
1/2 Tablespoon Lemon Juice
1/4 Teaspoon Salt
1/4 Teaspoon Turmeric

B:
1/2 Cinnamon Stick
1/4 Cayenne Pepper
(more if you want it spicier!)

C:
1/2 Tablespoon Powdered Coriander
1/2 Teaspoon Powdered Cumin
1/4 Teaspoon Turmeric

D:
100cc Coconut Milk
50cc Soup Stock (Cube or Powdered)
1/3 Teaspoon Salt

1. Remove bones from sea bass fillets, and cut into bite-size pieces.
2. Mix ingredients in A, then toss with sea bass. Let sit for 30 minutes to 1 hour.
3. Half onion, then slice into 1/4 inch strips. If the strips are long, halve them.
4. Cut paprika lengthwise into thick strips. Remove skin from tomato with hot water and dice.
5. Coat a frying pan with a tablespoon of cooking oil. Add B and cook over low heat.
6. When the ingredients become fragrant, add the onion and increase heat to medium. When the onions soften, add paprika.
7. Sauté, then add garlic and ginger. Once the garlic and ginger are fragrant, add C and sauté over low heat.
8. Add tomato to 7. Sauté until tomato begins to break down, then add D and set heat to medium.
9. When contents begins to boil, add sea bass in its dressing.
10. Simmer for 6-7 minutes, and you're done! (Remember to remove the cinnamon stick and cayenne pepper!)

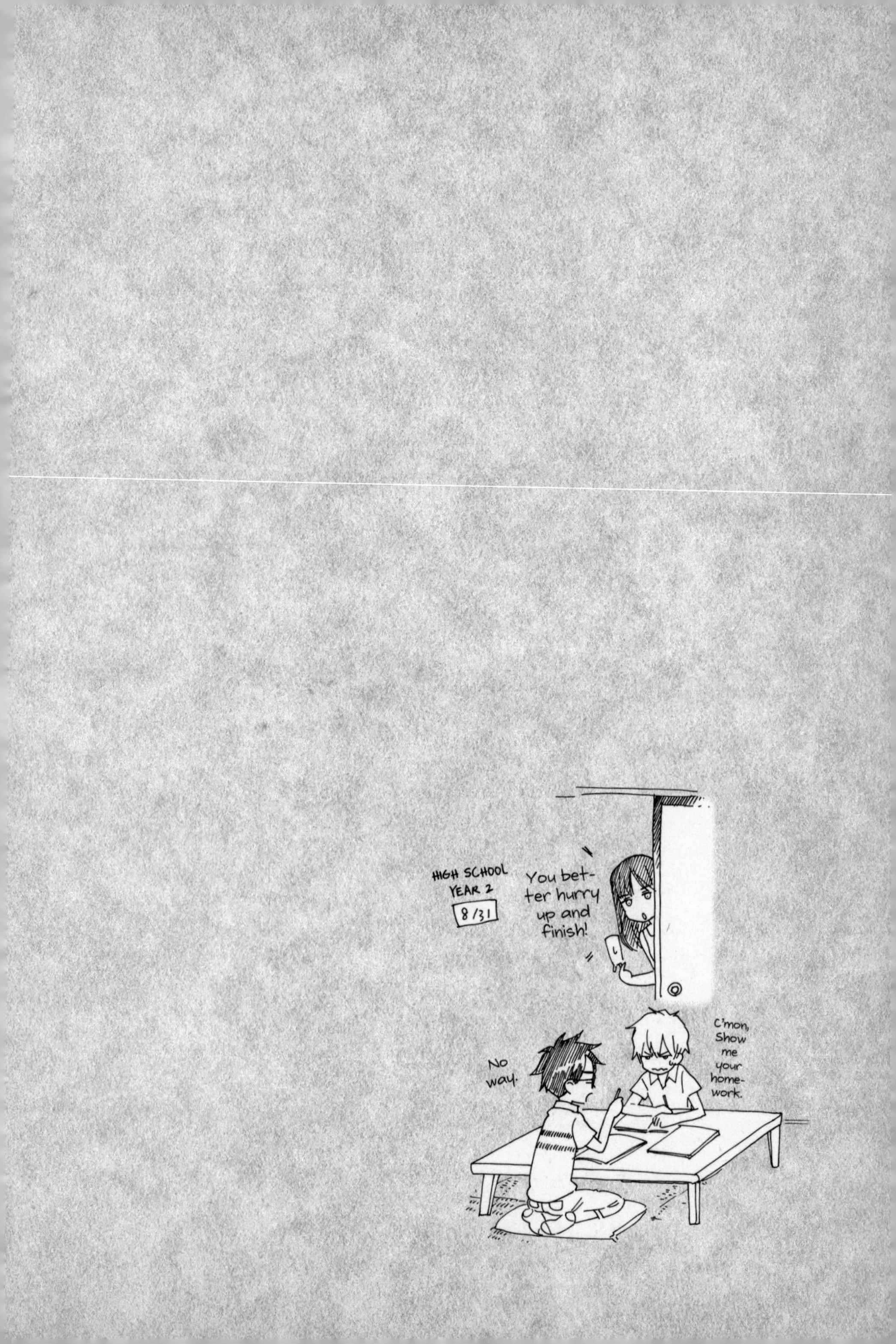
You better hurry up and finish!
HIGH SCHOOL YEAR 2
8/31
C'mon, Show me your homework.
No way.

BREAKFAST TIME

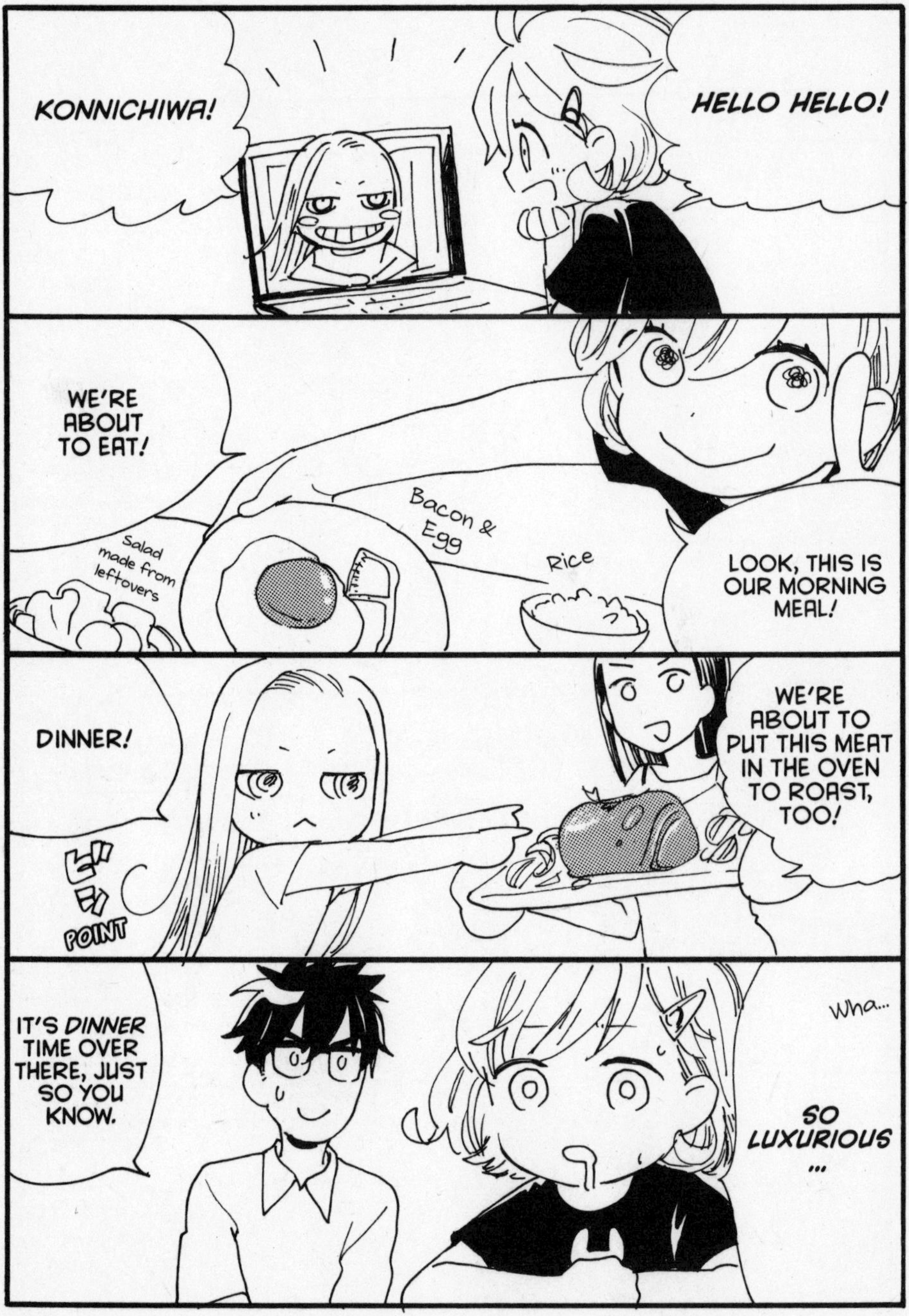
HELLO HELLO!
KONNICHIWA!
WE'RE ABOUT TO EAT!
Bacon & Egg
Rice
Salad made from leftovers
LOOK, THIS IS OUR MORNING MEAL!
WE'RE ABOUT TO PUT THIS MEAT IN THE OVEN TO ROAST, TOO!
DINNER!
POINT
Wha...
SO LUXURIOUS ...
IT'S DINNER TIME OVER THERE, JUST SO YOU KNOW.

WONDERFUL OLDER SISTER

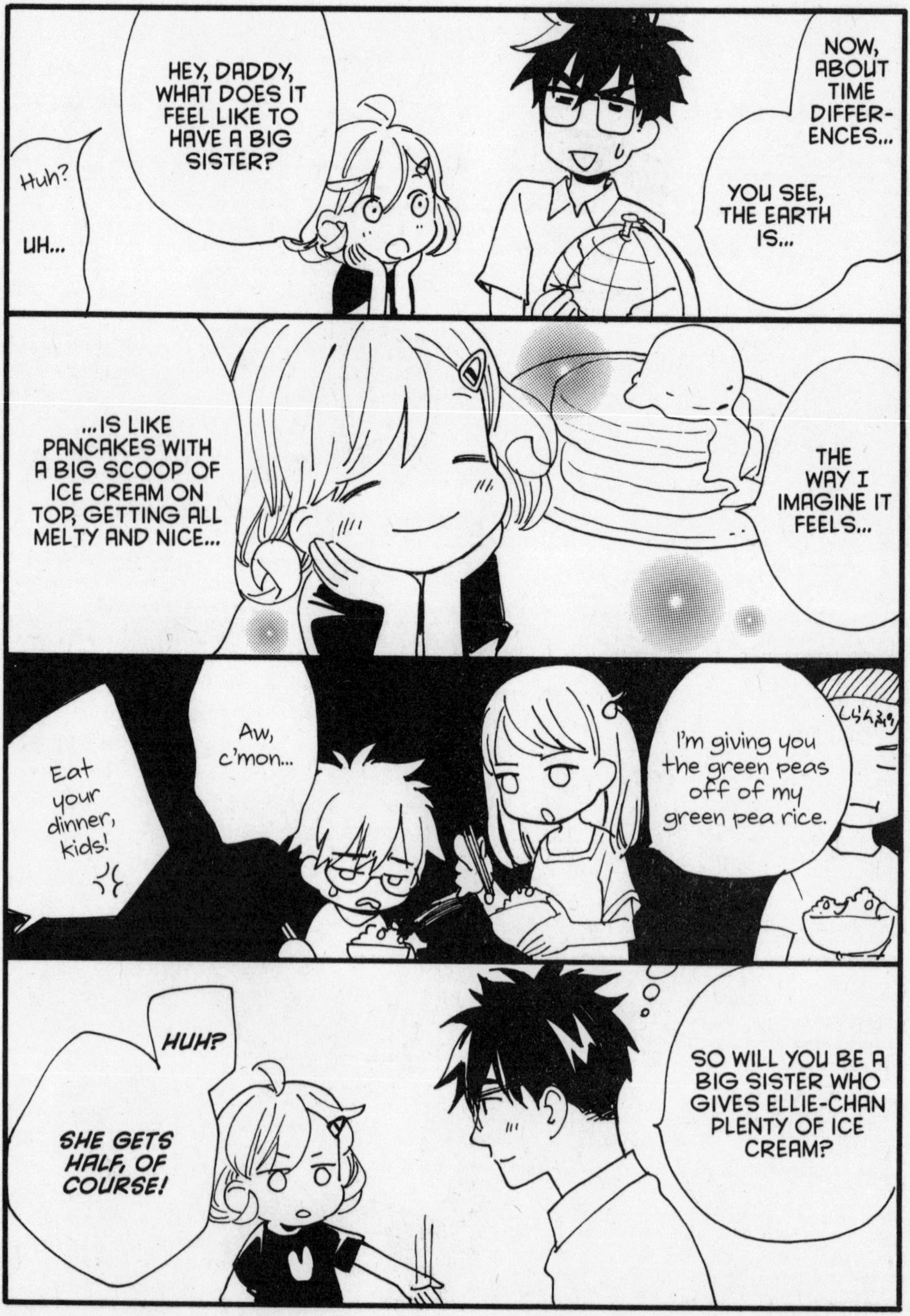
NOW, ABOUT TIME DIFFERENCES...
YOU SEE, THE EARTH IS...
HEY, DADDY, WHAT DOES IT FEEL LIKE TO HAVE A BIG SISTER?
Huh?
UH...
THE WAY I IMAGINE IT FEELS...
...IS LIKE PANCAKES WITH A BIG SCOOP OF ICE CREAM ON TOP, GETTING ALL MELTY AND NICE...
I'm giving you the green peas off of my green pea rice.
Aw, c'mon...
Eat your dinner, kids!
SO WILL YOU BE A BIG SISTER WHO GIVES ELLIE-CHAN PLENTY OF ICE CREAM?
HUH?
SHE GETS HALF, OF COURSE!

THE CUTER ONE

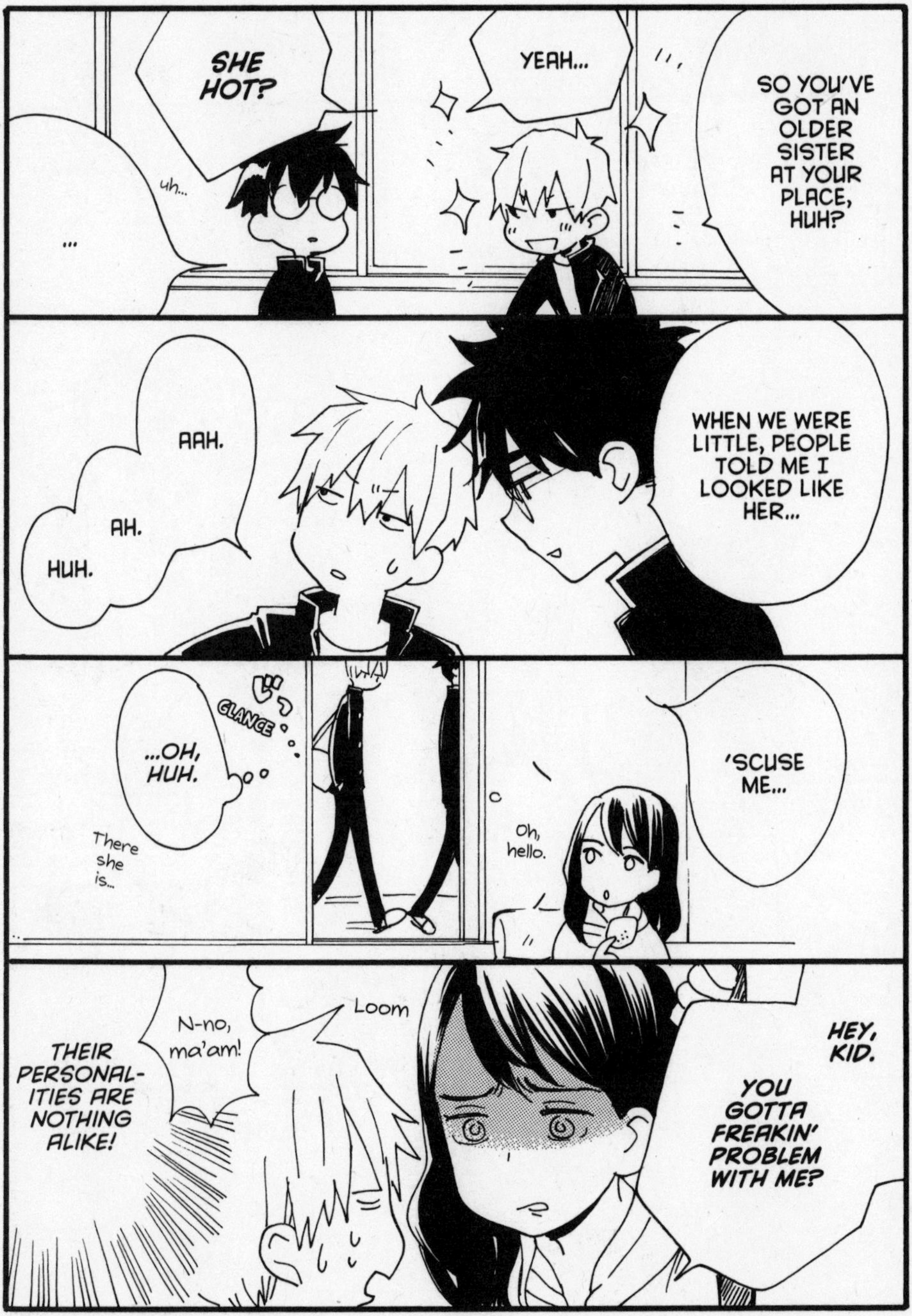
SO YOU'VE GOT AN OLDER SISTER AT YOUR PLACE, HUH?
YEAH...
SHE HOT?
uh...
...
WHEN WE WERE LITTLE, PEOPLE TOLD ME I LOOKED LIKE HER...
AAH.
AH.
HUH.
'SCUSE ME...
Oh, hello.
GLANCE
...OH, HUH.
There she is...
HEY, KID.
YOU GOTTA FREAKIN' PROBLEM WITH ME?
Loom
N-no, ma'am!
THEIR PERSONAL-ITIES ARE NOTHING ALIKE!

THE CUTER ONE

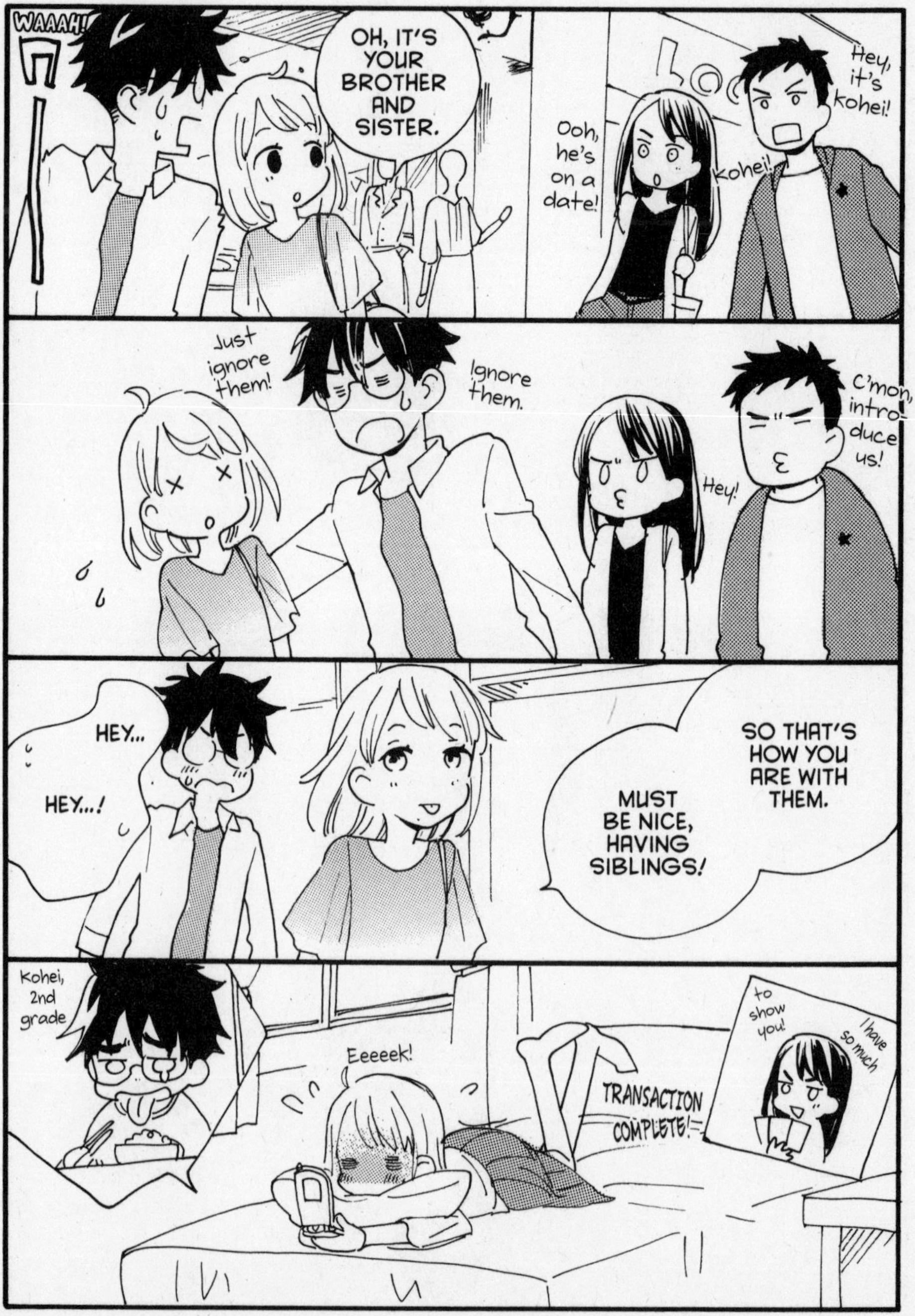
Hey, it's kohei!
Ooh, he's on a date!
Kohei!
OH, IT'S YOUR BROTHER AND SISTER.
WAAAH!
C'mon, intro-duce us!
Hey!
Ignore them.
Just ignore them!
SO THAT'S HOW YOU ARE WITH THEM.
MUST BE NICE, HAVING SIBLINGS!
HEY...
HEY...!
I have so much to show you!
TRANSACTION COMPLETE!
Eeeeek!
Kohei, 2nd grade

Afterword

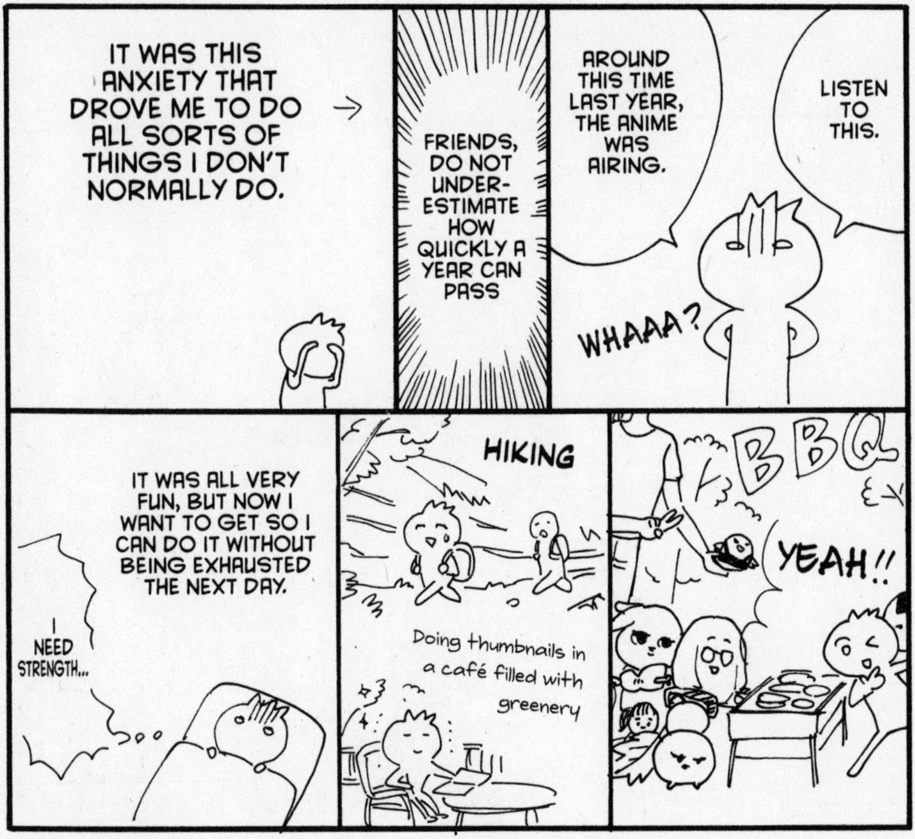

LISTEN TO THIS.
AROUND THIS TIME LAST YEAR, THE ANIME WAS AIRING.
WHAAA?
FRIENDS, DO NOT UNDER-ESTIMATE HOW QUICKLY A YEAR CAN PASS
IT WAS THIS ANXIETY THAT DROVE ME TO DO ALL SORTS OF THINGS I DON'T NORMALLY DO.
→
BBQ
YEAH!!
HIKING
Doing thumbnails in a café filled with greenery
IT WAS ALL VERY FUN, BUT NOW I WANT TO GET SO I CAN DO IT WITHOUT BEING EXHAUSTED THE NEXT DAY.
I NEED STRENGTH...

★SEE YOU AGAIN IN VOLUME 10!★ GIDO AMAGAKURE

! THANK YOU ALL SO MUCH! !

W-YAMA-SAN, GON-CHAN, TSURU-SAN, M-CHAN, MY FAMILY
T-SHIRO-SAMA, K-YAMA-SAMA, JUN ABE-SAMA
PHOTOGRAPHIC RESEARCH COOPERATION: TABEGOTOYA NORABO-SAMA
COOKING ADVISOR: AKARI TAITO-SAMA
CANNELONI RECIPE: HEATHER COOLING

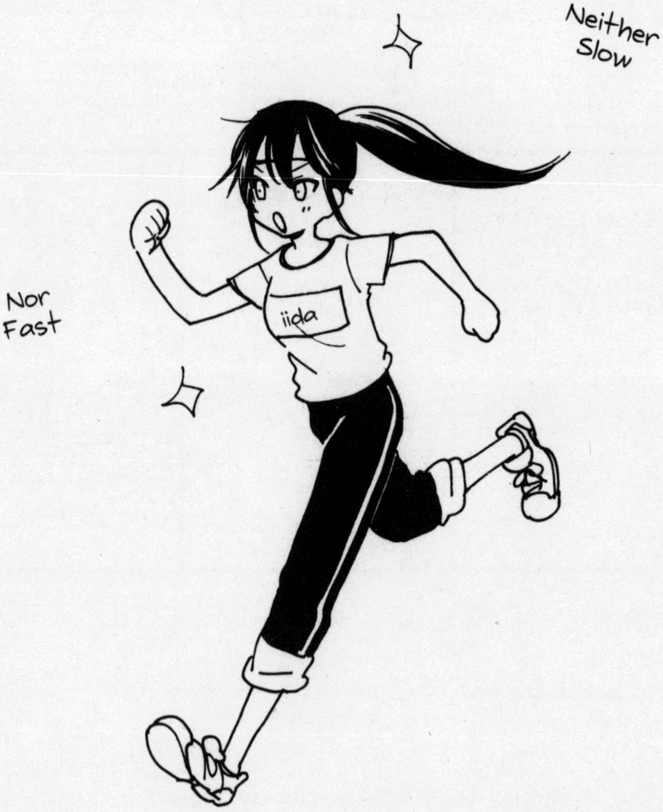
Neither Slow
iida
Nor Fast

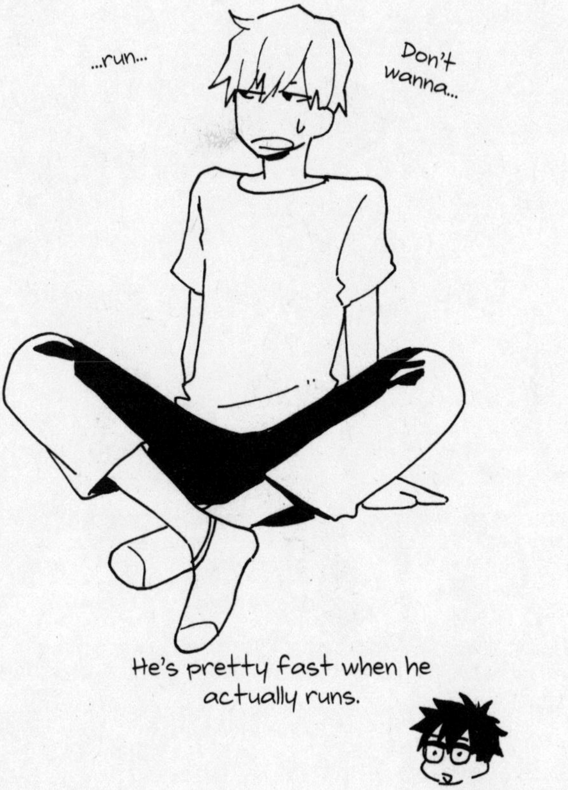
Don't wanna...
...run...
He's pretty fast when he actually runs.
Not fast.

KC

KODANSHA COMICS

A new series from the creator of *Soul Eater*, the megahit manga and anime seen on Toonami!

"Fun and lively... a great start!"
   -Adventures in Poor Taste

FIRE FORCE

By Atsushi Ohkubo

The city of Tokyo is plagued by a deadly phenomenon: spontaneous human combustion! Luckily, a special team is there to quench the inferno: The Fire Force! The fire soldiers at Special Fire Cathedral 8 are about to get a unique addition. Enter Shinra, a boy who possesses the power to run at the speed of a rocket, leaving behind the famous "devil's footprints" (and destroying his shoes in the process). Can Shinra and his colleagues discover the source of this strange epidemic before the city burns to ashes?

The award-winning manga about what happens inside you!

"Far more entertaining than it ought to be... what kid doesn't want to think that every time they sneeze a torpedo shoots out their nose?"
–Anime News Network

Strep throat! Hay fever! Influenza! The world is a dangerous place for a red blood cell just trying to get her deliveries finished. Fortunately, she's not alone…she's got a whole human body's worth of cells ready to help out! The mysterious white blood cells, the buff and brash killer T cells, even the cute little platelets— everyone's got to come together if they want to keep you healthy!

Cells at Work!

はたらく細胞

By Akane Shimizu

HAPPINESS

—ハピネス—

By Shuzo Oshimi

From the creator of *The Flowers of Evil*

Nothing interesting is happening in Makoto Ozaki's first year of high school. His life is a series of quiet humiliations: low-grade bullies, unreliable friends, and the constant frustration of his adolescent lust. But one night, a pale, thin girl knocks him to the ground in an alley and offers him a choice. Now everything is different. Daylight is searingly bright. Food tastes awful. And worse than anything is the terrible, consuming thirst...

Praise for Shuzo Oshimi's *The Flowers of Evil*

"A shockingly readable story that vividly—one might even say queasily—evokes the fear and confusion of discovering one's own sexuality. Recommended." —The Manga Critic

"A page-turning tale of sordid middle school blackmail." —Otaku USA Magazine

"A stunning new horror manga." —Third Eye Comics

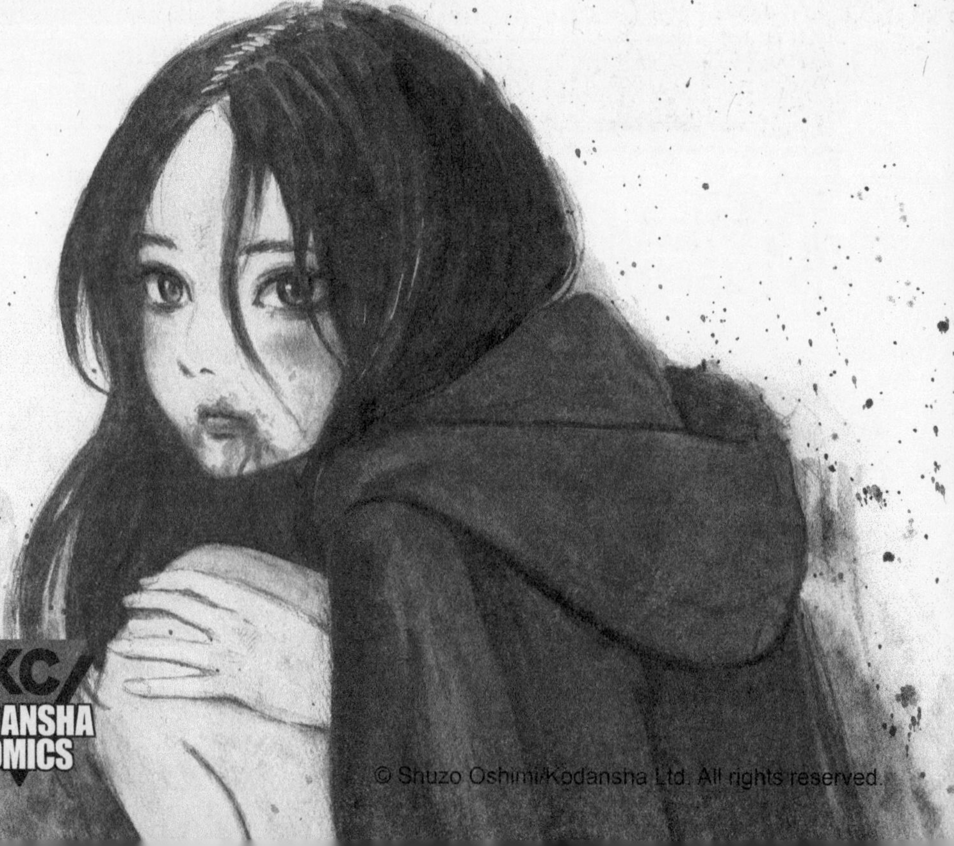

KC KODANSHA COMICS

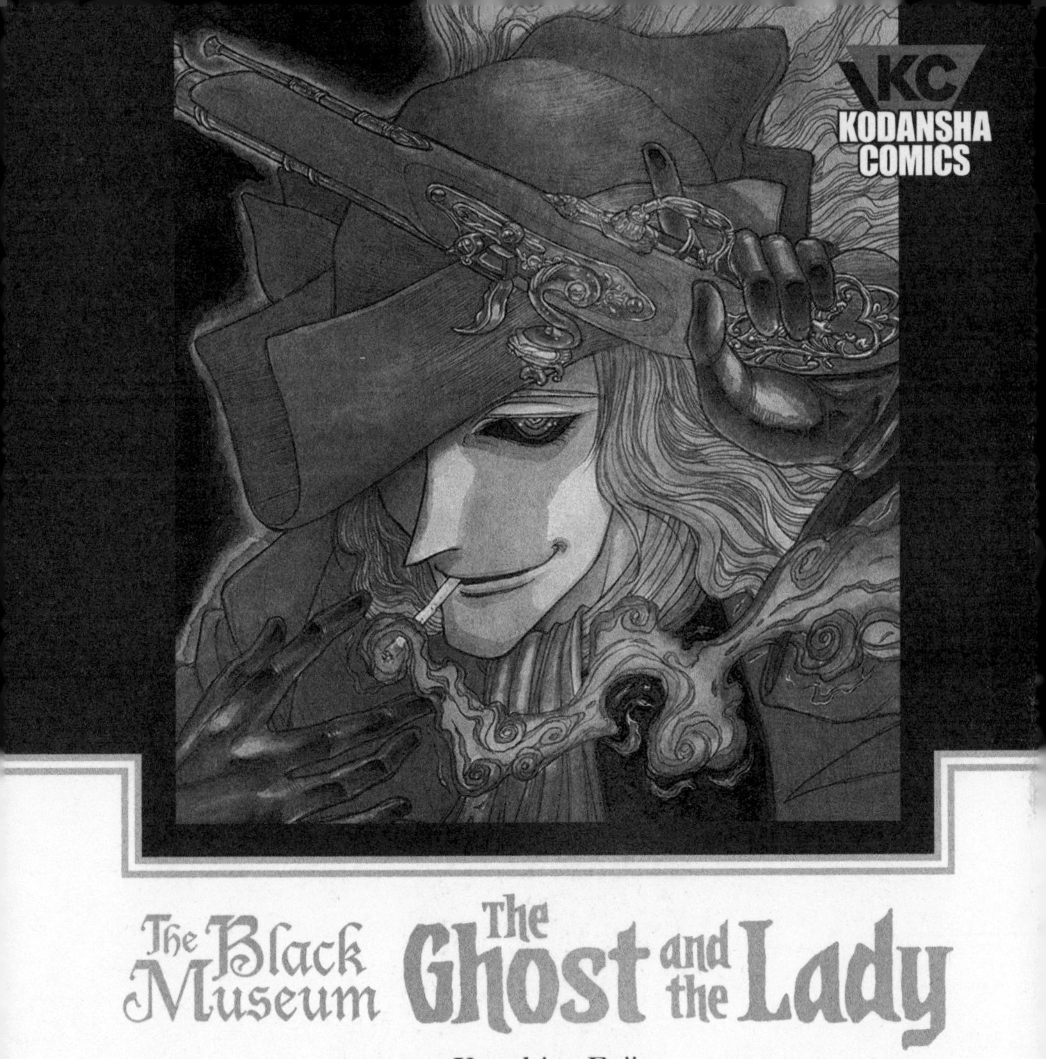
KC
KODANSHA COMICS

The Black Museum: The Ghost and the Lady

By Kazuhiro Fujita

Deep in Scotland Yard in London sits an evidence room dedicated to the greatest mysteries of British history. In this "Black Museum" sits a misshapen hunk of lead—two bullets fused together—the key to a wartime encounter between Florence Nightingale, the mother of modern nursing, and a supernatural Man in Grey. This story is unknown to most scholars of history, but a special guest of the museum will tell the tale of The Ghost and the Lady...

Praise for Kazuhiro Fujita's *Ushio and Tora*

"A charming revival that combines a classic look with modern depth and pacing... **Essential viewing both for curmudgeons and new fans alike.**" — Anime News Network

"**GREAT!** The first episode of Ushio and Tora captures the essence of '90s anime." — IGN

New action series from Hiroyuki Takei, creator of the classic shonen franchise Shaman King!

In medieval Japan, a bell hanging on the collar is a sign that a cat has a master. Norachiyo's bell hangs from his katana sheath, but he is nonetheless a stray — a ronin. This one-eyed cat samurai travels across a dishonest world, cutting through pretense and deception with his blade.

Nekogahara

STRAY CAT SAMURAI

By
Hiroyuki Takei

KODANSHA COMICS

Japan's most powerful spirit medium delves into the ghost world's greatest mysteries!

Story by Kyo Shirodaira, famed author of mystery fiction and creator of *Spiral*, *Blast of Tempest*, and *The Record of a Fallen Vampire*.

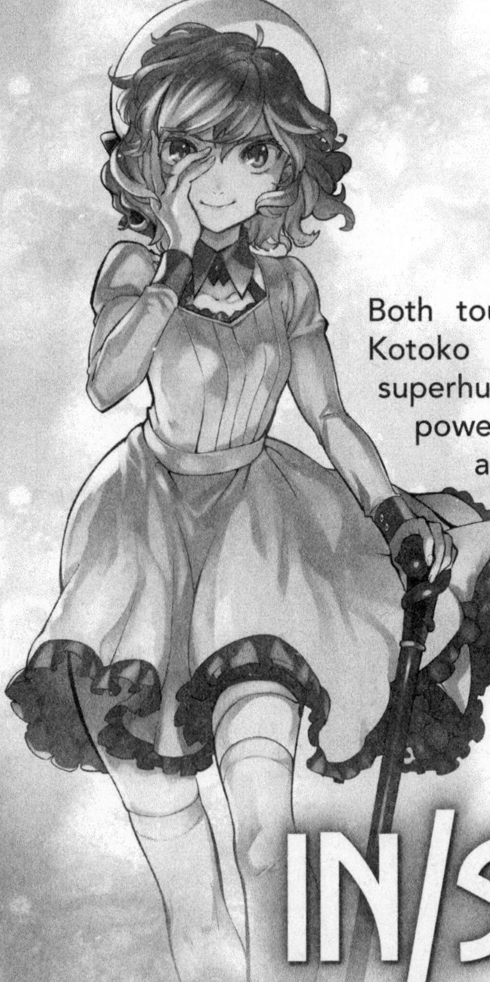

Both touched by spirits called yôkai, Kotoko and Kurô have gained unique superhuman powers. But to gain her powers Kotoko has given up an eye and a leg, and Kurô's personal life is in shambles. So when Kotoko suggests they team up to deal with renegades from the spirit world, Kurô doesn't have many other choices, but Kotoko might just have a few ulterior motives...

IN/SPECTRE

STORY BY KYO SHIRODAIRA
ART BY CHASHIBA KATASE

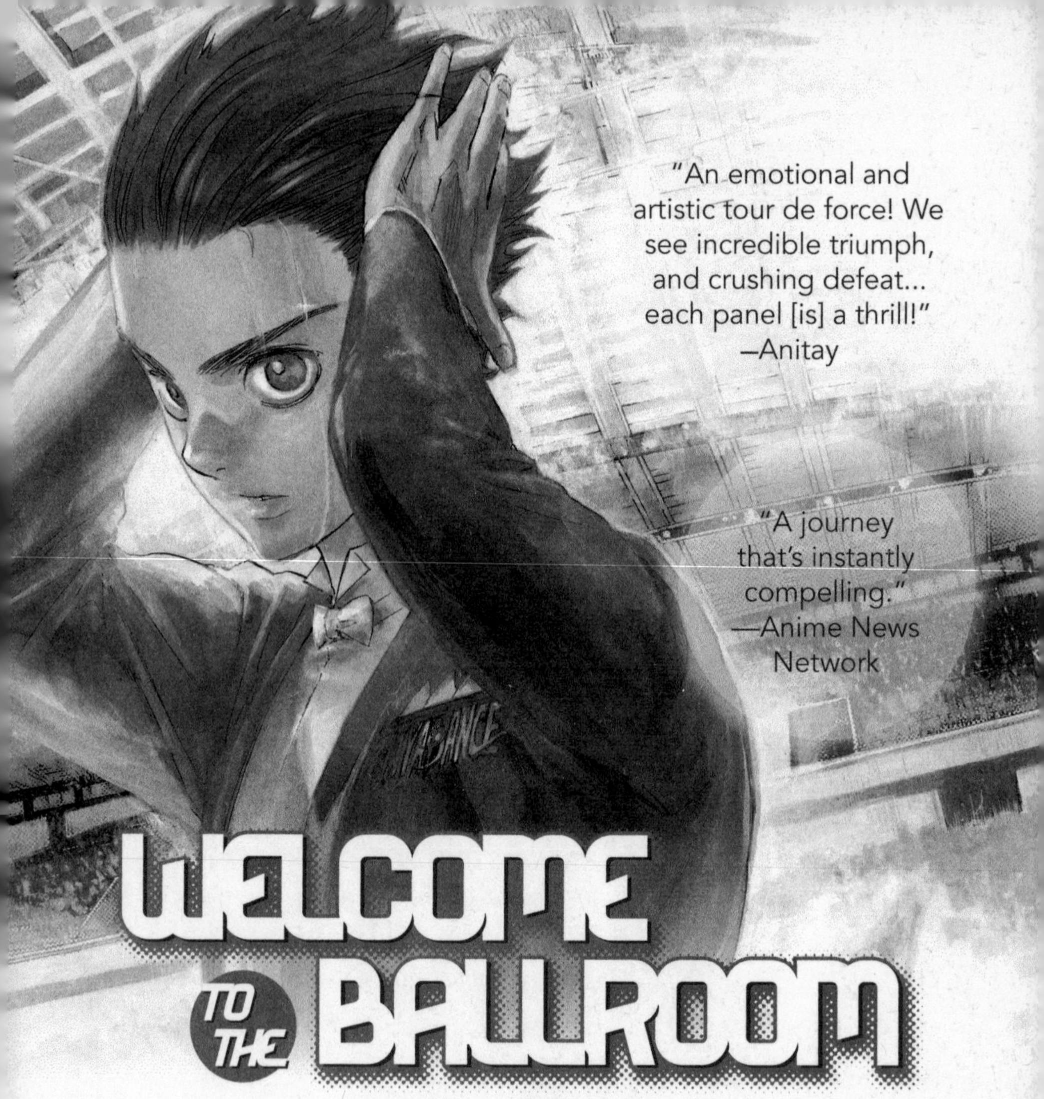

"An emotional and artistic tour de force! We see incredible triumph, and crushing defeat... each panel [is] a thrill!"
–Anitay

"A journey that's instantly compelling."
—Anime News Network

WELCOME TO THE BALLROOM

By Tomo Takeuchi

Feckless high school student Tatara Fujita wants to be good at something—anything. Unfortunately, he's about as average as a slouchy teen can be. The local bullies know this, and make it a habit to hit him up for cash, but all that changes when the debonair Kaname Sengoku sends them packing. Sengoku's not the neighborhood watch, though. He's a professional ballroom dancer. And once Tatara Fujita gets pulled into the world of ballroom, his life will never be the same.

KC KODANSHA COMICS

Based on the critically acclaimed classic horror manga

The first new *Parasyte* manga in over 20 years!

NEO Parasyte f

BY ASUMIKO NAKAMURA, EMA TOYAMA, MIKI RINNO, LALAKO KOJIMA, KAORI YUKI, BANKO KUZE, YUUKI OBATA, KASHIO, YUI KUROE, ASIA WATANABE, MIKIMAKI, HIKARU SURUGA, HAJIME SHINJO, RENJURO KINDAICHI, AND YURI NARUSHIMA

A collection of chilling new *Parasyte* stories from Japan's top shojo artists!

Parasites: shape-shifting aliens whose only purpose is to assimilate with and consume the human race... but do these monsters have a different side? A parasite becomes a prince to save his romance-obsessed female host from a dangerous stalker. Another hosts a cooking show, in which the real monsters are revealed. These and 13 more stories, from some of the greatest shojo manga artists alive today, together make up a chilling, funny, and entertaining tribute to one of manga's horror classics!

INUYASHIKI

A superhero like none you've ever seen, from the creator of "Gantz"!

Ichiro Inuyashiki is down on his luck. He looks much older than his 58 years, his children despise him, and his wife thinks he's a useless coward. So when he's diagnosed with stomach cancer and given three months to live, it seems the only one who'll miss him is his dog.

Then a blinding light fills the sky, and the old man is killed... only to wake up later in a body he almost recognizes as his own. Can it be that Ichiro Inuyashiki is no longer human?

COMES IN EXTRA-LARGE EDITIONS WITH COLOR PAGES!